From the River to the Sea

From the River to the Sea

Palestine and Israel in the Shadow of "Peace"

Edited by
Mandy Turner

LEXINGTON BOOKS
Lanham • Boulder • New York • London

Published by Lexington Books
An imprint of The Rowman & Littlefield Publishing Group, Inc.
4501 Forbes Boulevard, Suite 200, Lanham, Maryland 20706
www.rowman.com

6 Tinworth Street, London SE11 5AL, United Kingdom

Copyright © 2019 The Rowman & Littlefield Publishing Group, Inc.

Cover image description: Occupied Palestinian Territories, Gaza, June 2013
High school students enjoy a field trip on the Mediterranean Sea off the coast
of Gaza, where a ten-minute boat ride is the epitome of freedom. Gazans are
not allowed to travel outside of the enclave due to the siege, including limiting
fishermen and all boats to (approximately) six nautical miles off the coast.

All rights reserved. No part of this book may be reproduced in any form or by
any electronic or mechanical means, including information storage and retrieval
systems, without written permission from the publisher, except by a reviewer who
may quote passages in a review.

British Library Cataloguing in Publication Information Available

Library of Congress Cataloging-in-Publication Data

Names: Turner, Mandy, editor.
Title: From the river to the sea : Palestine and Israel in the shadow of
    "peace" / edited by Mandy Turner.
Description: Lanham, Maryland : Lexington Books, 2019. | Includes
    bibliographical references and index.
Identifiers: LCCN 2019001206 (print) | LCCN 2019006475 (ebook) | ISBN
    9781498582889 (electronic) | ISBN 9781498582872 | ISBN
    9781498582872 (cloth : alk. paper)
Subjects: LCSH: Arab-Israeli conflict—1993– | Palestinian Arabs—Politics
    and government—1993– | Palestinian Arabs—Economic conditions. |
    Muna?z?zamat al-Ta?hr?ir al-Filas?t?in?iyah.
Classification: LCC DS119.76 (ebook) | LCC DS119.76 .F795 2019 (print) | DDC
    956.9405/5—dc23
LC record available at https://lccn.loc.gov/2019001206

Contents

Acknowledgments and Preface   vii
    Mandy Turner

Introduction: From The River to the Sea: Charting the Changes in Palestine and Israel Since 1993   1
    Mandy Turner

1   The Oslo Agreements—What Happened?   17
    Diana Buttu

2   The Localization of the Palestinian National Political Field   41
    Jamil Hilal

3   Lost in Transition: The Palestinian National Movement After Oslo   63
    Tariq Dana

4   The Structural Transformation of the Palestinian Economy after Oslo   95
    Raja Khalidi

5   The Politics of Exclusion of Palestinians in Israel Since Oslo: Between the Local and the National   125
    Mansour Nasasra

6   A New Nationalistic Political Grammar: Jewish-Israeli Society 25 Years After Oslo   159
    Yonatan Mendel

7   From Singapore to the Stone Age: The Gaza Strip and the Political Economy of Crisis   179
    Toufic Haddad

8	Occupied East Jerusalem Since the Oslo Accords: Isolation and Evisceration *Mansour Nasasra*	213
9	The Politics of Being "Ordinary": Palestinian Refugees in Jordan After the Oslo Agreement *Luigi Achilli*	245
10	No "Plan B" Because "Plan A" Cannot Fail: The Oslo Framework and Western Donors in the OPT, 1993–2017 *Mandy Turner*	271
11	The Single-State Solution: Vision, Obstacles, and Dilemmas of a Re-Emergent Alternative in Flux *Cherine Hussein*	303

Index	333
About the Contributors	341

Acknowledgments and Preface

There are many people who should be thanked for helping to bring this book to life. First of all, I would like to thank the chapter contributors who worked hard to research and reveal the historical processes and recent trends in each of their respective case study areas. It was a pleasure to work with such a professional *and committed* group of people; it made the process of coordinating this project and editing the final product easier and more enjoyable. I am also extremely grateful to the immensely talented Tanya Habjouqa for the cover photograph for this book, which first appeared in *Occupied Pleasures* (Foto-Evidence, 2015), an extraordinary collection of photos of everyday Palestinian life. In this photo, Palestinian high school students take a field trip off the coast of Gaza. For these teenagers, "A ten-minute boat ride," says Habjouqa, "is the epitome of freedom." Second, I would like to thank the funders who made the research possible—the first grant was from the British Academy ("Twenty Years of the Oslo Peace Paradigm," 2013–2015) and the second grant was from the London School of Economics and Political Sciences' Middle East Centre ("Promoting Teaching and Research in Political Economy in Palestine," 2015–2017). Third, I would like to thank the wider group of people that greatly assisted in the project by attending our workshops and offering constructive criticism while we discussed earlier drafts of the chapters, and others who provided written peer review comments. These include: Adnan Abdelrazek, Valentina Azarova, Sam Bahour, Ray Dolphin, Dana Erekat, Michael Dumper, Rema Hammami, Michael Pugh, Mtanes Shehadeh, Dimi Reider, Sophie Richter-Devroe, and Elian Weizman—your help was indispensable. I would also like to thank Alaa Tartir and Toby Dodge, as well as the staff of the London School of Economics' Middle East Centre, for providing the support, funds and facilities to present our initial findings at a half-day conference on 2 September 2015 at the LSE. And fourth, last but not least, I would like to thank the staff at Rowman and Littlefield/Lexington Books, particularly Joseph, C. Parry, senior acquisitions editor, and assistant editor, Bryndee Ryan, who enthusiastically embraced the proposal for this book.

Few conflicts provoke as much passion and anger as the one that has raged between Israel and the Palestinian people since 1948 (and arguably since the emergence of Zionism and its implantation into Palestine during the British Mandate period). In recent years, as the promise of peace has become increasingly hollow, negotiations have collapsed, and sovereign statehood for Palestinians has been denied, exchanges have become ever more bitter—perhaps even returning to the level of acrimony that dominated the decades before peace talks began in the early 1990s. Israel has become increasingly insistent on its "right" to the land of Palestine as promised, it and its supporters argue, in the Bible—and has continued to create "facts on the ground" toward this end, in contravention of international law. Meanwhile, Palestinians continue to insist on their right to self-determination, while resisting their oppression and dispossession in a number of different ways and through a variety of avenues—none of which, so far, have been successful.

One of the by-products of this struggle over the land from the Jordan River to the Mediterranean Sea, and the discourses surrounding it, has been the creation of a toxic environment in which those who support the Palestinian people's right to self-determination are accused of anti-Semitism by Israel and its supporters in an attempt to scare and silence. Many musicians, writers, journalists and academics who have dared to step into the lion's den of this conflict and its competing narratives have been subjected to criticism and abuse, as well as pressures and practices that have had destructive impacts on careers and lives. There are too many to list here, but these include such diverse names as: Roger Waters, the Young Fathers, Toni Morrison, Linda Sarsour, Chris McGreal, Ben White, Rabab Abdulhadi, Steven Hawking, Richard Falk, Steven Salaita, and Norman Finkelstein—all of whom (and many more) have been attacked for speaking out against Israel's repressive practices and denial of rights to Palestinians. Indeed, Marc Lamont Hill, a professor at Temple University in Philadelphia and a well-known social activist and TV personality, was attacked for using the same phrase—"from the river to the sea"—that is the title of this book, during his speech at the 2018 UN Day of Solidarity with the Palestinian People on November 28. In response to an outcry from Israel and its supporters, CNN ended its contract with Lamont Hill, who was a frequent contributor to its news programs, although calls for Temple University, his main employer, to dismiss him failed.

There are many other examples of how this strategy of silencing operates in practice, but another three I will briefly mention include: the criminalization of the non-violent organization, the Palestinian Boycott, Divestment and Sanctions movement (BDS), by Israel and by many Western states; the intimidation tactics employed against academics and students on US campuses from the website, Canary Mission; and the extensive attempts to force Western political parties (both those in power and those in opposition) to adopt the International Holocaust Remembrance Alliance (IHRA) definition of anti-Semitism which redefines hatred of Jews to include criticism of Israel and has already been used in the UK to close down events and censor speakers at universities, as well as to attempt to force a change in the position of the UK Labour Party leader, Jeremy Corbyn, on Israel and Palestine.

It is thus commonplace, as a researcher of this situation, to be at the receiving end of comments that are ill-informed and ideologically driven; indeed, the exchange of examples of such experiences happens regularly between researchers. It is also routine to be accused of "bias"—as if somehow the study of society and social life can be "scientific" and "neutral." It has been a guiding principle throughout my intellectual life that research can be "objective" but it cannot be "neutral"—so I do not apologize for the common thread that underpins this edited book, i.e., how the past 25 years has witnessed the imposition of a victor's peace for Israel and has denied rights (both national and human) to Palestinians, under the guise of a "peace process." For all the contributors to this book, these facts are undeniable. Unfortunately, though, these facts are not enough because there is a broader ideological battle that continues to rage.

My aim with mentioning this in an acknowledgments and preface page is not to elicit sympathy or to plead a special case, but merely to provide evidence for my belief that the reason why there has been no peaceful and just solution is not because people are ignorant of the facts—indeed, far from it. The reason why this situation evolved and continues is because the dispossession and repression of Palestinians by Israel has been made permissible by an international environment that has *enabled* it and *sustained* it, despite all the violence and deaths that the situation has engendered. Many critics charge that there is a lack of political will from powerful states (who frequently declare their, often unconditional, support for Israel) to properly tackle the issue and support the rights of an oppressed people to a life free of violence. I used to believe this, but now consider that the political will is indeed there—but unfortunately this "will" is not directed toward a solution that will implant and support Palestinian rights, but is directed to supporting Israel no matter what it does.

I am under no illusion, as indeed are the other contributors to this book, that more research and more words will change this situation. What is required is a transformation in international public perception and opinion that, in turn, fuels an increase in solidarity actions and movements in support of Palestinian rights. We hope, at least, that this book helps toward this aim by offering documentation and analyses of the experiences and responses of the people who have been affected by the festering wound created by this conflict.

We, the contributors, have debated and discussed our research for this book in a variety of different venues and over many years—and we have not always agreed. Indeed, some of the chapters come to different conclusions about what the future holds for the land and the people from the River to the Sea. However, all of us are in firm agreement that this is an unjust and violent colonial situation that must be documented, opposed and resolved in a way that advances human dignity and rights.

Mandy Turner, East Jerusalem, November 2018

Introduction

From the River to the Sea—Charting the Changes in Palestine and Israel Since 1993

Mandy Turner

> "We stand here. Sit here. Remain here. Immortal here.
> And we have only one goal:
> to be."
>
> —Mahmoud Darwish, *A State of Siege* (2002) in *The Butterfly's Burden*, translated by Fady Joudah (Bloodaxe Books, 2007, p. 143).[1]

One month after the signing of the 1993 Declaration of Principles on Interim Self-Government Arrangements (DOP) between Israel and the Palestine Liberation Organization (PLO), the *London Review of Books* published a scathing critique by leading Palestinian academic, Edward Said. Entitled "The Morning After," Said attacked the agreement as "an instrument of Palestinian surrender, a Palestinian Versailles."[2] While many participated in the euphoria surrounding Israel's recognition of the PLO, relished the anticipation of an end to 26 years of occupation and six years of Intifada, and welcomed famous handshake on the White House lawn between PLO chairman, Yasser Arafat, and Israeli prime minister, Yitzhak Rabin, Said's words seemed harsh. But now, 25 years later, they have proven to have been prophetic. Far from bringing peace, the DOP—and the geographical, economic, and political framework that was its result (herein referred to as the Oslo framework)—has failed to halt Israel's vice-like grip over Palestinian natural resources and Palestinian lives. Rather, it gave breathing space for Israel to deepen its colonization and statebuilding practices over the whole of Mandate Palestine, but this time under the guise of a peace process endorsed, supported, and funded by the international community.

Dozens of books and articles have been written on whether this was Israel's original intention, and that the DOP should actually be understood as the most recent and successful attempt to implement the Allon Plan—a strategy proposed in 1967 by Israeli minister of labor, Yigal Allon, to annex East Jerusalem and most of the Jordan Valley, but leave the heavily populated areas of the West Bank under Arab control (with either Palestinian or Jordanian leadership).[3] Others argue that the DOP offered a genuine window of opportunity for a two-state solution, but that this was slammed shut by the assassination of Rabin in November 1995 at the hands of a Jewish-Israeli ultra-nationalist opposed to peace with Palestinians.[4] That the PLO participated in what was clearly a problematic process which left all the important issues to final status negotiations can be explained by a number of factors. However, the most important one was quite simply because the PLO was bankrupt and isolated after the withdrawal of financial and political assistance from the Gulf States due to its support for Iraq's invasion of Kuwait in 1990.[5] But whatever the reasons for why Israel and the PLO signed the DOP, one thing is clear: that its impacts and implications have been far ranging and transformative: spatially, politically, and economically.

Spatial practices were imposed that again divided Palestinians from each other: Palestinians in the West Bank and Gaza were cut off from Palestinians in Israel and East Jerusalem, and eventually from each other. And after 25 years of physical restrictions on movement in the OPT, imposed and policed through the closure regime, which was designed to expand and protect Israeli settlements (that have continued to grow exponentially), the West Bank has become internally fragmented. Politically, the creation of the Palestinian Authority as an institution of limited self-rule for Palestinians in the West Bank and Gaza, splintered the nationalist movement. Thereafter the official focus of liberation lay on the territories occupied since 1967 whereas the PLO had been established to represent *all* of the Palestinian people—from those in the OPT, to those inside Israel, to those in the *shatat* (diaspora) including refugees. While the PLO remains the negotiating partner to the peace process as well as the internationally-recognized representative of the Palestinian people at the diplomatic level, the terms "the PA" and "the PLO" are often used interchangeably and there is confusion over their separate functions particularly because of their interconnectedness, the fact that Fatah dominates both, and that there has been a de facto shift in political power toward the Palestinian Authority. The marginalization of Palestinians inside Israel and in the *shatat* from the Palestinian nationalist movement is particularly embodied in this shift.[6]

These spatial and political practices, that were designed to divide and rule, created the context for different forms of economy to emerge: the fragmented West Bank economy with small pockets of prosperity surrounded by a sea of marginalized communities; the disintegrating East Jerusalem economy isolated from the rest of the West Bank and marginalized within the Israeli economy; and the Gazan economy under siege and blockade reduced to being completely dependent on donor aid for survival. Inside Israel, the Palestinian-Arab economy continued to be subjected to contradictory processes that both marginalized it *and* integrated it within the wider Israeli economy largely to its detriment. There were also impacts in the social sphere, particularly through Israel's law restricting family reunification (i.e., that prevents Palestinians from East Jerusalem or Israel from living with spouses from the West Bank or Gaza inside Israel or East Jerusalem),[7] and through restrictions on movement. And it is in response to these different contexts that distinct and divergent responses were crafted to the restrictions and problems that were faced—often in innovative and unexpected ways. Familial, community, economic, and political relations have sometimes been sufficiently robust in continuing to knit Palestinian communities together thus leading to new forms of (re-)integration.

Israel, on the other hand, has experienced exceptional levels of economic growth prompted by policies that internationalized its economy coupled with the expansion of trade with large parts of the world through the establishment of relations made possible by the DOP and the peace process, and compounded by a wave of immigration in the 1990s from the former Soviet Union.[8] Such neoliberal capitalist policies were, as they have been in other parts of the world, accompanied by a rapid increase in inequality that has disproportionately impacted communities along communal lines—the worse affected being (in order): Palestinians-Arab citizens of Israel, the Haredim, and the Mizrahim.[9] And while the OPT is highly dependent economically on Israel, the converse is not true. Some commentators argue that the economic impact on Israel is to be found in the costs of maintaining the occupation through state subsidies for Jewish settlements in the West Bank and the military costs of defending them.[10] But there are, of course, a multitude of ways that Israel profits from its colonization and occupation, such as through access to natural resources in the OPT, i.e., water and fertile land,[11] and through its leading role as an exporter of "homeland security" products and weapons.[12] The massive scale of land expropriations from Palestinians, upon which the Israeli state itself was built in the immediate years following 1948,[13] continued in the West Bank and Gaza after 1967, thus indicating the continuity in the mechanisms used by Israel to expand its control over the whole of Mandate Palestine. Politically, Israel has shifted to the right in the past few decades—a process that has put settlers and their supporters deep within the government, with concomitant impacts in terms of policies. Many of the settlements (particularly large ones such as Ma'ale Adumim, Ariel, and those surrounding Jerusalem) are now largely not regarded by Jewish-Israelis to be problematic or illegal. Indeed, so many Jewish-Israelis now know someone (colleague, relative, friend) who lives in a settlement, that the "green line" has been virtually erased in their collective mind-set. Meanwhile, the Israeli state has continued with its strategy of conflict management and counterinsurgency (rather than conflict resolution, as promised by the peace process) against Palestinians with overwhelming support from Jewish-Israelis.

It is therefore the goal of this book to analyze the impacts of the framework and peace paradigm implemented by the DOP that has led to a restructuring of the lives of all peoples living between the Jordan River and the Mediterranean Sea—hence the title of this book. However, this framework impacted differently depending upon which community and what geographical area, with each experiencing a different mixture of processes of domination, disintegration, and reintegration. This edited book thus breaks down and analyzes the structural and ideational impact of the DOP and the Oslo framework in each of the different communities—as well as the variety of strategies that different communities developed to cope with them.

The communities selected for analysis include: Palestinians in the West Bank; Palestinians in East Jerusalem; Palestinians in the Gaza Strip; Palestinians in Israel; Palestinian refugees in Jordan; and Jewish-Israelis. The development of these communities from that initially widely acclaimed peace accord until 2018 is traced through the different chapters—and each reveals how the Oslo framework instituted certain processes of both separation *and* unification. While Palestinian refugees do not live between "the River and the Sea," it is both intellectually and politically misguided to ignore their experience of the DOP, and how they dealt with their (largely) practical exclusion from the two-state solution narrative and project as it has developed over the past two and a half decades. While other communities could have been analyzed (for example, the Bedouin and the Druze) and indeed different communities *within* communities (for example Christians, Muslims, different types of Jews: Mizrahim, Ashkenazim, and Haredim), the communities selected for this book were chosen because they represent the major fissure and line of dissent between the Jordan River and the Mediterranean Sea—the whole area that is under the control of Israel. Because of Israel's character as a Zionist state with privileged legal and political status for Jews, it has imposed different legal-political statuses on state-defined sets of peoples that thereafter structured their lives and created different political economies and life experiences.[14] Indeed, the Nation State Law that was passed by the Knesset (Israel's parliament) in July 2018 codified into Israeli law that only the Jewish people had the right to exercise national self-determination, it downgraded Arabic from its previous status as an "official language" to one with "special status," and it established "Jewish settlement as a national value." Critics have called it "a law of Jewish supremacy"[15] and "another step in the direction of annexing the territories."[16] Other divisions (while they obviously have impacts) were therefore regarded to be not as important for this analysis.

The premise underpinning this book was that in order to see a route out of the present impasse, a realistic analysis of the situation that currently exists is required. And so the in-depth analyses of the selected communities have been supplemented with chapters that analyze the economy of the OPT; the development of Palestinian nationalism historically through the PLO and more recently; the emergence of the Palestinian Authority and how the main Palestinian political factions responded to the DOP; the rationale, policies, and impact of the Western donors and the aid regime; and activists proposing an alternative strategy to that offered by the partition framework imposed by the DOP and the two-state solution. The methodology used in all the chapters was largely qualitative—based on in-depth interviews, archival research, the drawing together of work by other expert scholars, and a deep knowledge of the societies concerned. The chapters were written by researchers across the study-fields of economics, oral history, sociology, political economy, international relations, and law. Indeed, only research based on interdisciplinarity can help us to uncover and analyze what has really happened between the River and the Sea.

STRUCTURE OF THE BOOK

The book begins with a chapter by Diana Buttu on how to understand the DOP and subsequent agreements, as well as the years of peace negotiations. In theory, the DOP was meant to, if properly implemented, create confidence between Israel and the Palestinians so that they would be able to address the issues of the borders of the future Palestinian state, the rights and potential return of more than 7 million Palestinian refugees, the halting and removal of Israeli colonies in the OPT, and the status of Jerusalem. As Buttu shows in her analysis, however, in reality the DOP served to divide the Palestinian polity and land, and had a negative impact on Palestinian decision-making. An interim administration (the Palestinian Authority) was created purportedly as a precursor to sovereign statehood, but which became, in reality, a security contractor for Israel. The chapter outlines the different agreements signed between Israel and the PLO, what they meant, and how they were implemented. Buttu concludes by arguing that it is futile for the Palestinian nationalist movement to continue to seek liberation within a process that has locked it into a dead-end system.

Taking this as a starting point, the next two chapters analyze the impact of the agreements on the Palestinian political field, i.e., on the PLO and on Palestinian political factions (including the creation of the Palestinian Authority). Chapter two by Jamil Hilal offers a sociological analysis of the national Palestinian political field through various historical periods. It reconstructs its various articulations and the forces that drove the Palestinian national movement, as well as its internal workings, and examines the processes that led to its collapse into localized political fields formed by Palestinian communities responding to the exigencies of the situations in which they are dispersed. Hilal argues that while this collapse has had a drastic impact on the political, economic, and cultural dynamic of the Palestinian national movement, he maintains that the processes of localization are also reinvigorating this dynamic in a similar fashion to that which followed the Nakba of 1948. The chapter concludes by arguing that the ongoing responses of Palestinian communities to their vulnerable conditions could lead to the eventual (re)construction of a new national political field.

Chapter three by Tariq Dana follows on and adds to this analysis of the national movement by focusing on the creation of the Palestinian Authority and the responses of the various established Palestinian political factions operational in the OPT (both inside and outside of the PLO) to the era instituted by the signing of the DOP. The transformations that this provoked in the structures, functions, perceptions, political vocabulary, and behavior of Palestinian political actors profoundly impacted on the ability of the Palestinian body politic to function as an independent anti-colonial liberation movement and as the representative body of Palestinian national aspirations. Complementing the wider historical and conceptual analysis offered by Hilal in chapter two, yet disagreeing with his conclusions, Dana argues that the existing political forces failed to present alternative strategies to rebuild the national movement, in response to the current crisis, nor have any new political and social movements emerged to challenge the status quo. Only time will tell if Hilal or Dana are right in their differing prognoses about the long-term impacts of the fracturing of the national movement that has taken place over the past 25 years.

Moving from the political to the economic realm, chapter four by Raja Khalidi charts the structural transformation of the Palestinian economy after the DOP. It examines how the economic promises of the Paris Protocol delivered neither development for the OPT nor peace, but rather it entrenched an Israeli matrix of economic control that was enhanced by a neoliberal Palestinian economic policy program. Khalidi analyzes both the economic impacts of Israel's policies of colonization and occupation, as well as the PLO's embrace of globalization and neoliberalism. He argues that an analysis of the processes of class formation that have been taking place in the past 25 years in the OPT are crucial to understanding the transformation toward the neoliberal forms that dominate current economic thought and practice in the OPT and which have allowed the logic of stabilization and "economic peace" to go unopposed. The impacts of these dual processes of Israeli colonization and Palestinian neoliberalism, Khalidi concludes, have devastated the economic life of the OPT as encapsulated by key aggregate performance indicators since 1994 which demonstrate structural deformation, economic vulnerability, and communal impoverishment, despite signs of some individual enrichment. The chapter concludes that "development" cannot take place within such a context, and while "economic peace" may largely reign at present and the status quo could certainly be sustained longer, the processes of Palestinian wealth creation and economic interchange that encompass the West Bank, Jerusalem, the Galilee, and Gaza, "will also shape the future dynamics of conflict in the territory from the River to the Sea" (p. 120).

Chapter five by Mansour Nasasra focuses on the response of Palestinians inside Israel to the DOP, and the subsequent impact it had on their communities and politics. Through extensive interviews with political leaders and civil society activists, Nasasra argues that because there was no avenue for expressing the views of Palestinians inside Israel, nor even of recognizing their needs in the Oslo negotiations, this pushed them toward a reconceptualization of their politics in the context of campaigning for equal rights as a national indigenous minority. Using the equality paradigm as a leading strategy in their struggle, this spurred the rise of civil society activism to lobby for representation in decision-making bodies, cultural and linguistic rights, and a more just allocation of material resources. The key impact of the DOP on the Palestinian-Arab citizens of Israel has therefore been an acceleration of the "localization" of their struggle into one focused on (national) minority rights and justice within the Israeli state—a process that has been made more difficult by measures that insist on Israel as a specifically *Jewish* state, such as the passing of the 2018 Nation-State Law (more of which below). These trends toward "localization" are represented by a process that Nasasra calls the "nationalization" of Palestinian-Arab citizens' voting patterns in favor of Arab parties compared to the "Zionization" of their voting patterns in the 1990s and before, which were mainly cast for the Labor Party. The success of the Joint List in the March 2015 Israeli legislative elections and subsequently, has shown that Palestinian-Arab citizens of Israel could become a significant political force in Israeli politics. Simultaneously, however, they have also continued to identify with the wider Palestinian struggle for national rights and self-determination.

Remaining within the "green line," chapter six by Yonatan Mendel looks at the dynamics of the DOP in Jewish-Israeli society. At the heart of the Israeli debate, he argues, is a curious popular perception that Israel made a generous offer to end the conflict by signing the DOP and that the fault for its failure to bring peace lies with the Palestinians, despite the fact that, for over two decades, the Israeli state endorsed support for the two-state solution in principle, while undermining it in practice. Mendel charts two other developments in Israeli politics crucial for understanding the current situation. The first is the delegitimization of Palestinian citizens of Israel by Zionist politicians and the media, which portrays them as a "threat" to Israel as a Jewish state. The second is the fact that none of the other Zionist parties now pose any real opposition to the dominance or program of Likud, and instead try to gain political support by adopting similar policies. There is now a consensus across the Zionist political spectrum that the Israeli state should concentrate on the aspirations and desires of Jewish citizens only—a sentiment that strikes a popular chord with the Jewish-Israeli public as shown by recent polls that indicate significant support for discriminatory practices against Palestinians, and as embodied in the 2018 Nation-State Law. Mendel concludes this broad vista of Jewish-Israeli politics and society since the DOP by arguing that the lack of a just and comprehensive solution to the conflict has led to an acute shift toward right-wing and extreme national-religious groups, and that there currently exists very little incentive for Israel to change its relations with Palestine, particularly given that the second decade of the twenty-first century has been a period of remarkable stability for Israel.

Chapter seven by Toufic Haddad focuses on the Gaza Strip. Originally touted as a potential "Singapore on the Mediterranean," Haddad surveys the role of crisis in the transformation of the Gaza Strip from an optimistic object of development to a subject of humanitarian appeal. By tracing significant political, economic, and social transformations that took place across three distinct periods (the Oslo years, the Second Intifada period, and the era of Hamas governance) it explores the factors that have generated a perpetual state of crisis; how these have influenced or transformed social relations between actors and groups; and the implications of these transformations on relations between Gaza, the West Bank, Israel, and the national movement *in toto*. A clear message from this analysis is that the Gaza Strip can only be understood historically and politically as the product of the 1948 war, and that it has consistently experienced the most brutal of Israel's efforts to quash Palestinian nationalism. Utilizing Harvard economist Sara Roy's concept of de-development, Haddad concludes with an appeal for greater understanding of the political economy of crisis and how to resist it, particularly before it further contributes to the devastating environment being created in the Gaza Strip.

Chapter eight, the second one written by Mansour Nasasra, focuses on East Jerusalem. It charts how the experience of 25 years of the Oslo framework has marginalized East Jerusalemite Palestinians while a number of struggles take place around them (but largely beyond their control): between Israel and the PA/PLO; between Israel and Jordan; and between Jordan and the PA/PLO. Nasasra argues that this community is trapped between Israeli sovereignty aspirations (embodied in its policies of separating East Jerusalem from the rest of the West Bank, and its processes of "Judaization") and the lack of local Palestinian leadership (prevented from operating by Israeli military order, as well as by the shrinking and closure of political, economic and cultural institutions due to its separation from the rest of the West Bank). These processes are likely to accelerate in the context of a US administration that has thus far endorsed Israel's actions regarding Jerusalem. However, simultaneously with these accelerating forms of disintegration and fragmentation, the chapter shows that some surprising new forms of (re-)integration are taking place, i.e., with the Palestinian Arab citizens of Israel who have increasingly come to play a political role, particularly in the Knesset, in leading a political campaign on behalf of Palestinian East Jerusalem.

Chapter nine moves outside of the geographical space of Israel and Palestine to a community that has played a constant and essential role in the Palestinian nationalist narrative and movement: Palestinian refugees in neighboring Arab states. There are, of course, refugee camps inside the OPT (indeed, refugees in Gaza make up around 70 percent of the population) but each refugee community has had experiences specific to the country in which they have been hosted. This simple fact makes generalizations difficult, so the chapter by Luigi Achilli offers an analysis of the specific consequences of the DOP on Palestinian refugees living in camps in Jordan. Achilli begins the chapter by locating Palestinian refugees and refugee camps in the Middle East at the very heart of the Palestinian national movement, but which were then marginalized by the Agreements. Achilli shows how, by undermining the very basis upon which lay the refugees' hope of return, the DOP triggered among refugees a profound rethinking of their status in Jordan. The group of refugees analyzed by Achilli focused their attention on remaking their social world by striving to stay away from politics and live what they describe as an "ordinary life" (ḥayā 'ādiye). Achilli thus concludes that infusing nationalism with daily interests and needs has allowed refugees to accommodate the meanings, values, and promises of Palestinian nationalism with the reality of living in Jordan, which has tended to look unfavorably upon overt displays of "Palestinianness."

Chapter 10, by Mandy Turner, has a slightly different focus. Other chapters in the book explore the experiences and responses of Israeli and Palestinian communities to the significant geographic, economic, and political changes that came in the aftermath of the signing of the DOP. This chapter instead analyzes Western donor and multilateral involvement based on the observation that they have played a crucial role in creating and sustaining the DOP and the Oslo framework. Based on extensive interviews with high-ranking Western aid officials, Turner offers an analysis of the main Western aid actors and their strategies; it assesses the most important impacts of the past 25 years of their activities in the OPT; and it looks at what they think of the Oslo framework and the two-state solution nearly 20 years after the interim period was supposed to end. She concludes that, despite being acutely aware of the problems with the two-state solution and the Oslo framework, donors and multilaterals believe there is no alternative plan, which she labels (following donors themselves and the media) as constituting a potential "Plan B." The chapter shows how, even when the peace process appears to be dead, the façade that it is leading somewhere continues because it cannot be acknowledged to have failed. Turner concludes that, by continuing to contribute to and justify such a situation of stasis, the donors and multilaterals have played a crucial role in creating and sustaining the particular type of colonial "peace" that exists in 2018.

These 10 chapters all focus on understanding the logic and impact of the DOP and its resultant framework and paradigm, based as it was on the idea of separation and a two-state solution. While this framework continues to dominate and structure people's lives, the final chapter by Cherine Hussein looks at the alternative paradigm and solution of a single democratic state as proposed by some activists. Based on extensive interviews with one-state intellectuals and activists, Hussein explores its viability as a grassroots movement in-the-making that offers an alternative end-goal to the conflict. First, she maps the idea's re-emergence, its critique of Zionism and the DOP, and the prominent role of the Palestinian Diaspora within it. Second, she assesses the visions and divisions of activists and intellectuals in Palestine and Israel. And third, she analyzes whether this "alternative" perspective can create a unified movement in the near future. Hussein concludes that the single democratic state idea has been largely successful in creating an alternative vision capable of unifying its supporters both within Palestine and Israel and amongst the Diaspora. However, it has yet to find success in translating this vision into a grassroots popular resistance movement capable of reunifying the fragmented Palestinian national collective, and galvanizing political leadership or momentum necessary to organize opposition to the DOP, the Oslo framework, and the partition strategy that underpins the two-state solution.

CONCLUSION: BEYOND OSLO? WHAT NEXT?

As shown by the chapters in this book, the DOP and the Oslo framework have instigated new experiences or further compounded old processes of oppression, marginalization, fragmentation, and dispossession for Palestinian communities. But what these analyses also show is that the responses of the different communities to these processes have also created the foundations for new forms of political expression, mobilization, and interaction. For instance, while in the past the occupation was the focal point for anger from the Palestinian public in the OPT, it is now common to read newspaper articles and see placards displayed and slogans being chanted on demonstrations that call for the end of the Oslo framework, particularly security coordination between Israel and the Palestinian Authority. This happened, for example, on July 30, 2013, when protestors marched to the offices of Palestinian Authority president, Mahmoud Abbas, in Ramallah, chanting "*Al-Sha'b yurid isqat Oslo*" [the people want the fall of Oslo].[17] Furthermore, more commentators and pollsters are documenting the decline in support for the two-state solution amongst young Palestinians, and a rise in the belief that what will emerge will be a bi-national state.[18] However, despite some rhetoric from the Palestinian Authority leadership regarding this issue, it remains unlikely they will follow this path as this will prompt donor aid withdrawal and thus its own collapse. Israel, meanwhile, has further retreated to the right, and is increasingly insistent that it will not allow a sovereign Palestinian state to emerge. However, this could be Israel's undoing, as the international consensus since the 1947 UN Partition Plan has been for two states with a special status for Jerusalem. If one of the parties to the conflict (or even both) does not want the two-state solution, then what comes next?

There have also been changes in the diplomatic realm. Indeed, recent developments could lead to the wholesale abandonment of the pretense and façade of the two-state solution. In 2017, US president, Donald Trump, appointed David Friedman as US ambassador to Israel; Friedman is opposed to a Palestinian state, and is closely aligned with the Israeli settler movement.[19] Furthermore, Trump instituted a dramatic break in 70 years of US foreign policy by implementing the 1995 Jerusalem Embassy Act that recognized Jerusalem as the capital of Israel and supported moving its embassy there from Tel Aviv (which it duly did on May 14, 2018), thus endorsing Israel's claim to sovereignty over the whole city.[20]

At the time of writing, however, the DOP and the Oslo framework remain firmly in place—as also does the official two-state policy as constituting the route to peace. As analyzed in the chapter by Turner, high-ranking aid officials from Western donors and UN agencies continue to insist that the two-state solution is *the* only solution. Furthermore, the official policies of both Israel and the PLO (despite rhetoric to the contrary) remain that the conflict will be resolved by two states for two peoples. But if a sovereign Palestinian state does not emerge then what will exist under current conditions from the River to the Sea is an apartheid state, as warned by US secretary of state, John Kerry, in April 2014,[21] and countless other commentators.[22] In fact, many believe that it already is,[23] including a panel of experts from the UN's Economic and Political Commission for Western Asia[24] and South Africa's statutory research agency, the Human Sciences Research Council of South Africa.[25]

Despite stringent and extensive actions by Israel to control and oppress Palestinians—ranging from counterinsurgency techniques such as military violence, administrative detention, assassinations, and house demolitions; to more bureaucratic methods such as controls on movement, travel, and citizenship rights—it is clear that Palestinians, as encapsulated by Mahmoud Darwish's poem which is the epigraph to this introduction, continue to "stand here. Sit here. Remain here." As, indeed, do Jewish-Israelis. The key question thus remains: how to liberate Palestine from the violence of Israeli settler colonialism and to build a future based on the defeat and eradication of the inequality and oppression that this system has created.

ACKNOWLEDGMENTS

I would like to thank Michael Pugh for comments made on an earlier draft. Any errors left and opinions expressed, however, are my own.

NOTES

1. Reproduced by kind permission of Fady Joudah.
2. Edward Said, "The Morning After," *London Review of Books* 15, No. 20 (21 October 1993): 3–5.
3. For two examples of this perspective, see Gilbert Achcar, *Eastern Cauldron: Islam, Afghanistan and Palestine in the Mirror of Marxism* (London: Pluto Press, 2004): 205–222; and Adam Hanieh, "A Roadmap to the Oslo Cul-de-sac," *Middle East Research and Information Project*, May 15, 2003.
4. Dan Ephron, *Killing a King: The Assassination of Yitzhak Rabin and the Remaking of Israel* (New York: W. W. Norton, 2015).
5. Peter Ezra Weinberger, *Co-Opting the PLO: A Critical Reconstruction of the Oslo Accords, 1993–1995* (Lanham, MD: Lexington Books, 2006); Mandy Turner, "Israel and the Palestinians," in *Routledge Handbook on Peace Processes*, eds. Roger Mac Ginty and Alp Ozerdem (New York: Routledge, 2019, forthcoming).
6. PLO Vs PA, PASSIA, September 2014, http://www.passia.org/images/meetings/2014/oct/28/PA-PLO2.pdf.
7. Jonathan Lis, "Law Restricting Family Reunification Extended at Shin Bet's Request," *Ha'aretz*, June 2, 2016, http://www.haaretz.com/israel-news/1.722708.

8. Paul Rivlin, *The Israeli Economy from the Foundation of the State through the 21st Century* (Cambridge: Cambridge University Press, 2011): 94–117.

9. Rivlin, *The Israeli Economy*, 202–228.

10. Shir Hever, *The Political Economy of Israel's Occupation: Repression Beyond Exploitation* (London: Pluto Press, 2010): 51–71.

11. Clemens Messerschmit, "Hydro-apartheid and Water Access in Israel-Palestine: Challenging the Myths of Cooperation and Scarcity," in *Decolonizing Palestinian Political Economy: De-development and Beyond*, eds. Mandy Turner and Omar Shweiki (Basingstoke: Palgrave Macmillan, 2014): 53–76.

12. Jeff Halper, *War Against the People: Israel, the Palestinians, and Global Pacification* (London: Pluto Press, 2015).

13. Geremy Forman and Alexandre (Sandy) Kedar, "From Arab Land to 'Israel Lands': The Legal Dispossession of the Palestinians Displaced by Israel in the Wake of 1948," *Environment and Planning D: Society and Space* 22 (2004): 809–830. A dunum constitutes 1,000 square metres.

14. Yoav Peled, "The Evolution of Israeli Citizenship: An Overview." *Citizenship Studies* 12, no. 3 (2008): 335–345. Mandy Turner, "Creating a Counterhegemonic Praxis: Jewish-Israeli Activists and the Challenge to Zionism," *Conflict, Security & Development* 15, no. 5 (2015): 549–574.

15. Peter Beaumont, "EU Leads Criticism After Israel Passes Jewish 'Nation State' Law, *The Guardian*, July 19, 2018, https://www.theguardian.com/world/2018/jul/19/israel-adopts-controversial-jewish-nation-state-law.

16. Mordechai Kremnitzer, "Jewish Nation State Law Makes Discrimination in Israel Constitutional," *Ha'aretz*, July 20, 2018. https://www.haaretz.com/israel-news/.premium-nation-state-law-makes-discrimination-in-israel-constitutional-1.6291906.

17. Crispian Balmer and Noah Browning, "Palestinians Take anti-Oslo Protest to Abbas HQ," *Reuters News Agency*, July 3, 2012, http://www.reuters.com/article/us-palestinians-abbas-demonstration-idUSBRE8620XS20120703.

18. Miriam Berger, "Middle East Peace: Can Young Palestinians' Rejection of PA Lead to a Binational State with Israel," *Newsweek*, July 11, 2018, http://www.newsweek.com/2018/07/20/palestinians-israel-abbas-gaza-west-bank-peace-pa-palestinian-authority-hamas-1016978.html.

19. Peter Beaumont and Julian Borger, "Donald Trump's Israel Ambassador is Hardline Pro-Settler Lawyer," *The Guardian*, December 16, 2016, https://www.theguardian.com/us-news/2016/dec/15/trump-israel-ambassador-david-friedman.

20. Mandy Turner and Mahmoud Muna, "The United States Recognition of Jerusalem as the Capital of Israel and the Challenge to the International Consensus," *Middle East Information Project* (MERIP), May 16, 2018, https://www.merip.org/mero/mero051618.

21. Peter Beaumont, "Israel Risks Becoming Apartheid State if Peace Talks Fail, Says John Kerry," *The Guardian*, April 29, 2014, https://www.theguardian.com/world/2014/apr/28/israel-apartheid-state-peace-talks-john-kerry.

22. John Dugard, "Two States or Apartheid," *Huffington Post*, no date, https://www.huffingtonpost.com/john-dugard/post_356_b_258206.html; Jimmy Carter, "Israel, Palestine, Peace and Apartheid," *The Guardian*, December 12, 2006, https://www.theguardian.com/commentisfree/2006/dec/12/israel.politicsphilosophyandsociety.

23. Ilan Pappe (ed.), *Israel and South Africa: The Many Faces of Apartheid* (London: Zed books, 2015); Desmond Tutu, "Apartheid in the Holy Land," *The Guardian*, April 29, 2002, https://www.theguardian.com/world/2002/apr/29/comment.

24. UN Economic and Social Commission for Western Asia, "Israeli Practices Toward the Palestinian People and the Question of Apartheid," Palestine and the Israeli Occupation Issue Number 1 (2017) E/ESCWA/ECRI/2017/1, https://www.middleeastmonitor.com/wp-content/uploads/downloads/201703_UN_ESCWA-israeli-practices-palestinian-people-apartheid-occupation-english.pdf.

25. Human Sciences Research Council of South Africa, *Occupation, Colonialism, Apartheid?: A Re-assessment of Israel's Practices in the Occupied Palestinian Territories Under International Law* (Cape Town, 2009), http://www.alhaq.org/attachments/article/236/Occupation_Colonialism_Apartheid-FullStudy.pdf.

BIBLIOGRAPHY

Achcar, Gilbert. *Eastern Cauldron: Islam, Afghanistan and Palestine in the Mirror of Marxism* (London: Pluto Press, 2004).

Balmer, Crispian, and Noah Browning. "Palestinians Take Anti-Oslo Protest to Abbas HQ," *Reuters News Agency*, July 3, 2012, http://www.reuters.com/article/us-palestinians-abbas-demonstration-idUSBRE8620XS20120703.

Beaumont, Peter. "EU Leads Criticism After Israel Passes Jewish 'Nation State' Law," *The Guardian* July 19, 2018. https://www.theguardian.com/world/2018/jul/19/israel-adopts-controversial-jewish-nation-state-law.

———. "Israel Risks Becoming Apartheid State if Peace Talks Fail, Says John Kerry," *The Guardian*, April 29, 2014, https://www.theguardian.com/world/2014/apr/28/israel-apartheid-state-peace-talks-john-kerry.

Beaumont, Peter, and Julian Borger. "Donald Trump's Israel Ambassador is Hardline Pro-Settler Lawyer," *The Guardian*, December 16, 2016, https://www.theguardian.com/us-news/2016/dec/15/trump-israel-ambassador-david-friedman.

Berger, Miriam. "Middle East Peace: Can Young Palestinians' Rejection of the PA Lead to a Binational State with Israel," *Newsweek*, July 11, 2018, http://www.newsweek.com/2018/07/20/palestinians-israel-abbas-gaza-west-bank-peace-pa-palestinian-authority-hamas-1016978.html.

Carter, Jimmy. "Israel, Palestine, Peace and Apartheid," *The Guardian*, December 12, 2006. https://www.theguardian.com/commentisfree/2006/dec/12/israel.politicsphilosophyandsociety.

Darwish, Mahmoud. *A State of Siege* (2002) in *The Butterfly's Burden*, translated by Fady Joudah (Hexham, UK: Bloodaxe Books, 2007).

Dugard, John. "Two States or Apartheid," *Huffington Post*, no date, https://www.huffingtonpost.com/john-dugard/post_356_b_258206.html.

Ephron, Dan. *Killing a King: The Assassination of Yitzhak Rabin and the Remaking of Israel* (W. W. Norton, 2015).

Forman, Geremy, and Alexandre (Sandy) Kedar. "From Arab land to 'Israel Lands': The Legal Dispossession of the Palestinians Displaced by Israel in the Wake of 1948," *Environment and Planning D: Society and Space* 22 (2004): 809–830.

Halper, Jeff. *War Against the People: Israel, the Palestinians, and Global Pacification* (London: Pluto Press, 2015).

Hanieh, Adam. "A Roadmap to the Oslo Cul-de-sac," *Middle East Research and Information Project*, May 15, 2003.

Hever, Shir. *The Political Economy of Israel's Occupation: Repression Beyond Exploitation* (London: Pluto Press, 2010): 51–71.

Human Sciences Research Council of South Africa. *Occupation, Colonialism, Apartheid? A Re-assessment of Israel's Practices in the Occupied Palestinian Territories Under International Law* (Cape Town: HSRCSA, 2009), http://www.alhaq.org/attachments/article/236/Occupation_Colonialism_Apartheid-FullStudy.pdf.

Kremnitzer, Mordechai. "Jewish Nation State Law Makes Discrimination in Israel Constitutional," *Ha'aretz*, July 20, 2018, https://www.haaretz.com/israel-news/.premium-nation-state-law-makes-discrimination-in-israel-constitutional-1.6291906.

Lis, Jonathan. "Law Restricting Family Reunification Extended at Shin Bet's Request," *Ha'aretz*, June 2, 2016, http://www.haaretz.com/israel-news/1.722708.

Messerschmit, Clemens. "Hydro-apartheid and Water Access in Israel-Palestine: Challenging the Myths of Cooperation and Scarcity," in *Decolonizing Palestinian Political Economy: De-development and Beyond*, Mandy Turner and Omar Shweiki (eds.) (Basingstoke: Palgrave Macmillan, 2014): 53–76.

Pappe, Ilan (ed.). *Israel and South Africa: The Many Faces of Apartheid* (London: Zed Books, 2015).

Peled, Yoav. "The Evolution of Israeli Citizenship: An Overview." *Citizenship Studies* 12, no. 3 (2008): 335–345.

PLO Vs PA, PASSIA. September 2014, http://www.passia.org/images/meetings/2014/oct/28/PA-PLO2.pdf.

Rabbani, Mouin. "Quick Thoughts on Trump Pledge to Move the US Embassy to Jerusalem," *Jadaliyya*, December 16, 2016, http://turkey.jadaliyya.com/pages/index/25689/quick-thoughts_mouin-rabbani-on-trump-pledge-to-mo.

Rivlin, Paul. *The Israeli Economy from the Foundation of the State through the 21st Century* (Cambridge: Cambridge University Press, 2011): 94–117.

Said, Edward. "The Morning After," *London Review of Books* 15, no. 20 (October 21, 1993): 3–5.

Turner, Mandy. "Creating a Counterhegemonic Praxis: Jewish-Israeli Activists and the Challenge to Zionism," *Conflict, Security & Development* 15, no. 5 (2015): 549–574.

———. "Israel and the Palestinians," in *Routledge Handbook on Peace Processes*, eds. Roger Mac Ginty and Alp Ozerdem (New York: Routledge, 2019, forthcoming).

Turner, Mandy, and Mahmoud Muna. "The United States Recognition of Jerusalem as the Capital of Israel and the Challenge to the International Consensus," *Middle East Information Project* (MERIP), May 16, 2018, https://www.merip.org/mero/mero051618.

Tutu, Desmond. "Apartheid in the Holy Land," *The Guardian*, April 29, 2002, https://www.theguardian.com/world/2002/apr/29/comment.

UN Economic and Social Commission for Western Asia, "Israeli Practices Toward the Palestinian People and the Question of Apartheid," Palestine and the Israeli Occupation Issue Number 1, 2017. E/ESCWA/ECRI/2017/1, https://www.middleeastmonitor.com/wp-content/uploads/downloads/201703_UN_ESCWA-israeli-practices-palestinian-people-apartheid-occupation-english.pdf.

Weinberger, Peter Ezra. *Co-Opting the PLO: A Critical Reconstruction of the Oslo Accords, 1993–1995* (Lanham, MD: Lexington Books, 2006).

Chapter One

The Oslo Agreements—
What Happened?

Diana Buttu

In 1993, the Palestine Liberation Organization (PLO) abruptly reversed its long-standing decision not to negotiate with Israel.[1] This policy reversal, announced on the steps of the White House lawn, was accompanied by the now-famous handshake between PLO chairman Yaser Arafat and Israeli prime minister Yitzhak Rabin and culminated months of secret negotiations between Israeli and Palestinian political figures. The "peace process" as it was dubbed, had commenced.

The negotiations process was sold to Palestinians as the means to end Israel's military control over the West Bank and Gaza Strip leading to a permanent settlement based on UN Security Council Resolutions 242 and 338, resolutions that call for the withdrawal of Israeli armed forces from occupied Palestinian land and, as Palestinians believed, the establishment of a Palestinian state.[2] Yet while more than twenty-five years have passed, the majority of this time has been marked by periods *lacking* any negotiations, in which Israeli and Palestinian negotiators have not even feigned that meaningful negotiations are being conducted or that progress has been achieved. With the election of US president Donald Trump in 2016, and his subsequent 2017 recognition of Jerusalem as Israel's capital, it appears that negotiations likely never will restart.[3]

Despite this history, the Oslo Agreements have exerted an enormous, and lasting, impact on Palestinians, Palestinian decision-making and on the prospects for liberation.

The Oslo Agreements were marketed as a gradual, confidence-building process between Israel and Palestinians, which, if properly implemented, would create the proper political conditions so that the parties would be able to address, in future, the larger issues, including the fate of more than 6 million Palestinian refugees, existing and expanding Israeli colonies, borders of an independent Palestine and the status of Jerusalem. In reality, however, the Oslo Agreements served to divide the Palestinian polity and land, while leaving their indelible marks on Palestinian decision-making. Critics of the Oslo Agreements included Edward Said, who, writing a month after the signing of the first Israel-Palestinian agreement in 1993, made clear that this approach would scar the Palestinian landscape and decision-making, as well as prospects for Palestinian freedom.[4] The critics proved to be correct. This chapter will examine the new realities brought about by the signing of the Oslo Agreements and their continued impact.

To understand the impacts of the Oslo process, it is first necessary to outline the purported purposes of the major Oslo process agreements. These agreements were as follows:

- 1993: Israel-PLO Letters of Recognition. In these letters, the PLO affirmed that it: (i) recognized Israel's right to exist in peace and security; (ii) accepted UN Security Council Resolutions 242 and 338; (iii) agreed to engage in negotiations with Israel; (iv) renounced terrorism; and (v) agreed to amend the Palestinian National Covenant. Israel, in exchange, recognized the PLO and agreed to commence negotiations.[5]
- 1993: Declaration of Principles on Interim Self-Government Arrangements (DOP). This agreement outlined the permanent status issues to be negotiated: Jerusalem, borders, settlements, water, security and refugees. The DOP spelled out that the "transitional period" was to last no more than 5 years and lead to the implementation of UN Resolutions 242 and 338. The DOP also called for elections and outlined the first Israeli troop redeployment.[6]
- 1994: Gaza-Jericho Agreement. This agreement outlined the limited powers and responsibilities of the Palestinian Authority and specified the redeployment of the Israeli army from parts of the Gaza Strip and Jericho city. It also launched the start of the five-year transitional period and the transfer of limited powers to the Palestinian Authority.[7] Part of this agreement includes the Paris Protocol on Economic Relations, which integrated the Palestinian economy into that of Israel. It was later incorporated in the 1995 Interim Agreement (see chapter by Raja Khalidi in this book).
- 1995: The Interim Agreement on the West Bank and the Gaza Strip. This agreement set out the major and specific substance of the Oslo Agreements, establishing the powers and authorities of the Palestinian Authority, and delineating Areas A, B and C in the West Bank.[8]
- 1997: Protocol Concerning the Redeployment in Hebron. This agreement, paralleling its 1995 Interim Agreement predecessor, divided Hebron into two zones of authority: H1 nominally controlled by the Palestinian Authority, but maintaining Israel's right to re-enter, and H2, where a small

number of Israeli settlers live among a large Palestinian population, fully controlled by Israel.[9]
- 1998: Wye River Memorandum. This memorandum was negotiated as a means of renegotiating actions, especially Israeli troop redeployments, specified in the 1995 Interim Agreement that had not been implemented by Israel and specifically set out a revised timetable for Israel's redeployments.[10]
- 1999: Sharm el-Sheikh Memorandum. This memorandum also was negotiated following Israel's failure to abide by provisions of the Interim Agreement. Once again, it set out a specific timetable for Israel's troop redeployments. It was signed four months after the deadline for the conclusion of a final status agreement had passed.[11]

These hundreds of pages of agreements had, at their core, four main principles: (i) Palestinian recognition of Israel in exchange for Israel's recognition of the PLO; (ii) the division of the West Bank and Gaza Strip into small and disconnected cantons, with Israeli redeployment from these cantons—"containment"; (iii) establishment of a pseudo Palestinian government that exercised limited powers in those areas, while simultaneously establishing a Palestinian security force capable of ensuring that Palestinians would not engage in any resistance against Israel's military rule; and (iv) entrenchment of the "two state" framework, with negotiations earmarked as the only permissible means of ending Israel's military rule.

RECOGNITION OF ISRAEL, NO RECOGNITION OF PALESTINE

A primary objective of Israeli negotiators from the outset of the secret Oslo talks was to seek and obtain Palestinian recognition of Israel to facilitate international recognition of Israel. So important was this recognition of Israel that Israel's formal entry into the "peace process" was initiated only following the PLO's recognition of Israel's "right to exist in peace and security," notably in the 1993 Letters of Mutual Recognition, which, at their core do not entail mutual recognition but, rather, a one-sided recognition by the PLO of Israel's right to exist. This recognition was enshrined in all subsequent agreements signed between Israel and the PLO and required the amending of the PLO Charter to reflect the changed PLO position. As Said noted shortly after the signing of the Declaration of Principles, Amos Oz proclaimed that the DOP was "'the second biggest victory in the history of Zionism' with the first, of course being the establishment of the State of Israel following the ethnic cleansing of Palestine."[12]

Though the PLO has not revoked this recognition, in the face of Trump's recognition of Jerusalem as Israel's capital, the PLO has indicated that it is considering "suspending" it but without clearly stating what suspension entails.[13] For its part, to date, Israel has yet to recognize Palestine's right to exist—indeed, the 1993 letter of recognition merely states that the "Government of Israel has decided to recognize the PLO as the representative of the Palestinian people"[14] and, to date, no Zionist political party has recognized Palestine's right to exist. Indeed, with the passage of time, Israel has endeavored to move the recognition goalpost: not content with the Palestinian recognition of Israel's "right to exist," Israeli politicians have gone on to demand Palestinian recognition of Israel as a "Jewish state," a demand that effectively would extinguish the Palestinian right of return by subjugating this right to Israel's demand to remain a majority "Jewish state."[15]

The PLO's recognition of Israel's "right to exist" opened significant new markets for Israel and paved the way for wider international acceptance of Israel: between 1993 and 1999, 29 countries established diplomatic ties or trade offices with Israel including Jordan, Morocco, Tunisia, Oman, Qatar and Mauritania, all members of the Arab League that previously had boycotted Israel. This recognition also served to further shield Israel from diplomatic scrutiny. For example, in casting the 1995 US veto before the UN Security Council on a resolution condemning Israel's continued settlement expansion, in defiance of the letter and spirit of the Oslo Agreements, Madeleine Albright, the US ambassador to the UN, stated that, "This council is not able—and should not seek—to try to resolve sensitive issues in the Middle East peace process. That is for the parties, who must live with the outcome of those negotiations."[16]

Moreover, US assistance to Israel also increased significantly. For example, in late 1998, "Israel requested $1.2 billion in additional US aid to fund the movement of troops and military installations out of areas of the West Bank as called for in the October 23, 1998, Wye Agreement," and received this increased assistance in full despite that Israel never implemented the troop deployments it had agreed to undertake in the Wye River memorandum agreement.[17]

CONTAINMENT

In addition to augmenting Israel's international stature and economic relations, the Oslo Agreements conveniently assisted Israel in more tightly controlling and suppressing the Palestinian population—or what it refers to as the "demographic threat" or "demographic problem."[18] Israel accomplished this with a two-pronged approach consisting of separation and containment. With regard to separation, Israel quickly moved to separate Jerusalem from the rest of the West Bank by insisting that Jerusalem should be addressed only as a "final status" issue, to be negotiated in the future, that is, and effectively removing any Palestinian decision-making or control over the greater Jerusalem area until such future time. The second method—that of containment—involved the delineation of territory quasi-governed by the Palestinian Authority by erecting Israeli checkpoints beyond which Palestinians could henceforth pass only by obtaining permits from Israel to cross.

With the 1995 Interim Agreement, the West Bank, excluding greater Jerusalem, was classified into three categories: (i) Area A: eight unconnected cities comprising around 17.2 percent of the West Bank land area but where an estimated 80 percent of the West Bank Palestinian population (excluding East Jerusalem Palestinians) reside. Pursuant to the Interim Agreement, the Palestinian Authority is responsible for "internal" security, though Israel routinely reinvades these areas; (ii) Area B: comprising around 23.8 percent of the West Bank, where an estimated 18 percent of the Palestinian population resides, and where the Palestinian Authority has "civic" responsibility but Israel controls security; and (iii) Area C: comprising around 59 percent of the West Bank,[19] where Israel explicitly retains full responsibility for security and public order, as well as territory-related civil matters such as resource allocation, building and construction permits and planning. Unlike Areas A and B, which are disconnected islands, Area C is contiguous; it surrounds and divides Areas A and B. Also unlike Areas A and B, Area C's Palestinian population is sparse, comprising 2 percent of the Palestinian West Bank population but incorporating the vast majority of Palestinian farm land and resources. With the stroke of a pen, and with PLO acquiescence, Israel effectively achieved what it had long sought: the containment of the maximum number of Palestinians on the minimum amount of Palestinian land. In the West Bank, excluding Jerusalem, an estimated 98 percent of the Palestinian population came under some form of Palestinian Authority jurisdiction, yet with the Palestinian Authority exercising partial control over a mere 40 percent of West Bank territory. In the words of US president George Bush, the West Bank now resembled "Swiss cheese."[20]

These containment measures were replicated by Israel in the Gaza Strip. There, the Palestinian Authority was granted full responsibility for internal security and public order, except in Israeli settlements and the roads connecting the settlements, where Israel retained the sole power. Israel retained full control over all border crossings, including the Rafah-Egypt crossing, Palestinian airspace and Palestinian maritime areas and boundaries. Even after the 2005 "disengagement," Israel continued to retain full control over all Gaza

Strip air space, maritime space and boundaries and Israel reserved the right to "take any measures necessary against vessels suspected of being used for terrorist activities or for smuggling arms, ammunition, drugs, goods, or for any other illegal activity."[21] Thus, like Areas A and B in the West Bank, areas of the Gaza Strip placed under Palestinian jurisdiction remain surrounded and controlled by Israel.

This Israeli process of containment, sold as "territorial jurisdiction," meant that the PLO had to agree to the erection of checkpoints around 22 separate Area A enclaves, with Israel controlling movement into, out of and between all of them. Although the Oslo Agreements speak of the West Bank and the Gaza Strip as "a single territorial unit, whose integrity will be preserved during the interim period," the process of dividing those two areas accelerated under every successive Oslo Agreement and continues until today.

The process of separating the West Bank and the Gaza Strip began in 1991. Prior to the Gulf War in 1991, Palestinians had virtually complete freedom of movement both within, and between, the Gaza Strip, Jerusalem and the remainder of the West Bank, as well as throughout Israel. In 1991, however, Israel began to impose movement restrictions on the Gaza Strip, with Gaza Palestinians now needing permits to leave the Gaza Strip. In March 1993, this process was further extended to encompass Jerusalem, where Palestinians now needed "entry to Israel" permits to visit Jerusalem, including occupied East Jerusalem.

As the mislabeled "peace process" continued to emerge, Palestinian freedom of movement was further hindered with the restrictions imposed "temporarily" in March 1993 becoming permanent. In addition, economic development was, and remains today, severely hindered. This has been accomplished through Israel's continuous full control over borders, air and sea space, the large scale erection of Israeli checkpoints and obstacles to movement and the associated imposition of Israel's labyrinthine permitting regime, which together effectively strangle freedom of movement for Palestinians and the Palestinian economy.

Beginning in 1993, before the signing of the Declaration of Principles, Israel began establishing checkpoints in the Gaza Strip, Jericho and in Jerusalem, which later were extended throughout the West Bank. Today, the West Bank is littered with obstacles to movement with the UN Office for the Coordination of Humanitarian Affairs documenting in 2016 that Israel had erected over 572 fixed roadblocks in the West Bank, including 44 permanently staffed checkpoints, 52 partially staffed checkpoints and 376 roadblocks, earth mounds and gates. In addition, one or more of the main entrances to 10 of the 11 major West Bank cities remains blocked.[22]

Alongside the checkpoints came a new Israeli "permit regime" to strictly control Palestinian movement. Palestinians now needed permits to visit the Gaza Strip, to work in or visit Israel, and to visit, work or reside in Jerusalem as it had now been separated from the rest of the West Bank and increasingly treated by Israel as declared Israeli territory. Such permits were contingent upon obtaining security clearance and, given Israel's high rate of incarceration of Palestinians, such clearance was difficult to obtain.

While the process of closures and movement restrictions increased, Israel also used this period to continue the process of confiscating Palestinian land, to increase home demolitions and expand Israeli settlements: from 1993 to 2000, the total Jewish settler population in the West Bank (excluding East Jerusalem) increased from 115,600 to 198,300 and the number of housing units in these settlement areas rose by 50 percent.[23] Thus, during these "peace process" years, settler activity proceeded at breakneck speed as Israel rushed to build and expand settlements to be used as "facts on the ground" during negotiations.[24] In his final speech to the Knesset before his assassination a month later in November 1995, Yitzhak Rabin made clear his position on the construction of settlements in the interim period:

> I want to remind you: we committed ourselves, that is, we came to an agreement, and committed ourselves before the Knesset, not to uproot a single settlement in the framework of the interim agreement, and not to hinder building for natural growth.[25]

According to Israel's own statistics, there are now more than 400,000 settlers in the West Bank alone. When the settlers of East Jerusalem are included, the population increases to more than 600,000.[26] Illegal under international law and built on land illegally seized from Palestinians, Israel's settlements now control nearly 60 percent of the land surface of the West Bank, including East Jerusalem.[27]

As Israel solidified and expanded its hold on Palestinian land, Israel and the PLO entrenched the system of dual laws in a single jurisdiction: one law for Palestinians and another law for Israelis. In short, apartheid. Unlike in other countries around the world, where territorial jurisdiction is supreme, in the case of the Oslo Agreements, personal jurisdiction takes precedence. What this means is that the Palestinian Authority does not have any jurisdiction over Israelis, even if they violate the law while in Palestinian Authority-controlled areas. The Interim Agreement provides that "the territorial and functional jurisdiction of the [Palestinian] Council will apply to all persons, except for Israelis, unless otherwise provided in this Agreement." Israelis may only come under the jurisdiction of Palestinian judicial authorities in civil matters when such Israelis explicitly consent in writing to that jurisdiction, when they maintain ongoing businesses in territory under the Palestinian Authority's control, or when the subject matter of the action is real property located in Palestinian Authority areas. In other words, Israeli civilian and criminal law (but not Israeli military law) applies to Israelis, irrespective of whether they are in the West Bank or Israel, while Palestinians are subject to both Palestinian civil law (if in Area A or B) and Israeli military law (irrespective of whether they are in Areas A, B or C).[28]

In sum, Israel effectively managed to rid itself of responsibility for over 98 percent of the Palestinian population of the West Bank by granting to the Palestinian Authority narrowly drawn powers, pertaining to civil affairs, basic service provision and internal policing, in 22 separate enclaves which are entirely surrounded and controlled by Israel. With Palestinian citizens of Israel no longer of concern to the PLO, and with the Palestinian refugees and Jerusalem off the table, Israel's efforts to contain the demographic threat appear to have succeeded.

A SECURITY SUBCONTRACTOR FOR ISRAEL

Israel's intentions in entering the Oslo Agreements were to reap the rewards of recognition, contain the "demographic threat" and use the peace process to consolidate its hold on Palestinian land while simultaneously relieving itself of any responsibility toward Palestinians. But while these rewards were important, their importance was overshadowed by the demand that the Palestinian Authority maintain a security force capable of crushing any Palestinian resistance. By creating a Palestinian government responsible for maintaining internal security but without sovereignty, the Oslo Agreements effectively transformed Palestinians from a population resisting Israel's occupation to a population quasi-governed by an authority responsible for protecting the occupier. The value of this was clearly understood—as expressed by Israeli prime minister Yitzhak Rabin: "[t]he Palestinians will be better at establishing internal security than we were," adding that "they will rule by their own methods, freeing, and this is most important, the Israeli soldiers from having to do what they [the Palestinians] will do."[29]

Countless provisions relating to security are contained in agreements, detailing everything from the permissible size of the Palestinian police force and its permitted weaponry to the jurisdiction within which the Palestinian force may operate. The Oslo Agreements methodically delineated the limited powers of the Palestinian Authority's security force while allowing others to view it as having the trappings of an army.

This security force, deployed in the areas from which Israel redeployed, had, as its primary focus, the task of maintaining security for Israel and the hundreds of thousands of Israeli settlers implanted by Israel in the occupied West Bank and Gaza Strip in the years prior to, and especially following, the 1993 DOP. Unlike previous international diplomatic efforts that focused on the "land for peace" formulation, the Oslo Agreements created a new formulation: "security for peace."

By 1999, the Palestinian Authority's security services numbered 35,000 making the Palestinian people of the West Bank and Gaza Strip among the highest *per capita* policed populations in the world.[30] To create this bloated security force, the Palestinian Authority co-opted many Fatah party activists and turned them into security personnel responsible for policing Palestinians. The formula worked: from November 1997 to October 2000, not a single Israeli was killed inside Israel, thereby providing Israel with the "quiet" it had long desired.[31] This "quiet" came at a price for Palestinians: for example, in 1998, the Palestinian Authority rounded up an estimated 450 members of Hamas and Israeli Jihad activists, and placed the quadriplegic Hamas spiritual leader under house arrest.[32] Even the US Department of State in its annual country reports on human rights practices stated in 1999 that:

> Both Israel and the PA were responsible for serious human rights abuses; however, while there were several marked improvements in Israel's human rights record in the occupied territories, the PA's human rights record worsened in several areas. . . . PA security officials committed abuse, and in some cases torture, against prisoners and detainees. Palestinian security forces killed three persons in violent confrontations. PA security forces used excessive force, and in some cases, live ammunition against Palestinian demonstrators and shot at demonstrators and individuals indiscriminately. Two other Palestinians died in PA custody.[33]

Nonetheless, this crackdown on Palestinians continued to be lauded by others within the US Department of State, namely, then-assistant U.S. secretary of state, Martin Indyk, who stated in June 1999:

> We have always said that the Palestinians have done a good job on some of the issues, particularly on the security cooperation issue and combating terrorism. We weren't the only ones to say that; Prime Minister Netanyahu, at one point, called Yasir Arafat and thanked him for the efforts that he'd been undertaking.[34]

New York Times pundit Thomas Friedman echoed Indyk in 2014, noting that, "[t]he fact is, the only time Israelis have enjoyed extended periods of peace in the last decade has been when Palestinian security services disciplined their own people, in the heyday of Oslo."[35]

In short, the Oslo Agreements effectively transformed the Palestinian Authority into Israel's security subcontractor, with the Palestinians consenting to provide security for their occupier, Israel. This not only turned international humanitarian law on its head, but demanded that the Palestinian Authority commit gross human rights abuses against its own people to secure US and Israeli approval. Resistance of any kind was now a "violation" of the Oslo Agreements and reason for the PA to crack down on Palestinians.

In 2011, Mamdouh Aker, the former commissioner-general of the Palestinian Independent Commission for Human Rights noted that:

> For three years I have been warning that certain characteristics will drag us toward becoming a police state, unless we pay attention: Arbitrary, illegal arrests. Torture of detainees—due to our complaints, there has been an improvement for several months, but now there appears to be a return to this miserable procedure. Screening of candidates for public posts by the intelligence and preventive security apparatus. Arrests of civilians by the security apparatus—there was a promise that this would end, but we will still wait for an explicit guarantee from the high political level. A lack of compliance with court rulings.[36]

Today, more than one quarter of the Palestinian Authority's budget is spent directly on security, which is more than the amount spent on education and health care combined.[37] Moreover, although negotiations ended long ago, and with the election of Donald Trump as president of the US the unlikelihood of new negotiations recommencing, the Palestinian Authority not only has maintained its security collaboration with Israel but has increased it, even in the face of increasingly vociferous Palestinian calls to end it. For example, in March 2015, the PLO Central Council called upon the Abbas-led Palestinian Authority to end security collaboration in the face of Israel's withholding of Palestinian Authority tax revenues.[38] A similar statement also was made in January 2018.[39] Yet, despite calls from civil society organizations, political factions and the PLO, Abbas continues to collaborate extensively with Israel on a full range of security issues. In February 2018, Israel's army minister announced: "The Palestinian officers and the security coordination deserve a good word. The Palestinians also understand that the security coordination is a mutual interest, which is why we work to preserve it."[40]

NEGOTIATIONS, NEGOTIATIONS—UNTIL VICTORY

Just as the Oslo Agreements had the effect of creating a security force capable of serving as Israel's subcontractor, they also had the effect of enabling a change in the status of the Occupied Palestinian Territory (OPT) and fostered in the PLO a penchant for negotiations. In the words of Edward Said, the PLO, "have in effect discounted their unilateral and internationally acknowledged claim to the West Bank and Gaza: these have now become 'disputed territories.'"[41] And the PLO appeared to relish in the perpetual negotiations process. Rather than stepping away from or devising new strategies, the PLO continued to participate in endless talks, even when it became painfully evident that the negotiations not only were leading nowhere but provided Israel with cover to accelerate its settlement expansion in the occupied West Bank, including East Jerusalem.

Indeed, within months of signing the 1993 Declaration of Principles, Israel's attitude toward negotiations became clear when, in December 1993, Prime Minister Yitzhak Rabin declared, in relation to the deadlines spelled out in the Declaration of Principles, that "[t]here are no more holy dates."[42]

The failure to meet deadlines forced Palestinians to renegotiate agreements to press for previously promised Israeli redeployments. The renegotiation of agreements increasingly blurred the core idea of the Oslo Agreements as a temporary, five-year process that would end Israel's occupation, instead turning it into a series of never-ending negotiations. For example, the 1993 Declaration of Principles provided for Palestinian Authority elections to take place "not later than nine months after the entry into force [of the Declaration of Principles]."[43] The Declaration of Principles entered into force on October 13, 1993, one month after its signing. Accordingly, the first elections should have taken place in July 1994. They did not take place, however, until January 20, 1996, and the Council only held its inaugural session on March 7, 1996.

These delayed elections exacted a steep price for Palestinians because they also had repercussions for Israel's military redeployment. The 1995 Interim Agreement required Israel to complete its military withdrawal within 18 months of the inauguration of the Palestinian Legislative Council, i.e., by September 7, 1997.[44] This withdrawal was to encompass "West Bank and Gaza Strip territory, except for issues that will be negotiated in the permanent status negotiations," these being "Jerusalem, settlements, specified military locations, Palestinian refugees, borders, foreign relations and Israelis." Yet, by October 23, 1998, only 2 percent of the West Bank had been turned over to Palestinian control (Area A). When it became clear that Israel was not planning to redeploy, the US intensified its efforts to "revive the peace process." Beginning in 1998, with the Wye River Memorandum, the new agreements specified a revised timetable for the phased implementation of the first and second redeployments as outlined in the 1995 Interim Agreement. Again Israel failed to redeploy despite the fact that Palestinian security forces had ensured total "quiet" for Israel. In a further apparent attempt to "revive the peace process" the US pushed the PLO and Israel to sign the 1999 Sharm el-Sheikh Memorandum, which Israel also failed to adhere to. In other words, what was supposed to be a redeployment from "West Bank and Gaza Strip territory, except for issues that will be negotiated in the permanent status negotiations" by 1997, turned into a redeployment from a mere 17.2 percent of the West Bank, excluding Jerusalem, leaving the vast majority of the West Bank in Israel's hands and enabling it to maintain perpetual control over the Gaza Strip to this day.

The perpetual negotiations were not simply concerned with redeployments, however. They also continuously pushed back the date for conclusion of final status negotiations. According to the 1993 Declaration of Principles, the "transitional period" was to be for a period "not exceeding five years" and thus should have concluded no later than September 1998. Yet, when Israel failed to commence negotiations, the parties renegotiated the final date for reaching a permanent settlement. The 1995 Interim Agreement stated that the parties would work to reach a permanent status agreement by May 4, 1999.[45] Following the failure to conclude a permanent agreement in May 1999, the parties agreed in the September 1999 Sharm El-Sheikh Memorandum to make yet another "determined effort" to reach a Framework Agreement on Permanent Status by February 13, 2000, and a Comprehensive Agreement on Permanent Status by September 13, 2000.[46]

The myriad delays, however, were not by accident but, rather, by design: Israel used this period to build new settlements and expand existing settlements, in violation of the signed agreements, international law and even statements by US officials.[47]

The construction of settlements served Israel well because their burgeoning numbers amounted to Israel creating new facts on the ground, an increasingly entrenched colonial presence and extensive supporting infrastructure from which Israel would force Palestinians to "negotiate" their independence.

For the PLO, while the delays were a source of consternation, it undertook no actions to devise, much less deploy, alternatives to negotiations and continued to crack down on Palestinians dissenting against the Oslo process. In part, this was because the negotiations were a convenient means by which the PLO could focus on the establishment of a "Palestinian state" rather than on mechanisms to press for Israel's complete withdrawal. Indeed, this was part of the design of Oslo: while the PLO had (implicitly as far back as the 1970s and explicitly in 1988 with the Palestinian Declaration of Independence) accepted UN Security Council Resolution 242, the Oslo Agreements shifted attention from Israel's withdrawal from the OPT and the return of Palestinian refugees, toward the establishment of a "Palestinian state" as the means of implementing this UN Resolution. This distinction is neither a hair-splitting or semantic one given the differing interpretations of this UN Resolution.

For Palestinians and the international community, the UN Security Council Resolution 242 calls for Israel's complete withdrawal from all of the territories it occupied.[48] Israel argues that the Resolution provides latitude for Israel to determine the territories from which it can withdraw based upon its "security needs."[49] By refocusing on the establishment of a "Palestinian state," the peace process diverted attention away from Israel's colonization of Palestinian land and from Israel's international requirement to withdraw from the land it occupied in 1967. It also conveniently allowed the PLO/PA to ignore new settlement construction and instead focus on creating the symbols of statehood as a means of building support for the PA and quashing dissent that derided the failed peace process and demanded its cessation.

The full impact of Israel's expansion of settlements became apparent under Yitzhak Rabin's tenure and has been further solidified ever since. During each round of negotiations during Rabin's life, Israel made clear that it had no intention to completely withdraw from all of the territory that it occupied in 1967 and that it intended to perpetually hold onto Palestinian land. In his 1995 speech before the Knesset, Rabin stated:

> We would like this to be an entity which is less than a state, and which will independently run the lives of the Palestinians under its authority. The borders of the State of Israel, during the permanent solution, will be beyond the lines which existed before the Six Day War. We will not return to the 4 June 1967 lines.
>
> And these are the main changes, not all of them, which we envision and want in the permanent solution:
>
> A. First and foremost, united Jerusalem, which will include both Ma'ale Adumim and Givat Ze'ev—as the capital of Israel, under Israeli sovereignty, while preserving the rights of the members of the other faiths, Christianity and Islam, to freedom of access and freedom of worship in their holy places, according to the customs of their faiths.
> B. The security border of the State of Israel will be located in the Jordan Valley, in the broadest meaning of that term.
> C. Changes which will include the addition of Gush Etzion, Efrat, Beitar and other communities, most of which are in the area east of what was the "Green Line," prior to the Six Day War.
> D. The establishment of blocs of settlements in Judea and Samaria, like the one in Gush Katif.[50]

Despite this clear pronouncement, from he who has been lauded as the person who made the most significant moves (and for which he received a Nobel prize), Palestinian negotiators continued to maintain the façade that negotiations would yield a complete end to Israel's military occupation. For example, during the 2001 Taba negotiations, which followed the failed Camp David negotiations, the parties concluded that:

> The Israeli and Palestinian delegations conducted . . . deep and practical talks with the aim of reaching a permanent and stable agreement between the two parties. . . . Given the circumstances and time constraints, it proved impossible to reach understandings on all issues, despite the substantial progress that was achieved in each of the issues discussed. . . . The sides declare that they have never been closer to reaching an agreement and it is thus our shared belief that the remaining gaps could be bridged with the resumption of negotiations following the Israeli elections.[51]

Yet, examining the proposals put forth by Israel in all of the negotiations over the past decades, and based on experience in the negotiations process, it is clear that Israel consistently has sought to maintain: (i) permanent or semi-permanent control over major parts of Palestinian territory, particularly in Jerusalem and in the Jordan Valley, through the erection of military bases and settlements there; (ii) control over Palestinian airspace; (iii) eliminate the right of return for Palestinian refugees; (iv) control over Palestinian natural resources, including water; and (v) the presence of hundreds of thousands of Israeli settlers and settlements in the OPT particularly in Jerusalem, where Israel has refused even to discuss the removal of Israeli settlers and settlements.

The negotiations in the years subsequent to the Second Intifada maintained the same positions. Palestinian negotiators engaged in countless discussions of land swaps to accommodate Israeli settlements while Israeli negotiators continued to insist on no right of return for Palestinian refugees and no discussion on the future of Jerusalem.[52]

For its part, the PLO continued to entertain these positions and, as time passed, grew more desperate to achieve a "Palestinian state"—including a demilitarized one. The PLO's desperation was evidenced in pressing for land swaps to accommodate the presence of Israeli settlers, instead of Israel's withdrawal, from large and strategically essential parts of Palestinian territory. These land swaps initially were proposed by US officials during the 2000 Camp David negotiations and formalized in the 2001 Clinton Parameters. During the Taba negotiations in 2001, where Israeli negotiators accepted the concept of swaps,[53] by 2008 it became apparent that Israel was both refusing to recognize the 1967 boundaries and the idea of swaps,[54] and that Palestinian negotiators were mulling over the idea of accommodating more than 85 percent of Israeli settlers in the OPT.[55]

By 2008, Palestinian negotiators conceded all of the Jerusalem lands with Israeli settlements. In the words of PLO negotiator Ahmed Qurei: "We proposed that Israel annexes all settlements in Jerusalem except Jabal Abu

Ghneim (Har Homa). This is the first time in history that we make such a proposition; we refused to do so in Camp David." Qurei's words were echoed by the chief Palestinian negotiator, Saeb Erekat, who noted that: "[Our proposal] gives them the biggest Yerushalaim [*sic*, the Hebrew name for Jerusalem] in Jewish history, symbolic number of refugees return, demilitarised state . . . what more can I give?"[56]

Furthermore, the PLO signaled a potential change in its official position regarding the right of return for Palestinian refugees by agreeing to allow Israel to "agree to" any solution for Palestinian refugees. This marked a deviation from the international legal position that Palestinian refugees have a right to return to their homes as embodied in UN General Assembly resolutions, particularly UN General Assembly Resolution 194, as well as UN Security Council Resolution 242. By 2002, the PLO had amended its position—in an effort to entice Israel to support the Arab Peace Initiative—and assumed the significantly diluted position that an "agreed, just solution to the problem of Palestinian refugees" should be found.

Fortunately, despite the PLO's evident willingness to make sweeping concessions on territory, rights, resources and the ability to defend itself in the manner of every other sovereign state in the world, Israeli negotiators were unwilling to accept any Palestinian entity, including one as emasculated as that desperately proposed by Palestinian negotiators. In short, Israel was happy with maintaining the status quo rather than agreeing to even the most truncated, debilitated Palestinian quasi-state.

And despite the futility of negotiations, Palestinian negotiators continued to pursue this same policy from 2000 onward, with the same results. By 2011, as Mahmoud Abbas unveiled his "internationalization" plan, it was widely expected that this process would replace negotiations. Yet, Abbas made clear, and continues to make clear, that, in his view, bilateral negotiations are the only legitimate means for achieving an end to Israel's military rule.

As it stands today, Palestinians certainly are no closer to independence than they were more than two decades ago. Instead they are trapped in an abyss created by the Oslo Agreements, which appears actually to have moved them further away from the realization of Palestinian self-determination. To be clear, the Oslo Agreements are not international agreements, but rather temporal ones whose purpose expired long ago. Yet, although these agreements have expired, their impact remains. The Palestinian Authority continues to maintain security cooperation with Israel despite thousands of Palestinian lives taken by Israeli forces, and thousands of arrests. Moreover, the PLO refuses to adopt alternative strategies—whether violent or nonviolent, such as supporting the Boycott, Divestment and Sanctions Movement (BDS)—to hold Israel accountable and push for an end to Israel's military rule. Instead, the PLO continues to cling to the mirage of the "two-state solution" even while it is clear that neither the US nor Israel want to see any change to the existing "temporary" status quo. This mirage is only occasionally broken when the PLO unconvincingly threatens to disband the Palestinian Authority or abandon the two-state solution as a means of creating a sense of urgency with which to negotiate with Israel. Even the much-lauded "statehood" initiative remains little more than a tactic to press Israel to return to these futile negotiations, as stated repeatedly by Palestinian negotiators and leaders.[57] It is therefore unsurprising that 42 percent of Palestinians in the West Bank want to see the dissolution of the Palestinian Authority,[58] despite the fact that so many depend upon it and the evident lack of a cogent political alternative.

CONCLUSION

More than two decades after the start of the negotiations process, it is clear both what Oslo was and what it was not. It was neither a mechanism to liberate Palestine from Israel's clutches nor a temporary mechanism to build trust. Rather, Oslo entrenched three main phenomenon. First, it cemented Israel's apartheid regime. Second, it established a means by which Israel could separate itself from Palestinians while continuing to hold onto Palestinian land and demanding that Palestinians crush any resistance to Israel's colonial rule. And third, it established negotiations as the only legitimate means to end Israel's military rule with other options, whether resistance (armed or otherwise) and BDS, criminalized or labeled as illegitimate. These effects will take decades to undo, particularly as the Palestinian economy is now heavily dependent upon the existence of the Palestinian Authority, which is, in turn, dependent upon donor funds. Undoubtedly and unsurprisingly, therefore, Oslo will go down in Palestinian history books, as described by Edward Said, as the "Palestinian Versailles."[59]

NOTES

1. "The Khartoum Resolutions, August 29–September 1, 1967," https://ecf.org.il/media_items/513. The relevant portion of the resolutions provides that: "This will be done within the framework of the main principles by which the Arab States abide, namely, no peace with Israel, no recognition of Israel, no negotiations with it, and insistence on the rights of the Palestinian people in their own country."

2. The Declaration of Principles provides that: "It is understood that the interim arrangements are an integral part of the whole peace process and that the negotiations on the permanent status will lead to the implementation of Security Council Resolutions

242 and 338." While the text of the Oslo Accords did not mention an independent Palestinian state at the end of the transition period, Palestinians believed and were led to believe, that in return for giving up their claim to 78 percent of historic Palestine, they would gain an independent state in the remaining 22 percent, with a capital city in Jerusalem. This belief was not based on fiction: as indicated by Robert Malley, the former special assistant for Arab-Israeli affairs to President Bill Clinton from 1998 to 2001 at discussion during the Camp David summit of 2000 was the establishment of a Palestinian state. Found at: Robert Malley, "Fictions About the Failure At Camp David," *New York Times*, July 8, 2001, http://www.nytimes.com/2001/07/08/opinion/fictions-about-the-failure-at-camp-david.html.

3. Oded Revivi, "If the Oslo Accords Are Over, the Real Work of Peace Can Begin," *The Wall Street Journal*, Jan. 17, 2018, https://www.wsj.com/articles/if-the-oslo-accords-are-over-the-real-work-of-peace-can-begin-1516233947. In the piece, Abbas is quoted as saying: "'Today is the day that the Oslo Accords end,' Palestinian Authority President Mahmoud Abbas declared Sunday. 'We will not accept for the U.S. to be a mediator, because after what they have done to us'—namely, recognize Jerusalem as Israel's capital—'a believer shall not be stung twice in the same place.'"

4. Edward Said, "The Morning After," *London Review of Books*, October 21, 1999, http://www.lrb.co.uk/v15/n20/edward-said/the-morning-after.

5. Israel-PLO Recognition: Exchange of Letters between PM Rabin and Chairman Arafat, September 9, 1993, https://ecf.org.il/media_items/300.

6. Declaration of Principles on Interim Self-Government Arrangements, September 13, 1993, https://ecf.org.il/media_items/612.

7. Cairo Agreement—on the Gaza Strip and the Jericho Area, Cairo, May 4.

8. Israeli-Palestinian Interim Agreement on the West Bank and the Gaza Strip, Washington, D.C., September 28, 1995, https://ecf.org.il/media_items/624.

9. Protocol Concerning the Redeployment in Hebron (as initialed on January 15, 1997), http://ecf.org.il/media_items/631.

10. The Wye River Memorandum, October 23, 1998, http://ecf.org.il/media_items/634.

11. The Wye River Memorandum, October 23, 1998, http://ecf.org.il/media_item.

12. Edward Said, "The Morning After," *London Review of Books*, October 21, 1999, http://www.lrb.co.uk/v15/n20/edward-said/the-morning-after.

13. "PA Reconsiders Recognition of Israel," *Al Jazeera*, March 6, 2018, https://www.aljazeera.com/news/2018/01/palestinian-leadership-revokes-recognition-israel-180116060200939.html.

14. Israel-PLO Recognition.

15. Glenn Kessler, "Defining 'Jewish State': For Many, Term has Different Meanings," *The Washington Post*, October 2, 2010, http://www.washingtonpost.com/wp-dyn/content/article/2010/10/01/AR2010100104177.html.

16. https://www.nytimes.com/1995/05/18/world/us-vetoes-a-condemnation-in-un-of-israeli-land-seizure.html.

17. Jeremy Sharp, "U.S. Foreign Aid to Israel," June 10, 2015, http://securityassistance.org/sites/default/files/RL33222.pdf.

18. A central feature of Israeli practices since 1948 has been to contain, or minimize, the "demographic threat" or "demographic problem" that Palestinians pose to the maintenance of a Jewish majority in the borders of historical Palestine. In pursuit of this aim, Israel has used a number of different containment or minimization measures. In the mid-1940s, these measures involved the ethnic cleansing of more than 750,000 Palestinians, comprising 75 percent of the Palestinian population at that time. After 1948, Israel switched gears from outright ethnic cleansing to that of containing the "threat." From the time of Israel's 1948 proclamation until 1966, the remaining 150,000 Palestinians who had not fled or been expelled were subjected to martial law, with the concomitant establishment of checkpoints through which only those Palestinians with permits could pass, and a systematic land confiscation and expropriation process that continues to the present day. This containment measure ensured that Palestinians were cordoned off into Palestinian cities and towns surrounded by Israeli Jewish ones—this served as a model for Israel's actions in the West Bank after 1967. Though martial law ended inside Israel in 1966, with the start of Israel's military occupation of the West Bank and Gaza Strip in June 1967, martial law commenced anew there. Containment continued in the same form as in the past, by taking Palestinian land and transforming it into Israeli-only housing and areas of access.

19. This figure excludes the Israeli settlements, which comprise 1.7 percent of the West Bank. When the initial size calculation of the West Bank was made, it excluded the settlements owing to their relegation as a "final status" issue.

20. Khaled Abu Toameh, "Bush: Palestine Can't Be A Swiss Cheese," *Jerusalem Post*, January 10, 2008, http://www.jpost.com/Israel/Bush-Palestine-cant-be-a-Swiss-cheese.

21. Interim Agreement, Article XIV(1)(b)(4).

22. Office for the Coordination of Humanitarian Affairs, Humanitarian Facts and Figures, 2016 at 10. Found at: https://www.ochaopt.org/sites/default/files/factsheet_booklet_final_21_12_2017.pdf.

23. Israel Central Bureau of Statistics, "Table 2.7: Localities and Population By District, Sub-District, Area, Population Group and Religion, 1995," http://www.cbs.gov.il/archive/shnaton47/st02-07.gif and "Table 2.7: Localities and Population By District, Sub-District, Area, Population Group and Religion, 2000," http://www.cbs.gov.il/archive/shnaton52/st02_07.pdf.

24. Foundation for Middle East Peace, "Comprehensive Settlement Population 1972–2010," http://www.fmep.org/settlement_info/settlement-info-and-tfo/settlement-info-and-tables/stats-data/comprehensive-settlement-population-1972-2006.

25. Yitzhak Rabin, "Ratification of Interim Agreement" (speech, Israel Knesset, October 5, 1995), Israel Ministry of Foreign Affairs, http://www.mfa.gov.il/mfa/mfa-archive/1995/pages/pm%20rabin%20in%20knesset-%20ratification%20of%20interim%20agree.aspx.

26. Israel Central Bureau of Statistics, Table 2.13 (2014), http://www.cbs.gov.il/reader/shnaton/shnatone_new.htm?CYear=2015&Vol=66&CSubject=2. See also, Jerusalem Institute for Israel Studies, Table III/9—Population of Jerusalem,

by Age, Religion and Geographical Spreading, 2013. Found at: http://www.jiis.org.il/.upload/yearbook/2015/shnaton_C0915.pdf. See also Yotam Berger, "How Many Settlers Really Live in the West Bank?" *Haaretz*, June 15, 2017, https://www.haaretz.com/israel-news/.premium.MAGAZINE-revealed-how-many-settlers-really-live-in-the-west-bank-1.5482213.

27. B'Tselem, "Land Grab: Israel's Settlement Policy in the West Bank," 2002, 116, https://www.btselem.org/publications/summaries/200205_land_grab.

28. United Nations, Economic and Social Commission for Western Asia (ESCWA), "Israeli Practices toward the Palestinian People and the Question of Apartheid Palestine and the Israeli Occupation, Issue No. 1," March 15, 2017, https://electronicintifada.net/sites/default/files/2017-03/un_apartheid_report_15_march_english_final_.pdf.

29. Graham Usher, "The Politics of Internal Security: The PA's New Intelligence Services," *Journal of Palestine Studies* (Winter 1996).

30. International Institute for Strategic Security, Military Balance, 1998–9 at 138–9 (2000).

31. For a comprehensive list, see http://www.mfa.gov.il/MFA/Terrorism-+Obstacle+to+Peace/Palestinian+terror+before+2000/Fatal+Terrorist+Attacks+in+Israel+Since+the+DOP+-S.htm.

32. Lee Hockstader, "Arafat Says Crackdown On Hamas Is Not Over," *The Washington Post*, November 4, 1998, https://www.washingtonpost.com/archive/politics/1998/11/04/arafat-says-crackdown-on-hamas-is-not-over/51986192-8a00-401a-9a16-2fd57e9a8a12/?utm_term=.a4cee90ebe35.

33. US Department of State, "Human Rights Practices, 1999: The Occupied Territories," February 3, 2000, https://www.state.gov/j/drl/rls/hrrpt/1999/417.htm.

34. Press Conference by Assistant Sec. of State Martin Indyk, June 29, 1999.

35. Thomas Friedman, "Israel's Goals in Gaza?" *New York Times*, January 14, 2009, http://www.nytimes.com/2009/01/14/opinion/14friedman.html?ref=opinion&_r=0.

36. Amira Hass, "Why Isn't the PA Supporting the Egypt Uprising?" *Ha'aretz*, February 3, 2011.

37. See, for example, the 2011 budget as found in http://www.pmof.ps/en/index.php?pagess=home Table 6(a).

38. Diaa Hadid, "Palestinian Council Questions Security Arrangement With Israel," *New York Times*, March 5, 2015, https://www.nytimes.com/2015/03/06/world/middleeast/palestinian-council-questions-security-arrangement-with-israel.html.

39. Palestinian Boycott, Divestment and Sanctions National Committee, "PLO Endorses BDS, Makes Unprecedented Call for Sanctions," January 17, 2018, https://bdsmovement.net/news/plo-endorses-bds%C2%A0makes-unprecedented-call-sanctions.

40. Anna Ahronheim and Adam Rasgon, "Liberman Praises Security Coordination With Palestinians," *Jerusalem Post*, February 13, 2018, http://www.jpost.com/Arab-Israeli-Conflict/Liberman-praises-security-coordination-with-Palestinians-542483.

41. Edward Said, "The Morning After," *London Review of Books*, October 21, 1999, http://www.lrb.co.uk/v15/n20/edward-said/the-morning-after.

42. Clyde Haberman, "Rabin Says Israel May Not Meet Date To Begin Pullout," *New York Times*, November 27, 1993, https://www.nytimes.com/1993/11/27/world/rabin-says-israel-may-not-meet-date-to-begin-pullout.html.

43. Declaration of Principles, Article 3(2).

44. Under Article 3(2) of the DOP, elections for the Council were to be held "not later than nine months after the entry into force [of the DOP]." The DOP entered into force one month after its signing—on October 13, 1993, so the first elections should have taken place in July 1994. They did not take place, however, until January 20, 1996, and the Council held its inaugural session on March 7, 1996.

45. The preamble to the Interim Agreement states that, ". . . a transitional period not exceeding five years from the date of signing the Agreement on the Gaza Strip and the Jericho Area (hereinafter "the Gaza-Jericho Agreement") on May 4, 1994, leading to a permanent settlement based on Security Council Resolutions 242 and 338."

46. The Memorandum provides that: The two Sides will make a determined effort to conclude a Framework Agreement on all Permanent Status issues in five months from the resumption of the Permanent Status negotiations; The two Sides will conclude a comprehensive agreement on all Permanent Status issues within one year from the resumption of the Permanent Status negotiations; Permanent Status negotiations will resume after the implementation of the first stage of release of prisoners and the second stage of the First and Second Further Redeployments and not later than September 13, 1999.

47. The United States gave explicit assurances to the Palestinians at the inception of the process. In a letter dated October 30, 1991, the United States Government stated, "The United States has long believed that no party should take unilateral actions that seek to predetermine issues that can only be resolved through negotiations. In this regard the United States has opposed and will continue to oppose settlement activity in the territories occupied in 1967, which remains an obstacle to peace." "United States Letter of Assurances to the Palestinians, October 18, 1991" in Volume 2, *Documents on Palestine*, pg 8 (Mahdi Abdul Hadi ed., Jerusalem, 1997).

48. This position is bolstered by the provisions of the UN Charter which provide, in Article 2(4) that, "All Members shall refrain in their international relations from the threat or use of force against the territorial integrity or political independence of any state, or in any other manner inconsistent with the Purposes of the United Nations." Found at: http://www.un.org/en/documents/charter/chapter1.shtml.

49. For a detailed explanation of Israel's position, see Ruth Lapidoth, "The Misleading Interpretation of Security Council Resolution 242 [1967]," February 2012. Found at: http://jcpa.org/wp-content/uploads/2012/02/Kiyum-lapidoth.pdf.

50. Yitzhak Rabin, "Ratification of Interim Agreement" (speech, Israel Knesset, October 5, 1995), Israel Ministry of Foreign Affairs, http://www.mfa.gov.il/mfa/mfa-archive/1995/pages/pm%20rabin%20in%20knesset-%20ratification%20of%20interim%20agree.aspx.

51. "Israeli-Palestinian Joint Statement at Taba, January 27, 2001." Found at: http://www.mfa.gov.il/MFA/MFA-Archive/2001/Pages/Israeli-Palestinian%20Joint%20Statement%20-%2027-Jan-2001.aspx.

52. The Palestine Papers, found at: http://www.aljazeera.com/palestinepapers/.

53. Akiva Eldar, ""Moratinos Document"—The peace that nearly was at Taba," *Ha'aretz*, February 14, 2002, http://prrn.mcgill.ca/research/papers/moratinos.htm.

54. Meeting Summary: 5th Meeting on Territory—The Palestine Papers—Aljazeera Investigations, http://transparency.aljazeera.net/en/projects/thepalestinepapers/201218232341578673.html. During this meeting, it is reported that: "The Israeli side refused to engage on the basis of the 1967 line or to accept the principle of a swap—and it was clear that they had no mandate to do so. They also insisted that the border in Jerusalem be excluded from the work of the territory committee. However, there was no discussion of the eastern border, including the fate of the Jordan Valley."

55. "Summary of Ehud Olmert's 'Package' Offer to Mahmoud Abbas August 31, 2008," http://transparency.aljazeera.net/en/projects/thepalestinepapers/20121821046718794.html.

56. Gregg Carlstom, "The biggest Yerushalayimim," *Al Jazeera English*, January 23, 2011, http://www.aljazeera.com/palestinepapers/2011/01/2011122112512844113.html.

57. AFP, "Palestinians Open Door to Negotiation after Submitting Draft UN Resolution," *The Guardian* December 18, 2014, http://www.theguardian.com/world/2014/dec/18/palestinians-open-door-to-negotiatios-open-door-to-negotiation-after-submitting-draft-un-resolution.

58. "What is the Palestinian Authority for?" *Economist*, August 5, 2015, https://www.economist.com/news/middle-east-and-africa/21660493-authority-unable-protect-its-people-or-deliver-peace-what-it-good.

59. Edward Said, "The Morning After," *London Review of Books*, October 21, 1993, https://www.lrb.co.uk/v15/n20/edward-said/the-morning-after.

BIBLIOGRAPHY

Abu Toameh, Khaled. "Bush: Palestine Can't Be A Swiss Cheese," *Jerusalem Post*, January 10, 2008, http://www.jpost.com/Israel/Bush-Palestine-cant-be-a-Swiss-cheese.

AFP. "Palestinians open door to negotiation after submitting draft UN resolution," *The Guardian*, December 18, 2014, http://www.theguardian.com/world/2014/dec/18/palestinians-open-door-to-negotiatios-open-door-to-negotiation-after-submitting-draft-un-resolution.

Ahronheim, Anna, and Adam Rasgon. "Liberman Praises Security Coordination With Palestinians," *Jerusalem Post*, February 13, 2018, http://www.jpost.com/Arab-Israeli-Conflict/Liberman-praises-security-coordination-with-Palestinians-542483.

Berger, Yotam. "How Many Settlers Really Live in the West Bank?" *Haaretz*, June 15, 2017, https://www.haaretz.com/israel-news/.premium.MAGAZINE-revealed-how-many-settlers-really-live-in-the-west-bank-1.5482213.

B'Tselem. "Land Grab: Israel's Settlement Policy in the West Bank," 2002, 116, https://www.btselem.org/publications/summaries/200205_land_grab.

Burns, John F. "As Mideast Talks of Peace, Soft Voice Urges War," *New York Times*, August 27, 2000, https://www.nytimes.com/2000/08/27/world/as-mideast-talks-of-peace-soft-voice-urges-war.html.

Carlstom, Gregg. "The biggest Yerushalayimim," *Al Jazeera English*, January 23, 2011, http://www.aljazeera.com/palestinepapers/2011/01/2011122112512844113.html.

Crossette, Barbara. "U.S. Vetoes a Condemnation In U.N. of Israeli Land Seizure," *New York Times*, May 18, 1995.

Eldar, Akiva. "'Moratinos Document'—The peace that nearly was at Taba," *Ha'aretz*, February 14, 2002, http://prrn.mcgill.ca/research/papers/moratinos.htm.

Foundation for Middle East Peace. "Comprehensive Settlement Population 1972–2010," http://www.fmep.org/settlement_info/settlement-info-and-tfo/settlement-info-and-tables/stats-data/comprehensive-settlement-population-1972-2006.

Friedman, Thomas. "Israel's Goals in Gaza?" *New York Times*, January 14, 2009, http://www.nytimes.com/2009/01/14/opinion/14friedman.html?ref=opinion&_r=0.

Haberman, Clyde. "Rabin Says Israel May Not Meet Date To Begin Pullout," *New York Times*, November 27, 1993, https://www.nytimes.com/1993/11/27/world/rabin-says-israel-may-not-meet-date-to-begin-pullout.html.

Hadid, Diaa. "Palestinian Council Questions Security Arrangement With Israel," *New York Times*, March 5, 2015, https://www.nytimes.com/2015/03/06/world/middleeast/palestinian-council-questions-security-arrangement-with-israel.html.

Hass, Amira. "Israel's Closure Policy: An Ineffective Strategy of Containment and Repression," *Journal of Palestine Studies* 31 (2001/2), http://www.palestine-studies.org/jps/fulltext/41108.

———. "Why Isn't the PA Supporting the Egypt Uprising?" *Ha'aretz*, February 3, 2011.

Hockstader, Lee. "Arafat Says Crackdown On Hamas Is Not Over," *The Washington Post*, November 4, 1998.

International Institute for Strategic Security. "Military Balance, 1998–9" at 138–9 (2000).

Israel Central Bureau of Statistics. "Table 2.7: Localities and Population By District, Sub-District, Area, Population Group and Religion, 1995," http://www.cbs.gov.il/archive/shnaton47/st02-07.gif.

———. "Table 2.7: Localities and Population By District, Sub-District, Area, Population Group and Religion, 2000," http://www.cbs.gov.il/archive/shnaton52/st02_07.pdf.

———. "Table 2.13, 2014," http://www.cbs.gov.il/reader/shnaton/shnatone_new.htm?CYear=2015&Vol=66&CSubject=2.

Jerusalem Institute for Israel Studies. Table III/9—Population of Jerusalem, by Age, Religion and Geographical Spreading, 2013, http://www.jiis.org.il/.upload/yearbook/2015/shnaton_C0915.pdf.

Kessler, Glenn. "Defining 'Jewish State': For Many, Term has Different Meanings," October 2, 2010, http://www.washingtonpost.com/wp-dyn/content/article/2010/10/01/AR2010100104177.html.

Lapidoth, Ruth. "The Misleading Interpretation of Security Council Resolution 242 [1967]," February 2012, http://jcpa.org/wp-content/uploads/2012/02/Kiyum-lapidoth.pdf.

Malley, Robert. "Fictions About the Failure At Camp David," *New York Times*, July 8, 2001, http://www.nytimes.com/2001/07/08/opinion/fictions-about-the-failure-at-camp-david.html.

Office for the Coordination of Humanitarian Affairs, Humanitarian Facts and Figures, 2016 at 10. Found at: https://www.ochaopt.org/sites/default/files/factsheet_booklet_final_21_12_2017.pdf.

———. "The isolation of Palestinians in the Israeli-controlled area of Hebron city continues," https://www.ochaopt.org/content/isolation-palestinians-israeli-controlled-area-hebron-city-continues.

"PA Reconsiders Recognition of Israel," *Al Jazeera*, March 6, 2018, https://www.aljazeera.com/news/2018/01/palestinian-leadership-revokes-recognition-israel-180116060200939.html.

Palestinian Boycott, Divestment and Sanctions National Committee, "PLO Endorses BDS, Makes Unprecedented Call for Sanctions," January 17, 2018, https://bdsmovement.net/news/plo-endorses-bds%C2%A0makes-unprecedented-call-sanctions.

Rabin, Yitzhak. "Ratification of Interim Agreement" (speech, Israel Knesset, October 5, 1995), Israel Ministry of Foreign Affairs, http://www.mfa.gov.il/mfa/mfa-archive/1995/pages/pm%20rabin%20in%20knesset-%20ratification%20of%20interim%20agree.aspx.

Revivi, Oded. "If the Oslo Accords Are Over, the Real Work of Peace Can Begin," *The Wall Street Journal*, Jan. 17, 2018, https://www.wsj.com/articles/if-the-oslo-accords-are-over-the-real-work-of-peace-can-begin-1516233947.

Said, Edward. "The Morning After," *London Review of Books*, October 21, 1999, http://www.lrb.co.uk/v15/n20/edward-said/the-morning-after.

Selby, Jan. "The Political Economy of the Israeli-Palestinian and Indo-Pak Peace Processes: Non-Technical Summary (Research Summary)" 2007. ESRC End of Award Report, RES-228-25-0010. Swindon: ESRC, http://www.researchcatalogue.esrc.ac.uk/grants/RES-228-25-0010/outputs/read/36538120-f0b6-4bcf-bfcd-2971e88790a1.

Sharp, Jeremy. "U.S. Foreign Aid to Israel, June 10, 2015," http://securityassistance.org/sites/default/files/RL33222.pdf.

US Department of State, "Human Rights Practices, 1999: The Occupied Territories," February 3, 2000, https://www.state.gov/j/drl/rls/hrrpt/1999/417.htm.

Usher, Graham. "The Politics of Internal Security," *Journal of Palestine Studies* (Winter 1996).

"What is the Palestinian Authority for?" *The Economist*, August 5, 2015, https://www.economist.com/news/middle-east-and-africa/21660493-authority-unable-protect-its-people-or-deliver-peace-what-it-good.

Chapter Two

The Localization of the Palestinian National Political Field

Jamil Hilal

The theme of this chapter is the transformation and fragmentation of the Palestinian political field from its emergence as a national one in the second half of the 1960s into localized fields following the 1993 Declaration of Principles on Interim Self-Government Arrangements (hereafter referred to as the Oslo Accords). The concept of "political field" used here builds on that articulated by Pierre Bourdieu.[1] The "borders" of a political field are defined by the limits of national institutions, whether these are states or national liberation movements seeking independent statehood. Thus they are marked by parliaments, armies, a police force, security agencies, judiciary (courts, mandate of constitution, prisons, etc.), media, and national census centers, and so forth. A political field is defined also by political parties, movements, and political organizations competing for representation in national bodies and governments. Political fields encompass systems of rule, as well as procedures for the rotation and legitimization of power through procedures permitted by the system of government. Political fields tend to generate their own national and cultural symbols, their own historical narrative and constitutional frames of reference (constitutions or national charters). Civil society organizations—social movements, popular organizations, professional and workers' unions, and civil society organizations among others—function within (and attempt to shape) the political institutions of the field. The Palestine Liberation Organization (PLO) represented a Palestinian national field—with the Palestinian National Council (PNC) acting as the parliament of the Palestinian people, a National Charter (as a constitution), an executive committee as the leading body (central authority or government). The Palestinian national field also had political parties or factions, as well as journals, radio stations, prisons, hospitals, clinics, a formal army (the Palestine Liberation Army) and informal militias, sector-based organizations (women, students, etc.) and trade unions (for workers, teachers, writers, lawyers, doctors, etc.) and various functional departments.

Formed by the PLO during the late 1960s and developed during the 1970s and 1980s, the dissolution of these Palestinian national institutions in the 1990s—as an ostensible corollary of the establishment of the Palestinian Authority (PA) following the Oslo Accords—has left Palestinian communities exposed to the direct imperatives of the politics of the states in which they reside, as well as to their dictates. Given regional and international transformations, this change has had drastic impacts on the dynamics of the politics, economics, social organization, and culture of Palestinians in general, and on each of the Palestinian communities in particular.

The Palestinian Nakba of 1948 represented a historic turning point within Palestinian contemporary history. For Palestinians, it embodied the shattering of their society and the ethnic cleansing of Palestine. It concretized the defeat of the Palestinian national movement as it had developed during the British occupation of Palestine, and signaled the first collapse of the Palestinian political field.

This first collapse of the Palestinian political field in 1948 did not, however, entail the dissolution of the Palestinian cultural field nor the disappearance of Palestinian national identity. While national identity is shaped by processes related to the articulation and rearticulation of a collective national narrative (carried mainly but not solely within the cultural field), a political field is constructed and maintained by processes related to state formation and functioning, as well as to processes involved in the formation and running of national liberation movements (which are seeking independent statehood). Both the formation and maintenance of a nation-state or a national liberation movement involves the construction, organization, and running of national institutions that seek to articulate the historic narrative (through schools, mass media, cultural institutions, etc.) of their people. Such narratives are subject to revisions and challenges by both internal and external forces and agents.

The Nakba finalized the collapse of the Palestinian political field that had been formed and dominated by the Palestinian national movement created in the 1920s and shaped in the 1930s and 1940s. This collapse meant that the project of founding an independent Palestinian state was no longer viable as an Israeli state was erected on 78 percent of historic Palestine. The disappearance of the Palestinian political field explains why Palestinians seeking change joined predominantly pan-national or internationalist movements (such as the Arab National Movement, the Communist Party, the Ba'ath, and the Moslem Brotherhood) or immersed themselves, where possible, in political movements active in state-bounded political fields (particularly in Israel and Jordan). However, this should not be taken as evidence of the demise of Palestinian national identity, but as evidence of the demise of a particular Palestinian political field. Palestinians joined pan-national movements because there was no Palestinian national movement to join.[2]

While the Nakba witnessed the collapse of the Palestinian political field, it also initiated conceptualizations of a new national identity in which dispossession, ethnic cleansing, statelessness, discrimination, and refugee status became central components. This identity, which emerged in the 1950s, underwent further articulations in the 1960s and 1970s with the establishment of the PLO which emphasized armed struggle as a strategy to liberate the homeland. Here Palestinians were not presented simply as the victims of ethnic cleansing and dispossession, but as people seeking freedom and as being ready to die for the cause of liberating their country (this is what the word feda'i conveyed). Armed struggle acted as a catalyst for the construction of a new Palestinian national political field, and served to announce the presence of a people fighting for a national cause.[3] The struggle against colonization and dispossession has been a major theme in narrating Palestinian history, from the early stages of confronting Zionist settler-colonization and British military rule, right up to present-day confrontations with Israeli settler colonialism and racist policies. However, it took on a special urgency after the Nakba.

The Palestinian political field that was constructed in the late 1960s by the resistance organizations that allied themselves within the institutions of the PLO underwent considerable changes in the following decades. The ways in which this happened are the main focus of this chapter, which explores various phases in the history and development of the Palestinian political field, and its present-day fragmentation.

THE DISTINCTIVE FEATURES OF THE POST-NAKBA PALESTINIAN POLITICAL FIELD

Following the Nakba, it took more than a decade and a half for a new Palestinian national movement to emerge.[4] This was the movement that shaped and dominated the new Palestinian political field through the institutions of the PLO with all its political organizations and grassroots components and bodies. Palestinian resistance groups seized the political moment of the Arab states following their defeat in June 1967 to rebuild the PLO as the new national field with defined institutions, directives, organizational principles, and a new national charter. The political institutions of the PLO—with its armed, financial, informational, judicial, social, and economic bodies, in addition to a range of sector-based organizations (women, workers, students, etc.) and professional organizations (teachers, writers and journalists, engineers, etc.)—defined the contours and dynamics of the national field.

This new political field had a number of distinctive features that informed and dominated Palestinian politics for three decades.

The first distinctive feature was the transformation of the over-stressed pan-Arab features of the PLO to more distinctive Palestinian ones. Although the PLO was formed in 1964, under the auspices of the pan-Arabist states (Nasser's Egypt and the Ba'ath regimes in Syria and Iraq), it was captured in 1968 by the resistance organizations which had been inspired by post-Nakba Palestinian conditions and successful national liberation movements in other parts of the world. This capture and transformation of the PLO was symbolized by changing the title of the charter from the pan-Arab charter (almithaq alqaoumi) to the national charter (almithaq al-watani), thus announcing the emergence of a new Palestinian political field. Most important was that it signaled a change in the social composition of the leadership which replaced the previous semi-feudal (i.e., merchants and landowners) and upper middle class leadership with one that emerged from the dispossessed social classes that had utilized the free education made available by Arab states and the UN Relief and Works Agency for Palestinian Refugees in the Near East (UNRWA). This new leadership was predominantly middle class by virtue of its possession of "cultural capital" not economic assets.

The second distinctive feature was that the leading institutions of the PLO were established outside historic Palestine. This was the result of two main factors: the first was that, before 1967, the PLO was not mandated to represent Palestinians in Jordan (which included both the area and population of the West Bank); the second was that, after 1967, the newly reconstructed PLO was led by Palestinian resistance groups who could not operate on Palestinian territory following the Israeli military occupation of the West Bank and Gaza Strip in June 1967 (which had brought the whole of historic Palestine under Israeli control). This made it practically impossible to establish the PLO headquarters anywhere in historic Palestine.

But by locating leading PLO institutions on the territory of sovereign states (i.e., Jordan, Lebanon, Syria, and later Tunisia), tensions emerged between two "national" political fields driven by two incompatible rationales and goals: one driven by the desire to liberate an occupied homeland and the other focused on its own state security and legitimated by the right of sovereign states to monopolize the use and ownership of "means of violence" within their borders and in the defense of these borders. This tension between a state ethos and a national liberation movement ethos erupted in armed confrontations in Jordan, Lebanon, and Syria,[5] in addition to armed confrontations with the settler-colonial state (Israel).

The location of the PLO's leading institutions and those of its constituent factions (military, economic, informational, cultural, and security structures) on non-Palestinian territory (i.e., within the mandate of other states' political fields) was a significant factor—aided by other factors—that prompted the PLO leadership to seek, as early as 1974, a new strategy that moved away from the liberation of the whole of Palestine to one that sought state-building on the part of Palestine occupied in 1967. The change was initiated through the articulation of an interim political program (called the Ten Point Political Program), which was adopted in 1974 by the PNC, although not without opposition from some PLO factions led by the Popular Front for the Liberation of Palestine (PFLP) which formed what was called the Rejection Front.[6] The strategy was adopted after the October War of 1973 with an eye on the possibility of Israel withdrawing from the West Bank and Gaza Strip (WBG), which the PLO did not wish to see returning under the rule of Jordan and Egypt. It came also after military confrontations between the PLO forces and Jordanian and Lebanese armies.[7]

The imperatives of political geography together with strategic changes in regional and international power relations, acted as weighty pressures on the PLO to seek its own national territory to free itself from the constant migration of its headquarters from various Arab capitals and away from Palestine and Palestinian communities. Once the headquarters was moved to Tunis, the PLO leadership used this as a home base to rationalize joining, under restrictive conditions, negotiations in Madrid in 1991, and eventually to sign the Oslo Accords with the heavy imbalanced power relations they entailed. It is possible to argue that the Oslo Accords would not have been signed had the leadership had an insight into Israel's plans and of the US's commitment to the Israeli vision and policies. The path of the Oslo Accords hastened the fragmentation process of the Palestinian political field thus jeopardizing Palestinian national rights and exposing Palestinian communities to new hazards and new high risks. The fading away of political and organizational ties developed by the PLO in the 1970s and 1980s, that knitted together politically and organizationally the various Palestinian communities, heightened the exposure of Palestinian communities to new pressures and risks.

The third distinctive, indeed outstanding, feature of the Palestinian national political field was its encompassment of all Palestinian political factions, parties, or movements, except those operating within the Israeli political field, whose membership in the institutions of the PLO would have criminalized them by the Israeli state. Political groups active in the areas occupied in 1967 (which were extensions of groups and parties represented in PLO institutions) worked underground (apart from the Communist Party which later became the Palestinian People's Party) for the same reason. Its encompassment of all political parties and factions enabled the PLO to claim, rightly, that it represented the whole of the Palestinian people, to be acknowledged as their sole legitimate representative in 1974 by the Arab League, and to acquire in that year an observer status in the General Assembly of the United Nations.

The fourth distinctive feature of the Palestinian national political field was the high degree of autonomy (political, organizational, ideological, and financial) maintained by the Palestinian political parties and factions participating in the institutions of the PLO.[8] Each of the main factions: Fatah, the PFLP, the Democratic Front for the Liberation of Palestine (DFLP), and the Communist Party (later the Palestinian People's Party or PPP) had its own political agenda, organizational principles and structure, independent financial resources, autonomous military and security forces, as well as their own youth, women, students, and other rank and file organizations. Each celebrated its own foundation day, held its own conferences, published its own (usually) weekly journal, and issued its own political statements. In addition, each made sure of its right to be represented in the various national bodies that made up the PLO. This organizational edifice lasted formally until the signing of the Oslo Accords, although practically it had begun to wane in the 1980s, after the PLO's exit from Beirut.

The fifth distinctive feature was that although the rules of procedure of the PLO stipulate that the members of the PNC should be elected by secret ballot every three years, this was never implemented, not only because of the practical impossibility of holding elections for Palestinian communities subject to different state powers and regulations, but also because this would have excluded the representation of the smaller political organizations from membership of the PNC and from its other bodies. Such an implementation would therefore have undermined the representative character of the PLO. This highlights the fact that the decision-making process in the institutions of the PLO sought consensus and not majority votes. This consensus-seeking model noted, nevertheless, the existence of a large political organization (i.e., Fatah) that allows it—through a "quota system"—to have a weighted representation in the leading bodies of the PLO and its popular and professional organizations. Right up to the establishment of the PA, the Palestinian political field functioned by having a dominant organization (Fatah), with medium-sized political organizations (PFLP, DFLP, Communist Party [later the PPP], and a number of small political groups some of which were branches of the ruling Ba'ath parties in Syria and Iraq [al-Sa'qa and the Arab Liberation Front]).

A POLITICAL FIELD WITH CENTER-PERIPHERY FORMATION

The political, organizational, and ideological plurality that characterized the Palestinian political field coexisted with the centralization of the decision-making process. This was not what the political geography of the diverse Palestinian communities required, but what was promoted by the dominant political culture in the region at the time (Pan-Arab, left-wing, and Islamist), as well as in the socialist block with which the PLO had strong ties, and by Western liberal procedural democracy.

Others factors promoted the high levels of centralization of political decision-making as practiced by the leading institutions of the PLO, its political factions, as well as its mass and professional organizations and trade unions. A major dynamic in maintaining centralization was necessitated by the constant dangers posed by Israel as a settler-colonial state dedicated to overpowering the Palestinian national movement and defeating its aims. Another dynamic was presented by the tensions that characterized the relationships between the PLO and Arab governments particularly wherever PLO headquarters, institutions, and fighters were present, as this was viewed as undermining the sovereignty of the Arab states, and as providing excuses for Israel to attack not only Palestinian targets but also vital installations in the Arab country concerned.

The second half of the 1970s saw an intensification of the centralization, militarization, and bureaucratization of the central institutions of the PLO and the organizational structure of its constituent political factions and parties. A number of factors were important in assisting this process. First, in the wake of the PLO being widely acknowledged as the sole legitimate representative of the Palestinian people, was the establishment of numerous diplomatic missions in many capitals in the region and abroad, including all socialist countries which provided the PLO with access to valuable resources (educational, military training and equipment, and diplomatic support). Second, 1975 witnessed the outbreak of a long civil war in Lebanon in which the PLO was, up to the summer of 1982, directly involved, and thus this provoked further militarization. Third, following the 1973 October War with Israel, oil revenues shot up enormously which resulted in higher funding from some oil-producing Arab states (and remittances from Palestinians resident there) to the PLO. Availability of rent to the PLO and its factions promoted overstaffing of its institutions with full-time cadres and the regimentation of its military wings. The Lebanese civil war, the availability of funds and training, as well as the frequent Israeli raids and incursions on PLO positions, bases, and refugee camps, all sponsored the professionalization of Palestinian armed struggle. This induced the extension of centralization beyond the sphere of the military institutions of the PLO and its factions.

Within the political discourse dominant within the Palestinian national movement in the 1970s and 1980s, democracy meant basically adherence to pluralism (political, ideological, and organizational) within the institutions of the PLO and communities, which was translated into a system of representation that included all political organizations (through a "quota system") in the organization's leading bodies. In procedural terms this meant the holding of consultations among representatives of all political organizations, before deciding on matters of national importance. This practice ensured the unity of the institutions of the Palestinian national movement, but without engaging the active participation (political, organizational, and cultural) of the representatives of various Palestinian communities (as distinct communities) in the decision-making process. A focus on the latter would have necessitated envisioning a different system of representation that paid more attention to the needs and aspirations of Palestinian communities rather than confining the representation to political organizations. Thus decisions on national issues remained, effectively, the prerogative of the leaders of the PLO factions wherever their headquarters happened to be. This was formalized within the executive committee (as well as the Central Council) of the PLO in which the leadership of the various factions was represented. This highly centralized formula was in line with the dominant practice in the Arab world, most Third World countries, and socialist countries. Liberal political democracy was looked upon with suspicion as constituting a Western (and colonial) idea.

The imperatives of political geography, the dominant modes in the 1970s and 1980s of political culture and organization in Arab and socialist states, and the distrust of liberal democracy, all promoted and justified building and maintaining a highly centralized Palestinian political field—a field with a strong center of gravity (wherever the PLO leadership was located) that viewed dispersed Palestinian communities (in the Arab world, in Europe, the US, and elsewhere) as peripheries. Within this paradigm, the PLO related to Palestinian communities in Jordan and Israel through the political parties and civic societies active in these communities.[9] This center-periphery paradigm (that placed the leadership, wherever it was, as the center and all others at the periphery) that informed the functioning of the PLO institutions continued, in one form or another, up to the establishment of the PA in 1994.

THE TRANSFORMATIONS OF THE 1980s

A number of upheavals during the 1970s in the region also had substantial impacts. The early 1970s saw the PLO forced out of Jordan and seeking refuge in Lebanon, which soon erupted into a civil war that engulfed the PLO and brought in Syrian troops and control into the country. And the late 1970s saw the signing of the Camp David Agreement between Egypt and Israel (which impacted negatively on the regional and international standing of the PLO), and the triumph of the Iranian Islamic Revolution. These two events, together with the defeat of the Soviet presence in Afghanistan and the availability of huge rents from oil revenues, assisted the rise of political Islam in the region, including in the Palestinian political field which remained (up to the late 1980s) predominantly secular.

The forced departure of the PLO from Lebanon in the summer of 1982 weakened the control of the PLO leadership over the Palestinian political field. The unity of the main Palestinian institutions (political, mass, and professional) was shaken as a result of the scattering of Palestinian forces, and the distancing of the leading PLO institutions from their constituencies. In Tunis, these institutions were removed from direct daily contact with Palestinian communities, and the constituting factions (e.g., Fatah, the PFLP, the DFLP, the Communist Party, and other smaller factions) had to work within the limitations imposed by the states where they had offices and branches. The ability of the PLO and its factions to marshal Palestinians into unified political action was weakened by splits within Fatah (in 1983) and political differences as illustrated by the formation, in 1984, of the Democratic Alliance to oppose political moves taken by Arafat and his movement (Fatah).[10]

The flagging hold of the PLO on the national field following the forced exit of its institutions and fighters from Lebanon, and the political fractures that appeared within its ranks, rendered it more exposed to external interference and manipulation from Arab and international centers of power. The reunification of the PLO's leading institutions in 1987 was not a sign that it had regained its former mobilizational ability and standing, but an indication of the realization of a need to halt the ongoing loss of influence. In fact, the PLO's loosened grip over the political field in the occupied West Bank and Gaza after 1982 possibly helped lay some of the conditions necessary for the outbreak of the First Intifada at the end of 1987. The First Intifada empowered the local branches of the main political factions, as well as the mass and professional organizations active in the West Bank and Gaza Strip, to seize the initiative and form the Unified Command of the Intifada. This made the PLO leadership take notice and assume command from Tunis, a move that confined the initiative of the local leadership and led to processes that weakened the organized mass character of the Intifada and the high degree of collective solidarity it manifested. It was the First Intifada (which also saw the entry of Hamas into the Palestinian political field) that provided the impetus for the PLO to propose, at its PNC meeting in November 1988, its initiative based on a two-state solution, and to issue the Palestinian Declaration of Independence.

The momentum of the First Intifada indicated that the center of popular political struggle against the settler colonial state and for independent Palestinian statehood had moved to the West Bank and Gaza (WBG). But this fact was interpreted by the PLO political leadership as requiring the tightening of its grip on the WBG and on the Intifada.[11] This was reflected in the attitude of the PLO leadership that tended to deal with the local leadership of the Intifada in the WBG—as represented by the Unified Leadership of the Intifada—as something akin to "contractors" instead of political leaders of the WBG community confronting settler colonialism and engaged in a daily struggle to end Israel's occupation.

Politically, the PLO leadership signaled, through the Algiers' PNC resolutions in 1988, its readiness to enter into direct negotiations with Israel for the establishment of a Palestinian state in the WBG. The collapse of the Soviet Union (the main international ally of the PLO), the fractured and leaderless Arab world, and the heightened political and financial isolation imposed on the PLO as a result of its position on the Iraqi invasion of Kuwait, persuaded its leadership to yield to the limitations imposed on the negotiations, and to accept an agreement with inbuilt constraints on the establishment of an independent Palestinian state. This was clear in the PLO agreeing to the phasing of negotiations on the issues of: colonial settlement building, the future of East Jerusalem, borders, the implementation of the rights of refugees, control over natural resources, and Palestinian sovereignty. It was also clear in the PLO acknowledgment of the right of Israel to exist, which gave credence to the Zionist narrative by the representative of its victims. In return, however, Israel did not acknowledge the right of Palestinians to statehood, self-determination, and to return to their homeland. The readiness to accept the Oslo Accords was underpinned by an exaggerated apprehension by the PLO leadership of being sidelined by local elites from the WBG (an idea nurtured by the US and Europe), despite public and private insistence by all political elites in the WBG that the PLO was the sole legitimate representative of all the Palestinian people, including those in the WBG.

THE FRAGMENTATION OF THE NATIONAL POLITICAL FIELD

The construction of the PA radically altered the geography, demography, composition, and trajectory of the Palestinian political field. It formally discounted the national field for the aim of seeking statehood in the WBG. The building of the PA institutions went hand in hand with the marginalization of the institutions of the PLO as these were considered either obstructive or irrelevant to the process of state-building regarded as embryonic in the PA.

The paradigm of the PA narrowed the Palestinian political field as it thereafter viewed those living in WBG as constituting the Palestinian people. It also mapped the geography of Palestine to be conterminous with the WBG. Furthermore, it put on hold the right of return for Palestinian refugees, and created a mindset ready to interpret the Palestinian right to self-determination as entailing no more than the establishment of a Palestinian state on the WBG, combined with a readiness to accept a hazy interpretation of sovereignty. Given all this, it was understable for Palestinians to whom historic Palestine is inaccessible, and those holding Israeli nationality (i.e., Palestinians who remained in the areas on which Israel was declared in 1948) to feel, and rightly so, that the Oslo Accords had put them outside the mandate of the PA (see the chapter by Mansour Nasasra in this book). The Palestinian political field began to fracture.

For the Israeli establishment, the Oslo Accords presented no genuine change in policies toward the WBG, nor to Palestinian national rights. Not only did Israel continue implementing the same policies as before the Oslo agreement, in fact, it accelerated their implementation. Utilizing the Oslo II agreement, Israel proceeded to "Bantustanize" the West Bank by breaking it up into areas "A," "B," and "C"—retaining full control over area "C" which formed around 60 percent of the land; but it also disregarded the rights of the PA in Areas "A" and "B" as indicated by its reinvasion of the West Bank in 2002. Israel's control over the WBG continued to be fortified through various mechanisms. These include the building of more settler-colonies, the cleansing of Palestinians from Jerusalem, the construction of bypass roads and military checkpoints, the strengthening of control over the Jordan Valley, the tightening of the siege on Gaza, and the construction of the Separation Wall. These control mechanisms allowed Israel to fully utilize natural resources and to enforce a dependent economy in the WBG. Utilizing emergency laws (some of which had their origins in the British Mandate period), Israel continued its daily arrests of Palestinians in the West Bank (some of whom were detained in Israeli prisons without trial) and the demolition of Palestinian houses under various pretexts. Using the label of "terrorism," its army did not hesitate to shoot to kill Palestinians, including children under 18, and to detain them under flimsy charges.

Through Oslo, and its policies of separation, Israel has managed to create a specific system of apartheid with discriminatory laws and a system of "native reservations" or ethnic enclaves.[12] Economically, although it continues to keep the 1967 occupied Palestinian territory captive to its products, it no longer relies on the cheap labor of Palestinians. Israel has thus succeeded in employing the PA to transform its occupation of the WBG not only into a "deluxe" occupation that is economically, financially, and diplomatically advantageous, but also in using it as a major instrument for policing Palestinians in the WBG.[13]

LOCALIZING THE NATIONAL

The emerging political leadership of the PA did not seem to realize that the Palestinian national field was being changed in two major ways. First, it was being redefined as a local field geared toward state-building in the WBG while remaining under the full control of Israel, the colonizer. In other words, a self-governing authority (the PA) was established on a territory on which the right to a sovereign Palestinian state had not been conceded. Second, the disempowerment of the Palestinian national institutions and Palestinian mass and professional organizations meant the dismantlement of the national field before it established itself as an independent state. What happened is that the highly centralized paradigm of "a center with multiple peripheries" lost its center and was turning gradually into disconnected "peripheries" or "local community fields."

The "self-rule" formulation that the PA represented signaled a shift away from the modalities that had directed the decision-making process of the PLO in the 1970s and 1980s. The PA institutionalized a new modality whereby one political party (or coalition of parties) formed the "self-rule" government while another formed the opposition. A presidential-parliamentary model was adopted to guide the 1996 elections of the Palestinian Legislative Council (PLC), which resulted in Fatah gaining the overwhelming majority of its seats, a fact made possible because Hamas, Islamic Jihad, the PFLP and DFLP boycotted the elections. Following the Second Intifada and under pressure from the USA, EU, and Israel, as well as internal pressures, some limitations were instituted on the powers of the president of the PA (at that time, Yassir Arafat). These were the results of the signing of the Basic Law by the PA president, despite previously having delayed doing so for some years, which instituted the position of prime minister who was to be delegated some of the powers of the president. However, despite all the PA paraphernalia of "statehood" with the ministerial bodies, nomenclature and institutional hierarchies as found in sovereign states, this did not loosen the grip of Israeli colonial control. Nor did the PA gain any real powers on the ground following being granted the status of a non-voting member by the UN General Assembly in 2012. The fact that US president, Donald Trump, publicly recognized, in December 2017, Jerusalem as the capital of Israel and moved the American embassy from Tel Aviv to it in May 2018, demonstrated just how illusionary was the vision of a sovereign Palestinian state given the local, regional, and international conditions that defy its realization.

It is worth noting that the institutions erected by the PA differed significantly from those constructed by the PLO. The latter institutions were dominated by one major political organization (Fatah) that shared power with medium-sized political organizations such as the PFLP, the DFLP, and the Communist Party in the WBG as junior partners; and there was room left for the representation of smaller parties, i.e., the Popular Struggle Front (PSF), the Palestinian Liberation Front (PLF), the Arab Liberation Front (ALF), the PFLP-General Command, and al-Sa'iqa. The PA, on the other hand, came to be ruled by one major political party (Fatah) while opposed by another major party (Hamas), and both co-existed with what became small political parties (basically PFLP, DFLP, Islamic Jihad, PPP, Fida, PSF). In 2007, when Hamas took control of the Gaza Strip by force, the ruling party in the West Bank (Fatah) became the main opposition party in Gaza, and the ruling party in Gaza (Hamas) became the main opposition party in the West Bank. This followed the 2006 PLC elections in which Hamas succeeded in gaining a majority of the 132 seats, while in 2005 the Fatah candidate (Mahmoud Abbas) won the presidential election. In 2007, this developed into a situation of two self-governing authorities—one in the West Bank dominated by Fatah, and the other in Gaza dominated by Hamas. This dual authority situation was assisted by three main factors: the presidential-parliamentary system adopted by the PA, the international pressure directed at Hamas, and the different political and ideological perspectives of these two main competing parties each aided by opposed regional powers. The split between Fatah and Hamas finalized the fragmentation of the national political field into local fields according to its geographic components.

The transformation of the Palestinian political field began before the signing of the Oslo Accords. However, the establishment of the PA ushered in changes that radically altered the dynamics and scope of Palestinian politics. The highly centralized political field thereafter lost both its national character and mode of doing politics, and Palestinian communities thereafter started to develop strategies and responses to cope with their specific sociopolitical and economic situations.

In the WBG, the development of the PA into a sovereign, independent Palestinian state through a strategy of bilateral negotiations under the sponsorship of the US has proven to be illusionary after the elapse of a quarter of a century. Israel has accelerated and intensified its colonization of the West Bank and maintained a tight grip on its economy and natural resources. It retains full control over its borders, it has continued the construction of the Separation Wall and by-pass roads (for Israelis only), and it has maintained its strategically situated military checkpoints in the West Bank. Furthermore, the imposition of a suffocation siege on the "ghettoized" Gaza Strip, plus the re-establishment of control over areas "A" and "B" in the West Bank has made the majority of Palestinians realize that the Oslo process has been a dead-end as far as their national rights are concerned. Neither bilateral negotiations with

Israel nor the privileging of one type of resistance (regardless of whether it is armed struggle or negotiations) have proved to be effective strategies. Both strategies downgrade popular organized forms of action and confrontation, and both have proved ineffective in changing significantly the balance of power (militarily, economically, and even diplomatically) with Israel. Both are elitist strategies: one relies on negotiators (usually in closed rooms), and the other on highly-trained specialists who can operate long-range missiles. Both ignore the experience of the First Intifada in terms of popular organization and mobilization. Neither has sought to empower Palestinians in their various communities in the struggle for their national and civic rights. Both political parties (Fatah and Hamas) give priority to maintaining control over their respective territory still under Israeli control. Neither can "govern" their respective territories without dependency on external rent and political support. And neither can claim to represent the Palestinian people, or even the territory which they self-govern.

In Israel, the United Arab List—a coalition that includes communists, the pan-nationalist left, and Islamists—was formed by Palestinians with Israeli nationality to contest the Knesset elections in March 2015. It won 13 seats—an impressive result which it would not have attained had each party entered the election separately. This is one example of how each Palestinian community has found it necessary to tackle its own problems in the absence of overall national institutions representing the Palestinian collective. However, the United Arab List needs to be developed into a "historic bloc" if it is to be effective in confronting an increasingly right-wing and repressive Jewish-Israeli ruling establishment, including making the Arab Higher Follow Up Committee more representative through democratic and consensual procedure.

Meanwhile, Palestinians in Jordan remain without adequate representation as a community, and are thus without a voice that expresses their specific concerns within Jordan (particularly those without full civil rights), as well as toward Palestinian national issues and as Palestinians with historic rights. Palestinians in Syria and Lebanon remain very vulnerable to political change in their respective countries. Palestinian communities are incredibly vulnerable as a result of statelessness, as shown by the attacks on refugee camps in Jordan and Lebanon in the 1970s, their expulsion from Kuwait in the early 1990s, their continued discriminatory treatment in Lebanon, their mistreatment in Iraq and Libya in the past three decades, and their exposure in Syria following the developments there in 2011. When statelessness is coupled with the marginalization of their national institutions since the signing of the Oslo Accords, Palestinian have been left with a void in national strategy over how to deal with processes and events such as: the destruction and invasion of the Yarmouk refugee camp in Syria and the displacement of its population since 2013, the reinvasion of the West Bank in 2002, the slow ethnic cleansing of Palestinians in Jerusalem, the discriminatory laws against Palestinians in Israel, the siege and repeated wars waged by Israel against Gaza (in 2008, 2012, and 2014), the attacks by Israeli settlers against Palestinian civilians in the West Bank, and the killing and arrests of Palestinian children by the Israeli army.

The increased vulnerability and precariousness of Palestinian communities since the PLO left Lebanon, and more so since the Oslo Accords, have been amplified by changes in regional and international power relations. The weakened standing and effectiveness of the Palestinian national movement has gone hand in hand with the rapid shift of Israeli political society toward the right with the increased influence of West Bank colonial settlers in the Israeli government and Knesset.[14] (See the chapter by Yonatan Mendel in this book.) This has manifested itself in the heightening of collective repression against Palestinians and the implementation of a strategy to destroy the necessary prerequisites of a viable Palestinian state in the WBG.

The main two competing political movements—Fatah and Hamas—have erected their own pseudo-government structures, are both committed to neoliberal policies, and both have ensured that their cadres and militants are fully positioned as employees in their respective ministries and security apparatuses fulfilling roles in hierarchical bureaucracies with job descriptions alien to national liberation movements. The Palestinian left has lost much of its previous influence and organized constituency as it no longer has a place and role within the institutions of the PLO; previously it had enjoyed a national role from the late 1960s until it was marginalized in the early 1990s.[15] Regional and international changes, such as the collapse of the Soviet Union, the decline of the left in Europe, and the rise of political and Salafist Islam has also had a drastic impact on the left in Palestine and which has done nothing to overcome its factionalism. The left has thus lost the chance to form a "historic block" with its own political, socioeconomic, and cultural agendas, instead of mediating, ineffectively, between the two competing political movements of Hamas and Fatah.[16]

CONSTRUCTING A NEW PALESTINIAN POLITICAL FIELD

The fragmentation of the Palestinian political field, as a national field, has not and does not entail the demise of Palestinian national identity. In fact, replicating what happened following the defeat of the Palestinian national movement in 1948 (and the collapse of its Palestinian political field), new dynamics are emerging within the various Palestinian communities which are reminiscent of dynamics in the 1950s and 1960s. These new dynamics, as indicated by some of the activities at the various community levels (among Palestinians in 1948, within the West Bank, within the Gaza Strip, in Jordan, and in the refugee camps and diaspora or shatat) reflect the diverse conditions of these communities: of colonial occupation, repression, discrimination, exile, marginalization, as well as various forms of struggle for survival and for civil, human, and national rights.[17] It is possible that this emerging dynamism could lead to the gradual (re)construction of a new national political field and the emergence of a new national movement alert and attentive to the needs, rights, and aspirations of the various Palestinian communities as well as to Palestinian historic rights. Such a new political movement would need to explore and provide an answer as to how self-determination and emancipation can be realized in each Palestinian community as well as for Palestinians as a whole. In order to achieve this, it should focus on the following four issues.

First, it should rearticulate the Palestinian historic narrative as the history of a people that has been subjected to settler-colonialism, ethnic cleansing, dispossession, homelessness, and discrimination, as which has fought a long bloody struggle for self-determination, dignity, and freedom. This narrative is needed to rectify the distortions that have crept into the discourse of the PA, Arab states, international organizations, and most mass media regarding Palestinian history, geography, and demography.[18]

Second, it should develop national institutions that are democratic—in both the substantive sense and procedural sense (where the latter is feasible). These institutions should be representative: first, by including all political parties and movements; second, by ensuring the representation of all Palestinian communities without jeopardizing their acquired rights; and third, representative in terms of gender and class.

Third, the new national movement (in the inclusive democratic sense) should avoid the excessive centralization of the PLO (with its center-periphery paradigm) which ignored the specific conditions of each of the Palestinian communities thus ignoring their specific needs and aspirations. It needs to address the situation created by the PA whereby Palestinian communities have been left without a unifying national framework.[19] A new national institutional framework is required in which the aims and strategies needed for unifying the struggle for self-determination and collective national rights are articulated, while leaving each community to formulate (through its democratic representative body) the strategy that protects and furthers the interests and rights of its members within the imperatives of the overarching national strategy of self-determination.

And fourth, links between the various Palestinian communities need to be facilitated and strengthened by rebuilding mass and professional organizations (women, workers, students, journalists, writers, teachers, lawyers, engineers, doctors, etc.) that create interactive links between these communities and make joint and collective strategies possible. By implementing measures aimed at enhancing internal democracy and transparency, political parties would help to rebuild trust in their leaderships and strategies.

The task of constructing a vigorous and dexterous Palestinian national liberation movement to create and manage a new political field is by no means an easy one. It confronts many obstacles and entrenched interests. There is the question of what to do with the PA that has swallowed up the PLO and failed demonstrably to transform itself into an independent state. There is the question of the division between Fatah and Hamas, and how to constructively engage both in the project of rebuilding a new national movement while neutralizing their respective weaknesses, obsessions, and shortcomings.[20] There are also issues related to the implementation of the reconciliation agreements signed by the leaders of the two movements, and the need to reconstruct Gaza following the destruction imposed on it by Israeli wars and the suffocating siege. Relations between Fatah and Hamas should be viewed within the context of the regional and international alignments at each point in time. Indeed, the wider tectonic shifts in the region such as the collapse of state structures in Iraq, Syria, Libya, Yemen, and Lebanon (due to military intervention and occupation, the impact of globalized neo-liberal capitalism, and the rise of jihadist and Salafist movements) coupled with changing power relations (between Turkey, Iran, Israel, Saudi Arabia, and Egypt) as well as the shift toward the extreme right in Israel[21] will continue to impact on the Palestinian question. All of this makes the emergence of a new political movement (and thus the construction of a new Palestinian political field) much more difficult, but also absolutely crucial for renationalizing the locale—not through elite actions but through actions developed by each of the components that make up the Palestinians as a people who have been ethnically cleansed, dispossessed, and dehumanized.[22]

NOTES

1. Pierre Bourdieu, *Sociology in Question* (London: Sage Publications, 1993).

2. On the transformations of Palestinian national identity before and after the Nakba, see: Rashid Khalidi, Palestinian Identity; The Construction of Modern National Consciousness (New York: Columbia University Press, 1997). See also: Jamil Hilal, "Reflections on Contemporary Palestinian History," in Ilan Pappe and Jamil Hilal (eds.), *Across the Wall; Narratives of Israeli-Palestinian History* (London: I.B. Tauris, 2010).

3. On the role of armed resistance in the formation of the Palestinian national movement and how it gave new dimensions to national identity, see: Yezid Sayigh, *Armed Struggle and the Search for State: The Palestinian National Movement 1949–1993* (Oxford: Oxford University Press, 1999).

4. On the re-emergence of the Palestinian national movement after the Nakba, see Helga Baumgarten, "The Three Faces/Phases of Palestinian Nationalism, 1948–2005," *Journal of Palestine Studies*, 34, no. 4 (2005): 25–48. Also Helga Baumgarten, *From Liberation to the State: History of the Palestinian National Movement 1948–1988* (in Arabic) (Ramallah: Muwatin—The Palestinian Institute for the Study of Democracy, 2006).

5. In Tunisia, such confrontations did not take place because Palestinians were not permitted to have military bases or armed fighters, and had accepted, prior to the establishment of their institutions there (in 1982) to respect the right of the Tunisian state to monopolize the legitimate use of force, and to have absolute control on entry and exit of Palestinian cadres running the PLO institutions there.

6. The Rejection Front (full name: Front of the Palestinian Forces Rejecting Solutions of Surrender) was a political coalition formed in 1974 by Palestinian factions that rejected the Ten Point Program adopted by the PLO in its 12th Palestinian National Congress (PNC) session. The Ten Point Program authorized the PLO to "establish [an] independent combatant national authority for the people over every part of Palestinian territory that is liberated," which was regarded by some factions as a possible first step toward a two-state solution. At the same PNC session in 1974, the ultimate goal of the PLO was defined as the implementation of the Palestinian right of return and right of self-determination "on the whole of the soil of their homeland." The Rejectionist Front was strongly backed by Iraq. Most of its factions headed by the PFLP rejoined the PLO in 1978, following the formation of the Arab Steadfastness and Confrontation Front against the Camp David Agreement between Egypt and Israel. A similar formation—the Palestinian National Alliance—took place in September 1993 with the formation of the ten factions opposed to the Oslo agreement. The alliance was strongly backed by Syria. The most serious rift was in 1988, when the PLO recognized Israel, and most of the left-wing factions of the PLO again left, backed by Syria.

7. In 1976, armed confrontation took place between PLO forces and Syrian forces in Lebanon, and again in 1983. Apart from conflicts generated because the PLO institutions were not on their own national territory, there were other factors that made the idea of a two-state solution find support among the PLO. These included: (i) the removal of the PLO institutions and organizations (in 1970/71) from Jordan to Lebanon; (ii) the results of the October War in 1973 which suggested the possibility of Israeli withdrawal from the West Bank and Gaza Strip (not only Sinai) and for these not to revert back to Jordanian and Egyptian rule but to be under Palestinian sovereignty; (iii) political solutions proposed by influential international powers (like the Soviet Union, a major ally of the PLO) and international organizations; and (iv) the forced exit of the PLO institutions and forces from Lebanon in 1982 and the long siege of Beirut by Israeli forces allied to Lebanese right-wing forces.

8. On Palestinian political parties and movements, their programs, and their organization on the eve of the second Legislative Council election in January 2006, see

Jamil Hilal, *Palestinian Political Organizations and Parties* (in Arabic) (Ramallah: Muwatin—The Palestinian Institute for the Study of Democracy, 2006).

9. In Jordan, extensions of major Palestinian political organizations (Fatah, PFLP, DFLP and Communist Party) were established in the 1970s (after September in 1970) to work underground among Palestinians in the East Bank of Jordan as well as in the West Bank. In Israel, the PLO established informal relations with the Israeli Communist Party and other Israeli anti-Zionist groups in the early 1970s.

10. The Democratic Alliance was an alliance of a number of PLO factions that was established in early 1984. It included: the PFLP, the DFLP, the Palestinian Communist Party and a splinter of the Palestine Liberation Front (PLF). The Alliance opposed the Amman Agreement between Yassir Arafat and King Hussein in 1985 for joint political action. It was dissolved later when the PFLP and PLF left it in 1985 and joined the Palestine National Salvation Front instead, which was dissolved in 1988 with the convening of the meeting of the PNC in Algiers. The Alliance called for democratic reforms of the PLO (i.e., it suggested collective leadership of the PLO to curb the autocratic tendencies of the chairman of the Executive Committee of the PLO (i.e., Arafat).

11. See, for example, Mamdouh Nofal, "The Palestinian Political System between the Inside and Outside" (in Arabic), May 1, 1999 (http://www.mnofal.ps/articles/?nb=227), Personal blog.

12. On the policy of creeping apartheid, see: Oren Yiftachel, "Between Colonialism and Ethnocracy: 'Creeping Apartheid' in Israel/Palestine," *MERIP*, 27; no. 253 (2012): 7–37.

13. Israel has managed its relations with Palestinians "through a dual apparatus that combines both direct and soft measures." Both are used to manage the conflict rather than solving it "all the while changing facts on the ground. Forcing a one-sided solution." Honaida Ghanim (ed.), "MADAR Strategic Report 2015: The Israeli Scene 2014" (Ramallah: MADAR—The Palestinian Forum for Israeli Studies, 2015): 12; see also later strategic reports by MADAR.

14. See Honaida Ghanim (ed.), "MADAR Strategic Report 2017: 'The Israeli Scene 2016: The New Right in Israel Tightens its Grip on Israel's Present and Future'" (Ramallah, MADAR—The Palestinian Forum for Israeli Studies, 2017).

15. Public opinion polls in the WBG give all the left political parties combined less than 5 percent of support: see, for example, the public opinion poll carried out between December 7–10, 2017, by the Palestinian Center for Policy and Survey Research, "The Palestinian-Israeli Pulse: A Joint Poll" (Ramallah: PCPSR, 2017): http://www.pcpsr.org/sites/default/files/Table%20of%20Findings_English%20Joint%20Poll%204%20dec2017.pdf.

16. On this issue, see Jamil Hilal, "The Palestinian Left and the Multi-layered Challenges Ahead," *Rosa-Luxemburg-Foundation in Palestine Newsletter* (Ramallah: Rosa-Luxemburg-Foundation in Palestine, March 19, 2010) (http://www.palestine.rosalux.org/fileadmin/rls_uploads/pdfs/Standpunkte/Standpunkte_international/RLS_PAL_-_Hilal_Palestinian_Left.pdf).

17. On the perseverance of Palestinian political culture, see Jamil Hilal (ed.), *Palestinian Youth: Studies on Identity, Space and Community Participation* (Birzeit:

Centre for Development Studies, Birzeit University and American Friends Service Committee, 2017). See particularly the article by Hilal, "Reflections on Identity and Youth in Historical Palestine and the Diaspora."

18. See Jamil Hilal, "Reclaiming the Palestinian Narrative" (Al-Shabaka—the Palestinian Policy Network, January 7, 2013); http://al-shabaka.org/reclaiming-palestinian-narrative.

19. It has been argued that the institutions of the PLO should be reconstructed on a democratic and representative basis so as to continue the pluralist and secular tradition of the PLO, and to build on the fact that it is still acknowledged regionally and internationally as the sole representative of the Palestinian people, and is, formally, the body to which the PA is accountable. Others have argued that a fresh start independent from the heritage of the PLO to avoid its shortcomings and failings should be the aim. See Masarat (the Palestinian Center for Policy Research and Strategic Studies), "Rebuilding the Institutions of the Palestinian Liberation Organization" (Ramallah: Masarat, August 2013).

20. The 2013 Masarat document "Rebuilding the Institutions of the Palestinian Liberation Organization" was discussed at various stages by representatives of Fatah and Hamas and other political groups, and the version published took note of comments and suggestions expressed in joint meetings, but nothing agreed upon by the parties has been implemented.

21. On the impact of the Israeli parliamentary elections see Chris Whitman, "The Fall Out of the 2015 Israeli Elections: Diana Buttu Reflects on the Impact of the Elections on the Question of Palestine and Steps on how to Proceed Forward," PAL Papers (Ramallah: Rosa Luxemburg Stiftung Regional Office Palestine, April 2015).

22. For some thoughts on this issue, see Jamil Hilal "What's Stopping the 3rd Intifada?," Al-Shabaka (The Palestinian Policy Network), May 20, 2014 (http://al-shabaka.org/node/768). Also Jamil Hilal, "Rethinking Palestine: Settler-Colonialism, Neoliberalism and Individualism in the West Bank and Gaza Strip, *Contemporary Arab Affairs* 8, no. 3 (2015): 351–362.

BIBLIOGRAPHY

Baumgarten, Helga. "The Three Faces/Phases of Palestinian Nationalism, 1948–2005," *Journal of Palestine Studies*, 34, no. 4 (2005): 25–48.

Baumgarten, Helga. *From Liberation to the State: History of the Palestinian National Movement 1948–1988* (in Arabic) (Ramallah: Muwatin—The Palestinian Institute for the Study of Democracy, 2006).

Bourdieu, Pierre. *Sociology in Question*. London: Sage Publications, 1993.

Ghanim, Honaida (ed.). "MADAR Strategic Report 2015: 'The Israeli Scene 2014.'" Ramallah: MADAR—The Palestinian Forum for Israeli Studies, 2015.

Ghanim, Honaida (ed.). "MADAR Strategic Report 2017: 'The Israeli Scene 2016: The New Right in Israel Tightens its Grip on Israel's Present and Future'" Ramallah, MADAR—The Palestinian Forum for Israeli Studies, 2017.

Hilal, Jamil. "Reflections on Contemporary Palestinian History," in Ilan Pappe and Jamil Hilal (eds.), *Across the Wall; Narratives of Israeli-Palestinian History*. London: I.B. Tauris, 2010.

Hilal, Jamil. "What's Stopping the 3rd Intifada?," Al-Shabaka (The Palestinian Policy Network), May 20, 2014 (http://al-shabaka.org/node/768).

Hilal, Jamil. "Rethinking Palestine: Settler-Colonialism, Neoliberalism and Individualism in the West Bank and Gaza Strip," *Contemporary Arab Affairs* 8, no. 3 (2015): 351–362.

Hilal, Jamil. "The Palestinian Left and the Multi-layered Challenges Ahead," *Rosa-Luxemburg-Foundation in Palestine Newsletter*. Ramallah: Rosa-Luxemburg-Foundation in Palestine, March 19, 2010 (http://www.palestine.rosalux.org/fileadmin/rls_uploads/pdfs/Standpunkte/Standpunkte_international/RLS_PAL_-_Hilal_Palestinian_Left.pdf).

Hilal, Jamil (ed.). *Palestinian Youth: Studies on Identity, Space and Community Participation* (Birzeit: Centre for Development Studies, Birzeit University and American Friends Service Committee, 2017).

Hilal, Jamil. "Reclaiming the Palestinian Narrative" (Al-Shabaka—the Palestinian Policy Network, January 7, 2013) (http://al-shabaka.org/reclaiming-palestinian-narrative).

Hilal, Jamil. *Palestinian Political Organizations and Parties* (in Arabic) (Ramallah: Muwatin—The Palestinian Institute for the Study of Democracy, 2006).

Khalidi, Rashid. *Palestinian Identity; The Construction of Modern National Consciousness*. New York: Columbia University Press, 1997.

Masarat (the Palestinian Center for Policy Research and Strategic Studies). "Rebuilding the Institutions of the Palestinian Liberation Organization" (Ramallah: Masarat, August 2013).

Nofal, Mamdouh. "The Palestinian Political System between the Inside and Outside" (in Arabic), 1 May 1999 (http://www.mnofal.ps/articles/?nb=227), Personal blog.

Palestinian Center for Policy and Survey Research. "The Palestinian-Israeli Pulse: A Joint Poll" (Ramallah: PCPSR, 2017): http://www.pcpsr.org/sites/default/files/Table%20of%20Findings_English%20Joint%20Poll%204%20dec2017.pdf.

Sayigh, Yezid. *Armed Struggle and the Search for State: The Palestinian National Movement 1949–1993*. Oxford: Oxford University Press, 1999.

Whitman, Chris. "The Fall Out of the 2015 Israeli Elections: Diana Buttu reflects on the Impact of the Elections on the Question of Palestine and Steps on how to Proceed Forward," PAL Papers (Ramallah: Rosa Luxemburg Stiftung Regional Office Palestine, April 2015).

Yiftachel, Oren. "Between Colonialism and Ethnocracy: 'Creeping Apartheid' in Israel/Palestine," *MERIP*, 27, no. 253 (2012): 7–37.

Chapter Three

Lost in Transition

The Palestinian National Movement After Oslo

Tariq Dana

The signing of the Oslo Accords between Israel and the Palestine Liberation Organization (PLO) in 1993 inaugurated a new chapter of Palestinian politics that saw drastic changes in the national movement's structures, functions, perceptions, and political vocabulary and behavior. These drastic changes profoundly impacted on the ability of the Palestinian body politic to function as an independent anti-colonial liberation movement united in struggle for self-determination and obstructed its role as the representative body of Palestinian national aspirations. In fact, the reality of the Palestinian national movement after nearly a quarter century of the Oslo process is one lacerated by multiple forms of fragmentations, divisions, and conflicting agendas increasingly defined by narrow factional interests for power and privileges. Despite the ongoing deterioration and weakness, neither have the existing political forces sought to present alternative strategies to rebuild the national movement, nor have new political and social movements emerged to introduce new dynamics that may challenge the status quo. Israel, which systemically cleared the ground for the Oslo reality, has thus been able to deepen its colonization of the Occupied Palestinian Territory (OPT), further besiege the fragmented Palestinian communities—by geography, politics, and ever-increasing class and social divisions—and to intensify its "facts on the ground" to abort any chance for a two-state solution, which ostensibly was the ultimate goal of the Oslo Accords (see chapter by Diana Buttu in this book).

Two main perspectives explain the impact of the Oslo process on the national movement. The first, which is the most dominant, conceives the Oslo process as a *failure*. According to this perspective, the Oslo Accords were initially designed to introduce a new era of peaceful settlement based on a two-state solution, but things went wrong and the peace process failed. This "failure" caused deep harm to Palestinian national aspirations and rights, and led to negative consequences for the Palestinian national fabric. The blame is pinned on manifold factors: the flawed implementation of the Oslo Accords, the excessive power asymmetries between the Palestinians and Israel, the weakness and miscalculation of the Palestinian leadership, Israel's ongoing colonization practices, and the US's unconditional support for Israel.[1] In contrast, the second perspective conceives the Oslo process as a *success* if Israel's real intentions are properly understood. In this regard, Israel's real intention was to consolidate its colonial project and further its control over Palestinian life, while simultaneously creating the conditions to incapacitate and disarm the Palestinian national movement.[2] Accordingly, the Oslo process has successfully paved the way for the current situation where the numbers of settlers in the occupied West Bank have more than doubled and Israel's colonial control over land, resources, and borders has been institutionalized without effective resistance. Shortly after the signing of the Oslo agreements in 1993, the late Palestinian intellectual Edward Said noted the extent to which the agreements are inherently flawed and argued that the Oslo trap constituted "an instrument of Palestinian surrender, a Palestinian Versailles."[3] In fact, the Oslo framework constituted a successful method of counterinsurgency because it has fragmented what was left of the Palestinian body politic.[4] Now, after more than two decades of the Oslo Accords, Palestinians have the problem of their struggle facing the risk of being a "failed national movement."[5]

While failure of national liberation movements is hardly new, the failure of the Palestinian national movement is unique and unprecedented in the history of liberation movements. After decades of acting as a leading anti-colonial movement in the world—with success in building influential organizational structures characterized by ideological and political pluralism, and a revolutionary transnational reach that inspired and attracted supporters from distant parts of the world—the struggle and countless sacrifices that were made have ended in catastrophic failure whereby none of its stated objectives have been realized. While the seeds of failure could be attributed to a set of historical and structural factors since the formation of the PLO in the 1960s, the most crucial factor is undoubtedly the capitulation and self-defeat of the PLO as seen in how the 25 years of the Oslo process progressed with its humiliating terms and far-reaching consequences on all aspects of Palestinian life. Although the Palestinian political field today continues to be described as a national liberation movement, the highly restrictive Oslo framework and its related mechanisms of institutional, political, and economic control has led the national movement to abandon vital features and tasks integrally associated with liberation movements.

The adverse consequences of Oslo on the national movement are numerous, but three main features can explain much of the ongoing crisis:

First, it is unprecedented that an anti-colonial liberation organization voluntarily accepts to dissolve its capacity and embrace a state-building agenda under ongoing conditions of military occupation and settler-colonialism it has fought against for decades. The Oslo Accords redefined Palestinian-Israeli relations as stipulated by the mutual recognition between the PLO and the Israeli government in 1993. This mutual recognition institutionalized the relationship between the colonizer and colonized, evidenced in the establishment of the Palestinian Authority (PA) and the formation of official channels of political, economic, security, and civil coordination with the Israeli authorities, all of which were governed according to Israeli conditions.[6] The establishment of the PA as the center of Palestinian politics encapsulated the wider PLO force and its political pluralism in a narrowly defined institutional structure, limited in its resources, besieged in its geography, and governed by an exclusionary politics. This pushed the PA to be effectively exposed to Israeli pressure, which in turn left the Palestinian leadership with little room for maneuver and insubstantial political independence. As a result, the Palestinian leadership lost its capacity to lead the national movement, and instead it became an acquiescent elite whose survival is dependent on Israeli terms and conditions.

Second, the Oslo framework implanted the seeds of divisions and fragmentations within the Palestinian body politic and society at large, which culminated in the Hamas-Fatah division in 2007. This internal Palestinian schism is not only the consequence of factional conflict over the "legitimate" ruling party of the PA, but also demonstrates the divisive effects of the Oslo process along territorial, political, institutional, social, and ideological lines. The continuing division of the Palestinian political system has not empowered Hamas over Fatah nor vice versa, but has further damaged what was left of the fragile national unity, and provided Israel with a comfortable position from which to intensify the colonization of the OPT.[7] Furthermore, the West Bank, which became the favored site for international donors following the Hamas-Fatah schism, has witnessed an ever-increasing social and class division between the PA political and economic elite and the population at large. The PA elite has largely benefited from the reality introduced by Oslo, where international aid, privileges granted by Israel, monopolies over resources, involvement in private businesses, and corruption are major sources of personal enrichment.[8]

Third, the Oslo process exposed the OPT to systematic intervention by international donors, financial institutions, and international NGOs, ostensibly justified under the banners of peacebuilding and statebuilding. This allowed new patterns of external intervention effectively to influence internal Palestinian affairs through projecting "a variety of social and economic objectives and instrumentalities, underpinned by substantial commitments of financial support."[9] The goal has been to enforce political stability and security, and to maintain Western and Israeli geopolitical interests, all of which has come under the rubric of "supporting the peace process." These forms of international intervention have influenced the national movement at two levels. First, the state-building exercise, as embodied in the PA, has deprived the Palestinian body politic of the capacity to produce plans and programs according to the national perspective and local needs. Almost all of the PA designs, including its institutional framework, mode of governance, neoliberal economic policies, and security apparatus are a reflection of donors' diktats and conditions. Second, local civil society has been restructured toward an NGO sector to carry out predefined tasks in service of the "peace process." International donors, therefore, enforced the Oslo terms as a conditional political framework to which local civil society ought to refer for redefining their relations and interactions with the political dynamic on the ground. Thus, a large number of local organizations had to adapt to the perquisites of the Oslo political equation by replacing major political assignments previously associated with the dynamics of anti-colonial struggle with ostensibly apolitical approaches based on the politics of peacebuilding.[10]

This chapter will explore these aspects of the dramatic transformation of the Palestinian political field after Oslo. The chapter is divided into five sections. The first focuses on the ways in which the establishment of the PA contributed to the deterioration and weakening of the Palestinian national movement. The second section shows how the advent of the PA led to the disintegration of the PLO as a national liberation organization and the dismantling of its capacity as a representative body of the Palestinian people. The remaining three sections highlight the post-Oslo transformation of the three largest factions that represent the different political and ideological angles of Palestinian politics: Fatah representing the secular nationalist strand, Hamas as a representative of political Islam, and the Popular Front for the Liberation of Palestine (PFLP) as the leftist force.

THE DEMISE OF THE PLO

The acceptance of the PLO leadership to establish the PA in 1994 and to transfer the center of gravity of Palestinian politics into the OPT was motivated by the desire to transform the Palestinian struggle away from its revolutionary character into a pragmatic state-building program. Accordingly, the advent of the PA effectively pronounced the demise of the PLO. While the legitimacy of the PA is primarily gained from the PLO, the PA has marginalized the role of the PLO, effectively transformed it into a dysfunctional organization deprived of its main functions and roles. In theory, the PA was supposed to operate as a governing institutional branch subordinated to the PLO and its central decisions. In practice, however, the establishment of the PA marked the culmination of the PLO's internal and external crises, and obstructed its historical mandate as the sole legitimate representative of the Palestinian people. (See chapter by Jamil Hilal in this book.)

A primary striking consequence of the establishment of the PA has been the systematic marginalization of the PLO as a broad political structure characterized by political and ideological pluralism in favor of a narrowly defined semi-autonomous entity, besieged in its geography and political maneuvering, and dominated by an exclusionary political view subjected to terms imposed by Israel. The weighty shift toward the PA as the center of gravity for Palestinian politics instead of the PLO, has altered understandings of the nature of the Palestinian struggle for liberation and self-determination.[11] The PLO historically functioned as an umbrella organization under which the various factions operated for the cause of national liberation. The later dominant position of the PA over the PLO has radically changed this track toward formalized practices of state-building and institution-building, and prioritized service provision and the administration of daily life in the OPT.

While still internationally recognized as the sole legitimate representative of the Palestinian people, 25 years of the PA's predominance has substantially impeded the PLO's capacity to represent all Palestinians worldwide. The PA has also excluded Palestinian communities in exile from having any meaningful contribution in formulating national policy.[12] The issue of representation in the Palestinian context is associated with the principle of the struggle for self-determination. Against this backdrop, the UN recognized the PLO in 1974 as the sole legitimate representative of the Palestinian people. The PLO was the only national liberation movement in the world to enjoy such international status. This status allowed the organization to speak and act on behalf of Palestinians, spread its presence worldwide through establishing representative offices, entering into international agreements, and representing Palestinians at the UN and other international and regional organizations.

When the PA—which only represents Palestinians under its jurisdiction in the OPT—came to monopolize Palestinian politics, it essentially aborted the PLO's representative function, thus leaving millions of diaspora Palestinians unrepresented. One indication of this shift is the gradual transformation of PLO representative offices into embassies representing the PA or the "State of Palestine," thus effectively ending the PLO presence in many countries around the world. Likewise, when the PA decided to upgrade its status at the UN in September 2011, many legal analysts warned about the consequences of such a move on the PLO representative status in the UN. It was feared that a Palestinian statehood status would only represent Palestinian inhabitants of the West Bank and Gaza, and that "could jeopardize the effective and collective representation of all the Palestinian people—the Diaspora, refugees, Palestinians citizens of Israel and the Palestinians in the OPT—both inside and outside of the UN system."[13]

Another major aspect of the problematic PA-PLO relationship has been the overlapping jurisdictions and the absence of separation of powers and mandates. This dilemma is manifested in the elite domination over key overlapping positions within both the PLO and the PA without an internally elected mandate, which distorted the distinction between the PLO and the PA. The president of the PA is the chairman of the PLO, and most of the leadership positions of the PLO and the PA are intersecting in a manner that often creates confusion between the two organizations. It has become a regular occurrence to see a member of the Palestinian National Council (PNC) in a key position in the PA, or a member of the PLO executive committee occupying a leading post in the PA. Such a situation has encouraged a conflict of interest and therefore various corruption practices have spread across the PA and the PLO. Furthermore, the elite overlapping positions between the PLO and the PA go against the PLO's internal regulations that forbid combining the membership of the PLO National Council with another PLO position. The PLO Basic Law also forbids members of the PLO executive committee from other employment. The absence of effective mechanisms for accountability and democratic procedures within the PLO has deepened the crisis of legitimacy.

The deterioration of the PLO has been accompanied by repeated calls and initiatives to reform it and revive its centrality in Palestinian political life as an inclusive and representative body politic for all Palestinian factions and institutions. One central objective of these initiatives is to create a democratic and balanced representation of all factions, including Hamas and Islamic Jihad, which are not currently part of the PLO. Another objective is to reform the PLO apparatuses through engaging Palestinians in the process, wherever they reside. Nevertheless, attempts to reform the PLO have persistently failed to achieve any tangible result. While the PLO's revolutionary heritage has been exploited by the PA elites to legitimize their positions and exclusionary politics, which led the PLO to be effectively dysfunctional, many Palestinians believe that restructuring the PLO and reviving its role as a leading, unifying, and representative organization for all Palestinians is a prerequisite for rebuilding the national movement. For them, despite the misery of its post-Oslo status, the PLO shaped modern Palestinian national identity and legitimized the Palestinian struggle for liberation and self-determination at the regional and international levels.

Perhaps understandably, throughout the post-Oslo years little thought has been given to the possibility of establishing an alternative political framework that surpasses the PLO. However, the PLO's prolonged state of idleness and the persistent inability or unwillingness by the Palestinian leadership and factions to revive the umbrella organization, have driven some to call for the establishment of "alternative democratic leadership and to think collectively regarding how to construct a new national movement while preserving the assets that the Palestinian struggle built in previous decades."[14] While such calls are nascent and ambiguous, and which so far have not been developed into a strategic vision or practical plan, they might yet gain broader popularity, and new structures and leadership may emerge beyond the PLO.

FROM A NATIONAL MOVEMENT TO AN ACQUIESCENT AUTHORITY

As the PA emerged as the institutional embodiment of the Oslo process, it was forced to function according to various conditions and restrictions superimposed by the agreements. The PA thereafter established itself as the dominant political force in the OPT and as the official representative of Palestinian politics to the outside world. However, the PA's legitimacy was not supported by a broad Palestinian consensus, but rather its very existence and continuity were a result of a "process" that depended on Israel's consent, international diplomatic recognition, and donor financial support. Thus, the PA's dominance over Palestinian politics made it a driving force behind the dramatic transformation of the Palestinian political field.

The PA was designed to function as an interim administrative body responsible for overseeing civil and security affairs in Palestinian densely populated areas (Area A) in the West Bank and Gaza. This situation was governed by the logic of gradualism, which was translated into a transitional period of five years until a final status agreement with Israel was reached. All major issues that constitute the core of the conflict such as the status of Jerusalem, the Jewish settlements built on the occupied territories of 1967, the right of return of Palestinian refugees, and control over borders, were postponed to the final status agreement. With the collapse of the Camp David negotiations in 2000 and the subsequent events, particularly the Second Intifada, the Oslo process was declared dead.[15] However, despite the fact that the Oslo process has reached a dead-end, its conditions and manifestations are still powerfully evident on the ground, especially through the continuous existence of the PA and the implementation of policies strictly defined by the Oslo framework.

There is broad agreement that the advent of the PA has been central to understanding much of the crisis and weakness experienced by the Palestinian national movement in the past two decades. The PA has brought with it the seeds of divisions and fragmentations that profoundly impacted on the multiple structures and functions of the Palestinian political field, and reduced the Palestinian struggle for liberation and self-determination to a mere demand of statehood on parts of the territory occupied in 1967. These factors are either a direct result of the Oslo process and the various limitations it imposed on the PA mandate and functions, or are associated with the very nature of the PA, its characteristics, and policies.

The new geography introduced by the Oslo Accords has had a profound effect on the Palestinian political field and its ability to maintain a solid connection between its various units, institutions, and constituencies inside the OPT and in the Diaspora. On the one hand, the establishment of the PA meant a geographic shift in the center of gravity away from the Palestinian Diaspora to the "Palestinian center" in the West Bank and Gaza.[16] Such a move encapsulated the whole set of Palestinian leadership and institutions in a limited geographical context, fully governed by Israeli control over land and borders, and effectively suffocated by Jewish settlements and the closure regime.

On the other hand, the PA was set up to administer limited and non-contiguous areas in the West Bank and Gaza, mostly towns and cities that are densely populated. In accordance with the interim agreement, the West Bank was divided into three distinct areas with different jurisdictions and administrative and security arrangements (A, B, C). Area A consists of large towns and cities under full civilian and security control by the PA, and comprises roughly 18 percent of the West Bank. Area B consists of mostly Palestinian rural areas and is under PA administration and joint Palestinian-Israeli security control, and it comprises roughly 22 percent of the West Bank. Area C, under full Israeli military and administrative control, includes fertile agricultural lands, natural resources, and water aquifers.[17] This has augmented territorial fragmentation and consolidated Israel's control over the movements of people and goods, and facilitated Israel's imposition of various restrictions such as closure, curfews, and other mechanisms of control. As a result, the geographical reality introduced by Oslo has placed the West Bank in a sophisticated and all-encompassing "matrix of control."[18]

In addition, the PA was designed to function as a central institutional channel through which the Oslo political, economic, and security conditions, as well as international donors' visions, are transmitted and enforced over the Palestinian polity and society.[19] International intervention through technical and financial support to the PA is strictly associated with the Oslo framework and is often justified in terms of peacebuilding and state-building (see chapter by Mandy Turner in this book). This has brought the OPT into the forefront of internationally promoted experiments of governance, social engineering, economic development, security, and institution-building, which have been advanced by the highest-level practitioners, donor agencies, and international financial institutions. Such an extensive combination of post-conflict/neo-colonial set of experiments has transformed the OPT, particularly the West Bank, into a "laboratory of technologies of control."[20] In such a context, the PA capacity to produce social, economic, and institutional plans based on the real requirements of the local context as well as independent political decision-making has been largely eroded. Moreover, the strategies and practices of international intervention do not challenge the colonial order, but rather appear to have "complemented and meshed with the structures of domination and repression in subtle but crucial ways."[21]

Moreover, international intervention was accompanied by a major change in the political economy of the OPT, which is particularly associated with the effects of neoliberal policies pursued by the PA. In addition to economic dependency on Israel, the PA's neoliberal policies have created another structural form of dependency on international aid and foreign investments. This has also subjected Palestinian economic planning to international donors' diktats (and with the involvement of Israel) in determining various aspects of Palestinian economic strategy.

Neoliberalism found its way to the OPT from the outset of the Oslo process and the establishment of the PA which, since then, has faithfully been echoing donors' recommendations for a neoliberal institution-building and good governance schema.[22] Unlike other former colonized countries, the PA represents an unprecedented case in embracing neoliberalism from the very beginning of its establishment. In fact, international financial institutions such as the World Bank and other donor agencies played a leading role in guiding the newly established PA. However, the development of these policy prescriptions for the OPT began even before the PA was officially established, when the World Bank issued a report in 1993 titled *Developing the Occupied Territories: An Investment in Peace*, which emphasized the role of free market, private sector, export-led economic development, and good governance in guiding the Palestinian economy.[23]

The PA's neoliberal turn accelerated after President Mahmoud Abbas appointed Salam Fayyad as prime minister in 2007. Fayyad's neoliberal re-arrangement took it one stage further due to its technical professionalism, systemic implementation, and acceleratory dynamic. Hanieh notes that the PA's commitment to such a massive and rapid implementation of neoliberal policies exceeds measures imposed by IFIs on any other state in the region.[24] This includes the promotion of private sector-led development, export-led industrial zoning, the encouragement of foreign investments and finance, the expansion of banking deregulation and public debt, and the adoption of a regressive taxation regime. Furthermore, Fayyad's neoliberal implementation coincided with Israel's strategy of "economic peace" introduced by Israeli Prime Minister Benjamin Netanyahu in 2008. This produced a harmonious economic dynamic and encouraged joint economic ventures to flourish between Palestinian and Israeli businesses within Israel's colonial framework.[25]

This neoliberal dynamic has created a beneficial reality for certain political-economic elites whose interest is tied to maintaining the political status quo. This elite enjoys considerable influence over PA decision-making and it operates in close cooperation with the Israeli authorities and businesses. In addition, this elite considers the emergence of new counter political movements as a threat to its privileges, thus it often relies on Palestinian security to secure political stability and protect its businesses and assets.

Furthermore, authoritarian politics has been an integral feature of the PA, which has critically impacted on the development of political thought and ideological pluralism in the Palestinian political field. The centralization of political and economic power, and the repression of critical currents, has prevented the emergence and development of alternative visions and structures as well as paralyzed the roles of existing political actors in feeding the Palestinian political field with new ideas, perceptions, and dynamics.

The logic behind the creation and continuity of the PA is that it ought to be strictly governed by a compliant political class that fully accepts and implements conditions enforced by the Oslo Accords. The survival of the PA political class, or the PA elite, has become organically linked to the complex network of political and economic interests and privileges that became deeply rooted in the PA institutions. Thus, in order to preserve its interests, the PA elite monopolized the PA centers of power such as political decision-making, public institutions, financial resources, and the means of violence. This has resulted in an exclusionary politics that depends on a variety of techniques of co-optation and suppression.

The PA underwent two distinct phases of authoritarianism: the first is represented by Yasser Arafat's politics, and the second phase began with the post-Arafat uneasy transfer of power to Mahmoud Abbas and his narrow coalition of business elite and technocrats.

In the first phase of PA authoritarianism, political and economic power rested almost exclusively in the person of Arafat, first president of the PA and chairman of the PLO. He pursued a governance route similar to his ruling-style legacy in the PLO. While the institutional structure of the PA was initially supposed to be organized along the Western liberal paradigm of state-building, during the 1990s the state-building process was implemented in a disorganized fashion through ad hoc decisions made by Arafat, who ignored recommendations made by his professional team.[26] Israel, the US, and international donors turned a blind eye to those aspects of Arafat's governance as they supported strengthening his position against the opposition and affirming his control over the nascent PA. Accordingly, Arafat effectively dominated executive power and manipulated the legislative and judicial spheres. The Palestinian Legislative Council (PLC) is a case in point. It was formed to purportedly carry out the functions of a democratically elected parliament such as debating and passing legislation, and monitoring the executive branch. However, in practice the executive branch (i.e., Arafat) ignored various laws and instead depended on presidential decrees to advance his policies.

After Arafat's death in 2004, Mahmoud Abbas was elected as the PA president in 2005 and became the leader of Fatah and the PLO. Abbas's politics differed from those of Arafat in the sense that they were considered to be more compatible with both US and Israeli interests.[27] In addition, unlike Arafat, whose authoritarian character depended on his charismatic leadership, revolutionary legacy, and a broad consensus by the Fatah party over his leadership, Abbas's authoritarianism is based on networks of business and technocratic elite, and centralized control over the security branch. Furthermore, Abbas's authoritarianism is closely linked and coordinated with the US and Israel through a variety of mechanisms including political and financial backing, and security assistance. This means that the US and Israel are directly complicit in enhancing the PA's autocratic approach. In fact, this period witnessed unparalleled intensification of the level of authoritarianism and the deepening of anti-democratic practices including suppression of political dissidents, journalists, and activists.[28] This became particularly the case after the series of events that began with the international community's refusal to deal with the democratically elected government of Hamas in 2006, and the following military takeover of the Gaza Strip by Hamas in June 2007 that resulted in the institutional and political split between the West Bank and Gaza Strip. With international support for Abbas, these series of events marked a major turning point in the development of the PA's authoritarianism, whereby internal repression of political dissidents and assaults on civil and political liberties such as freedom of speech and the press were systemically carried out by PA security forces in close collaboration with Israeli security.

Moreover, the combination of authoritarianism and neoliberalism has promoted the PA's reputation for corruption whereby nepotism, misappropriation of public resources, and misuse of power are rampant within its ministries. As many as 95 percent of Palestinians living in the OPT believe there is corruption in PA institutions, according to a survey in 2016.[29] Similar surveys carried out since the establishment of the PA have persistently shown public mistrust in the PA. Corruption in the context of the PA has contributed to various institutional, economic, and social problems, including deepening inequality and harming of the social fabric, but its most alarming impact has been the deep corrupting effect it has caused to the national movement.

The most direct consequence of PA corruption on the national movement is particularly associated with the patron-client system that has constituted the backbone of PA institution-building since the beginning. The way in which the PA patron-client system works involves the systematic exploitation of political power and financial resources for the purpose of securing the hegemonic order. In particular, the PA patron-client system is seen as a powerful tool in three realms: for securing loyalties, reviving the politics of tribalism, and co-opting opposition.[30] First, the way the PA has managed to secure loyalty among its constituents is largely based on offering access to resources for economic survival rather than persuasion for its political, economic, and social programs. In particular, the PA's large public sector has been a vital source for creating dependency, ensuring hegemony, and securing loyalties. Second, the PA sought to accommodate large families through recognizing *Mukhtars* (head of tribes) and authorizing them to speak on behalf of their families in order to ensure their loyalty. In this way, the PA revived the politics of tribalism, which had been marginalized by the rise of the national movement in the OPT in the period prior to Oslo. Third, the patron-client system is also used to co-opt and naturalize political opposition. A number of political leaders were trapped into this network and incorporated into the PA project, which they initially claimed to reject. These leaders (independents, leftists and Islamists) are offered privileges, advantages, and access to prestigious posts in ministries and public institutions in exchange for political loyalty. In fact, some of those co-opted personalities have become key actors in PA politics.

Last but not least, security collaboration between the PA and Israel is another aspect that contradicts the basic feature of national liberation. The significance of security to both Israel and the PA can be clearly seen in a number of the principal agreements that were signed in the 1990s, most prominently the Declaration of Principles of 1993, the Cairo Agreement (Oslo II) of 1994, and the Wye River Memorandum of 1998 (see chapter by Diana Buttu in this book). Security has been and remains a defining feature of PA-Israeli relations, which is particularly expressed through the terms of "security coordination."

The security branch is a key institution that plays substantial roles in shaping the PA's character and behavior. It constitutes an essential mechanism for consolidating the PA's authoritarian character and enforcing its dominance over the Palestinian political field. The Palestinian security sector today is the most dominant in the PA. It absorbs 44 percent of a total of 145,000 civil servants, and it eats up a sizeable proportion of the PA financial resources, accounting for almost 30 percent–35 percent of the PA annual budget.[31]

The evolution and development of the PA security sector intersects with the dual phases of authoritarianism specified above. The first phase is associated with Arafat's control and direction of the security apparatuses during the 1990s, and the second phase witnessed a fundamental restructuring of security under the presidency of Abbas that began in 2005.

The first phase saw the formation of various competing security apparatuses under the full control of the president that concentrated their operations on internal policing as stipulated by the PA-Israeli agreements. During the 1990s, Israel permitted the PA security sector to quantitatively expand and even surpass the maximum number of 30,000 security personnel as specified by Oslo II. It was estimated that by 1996 the PA employed between 50,000–80,000 security officers in the West Bank and Gaza Strip. As such the PA became the most heavily policed territory in the world, with an officer-to-resident ratio of 1:50. In the late 1990s, the PA security forces were estimated to amount to a dozen operational branches, a figure which increased to more than 15 by 2004.[32]

By the end of the Second Intifada, the PA security apparatus was destroyed, scattered, and left largely dysfunctional by the Israeli reoccupation of Palestinian towns. In this context, rebuilding security constituted a top priority in Abbas's agenda, and ever since he assumed office in 2005, security has been a pillar of his presidency. Abbas wished to transform the Arafatist mode of security—which would sometimes forcefully resist the Israeli military—into a strictly inward-oriented security capable of enforcing stability and providing protection to the PA elite. These two objectives were only attainable through effective coordination with the Israeli security establishment, under the supervision of the US. International donors, particularly the US and the EU, played key roles in the PA's security reform, with a major focus on shaping the PA's security doctrine, training, vetting, and strategic planning, and the formation of professional security apparatuses with enhanced capacity for internal policing and "counterterrorism" operations.[33] The Euro-American involvement in restructuring the PA security forces is precisely defined in accordance with Israeli security needs. Indeed, Sayigh argues that "the United States and the European Union['s] . . . rhetoric about promoting democratic development and the rule of law is pious at best, and at worst disingenuous."[34] There is a growing agreement among observers that the way international assistance is directed to the Palestinian security forces has created a "police state." According to Aisling, "the seed of this deception which was to grow into a new police state in the region was the US and European acquiescence to Israel's self-definition of its own security needs and by extension, Israel's definition of the requirements for Palestinian security collaboration."[35]

FATAH: THE POLITICS OF ANTI-NATIONAL LIBERATION

The historic handshake between the PLO chairman and head of Fatah, Yasser Arafat, and the Israeli prime minister, Yitzhak Rabin, on the lawn of the White House in 1993 marked the beginning of a new era of transformation for Fatah. One year after the handshake, Arafat and many Fatah affiliates in exile in Tunisia and elsewhere were allowed to return to autonomous parts of the West Bank and Gaza to establish a self-governing authority in accordance with the terms of the Oslo Accords.

Fatah's weighty involvement in the Oslo compromise marks a turning point in its structure, functions, and characteristics which saw it embarking on a transition from a national liberation movement to a quasi-state party preoccupied with building institutions, distributing benefits, and securing hegemony under the ongoing occupation. Indeed, the PA is a Fatah-dominated project: its leadership, returnees, and supporters in the OPT have occupied key governmental positions and became the PA ruling elite.[36] A significant segment of Fatah cadres and militants have been attracted by opportunities and privileges offered by the PA and became the core of its bureaucracy, its large public sector, and its multiple security apparatuses. Fatah's multi-sectorial popular organizations that existed prior to Oslo and played vital roles during the First Intifada were integrated into the structure of the nascent PA.[37] Eventually Fatah became synonymous with the PA itself.

In order to accommodate the requirements of the Oslo political phase, Fatah political discourses became increasingly dominated by pragmatism and moderate political vocabulary. This served to direct public attention toward its state-building project, including emphasis on negotiations, diplomacy, peace-building, institution-building, security, and political stability. For many Palestinians, this marks a divergence from Fatah's early revolutionary principles that put it at the forefront of the Palestinian struggle.

This resulted in a dilemma, given the irreconcilable tensions between the functions of a national liberation movement and a state-building project, which in the Palestinian context has blatantly failed to coexist in harmony. In particular, being entangled in an internationally designed, Israeli-besieged, and financially conditioned "national project," Fatah has lost considerable ground, and its ability to pursue independent political decisions and effective maneuvering has been gravely undermined.

Fatah's historical dominance over the fate of the Palestinian cause is a result of exclusionary politics that has tended to marginalize and co-opt opposition, including critical voices within the movement itself. This logic has been translated into a form of politics employed by the PA that lacks popular participation and representation and which has contributed to its authoritarianism. Furthermore, neopatrimonial networks are a key feature of Fatah's internal hierarchies and its relations with members and the society at large. This has allowed the movement to exploit national institutions for personal ends, to concentrate power in the hands of its senior leadership, to punish dissidents, and to control its constituents.

Being ideologically based on Palestinian nationalism in its broadest sense, Fatah's internal fabric is comprised of diverse ideological leanings ranging from leftists to rightists, secularists, and conservatives. The movement's diversity paved the way for the emergence of rival trends in pursuit of competing political agendas. Despite these internal contradictions, which occasionally resulted in internal rifts, Fatah has generally maintained internal unity in times of crisis. However, in the Palestinian popular belief, there are considerable differences between the Fatah internal fabric under the leadership of Yasser Arafat and that under the leadership of Mahmoud Abbas. Apart from a couple of political rifts within the movement in the 1980s, Arafat's leadership symbolized the movement's cohesiveness and unity. Under Abbas's leadership, the movement has experienced precarious power struggles, particularly his rivalry with Mohammed Dahlan and its polarizing consequences on Fatah bases along personalized, geographical (West Bank, Gaza), and generational ("old guard," "young guard") lines. Originally, Abbas and Dahlan were close allies during the Arafat era. And when he was elected as PA president in 2006, Abbas appointed Dahlan as his adviser on national security and as secretary of the National Security Council. However, disputes over personal interests for power and wealth ended up in Dahlan being expelled from Fatah and the PA in 2011, and many of his supporters in the West Bank have been imprisoned and expelled from the movement. This divide is understood as an indication of the extent of the chaos and bitter succession crisis within Fatah.

Another form of the party's internal rivalry surfaces in times of national crisis and intensified Israeli aggression. For instance, Fatah's experience in the Second Intifada highlights two contradictory trends. The first was represented by Fatah's military wing, Al-Aqsa Martyrs Brigades, which favored challenging Israel militarily and cooperated closely with Hamas and Islamic Jihad. The second was led by the mainstream moderate trend that sought to put an end to the Second Intifada, reach a negotiable solution with Israel, continue security coordination with Israel, and maintain the existence of the PA—this was comprised of the higher echelon of Fatah and the PA. Tensions between these two trends have occasionally taken violent forms, and resulted in the emergence of armed militias in the last phase of the Second Intifada that caused a situation of chaos and fear in Palestinian towns. However, after the death of Arafat in 2004 and the end of the Second Intifada in 2005, Fatah experienced a new episode of transformation. The balance of power favored Fatah's moderate trend under the leadership of Abbas who, after his election as president of the PA in 2005, moved to disband Fatah's militant groups, absorbed them into the PA security apparatus, and neutralized leaders who could potentially pose a challenge to his authority.

Fatah's Sixth and Seventh General Congress held in Bethlehem in 2009 and in Ramallah in 2016, demonstrated the movement's political, structural, and ideological stagnation. The Congress had not met over the preceding two decades, despite party regulations that call for elections every five years. The holding of both Congresses was motivated by Abbas's desire to transform what remained of Fatah into a political party devoted to building a Palestinian state alongside Israel, to reassert his leadership despite the erosion of his public legitimacy, and to marginalize internal opponents. While most of Fatah's younger constituents hoped that the Congress would bridge the generational gap, the results consolidated Abbas's grip. A decisive factor was the role played by Israel, which prevented most Fatah delegates in exile from joining the event—only a few, closely associated with Abbas, participated. The reason for holding the Congress elections stemmed from two perceptions. First, Fatah's constituents perceived the Congress as an opportunity for change within the movement's organs and to bridge the generational gap between the "old guard" and "young guard." This, however, was not accompanied by a new political program or strategy reflecting a critical or reformist trend within the movement, but rather was based on the desire by the younger generation for power-sharing within the same Oslo paradigm. Second was Abbas's desire to transform the remaining aspects of the movement's national liberation character into an institutionalized political party devoted to building a Palestinian state alongside Israel. There were many reservations by Fatah cadres and external observers about the authenticity and transparency of the elections.[38] According to the author's conversations with many Fatah cadres during the periods of the Congress (August 2009 and December 2016), there is a broad belief that the elections primarily served as a mechanism to settle the party's power struggle in favor of Abbas and his circle.

While the outcomes of the Sixth and Seventh General Congress were conducive to some sort of stability for Abbas and his loyalists, this did not remedy the party's internal disarray and the leadership crisis.[39] The post-Oslo Fatah is caught between structural limitations and serious challenges. It represents an extreme case of the transformation that engulfed the very structure, fabric, and perception of the Palestinian national movement after Oslo. As the largest faction that dominated the politics, financial resources, and center of power of the PLO and the PA for almost half a century, Fatah has been discredited and blamed for the massive setbacks and persistent failure of the Palestinian national movement. Being a state-party without a state, governing an authority under military occupation, with persistent insistence on pursuing non-existent peace negotiations, Fatah politics has largely become irrelevant for a national liberation movement.

HAMAS: BETWEEN GOVERNANCE AND RESISTANCE

Despite its relatively recent rise compared with other Palestinian nationalist and secularist factions, the Islamic Resistance Movement (more popularly known by its Arabic acronym, Hamas [*Ḥarakat al-Muqāwamah al-'Islāmiyyah*]), became a significant pillar of the post-Oslo Palestinian political spectrum. Since its foundation during the First Intifada in 1987, Hamas has been the leading actor of political Islam in Palestine, representing an Islamic alternative that differs significantly from the PLO national project and its secularist character. Hamas's Islamist ideology is of dual character. The first is of a universal dimension rooted in the Muslim Brotherhood school of thought, which established its presence in Palestine in the 1940s. The second is reflected in the movement's peculiar status as a Palestinian militant group devoted to anti-colonial struggle and a civilian-social movement that seeks to influence society to accept and practice Islamic values.[40]

From the beginning, Hamas contested the PLO's historic status as the "sole legitimate representative of the Palestinian people" and positioned itself as a fierce competitor of Fatah. It rejected the Oslo Accords and their underlying negotiating process, and after the establishment of the PA in 1994 it sought to exercise counter-politics outside the PA structure. Thus, Hamas challenged the PA hegemony at different levels. First, it rejected the PA as a legitimate national project, and refrained from participating in the PA institutions and the general elections held in 1996. Second, the movement mobilized its popular base against the Oslo framework and advocated armed struggle against Israel. Hamas's influential counter-politics to the Oslo framework and considerable popular support has, therefore, allowed the movement to become dominant enough to enforce itself as an opposition force in the forefront of Palestinian politics.

Several factors contributed to Hamas's growing prominence during the 1990s. Politically, the expansion of Hamas came at a crucial time for the PLO factions, which were undergoing deepening crisis and a failure to pursue an effective liberation strategy. In particular, Hamas managed to fill the void left by the steady decline of the Palestinian left and its inability to produce a viable alternative to the PA project. In this context, Hamas represented an alternative political route to the PLO-Fatah-PA peace process and countered the Oslo process through discourses and actions that reflected its commitment to resistance. Ideologically, Hamas used a popularly appealing religious discourse, which depicts the movement as the vanguard of Islam in Palestine in a way that redefines Palestinian identity and struggle in Islamic terms. Socially, Hamas managed to establish and consolidate its cultural and ideological influence over various social groups. Its vibrant networks of charitable, cultural, medical, and educational associations operating at the grassroots level and among the poorest strata have enhanced Hamas's credibility and expanded its social base.[41] These social networks nurtured the movement's mobilizational and recruitment capabilities, and ensured loyal social constituents. Financially, the rising popularity of political Islam in the Arab and Islamic worlds opened the doors for donations and other forms of support from Palestinians in the Diaspora, as well as other states, wealthy individuals, Islamic organizations, and organized popular campaigns.[42] Organizationally, Hamas maintains a coherent internal structure and relations, which are based on strong discipline and organization. Its hierarchy is based on a sophisticated division between the political, military, social, and administrative branches, as well as external and internal leadership.[43] This has allowed the movement to maintain an influential presence on the ground even in periods of crisis and in the face of Israeli and PA hindrance.

When the Second Intifada erupted in September 2000, Hamas initially kept a low profile and was not actively involved in its early period. Part of the reason stems from Hamas's suspicious stance toward the uprising, fearing that it was driven by the PA leadership in order to improve its negotiating position. However, with its increasing militarization and signs that the uprising was spiraling out of the control of the PA, Hamas's military wing, the Izz ad-Din al-Qassam Brigades, joined the uprising and rapidly became a central actor in the military action against Israel. On the ground, Hamas's military wing cooperated closely with other Palestinian factions such as Islamic Jihad and Fatah militants.

By the end of the Second Intifada, Hamas began to moderate its position, hinting at accepting the two-state solution, announcing the end of suicide bombings, and declaring its willingness to join the formal political process. A significant shift in Hamas's perception toward the PA occurred in 2006, when it competed in the legislative elections and won a large majority in the Palestinian parliament; a striking victory that dramatically shook Fatah's historical dominance over official institutions. Hamas marketed its shifting position as a result of the realization that the Oslo reality had died by the bullets of the Second Intifada, and that the movement ought to play an active role in reshaping the post-Intifada political order.[44] While Hamas's overwhelming electoral victory was accompanied by official statements that explicitly demonstrated its acceptance of the two-state settlement, the international community, led by the United States, boycotted the democratically elected government and halted financial aid to PA institutions.

The halting of Western aid to the PA constituted one mechanism within a wider plan aimed at undermining the Hamas government and bringing back Fatah to power. In fact, while Western donors halted aid to the Hamas-led government, they continued to provide special financial assistance to President Abbas and his security apparatuses.[45] Israeli and Western interference in internal Palestinian affairs fueled tensions between Hamas and Fatah, which resulted in a semi-civil war in 2007 that ended Fatah control over the Gaza Strip. With two de facto divided governments in Gaza and the West Bank, the Palestinian political field reached its worst level of fragmentation since the emergence of the Palestinian national movement.

After the split, Hamas found itself in charge of governing the Gaza Strip, managing its institutions and security situation and the daily lives of millions of Palestinians under a crippling Israeli siege.[46] Hamas's move toward building a governing apparatus required that the movement concentrate its efforts in formalized governmental tasks and careful calculation of its political moves, a matter that obstructed its character as a resistance movement.

Hamas's governance of the Gaza Strip has had certain features. First, Hamas allows PLO and non-PLO military groups to operate in the Strip under its instructions and directions. This means that Hamas permits resistance groups to acquire arms and conduct military training, but it strictly forbids these groups from waging attacks against Israeli targets without its consent. Second, despite the fact that Hamas is a religious movement that seeks to create a disciplined society according to the Muslim Brotherhood's interpretation of Islamic society, its governance of Gaza has been controversial. On the one hand, secularists and nationalists criticize Hamas because of its conservative mode of governance, which tends to impose restrictive social rules and suppress civil liberties. On the other hand, ultraconservatives and Salafi Islamists view Hamas's governance of Gaza as unrepresentative of authentic Islamic rule. Third, while designated as a "terrorist group" by many Western governments and regarded as an illegitimate government by many others, Hamas attempted to embrace an active foreign policy to break the Israeli siege and challenge the Ramallah-based PA monopoly over external representation and diplomatic relations. For this purpose, the Hamas government organized training programs for diplomats, and attempted through different regional channels to reach European capitals and initiate dialogue with Western leaders. And fourth, Hamas's rule over Gaza is highly centralized and not representative of Palestinian political pluralism. Its security forces have occasionally violently suppressed opposition groups and arrested journalists, with Fatah members receiving the harshest treatment.

In terms of economic governance, the Hamas-controlled tunnel economy constituted a vital source for Gaza's survival amid the suffocating Israeli blockade. Through taxes and tariffs collected by Hamas on goods and materials flowing through underground tunnels with Egypt, Hamas managed to cover the government's expenditures and the payment of salaries for its civil servants. The tunnel economy in Gaza, as a new trade route, also caused considerable changes in Gaza's class structure as it marginalized the traditional business class and created a new class of nouveaux riche that depended on tunnel smuggling and trade.[47] After the toppling of the Muslim Brotherhood government in Egypt by the military junta in 2013, Egypt began to tighten its border closure with Gaza to an unprecedented extent, leading to a quasi-total collapse of the tunnel networks between Gaza and Egypt. (For more on Gaza and the rule of Hamas, see the chapter by Toufic Haddad in this book.)

Fearful of a Hamas takeover of the West Bank, the Fatah-dominated PA in Ramallah initially struggled to reassert its authority. It announced a state of emergency in June 2007 and moved to disband Hamas organizationally and militarily. The PA security forces arbitrarily detained Hamas officials, activists, and affiliated students, referring them to the military instead of the civilian judiciary, in contravention of the Palestinian Basic Law.[48] Furthermore, in its attempt to crack down on Hamas infrastructure in the West Bank, the PA security forces targeted Hamas-affiliated television and radio stations, and shut down dozens of charitable and social associations. Human Rights Watch reported that the PA's repressive campaigns against Hamas came "with the political and financial support of Israel, the United States and European Union, which likewise wanted to see Hamas's influence in Palestinian politics reduced or eliminated."[49] While the PA campaign has seriously damaged Hamas's infrastructure, it is difficult to assess its actual capabilities in the West Bank given its underground organizational structure

Nevertheless, Hamas's popularity has not significantly decreased; in fact, it tends to exceed Fatah's popularity especially in the periods following Israeli aggressions on the Gaza Strip. For example, the main finding of the Palestinian Public Opinion Poll, conducted four months after the 2014 war on Gaza, suggests that "the popularity of Hamas and Ismail Haniyeh remains higher.

Indeed, Hamas would easily win a new presidential election if one was held today; it would also likely do better than Fatah in a new parliamentary election."[50] Indications of Hamas's popularity have been evidenced in the student council elections that have taken place at Birzeit University in recent years—elections which are widely regarded as a bellwether for national politics, and which saw the Hamas-aligned student bloc winning most of the seats.

POPULAR FRONT FOR THE LIBERATION OF PALESTINE: EXPERIENCING POLYGONAL CRISIS

Once a leading political and military actor in the Palestinian national movement that left a substantial imprint on the evolution and development of the Palestinian left, the PFLP after Oslo underwent persistent crisis that pushed it to a marginal status in the Palestinian political milieu. Yet, while it is considered the largest leftist faction and the second largest faction within the PLO, the post-Oslo PFLP failed to revive its influence and popularity, despite several attempts to do so. By the early 1990s, the PFLP began to lose ground and political influence due to multiple crises resulting from various international, regional, and local realignments.[51] Strategically, the collapse of the Soviet Union and the dramatic shift in the global balance of power in favor of Western capitalist hegemony had a profound impact on the international left including the PFLP. While the PFLP had not consistently maintained warm ties with the USSR due to ideological differences, there is no doubt that the fall of the USSR dramatically weakened the PFLP, as was the case with the left worldwide. In addition, the demise of revolutionary anti-imperialist and anti-colonial movements around the world left the PFLP with fragmented and weak allies. Ideologically, the PFLP, as part of the international radical left, experienced a serious ideological crisis resulting from the collapse of the Soviet Union and its style of Communism, as well as the decline of the ideas and popularity of Arab nationalism (which had failed to achieve any of its promised objectives, either in unifying Arab nations or in liberating Palestine). The ideological retreat of revolutionary leftist ideas and secular Arab nationalism aided the rise of political Islam in Palestine, which has expanded at the expense of leftist factions. Politically, the Oslo process and the establishment of the PA constituted a central political challenge to all Palestinian rejectionist parties. While the PFLP uncompromisingly rejected the Oslo Accords and refrained from participating in the PA general elections in 1996 and the PA institutions, it failed to produce a viable theoretical and practical alternative to the political and institutional reality introduced by the Oslo process.

Many leftists, including many PFLP cadres, attribute the decline of PFLP popularity, in part, to factors associated with donors' intervention and conditions at the level of civil society. In particular, the construction of a professional NGO sector has replaced the democratic, critical, inclusive, and open-access popular movements that formed a significant part of the social and political force of the PFLP's grassroots linkages in the pre-Oslo era. The NGO sector has absorbed considerable segments of the PFLP leaders and cadres, who despite utter opposition to the Oslo reality, have found themselves trapped in implementing predefined agendas in service of PA state-building and the Oslo peace process.[52]

In an attempt to save itself from the brink of political irrelevancy, the PFLP held its Sixth National Conference in 2000. A significant outcome of this conference was the resignation of its founder and historical leader, George Habash, and the election of its second secretary general, Abu Ali Mustafa (nom du guerre of Mustafa Zibri). As part of a new strategy to revive the centrality of the PFLP in Palestinian politics, Abu Ali Mustafa returned to the OPT from Damascus. While this move marked an important shift toward relocating the PFLP centers of power to the OPT, Palestinians differed in their interpretation of the new strategy and the real objective behind Mustafa's return. Some interpreted it as an implicit acceptance of the two-state solution as introduced by the Oslo Accords, while others saw the return as a strategic option enforced by the new national and regional reality, which required new modes of resistance to be oriented and initiated from inside the territories.[53] Mustafa's return was featured with his slogan "we return to resist not to surrender."

This slogan of his return was translated on the ground into a renewal of the PFLP's organizational infrastructure and a reactivation of its militancy from the outset of the Second Intifada in 2000. In addition, under the leadership of Abu Ali Mustafa, the various leftist parties engaged in serious debates in an attempt for unification. However, his leadership inside the OPT lasted only briefly as he was assassinated by two Israeli rockets that targeted his office in Ramallah in 2001. Ahmad Sa'adat, who became the third secretary general of the PFLP, vowed to pursue the same revolutionary path and retaliate for Mustafa's assassination. Shortly afterwards, the PFLP's military wing, the Abu Ali Mustafa Brigades, was formed and claimed responsibility for the killing of the far-right Israeli government minister, Rehbavam Ze'evi, who was a leading advocate of the Zionist strategy of "transfer."[54]

The assassination of Ze'evi marked a turning point in the trajectory of the Second Intifada as it resulted in the immediate intensification of Israeli aggression and a partial military reoccupation of Palestinian towns and cities in the West Bank and Gaza. In addition, in response to combined Israeli and

US pressure, the PA banned the PFLP military wing and in 2002 it arrested Sa'adat and three party militants who were then held in a PA prison in Jericho under the supervision of US and British guards for almost five years. In 2006, the Israeli military stormed the Jericho prison, abducting Sa'adat and five fellow prisoners and transferred them to Israeli military prisons where they are still imprisoned.

While the PFLP's military role in the Second Intifada made a ripple in otherwise stagnant waters, the assassinations and arrests of its senior leaders and cadres, coupled with the organization's inability to renovate itself along new political and ideological lines, have imposed significant limitations on its attempt to revive the importance of leftist politics.

An important shift in the PFLP's stance toward political engagement in PA institutions occurred in the second presidential and legislative elections in 2005 and 2006, respectively. First, while the PFLP did not officially nominate any candidate to run for presidential elections, it backed the leader of the Palestinian National Initiative (PNI), Mustafa Barghouti, who came in second after Mahmoud Abbas. In the legislative elections in 2006, despite failed attempts to unify Palestinian leftist factions in one electoral list, the PFLP won three seats in the PNC. The PFLP motives to participate in the PA elections despite its rejectionist position to the Oslo framework stemmed from its belief (like Hamas) that the Oslo process had been killed in the Second Intifada, and it sought to counter Fatah dominance and contribute to reshaping the post-Intifada political reality.

However, the internal Palestinian schism and division between the West Bank and Gaza distorted the post-Intifada political reality. While disastrous for the cohesiveness of the Palestinian national movement, the vacuum left by the Fatah–Hamas chasm and the growing popular disappointment with the bipolar political division provided a historic opportunity for the PFLP and the left to reemerge as an alternative force, and advance an alternative political program and new national strategy. However, despite its persistent calls for national unity, the PFLP failed to take advantage of the division and present itself as a unifying force. Instead it found itself hostage to the political division, which occasionally resulted in incoherent statements between its Gaza and West Bank branches.

Part of the PFLP's inability to act as an influential actor in the post-Second Intifada era can be attributed to the PFLP's financial dependency on PLO allocations, which are fully controlled by Fatah and the president of the PA, Mahmoud Abbas. The PLO allocations distributed to the PLO factions are often used to pressurise these factions and weaken their opposition to the PA. This has proved to be problematic for PFLP political independence and has hindered its ability to influence political reality. For example, when the

PFLP pulled out of the PLO executive sessions in April 2014 in opposition to Abbas's willingness to continue negotiations and security coordination with Israel, Abbas ordered the suspension of the PFLP's financial allocations to pressure it to change its position.[55]

In November 2014, the PFLP held its Seventh General Congress under secret conditions. According to the PFLP statement, the main objectives were "to carry out a comprehensive review and evaluation of the Front's methods, work, overall policies and plans, and the formulation of a political vision and organizational methods for the new phase of struggle."[56] During the Congress, several leaders resigned and new younger members were elected for the party's Central Committee and General Political Bureau. While the PFLP's intention was to resurrect its former prominence in Palestinian politics, in reality, after the Seventh General Congress the party has not shown any sign of revival, nor can it survive its long-standing crises.

CONCLUSION: REBUILDING THE PALESTINIAN NATIONAL MOVEMENT BEYOND THE OSLO FRAMEWORK

In the past few years (2012–2017) there have been several waves of popular uprisings in various localities in the West Bank, Jerusalem, Gaza, and among 48 Palestinians. These waves were sparked by multiple connected issues such as Israel's continued colonization of the West Bank, the tightening of the blockade over Gaza, the Judaization of East Jerusalem, and the constant violations of the status quo regarding Al-Aqsa Mosque and religious sites in Jerusalem. While all of these issues can be interpreted as viable objective conditions sufficient for the outbreak of a fully fledged Intifada, the subjective conditions necessary to transform these waves into a sustained and organized revolutionary dynamic are effectively absent. In fact, Palestinian political factions and civil society organizations that have historically constituted the key source of leadership, mobilization, orientation, and organization have not shown any sign of organized engagement on the ground. Perhaps, at this point, it can be observed that the Palestinian political factions are unable or unwilling to lead a new Intifada for various objective and subjective reasons: internal divisions, interest politics and privileges, weak and competing leadership, detachment from the grassroots, lack of mobilization, and organizational fragmentations— all of which are a result of the exhausting Oslo process.

The Oslo framework and its associated institutions such as the PA and the kind of political, economic, security, and civil relations it built with Israel have always constituted mechanisms of co-option, subversion, and capitulation. The continuation of this status will therefore likely abort efforts to reconstitute the national movement and will block the emergence of new forces and leadership. Thus, it is impossible to imagine the Palestinian national movement—whether in the form of the PLO or a new organization—rising again under the same conditions that led to its deterioration, division, and decline.

Much has been written about the desired features for reconstituting the national movement—that it should be organizationally democratic, representative of the people, unifying for all factions, ideologically and politically pluralistic, inclusive and accountable, and should be based on anti-colonial principles of self-determination, liberation, social justice, and equality. Nevertheless, few, if any, have envisioned a national movement that advances a sophisticated strategy that completely breaks with the Oslo framework. And this really should constitute the main focus: if Palestinians do not begin by rebuilding their national movement beyond the Oslo framework, what remains of the national movement will likely suffer further fragmentation, disintegration, and degeneration.

NOTES

1. See for example: Rashid Khalidi, *Brokers of Deceit: How the US Has Undermined Peace in the Middle East* (Boston: Beacon Press, 2013). Ghassan Khatib, *Palestinian Politics and the Middle East Peace Process: Consensus and Competition in the Palestinian Negotiating Team* (New York: Routledge, 2011).

2. See, for example: Tariq Dana, "The Prolonged Decay of the Palestinian National Movement," *National Identities* (2017): 1–17, https://doi.org/10.1080/14608944.2017.1343813. Adam Hanieh, "The Oslo Illusion," *Jacobin Magazine*, April 24 2013, https://www.jacobinmag.com/2013/04/the-oslo-illusion/.

3. Edward Said, "The Morning After," *London Review of Books*, October 21, 1993, https://www.lrb.co.uk/v15/n20/edward-said/the-morning-after.

4. Mandy Turner, "Peacebuilding as Counterinsurgency in the Occupied Palestinian Territory," *Review of International Studies* 41, no.1 (2015), 73–98.

5. As'ad Ganem, *Palestinian Politics after Arafat: A Failed National Movement* (Bloomington: Indiana University Press, 2010).

6. Mandy Turner, "Peacebuilding as Counterinsurgency," 90.

7. Jamil Hilal, "Rethinking Palestine: settler-colonialism, neo-liberalism and individualism in the West Bank and Gaza Strip," *Contemporary Arab Affairs* 8, no. 3 (2015): 351–362.

8. Khalil Nakhleh, *Globalized Palestine: The National Sell-out of a Homeland* (Trenton, NJ: Red Sea Press, 2012).

9. Rex Brynen, *A Very Political Economy: Peacebuilding and Foreign Aid in the West Bank and Gaza* (Washington DC: United States Institute of Peace Press, 2000).

10. Tariq Dana, "The Structural Transformation of Palestinian Civil Society: Key Paradigm Shifts," *Middle East Critique* 24, no. 2 (2015): 191–210.

11. Al-Shabaka, "Open Debate on Palestinian Representation," Al-Shabaka Roundtable, May 1, 2011, https://al-shabaka.org/roundtables/open-debate-palestinian-representation/.

12. Helena Cobban, "The PLO and the Continuing Project to Win Palestinian National Liberation." Middle East Monitor, January 29, 2012, https://www.middleeastmonitor.com/20140129-the-plo-and-the-continuing-project-to-win-palestinian-national-liberation/.

13. Al-Haq, "Palestine's UN Initiatives: Questions and Answers: Palestine's UN Initiatives and the Representation of the Palestinian People's Rights," Ramallah, 2011: http://www.alhaq.org/advocacy/targets/united-nations/453-palestines-un-initiatives-questions-and-answers-on-the-representation-of-the-rights-of-the-palestinian-people.

14. Al-Shabaka, "Palestinian Youth Revolt: Any Role for Political Parties," Al-Shabaka Roundtable, November 23, 2015, https://al-shabaka.org/roundtables/palestinian-youth-revolt-any-role-for-political-parties/.

15. Edward Said, *The End of the Peace Process: Oslo and After* (New York: Vintage, 2007).

16. Ganem, *Palestinian Politics*, 2.

17. Geoffrey Aronson, "Recapitulating the Redeployments: The Israel-PLO Interim Agreements," *Jerusalem Fund*, Information Brief 32, April 27, 2000.

18. Jeff Halper, *An Israeli in Palestine: Resisting Dispossession, Redeeming Israel* (London: Pluto Press, 2008), 141.

19. Dana, "The Structural Transformation," 193.

20. Eyal Weizman, *Hollow Land: Israel's Architecture of Occupation* (London: Verso Books, 2012), 11.

21. Turner, "Peacebuilding as Counterinsurgency," 76.

22. Adam Hanieh, *Lineages of Revolt: Issues of Contemporary Capitalism in the Middle East* (Chicago: Haymarket Books, 2013), 116.

23. World Bank, *Developing the Occupied Territories: An Investment in Peace* (Washington, D.C: World Bank, 1993).

24. Hanieh, *Lineages of Revolt*, 115.

25. Tariq Dana, "The Symbiosis Between Palestinian 'Fayyadism' and Israeli 'Economic Peace': The Political Economy of Capitalist Peace in the Context of Colonisation," *Conflict, Security & Development* 15, no. 5 (2015): 455–477.

26. Anne Le More, *International Assistance to the Palestinians after Oslo: Political Guilt, Wasted Money* (London: Routledge, 2008), 66.

27. Philip Leech, "Who Owns 'The Spring' in Palestine? Rethinking Popular Consent and Resistance in the Context of the 'Palestinian State' and the 'Arab Spring,'" *Democratization* 22, no. 6 (2015), 1013.

28. Isam Abdeen, "Limits to the Powers of Palestinian Security Agencies to Detain Palestinian Civilians," *Al-Haq Organisation*, Ramallah. 2011.

29. Associated Press, "In Tough Times, Most Palestinians View Government as Corrupt," AP, May 24, 2016: https://apnews.com/3aabd1f5db4e4623a74c00fcd71589f3.

30. Inge Amundsen and Basem Ezbidi, "Clientelist Politics, State Formation and Corruption in Palestine 1994–2000," Development Studies and Human Rights, Bergen: Chr. Michelsen Institute, 2000.

31. Alaa Tartir, "Criminalizing Resistance: The Cases of Balata and Jenin Refugee Camps," *Journal of Palestine Studies* 46, no. 2 (2017), 8.

32. Le More, *"International Assistance,"* 75.

33. Tariq Dana, "The Beginning of the End of Palestinian Security Coordination With Israel?," *Jadaliyya*, July 4, 2014, http://www.jadaliyya.com/Details/30903/The-Beginning-of-the-End-of-Palestinian-Security-Coordination-with-Israel.

34. Yezid Sayigh, "Fixing Broken Windows: Security Sector Reform in Palestine, Lebanon, and Yemen," *Carnegie Middle East Center*, Carnegie Paper (Beirut, 2009), 26.

35. Aisling Byrne, "Building a Police State in Palestine," *Foreign Policy*, January 18, 2011, http://foreignpolicy.com/2011/01/18/building-a-police-state-in-palestine/.

36. Nigel Parsons, *The Politics of the Palestinian Authority: From Oslo to Al-Aqsa* (New York: Routledge, 2005).

37. Dana, "The Prolonged Decay," 12.

38. Mohammed Assadi, "Old Guard 'Hijacks' Fatah Congress, Say Reformers," *Reuters*, August 5, 2009, https://www.reuters.com/article/us-palestinians-israel-fatah/old-guard-hijacks-fatah-congress-say-reformers-idUSTRE57456G20090805.

39. Mel Frykberg, "Critics Slam Mahmoud Abbas' PLO Resignation as 'Farce,'" *Aljazeera*, August 22, 2015, https://www.aljazeera.com/news/2015/08/critics-slam-mahmoud-abbas-plo-resignation-farce-150827081457810.html.

40. Tareq Baconi, "The Demise of Oslo and Hamas's Political Engagement," *Conflict, Security & Development* 15, no. 5 (2015), 504.

41. Sara Roy, "The Transformation of Islamic NGOs in Palestine," *Middle East Report* (Spring 2000), 24–27.

42. Ziad Abu-Amr, "Hamas: A Historical and Political Background," *Journal of Palestine Studies* 22, no. 4 (1993): 5–19.

43. Somdeep Sen, "Bringing Back the Palestinian State: Hamas Between Government and Resistance," *Middle East Critique* 24, no. 2 (2015): 211–225.

44. Baconi, "The Demise of Oslo."

45. Mohammed Samhouri, "The 'West Bank First' Strategy: A Political-economy Critical Assessment." Brandeis University, Crown Center for Middle East Studies, Working Paper 2, October 2007, https://www.brandeis.edu/crown/publications/wp/WP2.pdf.

46. Benedetta Berti and Beatriz Gutiérrez, "Rebel-to-Political and Back? Hamas as a Security Provider in Gaza Between Rebellion, Politics and Governance," *Democratization* 23, no. 6 (2016): 1059–1076.

47. Nicolas Pelham, "Gaza's Tunnel Phenomenon: The Unintended Dynamics of Israel's Siege," *Journal of Palestine Studies* 41, no. 4 (2012), 6–31.

48. Addameer Prisoner Support and Human Rights Association, "Stolen Hope: Political Detention in the West Bank," Ramallah (February 2011), http://www.addameer.org/sites/default/files/publications/EN%2520PA%2520Violations%2520Report%25202009-2010_0.pdf.

49. *Human Rights Watch*, "Internal Fight: Palestinian Abuses in Gaza and the West Bank" (July 2008), https://www.hrw.org/sites/default/files/reports/iopt0708_1.pdf.

50. The Palestinian Center for Policy and Survey Research, "Palestinian Public Opinion Poll No 54" (3–6 December), http://www.pcpsr.org/en/node/600.

51. Jamil Hilal, "The Palestinian Left and the Multi-Layered Challenges Ahead," *Rosa Luxemburg Foundation* (April, 2010), http://www.rosalux.de/fileadmin/rls_up loads/pdfs/Standpunkte/Standpunkte_international/RLS_PAL_-_Hilal_Palestinian_Left.pdf.

52. Dana, "The Structural Transformation," 194.

53. "Interview With the New Leader of the Popular Front for the Liberation of Palestine (PFLP), Abu Ali Mustafa," *Al-Jazeera Archive*, May 10, 2000, http://abualimustafa.org/2001/01/interview-with-the-new-leader-of-the-popular-front-for-the-liberation-of-palestine-pflp-abu-ali-mustafa/.

54. Elia Zureik, "Demography and Transfer: Israel's Road to Nowhere," *Third World Quarterly*, 23, no. 4 (2003), 619–630.

55. Al-Akhbar, "PFLP Loses Funding after Lambasting Abbas," *Al-Akhbar*, May 22, 2014, http://english.al-akhbar.com/node/19876.

56. PFLP, "Statement on the Work of the Seventh National Conference of the PFLP." PFLP (December 18, 2013), http://pflp.ps/english/2013/12/18/statement-on-the-work-of-the-seventh-national-conference-of-the-pflp/.

BIBIOGRAPHY

Abdeen, Isam. "Limits to the Powers of Palestinian Security Agencies to Detain Palestinian Civilians." *Al-Haq Organisation*, Ramallah. 2011.

Abu-Amr, Ziad. "Hamas: A Historical and Political Background." *Journal of Palestine Studies* 22, no. 4 (1993): 5–19.

Addameer. "Stolen Hope: Political Detention in the West Bank." *Addameer Prisoner Support and Human Rights Association*. Ramallah (February 2011), http://www.addameer.org/sites/default/files/publications/EN%2520PA%2520Violations%2520Report%25202009-2010_0.pdf.

Al-Akhbar. "PFLP Loses Funding After Lambasting Abbas." May 22, 2014, http://english.al-akhbar.com/node/19876.

Al-Haq. "Palestine's UN Initiatives: Questions and Answers: Palestine's UN Initiatives and the Representation of the Palestinian People's Rights." Ramallah, 2011: http://www.alhaq.org/advocacy/targets/united-nations/453-palestines-un-initiatives-questions-and-answers-on-the-representation-of-the-rights-of-the-palestinian-people.

Al-Shabaka. "Palestinian Youth Revolt: Any Role for Political Parties," *Al-Shabaka Roundtable*. November 23, 2015, https://al-shabaka.org/roundtables/palestinian-youth-revolt-any-role-for-political-parties/.

Al-Shabaka. "Open Debate on Palestinian Representation." *Al-Shabaka Roundtable*. May 1, 2011, https://al-shabaka.org/roundtables/open-debate-palestinian-representation/.

Amundsen, Inge, and Ezbidi Basem. "Clientelist Politics, State Formation and Corruption in Palestine 1994–2000." Development Studies and Human Rights, Bergen: Chr. Michelsen Institute, 2000.

Aronson, Geoffrey. "Recapitulating the Redeployments: The Israel-PLO Interim Agreements." *Jerusalem Fund*, Information Brief 32, April 27, 2000.

Assadi, Mohammed. "Old guard "hijacks" Fatah congress, say reformers." *Reuters*, August, 5, 2009: https://www.reuters.com/article/us-palestinians-israel-fatah/old-guard-hijacks-fatah-congress-say-reformers-idUSTRE57456G20090805.

Associated Press. "In Tough Times, Most Palestinians View Government as Corrupt." AP, May 24, 2016: https://apnews.com/3aabd1f5db4e4623a74c00fcd71589f3.

Baconi, Tareq. "The Demise of Oslo and Hamas's Political Engagement." *Conflict, Security & Development* 15, no. 5 (2015): 503–520.

Berti, Benedetta, and Beatriz Gutiérrez. "Rebel-to-Political and Back? Hamas as a Security Provider in Gaza Between Rebellion, Politics and Governance." *Democratization* 23, no. 6 (2016): 1059–1076.

Byrne, Aisling. "Building a Police State in Palestine." *Foreign Policy*, January 18, 2011: http://foreignpolicy.com/2011/01/18/building-a-police-state-in-palestine/.

Brynen, Rex. *A Very Political Economy: Peacebuilding and Foreign Aid in the West Bank and Gaza* (Washington, DC: United States Institute of Peace Press, 2000).

Coalition on Integrity and Accountability (AMAN). "Public Opinion Poll on Corruption in Palestine 2016." Ramallah, Palestine (December 2016), https://www.aman-palestine.org/data/itemfiles/8892298ee2e24097be076a88db7f8f1b.pdf.

Cobban, Helena. "The PLO and the Continuing Project to Win Palestinian National Liberation." *Middle East Monitor*. January 29, 2012, https://www.middleeastmonitor.com/20140129-the-plo-and-the-continuing-project-to-win-palestinian-national-liberation/.

Dana, Tariq. "The Prolonged Decay of the Palestinian National Movement." *National Identities* (2017): 1–17, https://doi.org/10.1080/14608944.2017.1343813 .

———. "The Structural Transformation of Palestinian Civil Society: Key Paradigm Shifts." *Middle East Critique* 24, no. 2 (2015): 191–210.

———. "The Symbiosis Between Palestinian 'Fayyadism' and Israeli 'Economic Peace': The Political Economy of Capitalist Peace in the Context of Colonisation." *Conflict, Security & Development* 15, no. 5 (2015): 455–477.

———. "The Beginning of the End of Palestinian Security Coordination With Israel?" Jadaliyya, July 4, 2014: http://www.jadaliyya.com/Details/30903/The-Beginning-of-the-End-of-Palestinian-Security-Coordination-with-Israel.

Frykberg, Mel. "Critics Slam Mahmoud Abbas' PLO Resignation as 'Farce.'" *Aljazeera*, August 22, 2015, https://www.aljazeera.com/news/2015/08/critics-slam-mahmoud-abbas-plo-resignation-farce-150827081457810.html.

Ganem, As'ad. *Palestinian Politics after Arafat: A Failed National Movement*. Bloomington: Indiana University Press, 2010.

Halper, Jeff. *An Israeli in Palestine: Resisting Dispossession, Redeeming Israel*. London: Pluto Press, 2008.

Hanieh, Adam. *Lineages of Revolt: Issues of Contemporary Capitalism in the Middle East*. Chicago: Haymarket Books, 2013.

———. "The Oslo Illusion." *Jacobin Magazine*, April 24, 2013, https://www.jacobinmag.com/2013/04/the-oslo-illusion/.

Hilal, Jamil. "Rethinking Palestine: Settler-Colonialism, Neo-liberalism and Individualism in the West Bank and Gaza Strip." *Contemporary Arab Affairs* 8, no. 3 (2015): 351–362.

———. "The Palestinian Left and the Multi-Layered Challenges Ahead," *Rosa Luxemburg Foundation* (April 2010), http://www.rosalux.de/fileadmin/rls_uploads/pdfs/Standpunkte/Standpunkte_international/RLS_PAL_-_Hilal_Palestinian_Left.pdf.

Human Rights Watch. "Internal Fight: Palestinian Abuses in Gaza and the West Bank." *Human Rights Watch* (July 2008), 9, https://www.hrw.org/sites/default/files/reports/iopt0708_1.pdf.

International Crisis Group. "Palestine: Salvaging Fatah." *ICG Middle East Report* (November 2009).

Khalidi, Rashid. *Brokers of Deceit: How the US has Undermined Peace in the Middle East*. Boston: Beacon Press, 2013.

Le More. Anne. *International Assistance to the Palestinians after Oslo: Political Guilt, Wasted Money*. London: Routledge, 2008.

Leech, Philip. "Who Owns 'The Spring' in Palestine? Rethinking Popular Consent and Resistance in the Context of the 'Palestinian State' and the 'Arab Spring.'" *Democratization* 22, no. 6 (2015): 1011–1029.

Nakhleh, Khalil. *Globalized Palestine: The National Sell-out of a Homeland*. Trenton, NJ: Red Sea Press, 2012.

Parsons, Nigel. *The Politics of the Palestinian Authority: From Oslo to Al-Aqsa*. New York: Routledge, 2005.

PCPSR. "Palestinian Public Opinion Poll No 54." *Palestinian Center for Policy and Survey Research* (3–6 December), http://www.pcpsr.org/en/node/600.

Pelham, Nicolas. "Gaza's Tunnel Phenomenon: The Unintended Dynamics of Israel's Siege." *Journal of Palestine Studies* 41, no. 4 (2012): 6–31.

PFLP. "Statement on the Work of the Seventh National Conference of the PFLP." *PFLP* (December 18, 2013), http://pflp.ps/english/2013/12/18/statement-on-the-work-of-the-seventh-national-conference-of-the-pflp/.

Rabbani, Mouin. "Another Palestinian Uprising." *Middle East Institute*, August 5, 2015, http://www.mei.edu/content/article/another-palestinian-uprising.

Roy, Sara. "The Transformation of Islamic NGOs in Palestine." *Middle East Report* (Spring 2000): 24–27.

Said, Edward. *The End of the Peace Process: Oslo and After*. New York: Vintage, 2007.

———. "The Morning After." *London Review of Books*, October 21, 1993, https://www.lrb.co.uk/v15/n20/edward-said/the-morning-after.

Samhouri, Mohammed. "*The 'West Bank First' Strategy: A Political-economy Critical Assessment*." Brandeis University, Crown Center for Middle East Studies, Working Paper 2, October 2007: https://www.brandeis.edu/crown/publications/wp/WP2.pdf.

Sayigh, Yezid. "Fixing Broken Windows: Security Sector Reform in Palestine, Lebanon, and Yemen." *Carnegie Middle East Center*, Carnegie Paper (Beirut, 2009).

Tartir, Alaa. "Criminalizing Resistance: The Cases of Balata and Jenin Refugee Camps." *Journal of Palestine Studies* 46, no. 2 (2017): 7–22.

Turner, Mandy. "Peacebuilding as Counterinsurgency in the Occupied Palestinian Territory." *Review of International Studies* 41, no. 1 (2015): 73–98.

Weizman, Eyal. *Hollow Land: Israel's Architecture of Occupation*. London: Verso Books, 2012.

World Bank. *Developing the Occupied Territories: An Investment in Peace*. Washington, DC, 1993.

Zureik, Elia. "Demography and Transfer: Israel's Road to Nowhere." *Third World Quarterly*, 23, no. 4 (2003), 619–630.

Chapter Four

The Structural Transformation of the Palestinian Economy after Oslo

Raja Khalidi

LOOKING BACK, TODAY

In 1993, the Palestine Liberation Organization (PLO) accepted to create a Palestinian "Authority" (PA) to manage the "interim self-government arrangements" ushered in by the Oslo, Washington, Paris and Cairo Accords—supposedly for only five years. At the time, its leaders surely could not have imagined how little would have been achieved 25 years later, at least in terms of the national goals in whose service the PLO claimed it accepted the Accords. With the most recent breakdown in the peace process, a new outbreak of military confrontations in Gaza and popular uprisings in the rest of Palestine since 2014, recognition of the failures of Oslo and Palestinian-Israeli bilateral negotiations and relations has become almost trite.[1] This and other strategic defeats suffered by the Palestinian "national project" over the past two decades are well documented and are increasingly acknowledged as new facts on the ground, especially:

- the incessant expansion of Israeli colonies and related infrastructure throughout the occupied Palestinian territory (OPT);
- the iron-fist security control exercised by Israel throughout the occupied territory and policed in some areas of the West Bank by the PA itself; and,
- the physical, legal and political separation of Gaza and East Jerusalem from the rest of the occupied territory in the West Bank.

However, it is less widely accepted that the same period has witnessed a similar degree of failure in the performance of the Palestinian economy and in development policy making. Indeed, the conventional wisdom among most Palestinian and Israeli policy makers and elites, no less among international donor circles and peace process advocates, is that economic growth is generally impressive, that individual prosperity is increasingly evident, and that Palestinian economic and institutional development is truly underway. Within this narrative, and notwithstanding prolonged occupation and the absence of sovereignty, Palestinians have rarely had it so good and should be able to acquiesce in enjoyment of the fruits of economic peace instead and thus postpone national self-determination. True, the balance of power in the Israeli-Palestinian struggle might be so asymmetric as to preclude the latter for the foreseeable future. However, within this logic there is no reason to expect capital or markets to remain dormant as long as the former is an acceptable second-best path for an emerging Palestinian "middle class" and "national interests" as understood by the ruling power elites of the PA regime.

In fact, since Oslo the PA has declared its adherence to the principles of an "open, free-market" economy, even within the constraints of military occupation, settler colonial aggression, unfettered capital penetration of vulnerable and dependent captive populations and markets. The impact has debilitated the structure of the putative "national Palestinian economy" and its development prospects, social fabric and values, natural resources and overall national economic security.

By 2018, the Palestinian economy had the following features, echoing its structure in 1994:

- structural deformation;
- channels of trade dependency and resource extraction that track the path of Israeli liberalization;
- a largely ineffective public sector that has ceded the way to private enterprise while maintaining a strong internal security ethos;
- growing economic, social and regional inequalities and disparities; and,
- a liberal economic policy framework risks undermining the options for a viable development strategy for an independent Palestinian state.

It is only natural to apportion primary blame for this among the obvious external suspects (Israel, donor states, international financial institutions). But no doubt the PLO and the Palestinian leadership bear their share of responsibility for having locked the Palestinian people into the Oslo cage, while being increasingly unable to fulfil their role as public authorities to ensure the welfare and prosperity of the community. Indeed, a whole class of PA functionaries dependent upon the status quo for their daily bread, an energetic professional and commercial class divorced from politics and seeking a "normal" lifestyle, and a political system wedded to the idea of a peace process with Israel all have a responsibility for the current state of economic policy.

They are all acquiescent in a liberal market and governance model that has delivered neither communal development nor national liberation.[2]

Various sources have related this story partially and at different points over the years, but with hindsight today we can recount it with greater clarity and candidness and indeed with a sense of closure. Certainly, the standard concepts and tools for measuring and analyzing the growth and development of sovereign economies are inherently inadequate to describe an economy under prolonged occupation and can only paint a limited picture of the Palestinian reality, which after all did not begin with Oslo.[3] Most recent efforts, especially favored by the international community, have attempted to analyze the Palestinian economic dilemma in terms of conventional institutional economics and generic concepts such as "good governance" and "institution building" or more dubious themes of "state-in-the-making" and "statehood readiness."[4] This latter theme characterized much of the 2008–2013 PA economic policy making, public investment and national or regional level planning. Its predominance largely served to divert Palestinian collective efforts away from mobilizing to end occupation and in the direction of liberal goals such as the rule of law, safeguarding property rights, good citizenship, private enterprise and operation of the "free-market" (as if such a thing could exist in the warped Palestinian context) as adopted in the Palestinian Basic Law of 2002.[5]

Other analyzes have searched for appropriate frames of reference and concepts that better address Palestinian realities, such as the economics of settler colonialism, "de-development" or "the economic impact of prolonged occupation."[6] These approaches have been unable to effectively dislodge the mainstream narrative of a state-building process devoid of independence or sovereignty, as still maintained by both the PA and the international community, or of economic growth despite political stasis. However, the failures to impose Palestinian statehood be it through institution building, diplomatic maneuvers or waging "lawfare," gives greater explanatory power to alternative, critical analyzes today and to their relevance in addressing future challenges.[7]

THE PLO EMBRACE OF GLOBALIZATION AND THE PARIS PROTOCOL

The last phase of direct military administration of the occupied territory prior to the signing of the Oslo and Paris Accords entailed, on the one hand, initiatives to create economic incentives and, on the other, the application of security measures which continued to limit the scope of Palestinian productive and income generation activities. As early as 1992, UNCTAD had argued that the way out for the Palestinian people was through viable legal and economic frameworks, which could override Israeli occupation policies: "The Palestinian economy and its institutions need to be freed from arbitrary measures that distort economic structure and performance of the economy."[8] This is a refrain that is reproduced today in the international community's demand for "free movement and access" as a prerequisite for economic revival, indicative of how little the debate of that issue has changed.

The policy framework that has since then governed the Palestinian economy, and which has kept it bound to the Israeli economy and subject to its colonial security interests, has been one of the constants of the past 25 years that has allowed Israeli colonization to proceed apace.[9] The Protocol on Economic Relations (PER) was signed in Paris by Israel and the PLO in April 1994 and annexed to the Oslo I implementation agreements. This bilateral agreement always trumps any other economic agreements between Palestine and any other party. The essential ingredient in ensuring Palestinian economic dependency upon Israel was the acquiescence of the PLO in maintaining a common economic policy regime with the occupying power. As long as the PLO has been unwilling or incapable of breaking away from the Protocol straitjacket to pursue an alternative trade and economic regime, its complaints about its inadequate provisions or Israeli non-compliance ring hollow and the prospects for Palestinian development remain dim.

Nearly 25 years later the Protocol remains the economic law of the land and it reinforces the adverse growth path within which the West Bank and Gaza economies are locked. The Protocol's terms and operation, and the dependency it perpetuates, have been the subject of growing criticism since the 1990s from international agencies, Palestinian and Israeli economists, and even West Bank popular protests in 2012.[10] But the PLO's determination to not repudiate the PER's *de facto* or *de jure* validity has become yet another stumbling block on the path to Palestinian economic viability and development.

The economic model that the PLO espoused for its first 30 years of national liberation struggle as part of a global anti-colonial movement[11] was a far cry from that embodied in the Oslo/Paris scheme.[12] Most official and expert Palestinian economic thought and practice had until then revolved around a vision of public sector empowerment for the benefit of the broader dispossessed Palestinian masses. PLO officials promoted the idea of an economy that was productive in traditional sectors and reliant on its own capacities, and which could address the imperatives of disengagement from the economic domination and dependency engendered by decades of Israeli occupation and colonization. Throughout the PLO eras in Beirut and Tunis, Palestinian public economic, financial, research and social welfare institutions had continued to operate as a government in exile for the Palestinian people inside and outside their homeland, providing some sustenance for the former and supporting the steadfastness (*sumoud*) of the latter.

Despite the military and political defeat ultimately endured by the Palestinian national movement in Lebanon in 1982, this broader institutional landscape seemed to manifest the PLO's "viability" as a forerunner of the national state project in a future liberated Palestine that was still a twinkle in Palestinian planners' eyes. And yet within little more than a decade, the PLO had signed off in Paris on an economic policy package that aborted the plans and possibilities for an independent Palestinian economy and enshrined a "free market" economy designed in line with the spirit of globalization and trade liberalism. Just as the Accords were announced in 1993, the PLO had completed a "Program for the Development of the Palestinian National Economy 1994–2004" (PDP), designed by the eminent Professor Yusef Sayigh, whose heterodox economic thought remained rooted in the development and dependency economics that had held sway since the 1950s. Highlighting the crossroads that the PLO faced at that moment, the director of the PLO Economic Department responsible for spearheading the PDP effort in the preceding years (Ahmed Qurei, also known as Abu Alaa) was the same official who negotiated and signed the Oslo and Paris accords.

Nearly 25 years down the road, it is worth considering the limited options that the nationalist leadership (and an exhausted First Intifada) had by the early 1990s. These constraints were obvious both in terms of the ability to resist the terms of a dictated "peace settlement" despite two years of bilateral negotiations in Washington, and in terms of the limited capacities to manage the lives of some three million Palestinians with only a patchy record of (largely military and political) institution building in exile. The opportunity that Oslo offered for expatriate Palestinian capital to link up again with the PLO, except this time inside Palestine in a shared economic and investment program, meant that the PLO could only embrace the new world economic order of globalization and liberalization.

Even as a weakened, exiled PLO continued to raise the banner of resistance in the wake of its post-Gulf War isolation, the ensuing Madrid Peace Conference set in motion political negotiations that continue into their third decade. This drawn out "process" itself implies a trade-off between pursuing national liberation through resistance or through cooperation. But this is not adequate to explain the dramatic policy reversal that the PLO undertook when it signed the PER with Israel in Paris in 1994. Nor why for nearly 25 years the PLO has chosen the path of least resistance and has been reluctant to abandon an economic policy framework put in place in another era with limited, time-bound purposes that have been overtaken by time and events.

An important dimension of the dynamics of the retreat of Palestinian "developmentalism" was the rapidly transforming global and regional political scene at the time. The collapse of the Soviet bloc meant that while the PLO bought into the Madrid process in 1991 with USA-USSR cosponsorship, by the time the Oslo Accords were reached in 1993 the bilateral Israeli-Palestinian track had become dominant and the multilateral formula of Madrid (and Soviet camp support) became redundant. Meanwhile, PLO leaders were open to any formula that would return them to Palestine and that might achieve what they argued would be a short transition to independence.

In retrospect it is not difficult to see why the PDP, which represented the culmination of the thinking of an earlier generation, did not stand a chance once the World Bank arrived on the scene in 1993. The forceful entry into the Palestinian economy arena after 1993 of the Bretton Woods institutions (BWIs) and the powerful appeal of the World Bank's first (of many) publications on the subject, added an influential player to a scene that had, until then, been dominated by Israeli unilateralism.[13] By the 2000s the PLO had welcomed the engagement of influential Washington and Brussels players, who came armed with funding, political influence and a textbook of technical advice, not to mention their own secretariat in the form of the BWIs.

The Oslo Accords self-governing arrangements in the occupied territory were heralded by their signatories as a break with the past. The economic institutions that the PA was enabled to build within the scope of the Protocol did entail a withdrawal of the Israeli Civil Administration from those areas where the PA was granted jurisdiction—an unprecedented ceding to Palestinian hands of economic and local management functions that hitherto had been under direct Israeli control. While the PA strove to portray institutions as "national" in their role and purpose, the actual limits to their regulatory or enforcement authorities soon became apparent (in areas such as trade, fiscal management, banking, industrial zoning, agricultural resources, land use, etc.). Furthermore, while the reality of direct Israeli rule was replaced by Palestinian "home-rule" in the core "A" and "B" areas designated for PA jurisdiction under the Accords, the Israeli military remained in direct control of the surrounding "C" areas, while the Gaza Strip borders were and remain subject to Israeli control. Hence, while some *policy-management space* was gained, the pertinent issue relates to the restrictions placed on spatial and sovereign economic policy making and institutions.

The choice of appropriate trade regime with Israel was a source of much tension in the PER negotiations and has remained a subject of intensive academic analysis and debate.[14] Palestinian negotiators began by arguing for a free trade agreement (FTA) which would require drawing customs borders between the territory and Israel, and allow Palestinians to maintain differential trade relations with other partners. However, Israel preferred a formalization of the "customs union," which had existed defacto since 1967 and insisted on referral of all matters linked to borders to the permanent status negotiations. In conceding to the Israeli formula, with some exceptions, PLO negotiators rationalized their acceptance of the Paris arrangements as a "small Palestinian customs envelope within the large Israeli customs envelope," giving the illusion of some trade autonomy.

In their calculations, PLO negotiators apparently believed that the price of signing an Economic Protocol, whose terms were spelt out by Israeli professors and lawyers, was outweighed by the political advantages they believed they had gained in the larger framework of Oslo and the establishment of the PA. Ultimately the Protocol was a necessary and natural corollary of the Oslo obligations and limitations accepted by the PA. It was much less about optimal economic models for a people engaged in a national liberation struggle or an economic reconstruction process than about which economic arrangements were most suited to ensuring Israeli security interests and domination of the occupied territory through limiting the powers of the PA.

The PER inherently linked the Palestinian economy to the foreign trade regime of Israel and the latter's rights and obligations under the World Trade Organization (WTO) and the Agreement on Trade-Related Aspects of Intellectual Property Rights (TRIPs), thus binding Palestinian trade with third parties to these rules without enjoying any of the benefits of these agreements. This quasi-customs union exposed the fragile Palestinian economy to the winds of globalization without any protection or transition during liberalization of the Israeli economy in the 1990s. Therefore, the Palestinian economy paid the price of WTO membership since its markets were opened through Israel to products from all WTO members, without benefiting from WTO rules to regulate the trade practices of WTO members, including Israel.

As a result, Israel remained the occupied territory's main trading partner in the post-Oslo years and, under the PER, the PA has become critically dependent on Israeli rebates of customs and income taxes. However, Israel interprets 'imports' into the territory in a peculiarly restrictive way, i.e., it only counts those goods directly imported by *Palestinian* companies via Israel and *not* those imports into the territory that were first imported via an Israeli company for onward shipment to Palestinian traders. Reclaiming customs duties therefore does not apply to the latter type of imports, although they constitute the bulk of imports to Palestine. This, as well as other terms of the PER, limited the PA's access to a large part of revenues from imports, resulting in a recurrent loss of Palestinian fiscal revenue to Israel.[15]

While the Palestinian Monetary Authority would be the sole agent responsible for banking regulation in the territory, the issue of a Palestinian currency, which would carry with it the symbol of sovereignty, was postponed indefinitely under the PER, and the New Israeli Shekel (NIS) remained the main currency in circulation in the Occupied Palestinian Territory (OPT), alongside the dollar and the dinar. Although both sides were supposed to maintain normal labor movement with the other, the PER failed to guarantee unlimited Palestinian access to the Israeli labor market because it granted Israel the right to determine the extent and conditions of this labor movement. In fact, the Protocol explicitly gave the employing side (Israel) the "right to determine from time to time the extent and conditions of the labor movement into its area."[16]

Furthermore, the PER lacked any monitoring of implementation mechanisms, which was particularly harmful as such mechanisms could have been used to address the persistent leakage of revenues collected by Israel on behalf of the PA. The Joint Economic Committee, established by the Protocol to manage its implementation, was an unwieldy, politicized body which never served as an effective dispute resolution function and which failed to provide a governance role or address conflictual issues.

The interim period arrangements therefore perpetuated a skewed incorporation of the Palestinian economy with Israel and its settlements in the territory. However, the architects of the PER had envisaged the interim period as one of reconstruction and growth. Indeed, the PA adhered to the Protocol, just as it tolerated and discounted its acknowledged weaknesses as they became evident over the 1990s, on the assumption that Israel would implement the Accords and that would ensure a hospitable economic environment markedly different from the direct occupation period. Some accounts of PLO decision-making in this period point to an early realization by Arafat that the Israelis would not uphold their end of the "peace of the brave," especially after the assassination of Prime Minister Yitzhak Rabin. However, the PLO had locked itself into a deal that, as the weaker party, it could only play out in the hope that it could somehow outmaneuver Israel and consolidate its forces and resources to fight another day.[17]

Ultimately, political factors combined to create an environment by the end of the five-year interim period different from that proclaimed by the PER—fraught with violence, mistrust, uncertainty and unabated Israeli colonization. These engendered adverse repercussions, bringing down real income levels for the average Palestinian by 2000. These setbacks over time dampened public satisfaction with the interim economic and trade arrangements. Chronic Palestinian economic dependency upon Israel was perpetuated by the unchanging framework of the PER and the dysfunction of most of its machinery, especially during a time of great upheaval in the economy. By 2000, various Israeli-Palestinian and international study groups had advanced models for future improved economic relations between two sovereign states.[18] But these were soon dashed against the Israeli security-first logic during the Second Intifada that disregarded neighborly economic relations and which easily converted the Protocol's fiscal and trade control mechanisms into punitive tools deployed against a fragile PA.

After the suppression of the Second Intifada, Israeli policies of land and water confiscation expanded, now based on 'security concerns.' As early as July 2004, 86 percent of the land confiscated for the construction of the Separation Barrier in the West Bank was agricultural, leading to the loss of some of the region's most fertile agricultural lands and a maze of movement and access restrictions. Meanwhile, Israel's West Bank settler population expanded from 116,300 in 1993 to over 400,000 by 2014, while settlers in East Jerusalem increased from 152,800 to almost 190,000.[19] After almost 50 years of occupation, these 600,000 Israelis settled in the West Bank were equivalent to over 20 percent of the Palestinian population in the territory, an extraordinary demographic reversal, mirroring that which has occurred within Israel between its Jewish and its one-in-five Arab citizens, almost to the percentage point.

But even in the best possible scenario of a benevolent Israeli occupation, the PA had conceded, among the compromises of Oslo, to permit the segmentation of the West Bank into zones of supposedly full Palestinian ("A"), shared ("B") and solely Israeli ("C") jurisdiction. This spelt an early death for any serious possibility of ensuring a contiguous or cohesive Palestinian economic development effort that might set the scene for sovereignty and statehood or create the conditions for an end to occupation. PA planners have gone through excessive contortions to explain why they did not properly examine maps at the time of signing off on the zoning in 1995, or that they expected Israel to cede the bulk of Area "C" by 1999. Only by 2014 had the time finally come for the PA to design a dedicated program for the benefit of Area "C" as a priority development zone—through a strategy that remains without effect several years later.[20]

Article IV of the 1993 Declaration of Principles affirmed that "the two sides view the West Bank and the Gaza Strip as a single territorial unit, whose integrity will be preserved during the interim period."[21] The PER was intended to lay "the groundwork for strengthening the economic base of the Palestinian side and for exercising its right of economic decision making in accordance with its own development plan and priorities." It was a "contractual agreement that will govern the economic relations between the two sides and will cover the West Bank and the Gaza Strip during the interim period."[22]

On paper this was hailed by PLO advocates as an adequate starting point for maintaining a coherent and contiguous Palestinian economy in the whole occupied territory, including Jerusalem. However, perhaps the fatal weakness of the PER and the Oslo agreements (and some would argue, its core purpose from an Israeli vantage point), was the postponement of Palestinian sovereignty, which led to further dependency and irreversible loss for all aspects of the Palestinian economy. Amidst the euphoria surrounding the Oslo Accords, the lone voice of the late, eminent scholar Edward Said rings true today:

> By accepting that questions of land and sovereignty are being postponed till "final status negotiations," the Palestinians have in effect discounted their unilateral and internationally acknowledged claim to the West Bank and Gaza: these have now become "disputed territories.". . . Moreover, rather than becoming stronger during the interim period, the Palestinians may grow weaker, come more under the Israeli thumb, and therefore be less able to dispute the Israeli claim when the last set of negotiations begins. But on the matter of how, by what specific mechanism, to get from an interim status to a later one, the document is purposefully silent. Does this mean, ominously, that the interim stage may be the final one? [23]

STRUCTURAL TRANSFORMATION OF THE ECONOMY 1994–2014: THE SHAPE OF A FREE MARKET ECONOMY UNDER COLONIAL DOMINATION

Surveying Palestinian economic performance in the first few years after the PA was established, UNCTAD noted in 1997 that little had yet changed. This could have been written in 2018 because it retains the same accuracy and veracity:

> In the period 1995–1997 aggregate economic indicators exhibited trends consistent with those witnessed in previous years, with an overall adverse impact on the standards of living. The high exposure and vulnerability of the economy to external shocks continues to reveal major structural weaknesses. These include weak domestic employment capacity, uneven sectoral growth, weak intersectoral articulation, severe marketing bottlenecks, poorly coordinated and fragmented new investments in both public and private ventures, and structural imbalances among macroeconomic aggregates. These features become all the more critical when viewed against stagnation in income and growing poverty among marginalized segments of the population. Human resource development and growing unemployment since 1992 have posed critical challenges for the performance of the economy, with important political, social and economic ramifications.[24]

By 2014, in many *apparent* ways however, the Palestinian economy and society hardly resembled that which the PA had inherited after 1994.[25] Indeed, the changes witnessed in the previous two decades were wider, deeper and more varied than those experienced in previous decades under Israeli or even prior to 1967 under Jordanian and Egyptian rule. The West Bank and Gaza economies under the latter had retained many of the sectoral and labor force features, limited scope of capital formation, and links with the Jordanian economy that had developed prior to 1967. However, some of the transformations after Oslo/Paris have been relatively dramatic. The West Bank economy, if not Gaza and Jerusalem in recent years, has morphed into a very different system than before, be it in terms of the degree of de-industrialization, ad-hoc services sector growth, scale and diversity of capital formation, or overall living standards and "human development" indicators.

Prosperity, conspicuous consumption and efficient private and public services are notable in the urban centers of the PA areas in the West Bank, and basic education and health standards for much of the West Bank population are good. However, on the rural margins in out-of-bounds Area "C," in Jerusalem, and in Gaza, economic and social disintegration and poverty are the challenges faced by over 2.5 million Palestinians living in those areas combined. Such an outcome undermines the credibility of the Oslo/Paris project as a whole. On the other hand, the structure of the Palestinian "macro-economy" and the enduring weaknesses which have been nurtured by prolonged occupation, have changed minimally in 20, or even 30 years. This lends credence to the idea of the legacy of Oslo/Paris having ensured "individual prosperity and communal impoverishment," and little in the way of "development."[26]

Several forces and dynamics have driven this structural transformation and skewed development. These include especially the largely negative impacts of prolonged exposure to the much more advanced and powerful Israeli economy, the effects of globalization and rapid liberalization (on Israel and, by extension, Palestine), both of which were facilitated and indeed inevitable within the PER framework. Surely the relatively weak Palestinian natural resource base, small market and other features of lagging development were factors which favored investment and policy choices that emphasized tertiary (services) sectors instead of primary (agricultural and mining) or secondary (manufacturing) sectors and imports instead of domestic production. Since the 1990s, the influence of the economic policy prescriptions of the Washington Consensus and the BWIs pointed to such constraints on domestic productive capacity as the justification for the neoliberal economic policies that they successfully advocated as being appropriate in the Palestinian context and necessary to ensure the PA's viability and survival.[27]

Ultimately, in this respect, as in the debate over the PER, the PLO is complicit in the process by having freely adopted and implemented a range of policy preferences that were not suited to the Palestinian development challenge. The profit and rent seeking imperatives of Palestinian private capital increasingly call the shots in economic policy by maintaining PA fiscal solvency through supplier and banking credit lines. This trajectory has resulted in a stunted agricultural sector, an enfeebled industrial base, a captive trade sector, a highly indebted middle class, deep poverty and structural unemployment. These features cannot be ascribed solely to the adverse impact of prolonged occupation. The Palestinian political leadership and economic elites own agency in allowing this process to endure, take deep root and in "embedding neoliberalism"[28] in the life of all Palestinians, even amongst its fiercest intellectual critics, is one of the evident outcomes of the past two decades of economic peace.

AGGREGATE ECONOMIC DEMAND AND PERFORMANCE

In examining Palestinian economic growth, even without reference to gaps with Israel, its unstable path over the first 20 years of Oslo demonstrates a disarticulation of the macro-economy.[29] Table 4.1 presents the aggregate indicators that portray the major features of Palestinian economic performance between 1994 and 2013, the twenty-year period covered by this analysis.

The economy has regularly featured spurts in growth of Gross Domestic Product (GDP) and Gross National Income (GNI, which equals GDP plus non-domestic income from workers in Israel), and indeed has grown in nominal terms to almost four times its size in 1995. However, recurrent 3–4 year bouts of reversal (1988–1991, 2001–2005) and recovery (1994–1996, 2008–2011) are the primary feature of this growth trajectory, which had already emerged by the 1980s, leaving the economy fragile and highly vulnerable to shocks, be they fiscal, trade, price or security-based. Amidst the political uncertainties and continued adverse impact of occupation, and even after the latest growth spurt that peaked in 2011 at 12 percent, the slowdown in economic growth afterwards was consistent with the growth trajectory since occupation.

Adding donor and private transfers to GNI, gross national disposable income (GNDI) exceeded US$14 billion by 2013. While GDP's share of GNDI hovered around 79 percent from 1995 (the first year that significant aid reached the OPT and employment in Israel began to rise again) to 1999, during much of the 2002–2006 period it fell to as low as 73 percent as donor aid constituted more than a quarter of all Palestinian income. By 2013, the contribution of domestic sources of income had strengthened to 84 percent, reflecting a relative reduction of aid dependency if not a more robust domes-

Table 4.1. Economy of the Occupied Palestinian Territory: Selected Years[a]

	1995	1999	2002	2005	2006	2010	2011	2012	2013
Macroeconomic performance									
GDP ($ mil.)	3,282	4,271	3,555	4,831	4,619	8,913	10,465	11,279	12,476
Gross national income ($ mil.)	3,723	5,025	3,774	5,180	5,047	9,512	11,215	12,136	13,636
Gross national disposable income ($ mil.)	4,122	5,398	4,826	6,317	6,323	11,503	12,319	13,887	14,824
GDP per capita ($)	1,427	1,553	1,182	1,470	1,363	2,339	2,665	2,787	2,992
GNI per capita ($)	1,618	1,827	1,255	1,576	1,489	2,496	2,856	2,999	3,270
Real GDP growth (%)	6.0	8.8	-13.3	8.6	-5.2	9.3	12.2	5.9	1.9
Real GDP per capita growth (%)	-1.3	4.3	-15.7	5.3	-8.1	6.1	8.9	2.7	-0.1
Real GNI per capita growth (%)	0.7	4.1	-16.7	7.5	-6.5	5.4	9.0	3.6	-0.4
Final consumption expenditure/GDP (%)	118	118	123	133	145	122	119	118	116
Investment expenditure/GDP (%)	30	41	26	28	25	19	16	16	22
Household/Final consumption expend (%)	79	77	73	76	76	73	74	73	73
Buildings/Fixed investment (%)	75	67	63	66	61	72	79	78	81
Population and labor									
Population (mil.)[a]	2.34	2.96	3.23	3.51	3.61	4.05	4.17	4.29	4.42
Unemployment (%)[b]	32.6	21.7	41.2	29.0	29.8	30.0	25.8	26.7	27.0
Total employment (thousands)	417	588	452	603	636	744	837	858	885
In public sector	51	103	125	145	148	179	188	195	204
In Israel and settlements	68	135	42	56	55	78	84	83	99

(continued)

Table 4.1. Continued

	1995	1999	2002	2005	2006	2010	2011	2012	2013
External trade									
Net current transfers ($ mil.)	400	374	1,052	1,128	1,276	1,991	1,246	1,116	1,874
Exports of goods and services ($ mil.)	562	752	478	723	678	1,367	1,799	1,871	2,067
Imports of goods and services ($ mil.)	2,441	3,363	2,234	3,754	3,202	5,264	5,723	6,300	6,447
Trade balance ($ mil.)	−1,879	−2,612	−1,756	−2,851	−2,523	−3,897	−3,924	−4,429	−4,380
Trade balance (% of GDP)	−57	−61	−49	−59	−55	−44	−37	−39	−41
Trade balance with Israel ($ mil.)	−922	−1,598	−886	−1,945	−1,887	−2,818	−3,203	−3,712	−3,096
Trade balance with Israel (% of GDP)	−28	−37	−25	−40	−41	−32	−31	−33	−29
PA trade with Israel/total PA trade (%)[c]	92	69	53	83	73	77	69	67	60
A trade with Israel/total Israeli trade (%)[c]	4.3	3.7	1.8	2.5	2.2	2.8	2.7	2.9	2.7
Fiscal balance (% of GDP)									
Revenue net of arrears/clearance withheld	13.2	23.9	8.5	29.5	25.0	22.6	20.9	20.2	23.5
Current expenditure—commitment basis	15.3	22.6	29.0	43.0	49.3	36.9	33.1	32.4	33.5
Total expenditure—cash basis	25.6	29.9	35.4	49.2	55.0	41.5	31.3	29.1	31.0
Overall balance—cash bass	−12.3	−6.1	−27.0	−19.7	−30.0	−18.9	−10.4	−8.9	−7.5

[a] Except for the population figures, data exclude East Jerusalem.
[b] ILO's "relaxed definition" of unemployment includes discouraged workers.
[c] Palestinian and Israeli trade data refer to goods, and non-factor and factor services.

Sources: Palestinian Central Bureau of Statistics (PCBS), PA Ministry of Finance, IMF, International Labour Organization (ILO), and Israel Central Bureau of Statistics.

tic economy, something that if sustainable would constitute a rare achievement in an otherwise bleak economic history.[30]

However, the Palestinian population almost doubled in the same period. Therefore, against nominal growth in GDP and GNDI, the real (deflated to constant prices) gains in output and income in per-capita over time have been limited. Even with accelerated GDP growth after 2007 and per-capita growth that almost reached double digits in the same period, this apparent gain was short-lived. Real per capita GDP and GNI growth in 2012 declined to a third of the previous year's record—to 2.7 percent and 3.6 percent, respectively—and stalled by 2013 for the first time in seven years.

The distribution of GDP in terms of "aggregate demand" (total expenditure on consumption, investment and net exports) is indicative of the overall productive and consumptive structure of the Palestinian economy, as well as the process of its development and its response to shocks over time. In "normal" periods when GDP growth is relatively strong, the share of consumption (private and government) from total GDP has remained under or close to 120 percent (e.g., in the 1990s, and since 2010). However, in times of crisis, such as the early 2000s, domestic output declines and external income sources predominate, so the share of consumption in GDP grows, reaching as much as 145 percent of GDP in 2006.

Alongside this, the share of (private and public) investment in GDP reflects not only the growth of actual investment flows, but also the maturity and stability of the economy and its ability to productively absorb new finance, and hence the creation of future productive capacity. Generally, advanced economies feature investment rates below 20 percent, owing to their relatively sophisticated and efficient economic structure and higher standards of living, while developing and emerging economies on sustained growth and development paths feature rates averaging over 30 percent. Average Middle Eastern investment rates are under 30 percent of GDP while those of developing Asian economies remain high, above 40 percent.

The Palestinian investment rate, which was robust and growing in the 1990s, plummeted during the Second Intifada to 25 percent by 2006, and continued to fall. As this path certainly does not reflect greater economic security, efficiency or emergence from "de-development," its decline to 16 percent by 2012 (and recovery to 22 percent in 2013) is more symptomatic of the weak investment opportunities and unstable climate, underlying weakness of the productive economy and inability of public investment to lead and crowd-in private investment. If anything, private investment dominates the Palestinian economy, and is composed largely of household investment in residential and commercial property, the safe haven in which Palestinian household savings have historically always found refuge. By 2013, over 80 percent of fixed investment was still in buildings, clearly the least risky allocation of household and corporate savings.

High consumption expenditure and output growth fuel a chronically large external trade deficit, which was well above 55 percent for most of the period 1995–2006 and only began to fall after. This largely reflected the recovery of Palestinian exports of goods and services, whose total has trebled from a low in 2006 to just over $2 billion in 2013, whereas the level of imports has only doubled in the same period, to over $6 billion. With a trade deficit that exceeded $4 billion since 2011, the net trade balance has hovered within a few percentage points of 40 percent of GDP; some $3 billion of that deficit is with Israel, which remains the main Palestinian trade partner and source (or channel) of imports.

Alongside a less onerous trade deficit, the PA can credibly claim to have promoted and overseen a decreasing trade dependence on Israel. The deficit still accounted for 90 percent of all Palestinian trade in 1995, but fell to between 70–75 percent when the economy recovered after 2006 and, for the first time ever, hit as low as 60 percent by 2013. If such an achievement is pursued, no doubt this will make the important goal of Palestinian external trade market diversification within reach, while also undermining the economic arguments that have sustained belief in the necessity of the customs union with Israel. Clearly, as compared to its utility as a control tool, the Protocol remains of little, if any, economic significance to Israel, since the PA market accounts for less than 3 percent of total Israeli trade (exports and imports).

With the PA running a budget deficit that only in the past few years has been reduced to under 10 percent (from 30 percent in 2006), meaning anaemic public investment alongside risk-averse private investment, there are few prospects for any developmental surge in Palestine, or even sustained GDP/GNI growth. The few channels for private investment in residential construction become less attractive with over-supply, and excessive (increasingly debt-fuelled) private consumption becomes the preferred haven for the liberal Palestinian consumer. This is the macroeconomic testament of Oslo/Paris, and while it may be argued (as PA officials do) that at least the people have been kept alive, employed (more or less) and able to live normal lives, in Palestine, as far as economic development is concerned, these have really been two lost decades.

THE SUPPLY SIDE: THE INEXORABLE RISE OF THE SERVICES ECONOMY

In cautiously welcoming the opportunities that the Oslo and Paris Accords appeared to offer the Palestinian economy emerging in 1994 from the adverse impacts of the First Intifada and the first Gulf War, UNCTAD nevertheless affirmed at the time that the challenges of structural transformation were daunting:

> The Palestinian economy remains characterised by a distorted structure of output which has favored services, residential construction and traditional agriculture as against the relatively weak industrial sector, infrastructures including utilities and some private services. This structure, reflecting a weak domestic resource base and the impact of prolonged occupation, will no longer be sustainable under the new policy environment emerging in the (Palestinian) territory.[31]

Reading today that concise testimony of the economy bequeathed to the PLO by the Israeli occupying power, the extent to which so little has changed despite the almost 25 years that have elapsed is striking. There were some initial spurts in strengthening of "productive" sectors in the first years after Oslo/Paris, and Palestinian industrial growth has not been without its successes, especially in import substitution investments in the last few years brought about by changing global market systems and greater Palestinian competitiveness. However, over two decades, the twin impacts of progressive rounds of trade liberalization and the violent confrontations of the Second Intifada combined to thwart most potentials or opportunities for building the productive and autonomous Palestinian economy that the PLO had promised in its 1993 development plan. Instead, for better or worse, an economy dominated by private and public services remains the "motor" of growth and of sustaining aggregate demand in uncertain and turbulent times.[32]

Table 4.2 summarizes the shifts in the sectoral structure of the Palestinian economy in the 25 years after 1987, reflecting the shocks of both the Intifadas, the influence of the Oslo/Paris framework, and the impact of late twentieth-century globalization and liberalization. In some respects, the changes in the share of each sector in total GDP typify those witnessed by some smaller, poorer developing countries in the face of the same global forces unleashed in the 1990s, especially the decline of agriculture and weak industrialization. Undoubtedly, the constraints of prolonged occupation also have stunted the possibilities for development of the productive (primary and secondary) sectors and favored the predominance of services. In other aspects however, conscious Palestinian policy choices made under the Oslo terms of engagement and the liberal economic philosophy adopted by the PA dictated the course of events. It is safe to assume that all those factors conspired (and reinforced each other) to thwart any hope that PLO planners might have entertained before 1994 to build "the core of the independent Palestinian economy and of a Palestinian public sector liberated of bureaucracy and infused with the determination and spirit of revolution."[33] Instead, by 2014 the Palestinian

Table 4.2. Economy of the Occupied Palestinian Territory: Percentage Contribution to GDP by Economic Activity, Selected Years

Economic Activity	1987*	1994	2000	2010	2013
Agriculture, forestry and fishing	21.6	12.3	9.5	5.2	4.1
Mining, manufacturing, electricity, and water	8.9	21.2	15.7	12.6	15.7
Thereof:					
—Mining and quarrying	—	0.7	0.6	0.4	0.5
—Manufacturing	—	18.9	12.9	10.2	12.8
—Electricity, gas, steam, and air conditioning supply; water supply	—	1.6	2.2	2.0	2.4
Construction	17.6	10.5	5.6	4.4	4.5
Wholesale and retail trade, repair of motor vehicles and motorcycles	36.7*	17.3	11.7	15.9	17.1
Transportation and storage	—	4.5	5.1	1.9	1.8
Financial and insurance activities	—	1.0	4.1	3.7	2.8
Services	—	23.1	23.7	27.3	26.9
Thereof:					
—Accommodation and food service, real estate, and professional services	14.4		14.5	10.5	10.9
—Information and communication			—	6.3	5.9
Education		5.3	5.8	7.2	6.6
—Human health and social work activities		3.2	3.2	3.2	3.4
Public administration and defense	12.2*	10.0	13.3	14.8	14.8
Public Owned Enterprises		0.0	4.1		
FISIM		−0.6	−3.2	−2.8	−1.9
Customs Duties and VAT on Imports, net	3.0	0.6	10.4	17	14.2
Total	100.0	100.0	100.0	100.0	100.0

Sources: Palestinian Central Bureau of Statistics (PCBS), and Israel Central Bureau of Statistics for 1987.

economy retained in most sectors the stunted features that have long characterized performance under occupation, while the specific impacts of globalization and neoliberal economic policy aggravated or accelerated "normal" development processes in some sectors.

Most notable in this respect is the spectacular collapse of Palestinian agriculture as the mainstay of the domestic economy, from one-fifth of GDP before the First Intifada to as low as 5 percent in 2013. Already, by 1994 the share of agriculture was down to around 12 percent, but this decline accelerated under the pressure of forces originating in land, natural resources, marketing and price/income constraints, alongside the prevailing economic orthodoxy that Palestinian agriculture was not competitive in the new global market. Both PA funding and donor aid bypassed investment in agriculture and it is only in recent years that private investment on an industrial scale (increasingly linked to upstream food processing industries) have rediscovered the potential and strengths of Palestinian agriculture, both economically and socially.

Meanwhile, a burst of industrial sector growth that was favored by the lifting from 1992 of Israeli restrictions on manufacturing industry and growing sub-contracting links with Israeli producers was stopped in its tracks by the liberalization of the Israeli trade regime and the wave of cheap imports from abroad in the subsequent decade. From a share of as much as 21 percent of GDP in 1994, industry's contribution (including manufacturing, mining and utilities) had fallen to 15 percent by 2010, only to rebound to around 18 percent by 2014. In the same period, the share of manufacturing industry declined from 19 percent to 13 percent. Construction, which was a leading sector prior to Oslo (given the limited alternatives for growth), also witnessed significant decline, to 5 percent of GDP. While this is something which may appear hard to reconcile with the ongoing building boom in much of the urban West Bank in the past years, the relatively low cost (and value added) of building activities most likely encourages the continuing massive allocation of private investment resources to residential construction, and vice versa.

Against this backdrop of productive sector decline, the creation of a Palestinian government sector and the expansion of public services after Oslo led to a doubling of the contribution of the public services sector to GDP, to more than a quarter of the economy by 2013. Whereas the contribution of public health and education services has not grown significantly since 1994 and remained under 10 percent, the strongest growth has taken place in government (civil and security) administration, which accounted for above 15 percent of GDP in 2013.

No less significant has been the sustained growth and diversification in the range of private sector services, which already accounted for over a third of economic output before the First Intifada and continues to be the leading economic cluster, generating around 45 percent of Palestinian GDP by 2010. Palestinian services today are composed mainly of wholesale and retail commerce, tourism and real estate and professional services, and the newly emergent information and communication services. Together, public and private services, which accounted for 54 percent of GDP in 1994, today produce over two thirds of Palestinian domestic product. The reliance on economic activities which are heavily dependent on (and have been shaped by) the constraints of occupation, render the prospects for building domestic productive capacity more difficult and improbable.

ISRAELI-PALESTINIAN ECONOMIC RELATIONS: CHANNELS OF DEPENDENCY AND RESOURCE EXTRACTION

Certainly, the free-market economic policies adopted by the PA as part of adherence to the liberalized Israeli trade regime enabled much of the structural transformation reviewed above, or at least could not protect the Palestinian economy from the more destructive forces of globalization and exposure to international competition. However, these usual economic forces of development were never free to operate on their own, nor was the PA ever in a position (politically or institutionally) to confront them, assuming it had possessed the requisite economic policy determination and foresight to do so. Most mainstream Palestinian and international analyzes of the Palestinian economy and programs for its development, policy planning and institution building have consciously ignored the obvious "abnormality" of markets in the case of the OPT. Instead, the past two decades have been characterized by policy making solely within the realm of the possible, rarely the desirable.

By definition, the "interim self-government" arrangements in place since 1994 reduced the PA's role to managing the "possible" with no real tools or realistic horizon to shape the economy. Hence, aggregate growth has been woefully inadequate in terms of building the autonomous Palestinian economic base as promised by Oslo. Moreover, it is hard today to find the "*Palestinian public sector liberated of bureaucracy and infused with the determination and spirit of revolution*" as envisioned by the PLO a generation earlier. All told, this adds up to continued domination of the Palestinian economy by Israel's settler-colonial imperatives and enforced trade, monetary and fiscal dependency upon the Israeli economic model and its liberal market philosophy.

Israeli and other apologists for occupation have tried to argue that regardless of other impacts of the domination of the Palestinian people and territory by Israel, at least the effects of exposure of the smaller, resource-poor and open Palestinian economy to that of Israel should be beneficial to both sides, and eventually lead to integration. Claims about the benevolence of the occupation and the "prosperity of the inhabitants of the Areas" was the regular trope of Israeli diplomats in rebutting UN reports to the contrary and of Israeli economists who produced counter-reports documenting Palestinian strong economic growth rates.[34] This assumption of the normal functioning of market forces even under occupation became the underlying premise of the PER, and the quasi-customs union it entailed, and it remains the conviction of many Palestinian business and economic leaders that the future of Palestinian growth and development lies to the west, with and through Israel.

The main channel that ties the Palestinian economy to Israel, both in policy and material terms, is that of merchandise and services trade. The PA considers these flows as "external" trade (as they account for 60 percent of all Palestinian trade), while Israel continues to account for them as internal trade, within the one-state logic with which the Israeli Jewish economy trades with all sectors of the subjugated Palestinian population over which it rules. As shown in the preceding section, one of the economic achievements of the PA era was reduction of the Israeli economy's monopoly of Palestinian trade by a third, largely through PA efforts to diversify both import and export markets. However, as the occupying power in control of borders, Israel dominates international market access of 100 percent of Palestinian trade, as well as remaining the source or destination of much, though no longer most, Palestinian trade.

The trade deficit with Israel ($3.7 and $3 billion in 2012 and 2013, respectively) is equivalent to almost 30 percent (and in most years more) of GDP. In other words, for every dollar produced by the Palestinian economy, 30 cents end up back to Israel, in a perverse payment for this chronic dependence on the dominant trade partner (which so happens also to be the occupying power). Excluding exports of labor services to Israel, Palestinian merchandise and service exports to Israel account for 87 percent of all registered Palestinian exports, while Israel is the origin (or channel) of 72 percent of recorded merchandise and service imports. While not necessarily of economic significance to Israel, this resource capture provides a useful channel for control and sanctions when politically expedient (through withholding of PA trade tax revenues or through movement and access restrictions).

Recent official Israeli data suggest that a significant proportion of merchandise imports between the two sides recorded as being products of Israeli origin are in fact imports from abroad that are destined at once for the Israeli and Palestinian common market, and imported through Israeli shippers. This might constitute as much as 40 percent of all imports formally recorded as being from Israel including oil products (which account for 11 percent of all Palestinian imports).[35] Over and above the loss of fiscal revenue that these uncaptured, indirect imports represent for the Palestinian treasury, this decreasing share of the Israeli economy in Palestinian trade lends further credence to the observation that in fact the Palestinian economy trades mainly with the rest of the world, despite all the existing trade facilitation impediments. The Israeli economy is no longer the indispensable partner for Palestinian trade or economic development expected 25 years ago. While existing trade and fiscal arrangements do not reflect this reality, they certainly ensure Israeli colonial control over the OPT, its people, resources and prospects.

Foreign trade data also refute the hype among some economists and international agencies about the alleged advantages of building a service economy in a globalized market where Palestinian merchandise exports cannot hope otherwise to compete. In 2013, merchandise still dominated the Palestinian import and export flows, including to/through Israel, constituting 79 percent of all recorded exports and 96 percent of all Palestinian imports. Almost all Palestinian services exports are destined for Israel and 24 percent of all Palestinian exports to Israel are services (mainly construction, telecommunication and sub-contracting processing). Most Palestinian services imports from Israel are in the areas of transportation, communications and other business services. Under the distorted market conditions of the OPT, even the supposedly more flexible and "borderless" services trade relying on the so-called "knowledge economy" is inadequate to redress the chronic imbalances of Palestinian external trade or to build a productive economy (the bulk of the private services sector is engaged in commercial and not "producer-services").

The Paris Protocol binds Palestinian trade and industrial support policy to the ultra-liberal stance that Israel has adopted in the past decade, suitable to its development needs but alien to those of the OPT. The Protocol also enables a significant leakage of fiscal resources to the occupying power. The value of lost PA fiscal revenue on indirect imports to the Palestinian territory by Israeli importers/shippers who pay trade taxes on the goods to Israeli Customs has been estimated by UNCTAD and the World Bank, respectively, at around $310 and $285 million annually.[36] The foregone opportunities for public investment, fiscal solvency and trade sovereignty of this open wound are recurrent and significant, when compared to the fiscal needs of the PA, and when viewed alongside the other channels through which the cost to

Table 4.3. Major External Trade Indicators, 2013

Million US$	2013
Total Palestinian Exports	900.6
Total Palestinian Imports	5,163.9
Palestinian Net Trade balance	−4,263.3
Total Palestinian Imports From Israel	3,694.8
Total Palestinian Exports to Israel	786.4
Total Palestinian Imports by Pipes and nets	552.7
Total Palestinian Exports of Services to Israel	185.8
Total Palestinian Imports of Services From Israel	136.3
Percentages	
Merchandise exports/Total exports	0.79
Imports Israel/Total imports	0.72
Exports Israel/Total exports	0.87
Pipes/Total imports	0.11
Services Exports Israel/Total exports Israel	0.24
Services Imports Israel/Total imports Israel	0.04

Source: Palestinian Central Bureau of Statistics (PCBS); constructed by the author.

Israel of occupation is minimized (e.g., donor allocations to cover PA internal security expenditures). Additional fiscal resource leakage takes place in smuggling, which over and above indirect imports denies the PA Treasury of revenue and diminishes its customs control capacities. Official statistics do not capture these "under-the-radar" trade flows, like much of the informal/shadow economy that exists on the fringes of the formal economy. However, their existence is indicative at once of the inability of outdated trade arrangements to cater to economic realities, as well as the degree of entanglement of the Palestinian economy in the web of Israeli commercial, security and colonial control interests.

LABOR, LAND AND NATURAL RESOURCE EXTRACTION

Underlying the economic predominance that Israel enjoys over Palestinian markets and access to markets, are more profound processes that have entailed significant extraction of labor and natural resources from the OPT over the past five decades. The confiscation and colonization of Palestinian land and control over water resources went hand in hand since 1967 with the incorporation of (mainly unskilled) Palestinian labor into Israeli labor markets. This began with agriculture and construction (including in settlements) and extended for some periods into industry and various commercial and personal services branches, with demand shifting over time as Israel's economy grew and matured. Ensuring Israeli domination over each of these important Palestinian resources proceeded at a different pace and according to changing imperatives. But they fit together neatly, along with control of trade routes and fiscal resources and overall macroeconomic sovereignty (within the monetary union in place), in the matrix of control exercised by Israel, and which seems only to have tightened in recent years.

The "non-factor income" of Palestinian labor in Israel at one point in the 1980s contributed as much as a quarter of Palestinian GNI, with as many as 150,000 Palestinians working in Israel and its settlements. This has been reduced since the building of the Israel Security Barrier, and today over 110,000 Palestinians work with permits or illegally inside Israel. By 2013, income from labor in Israel contributed only 10 percent of GNI, reflecting both the reduced numbers and the low-paid occupations they fill. Here again, the Oslo/Paris framework failed to ensure the terms of movement upon which it was predicated, but also was unable in 25 years to promote a Palestinian productive economy that could wean its labor force from dependence on Israel or from providing the manpower which has built its settlements throughout the West Bank.[37]

Perhaps of greater strategic significance to Israel than either fiscal resource or rent extraction from its control of Palestinian trade and of greater vitality to fueling its colonial enterprise in the West Bank has been its increasingly suffocating embrace of Palestinian land, water and mineral resources. The World Bank has estimated the loss to the Palestinian economy of lack of access and control in Area "C" at $3.4 billion annually.[38] Through an elaborate fabric of colonies, roads, military bases and firing zones, checkpoints, barriers and utility networks emanating from inside Israel and now integrating the settlements in the OPT into Israel as one territory, Israel is effectively sovereign not only in the 60 percent of Area "C" (plus Jerusalem) that is formally outside PA jurisdiction. It equally constrains and shapes the path of urban and rural development in the rest of the West Bank and access to the natural resource base, without which any sustained growth, much less development, is an illusion. The growing isolation and separation of the Palestinian economy in East Jerusalem and its shrinking share of Palestinian national income[39] adds yet another dimension to the multiple levels on which Israel divides and separately rules different Palestinian regions.[40]

The fragmentation of the OPT, the daily struggle of ordinary Palestinians to defend land and water rights, the inability of the PA to access and exploit natural resources such as stone and marble, Dead Sea minerals, Gaza offshore gas or West Bank shale oil deposits, are among the concrete testaments to the naïveté, irresponsibility, ignorance or complicity of Palestinian negotiators since Oslo. By error of commission or omission, over the past 25 years the PLO treated these assets of national economic security as bargaining chips, expendables, revenue streams, "delayables" or otherwise secondary matters, when all that really mattered for the viability of any state-building effort was precisely such red-line issues.

LOOKING FORWARD: THE NEXT 25 YEARS OF OSLO?

Over the first 25 years of the Oslo/Paris regime, the Palestinian economy certainly has grown and in some macroeconomic respects, has strengthened. However, other aggregate indicators highlight the enduring constraints of any growth path under the "non-market" constraints that have always limited potentials for development. The volatility of the growth path, affected by external shocks of differing degree and source, has meant only limited irreversible welfare gains as measured by per capita income and output indicators. Under the fragile economic conditions created by occupation and colonialism there can be no structural transformation in the composition of aggregate demand or strengthened domestic demand and production of the sort that sustained growth might permit. That is a bare truth too often overlooked by conventional economic policy for Palestine, which remains in the realm of damage limitation that at best reinforces communal resilience rather than sovereign state building or development that decolonizes.

Despite the weaknesses, deformations and limitations inherent in the Palestinian economic edifice built since 1994, it is hard to discern what, if anything, may unmake what has been wrought. Only with a dramatic transformation in the Israeli-Palestinian struggle for sovereignty could a different relation than that currently in place be envisaged, and only through the rosiest of glasses.[41] Israel's system of military and colonial domination over some six million Palestinian Arabs and control of their livelihoods within the different domains of its sovereignty has been refined into a sophisticated system of divide and rule. This allows for differential degrees of civil and legal status and local government for Palestinians living in Gaza, Jerusalem, Ramallah and Area C in the OPT, and Haifa, Nazareth and the Naqab inside Israel. Whereas some 4.5 million Palestinians in the former areas remain stateless, though with significant autonomy in many areas of public services and government, around 1.5 million Palestinian Arabs are citizens of the State of Israel, though with no distinct political governing entity to represent them or provide them services beyond the local (municipal) level. In all cases, national self-determination is denied, and Palestinians are expected to acquiesce in, and suffice with, whatever civil, cultural or economic freedoms are granted by the sovereign. Economic peace, for the moment, reigns.

This would seem to be an unsustainable, if not unjust, situation that surely is a recipe for unending confrontation and rebellion. But such a likelihood does not necessarily mean that the balance of power will shift within a foreseeable horizon in favor of oppressed Palestinians, however much international law, global public opinion and their own sacrifices may weigh in that struggle. Conflict "management" has been elevated in the case of Israel-Palestine to an artform. In fact, just as permits, curfews, checkpoints, walls, closed military zones and prisons serve to operate and valorize the complex matrix of colonial control, so do economic facilitation, promises of material enrichment and the basic human instinct of self-preservation and seeking a normal life play an essential role in keeping the peace. Hence, to view the economic outcomes of Oslo as somehow separate from its politics and security arrangements misses the point of why the Palestinian people face today one of the greatest predicaments of the modern Palestinian national movement.

Sustained Israeli calculating, planning and policy making from before and since Oslo have been invested in devising a formula for governing Palestinians that is carefully balanced between economic, material and lifestyle inducements while denying political self-determination and sovereignty. For all the tactical maneuvering and brinksmanship of Yasser Arafat, and the sincere dedication to peace-making of Mahmoud Abbas, the Palestinian leadership has only become more beholden to the Oslo framework, the limited power it has created for them and the reduced liberation horizon that has entailed. In the meantime, most Palestinians have adapted their lives to this regime, some surviving in the worst of conditions (e.g., in Jerusalem or Gaza) and others flourishing in the best (Ramallah or Haifa). Therefore, in the absence of either significant Palestinian social upheaval that challenges an economic system that perpetuates poverty, unemployment and deprivation, or of effective, widespread contestation of Israeli colonization and occupation in the West Bank, there is no reason why the status quo cannot be sustained.

While Israeli economic peace policies might be crafted to maintain an explicit trade-off between prosperity and self-determination, or property rights and national rights, the law of unintended consequences is always at play in the Palestinian-Israeli struggle. On the one hand, the three most significant Palestinian mass uprisings against settler colonialism (1936, 1987 and 2000) came in the wake of relatively sustained periods of economic growth and improving quality of life. This might well imply, on the other hand, that the creation of wealth, accumulation of material and economic assets and the taste of a better life creates inducements to more of the same . . . and to seeking greater freedom in disposing and investment of capital . . . and to more jealously guarding acquired assets and rights. To paraphrase Mao-Tse-Tung, in the Palestinian case, political power may well be said to spring from the proliferation of industrial assembly lines.

This in turn points to a conceivable way forward out of the current dead-end. Could the creation of a Palestinian economy (however stunted) and the concentration in one space (however nonsovereign) of Palestinian capital (however much profit-oriented) be a necessary condition for growing autonomous Palestinian national economic power in an otherwise asymmetric conflict with Israel? Just as Israel's state security and economic system extend from Tel Aviv to its northern, eastern and southern borders, so do the strategic interests of Palestinian wealth creation and economic interaction encompass the West Bank, Jerusalem, Galilee and Gaza. If, alongside the imminent demographic balance between Arabs and Jews under Israel's sovereignty, some closing of economic gaps and imbalances can also be achieved through sustained Palestinian wealth creation, this might create the material conditions that could break the stranglehold that Oslo has held on Palestinian politics and economics. The lure of unfulfilled national self-determination may well continue to frame the struggle of the Palestinian people for their denied rights. But the imperatives of accelerating processes of capital accumulation, class formation and socioeconomic contestation will also shape the future dynamics of conflict in the territory from the River to the Sea.[42]

NOTES

1. Hussein Agha and Ahmad Samih Khalidi, "The End of This Road: The Decline of the Palestinian National Movement," *New Yorker* (August 6, 2017).
2. Raja Khalidi and Sobhi Samour, "Neoliberalism as Liberation: The Statehood Program and the Remaking of the Palestinian National Movement," *Journal of Palestine Studies*, 40, No. 2 (2011).
3. George T. Abed, *The Palestinian Economy: Studies in Development Under Prolonged Occupation* (London: Routledge, 1986).
4. These were exemplified by the reports presented by the key international organizations to the 2011 United Nations General Assembly discussion of the Question of Palestine, when the PLO first attempted to garner Security Council recognition of the State of Palestine. This entailed a veritable reporting simultaneous chorus of the World Bank attesting to the good governance capacities of this "middle-income economy," the IMF verifying the transparent and modern management of PA public finances (e.g., International Monetary Fund—IMF, *West Bank and Gaza: Report to the Ad-Hoc Liaison Committee* (Washington, DC: IMF. 2011).
5. Adam Hanieh, *Lineages of Revolt: Issues of Contemporary Capitalism in the Middle East* (Chicago: Haymarket Books, 2013).
6. Raja Khalidi and Sahar Taghdisi Rad, *The Economic Dimensions of Prolonged Occupation: Continuity and Change in Israeli Policy Toward the Palestinian Economy* (Geneva: UNCTAD, 2009); Omar Jabary Salamanca, Mezna Qato, Kareem Rabie, and Sobhi Samour, editors "Past Is Present: Settler Colonialism in Palestine," *Special Issue of Settler Colonial Studies*, No. 2.1 (2012).
7. Raja Khalidi, "Bringing it All Back Home: Twenty First Century Palestinian Development Studies," *Journal of Palestine Studies* Vol. 45, No. 4 (2016); Rayya Zein, "Developing a Palestinian Resistance Economy through Agricultural Labor," *Journal of Palestinian Studies* Vol. XLVI, No. 3 (2017).
8. United Nations Conference on Trade and Development, *Report on Assistance to the Palestinian People* (Geneva: UNCTAD, 1992).
9. United Nations Conference on Trade and Development, *The Palestinian War-torn Economy: Aid, Development and State Formation* (United Nations: Geneva, 2006).
10. Raja Khalidi, "After the Arab Spring in Palestine: Contesting the Neoliberal Narrative of Palestinian National Liberation," *Jadaliyya E-Zine*, March 2012.
11. Paul Thomas Chamberlin, *The Global Offensive: The United States, the Palestine Liberation Organization, and the Making of the Post-Cold War Order* (New York: Oxford University Press, 2012).
12. Raja Khalidi, "The Economics of Palestinian Liberation," *Jacobin Magazine*, October 15, 2014.
13. Ishac Diwan, Radwan Shaban (editors), *Development Under Adversity: the Palestinian Economy in Transition* (Washington, DC: World Bank, 1999).
14. Sobhi Samour, *Review Assessment of Palestinian Trade Policy Options* (Ramallah: Palestine Economic Policy Research Institute—MAS, 2016).

15. United Nations Conference on Trade and Development, *Palestinian Fiscal Leakage under the Paris Protocol* (Geneva: UNCTAD, 2013).

16. Article VII of the PER, 1994.

17. A theme explored in its various dimensions in Mushtaq H. Khan, Ingrid Amundsen and George Giacaman (editors), *State Formation in Palestine: Viability and Governance During a Social Transformation* (London: Routledge, 2004).

18. The Economic Permanent Status (EPS) project in 1998 was the first of such joint ventures, followed after 2001 by the Aix Initiative, and the similar Geneva Peace Initiative, all of which remained without effect.

19. For 1993 figures, Daniel Kurtzer, "The Settlement Facts," *Washington Post*, June 14, 2009. For 2014: Palestinian Central Bureau of Statistics (http://www.pcbs.gov.ps/Portals/_Rainbow/Documents/sett_2013_E_tab4.htm).

20. As suggested by the author in Vijay Prashad, "Palestine's Lost Present: A Journey in the Jordan Valley," *New Araby*, December 31, 2015.

21. The Declaration of Principles on Interim Self-Governance Arrangements, 1993, http://avalon.law.yale.edu/20th_century/isrplo.asp.

22. Protocol on Economic Relations Between the Government of the State of Israel and the PLO Representing the Palestinian People, April 9, 1994, https://www.paltrade.org/upload/agreements/Paris%20Economic%20Protocol.pdf.

23. Edward Said, "The Morning After," *London Review of Books*, October 21, 1993.

24. United Nations Conference on Trade and Development, *Report on UNCTAD's Assistance to the Palestinian People* (UNCTAD: Geneva, July 1997—TD/B/44/10).

25. Raja Khalidi, "Key Features of the Palestinian Economy: Challenges to Endurance and Existing Visions to Address Them," in MAS (ed.), *Toward a New Vision for the Revival of the Palestinian Economy, MAS Economic Conference 2016 Preparatory Papers* (Ramallah: Palestine Economic Policy Research Institute—MAS, 2016).

26. The concept of "de-development" was elaborated to describe the Gaza economy in the pre-Oslo period in: Sara Roy, *The Gaza Strip: The Political Economy of De-development* (Washington, DC: Institute for Palestine Studies, 2016).

27. World Bank, *Economic Monitoring Report to the Ad Hoc Liaison Committee Meeting* (Washington, DC: World Bank Group, April 2016).

28. Khalidi and Samour, "Neoliberalism as Liberation."

29. All figures in this section are taken from or based upon the data in tables 4.1–4.3.

30. Sahar Taghdisi-Rad, *The Political Economy of Aid in Palestine* (London: Routledge, 2011).

31. United Nations Conference on Trade and Development, "Developments in the Economy of the Occupied Palestinian Territory" (UNCTAD: Geneva, July 1994—TD/B/41(1)/3).

32. Raja Khalidi, *Political Economy Analysis of the Palestinian Private Sector* (Ramallah: Palestine Economic Policy Research Institute—MAS, 2019).

33. As advocated from the exile of Beirut prior to 1982 by an earlier incarnation of Yasser Arafat, quoted in Ahmad Qurie, *The Productive Experience of the Palestinian Revolution* (Amman: Arab Institute for Studies and Publishing, 2007).

34. Raja Khalidi, "The United Nations, Palestine, Liberation and Development" in Vijay Prashad and Samir Makdisi (eds.), *Land of Blue Helmets* (Oakland: University of California Press, 2017).

35. United Nations Conference on Trade and Development, *Palestinian Fiscal Revenue Leakage to Israel under the Paris Protocol on Economic Relations* (Geneva: UNCTAD, 2014).

36. UNCTAD, "Palestinian Fiscal"; World Bank, "Economic Monitoring."

37. United Nations Conference on Trade and Development, *The Occupied Palestinian Territory: Twin Deficits or an Imposed Resource Gap?* (Geneva: UNCTAD, 2017).

38. World Bank, *Area C of the West Bank and the Future of the Palestinian Economy*, Washington, DC: World Bank Group, January 15, 2014.

39. United Nations Conference on Trade and Development, *The Palestinian Economy in East Jerusalem: Enduring Annexation, Isolation and Disintegration* (Geneva: UNCTAD, 2013).

40. Raja Khalidi, "What is the 'Palestinian Economy'?" in Gulistan Gurbey, Sabine Hoffman and Ferhad Ibrahim Seyder (eds.), *Between State and Non-State: Politics and Society in Kurdistan-Iraq and Palestine* (New York: Palgrave Macmillan, 2017).

41. Raja Khalidi, "An Israel-Palestine Parallel State Economy by 2035," in Mark Levine and Matthias Mossberg (eds.), *One Land, Two States: Israel and Palestine as Parallel States* (Berkeley and Los Angeles: University of California Press, 2014).

42. This trade-off is explored further in Raja Khalidi (2018) "Nation and Class: Generations of Palestinian Liberation," *Rethinking Marxism* Vol. 30, No. 3, 368–392.

BIBLIOGRAPHY

Abed, George T. *The Palestinian Economy: Studies in Development Under Prolonged Occupation.* London: Routledge, 1988.

Agha, Hussein J. and Khalidi Ahmad Samih. "The End of This Road: The Decline of the Palestinian National Movement." *New Yorker*, August 6, 2017.

Chamberlin, Paul Thomas. *The Global Offensive: The United States, the Palestine Liberation Organization, and the Making of the Post-Cold War Order.* New York: Oxford University Press, 2012.

Diwan, Ishac and Radwan A. Shaban (eds.). *Development Under Adversity: the Palestinian Economy in Transition.* Washington, DC: World Bank, 1999.

Hanieh, Adam. *Lineages of Revolt: Issues of Contemporary Capitalism in the Middle East.* Chicago: Haymarket Books, 2013.

International Monetary Fund—IMF. *West Bank and Gaza: Report to the Ad-Hoc Liaison Committee.* Washington, DC: IMF, 2011.

Khalidi, Raja. "After the Arab Spring in Palestine: Contesting the Neoliberal Narrative of Palestinian National Liberation." *Jadaliyya E-Zine*, March 2012.

———. "The Economics of Palestinian Liberation." *Jacobin Magazine*, October 2014.

———. "An Israel-Palestine Parallel State Economy By 2035," in *One Land, Two States, Israel and Palestine as Parallel States*, edited by Mark Levine and Matthias Mossberg. Berkeley and Los Angeles: University of California Press, 2014.

———. "Key Features of the Palestinian Economy: Challenges to Endurance and Existing Visions to Address Them," in *Toward a New Vision for the Revival of the Palestinian Economy, MAS 2016 Economic Conference Preparatory Papers.* Ramallah: Palestine Economic Policy Research Institute, 2016.

———. "Bringing It All Back Home: Twenty-first Century Palestinian Development Studies." *Journal of Palestine Studies*, Vol. 45, No. 4, 2016.

———. "The United Nations, Palestine, Liberation and Development," in *Land of Blue Helmets*, edited by Vijay Prashad and Samir Makdisi. Oakland: University of California Press, 2017.

———. "What is the 'Palestinian Economy'?" in *Between State and Non-State: Politics and Society in Kurdistan-Iraq and Palestine*, edited by Gulistan Gurbey, Sabine Hoffman and Ferhad Ibrahim Seyder. New York: Palgrave Macmillan, 2017.

———. "Nation and Class: Generations of Palestinian Liberation," *Rethinking Marxism*, Vol. 30, No. 3, 368–392, 2018.

———. *Political Economy Analysis of the Palestinian Private Sector.* Ramallah: Palestine Economic Policy Research Institute—MAS, 2019.

Khalidi, Raja and Sobhi Samour. "Neoliberalism as Liberation: The Statehood Program and the Remaking of the Palestinian National Movement." *Journal of Palestine Studies*, Vol. 40, No. 2, 2011.

Khalidi, Raja and Sahar Taghdisi-Rad. *The Economic Dimensions of Prolonged Occupation: Continuity and Change in Israeli Policy Toward the Palestinian Economy.* Geneva: UNCTAD, 2009.

Khan, Mushtaq H., Ingrid Amundsen and George Giacaman, eds. *State Formation in Palestine: Viability and Governance During a Social Transformation.* London: Routledge, 2004.

Qurei, Ahmad. *The Productive Experience of the Palestinian Revolution.* Amman: Arab Institute for Studies and Publishing, 2007 (in Arabic).

Roy, Sara. *The Gaza Strip: The Political Economy of De-development.* Washington, DC: Institute for Palestine Studies, 2016.

Samour, Sobhi. *Review Assessment of Palestinian Trade Policy Options.* Ramallah: Palestine Economic Policy Research Institute—MAS, 2016.

Taghdisi-Rad, Sahar. *The Political Economy of Aid in Palestine.* London: Routledge, 2011.

United Nations Conference on Trade and Development. *Report on Assistance to the Palestinian People.* Geneva: UNCTAD, 1992.

———*The Palestinian War-torn Economy: Aid, Development and State Formation.* Geneva: UNCTAD, 2006.

———*The Palestinian Economy in East Jerusalem: Enduring Annexation, Isolation and Disintegration.* Geneva: UNCTAD, 2013.

———*Report on UNCTAD Assistance to the Palestinian People: Recent Developments in the Economy of the Occupied Palestinian Territory.* Geneva: United Nations, July 2015.

———*The Occupied Palestinian Territory: Twin Deficits or an Imposed Resource Gap?* Geneva: UNCTAD, 2017.

World Bank. *Economic Monitoring Report to the Ad-Hoc Liaison Committee Meeting.* Washington, DC: World Bank Group, April 2016.

Zein, R. "Developing a Palestinian Resistance Economy through Agricultural Labor." *Journal of Palestinian Studies*, Vol. 46, No. 3, 2017.

Chapter Five

The Politics of Exclusion of Palestinians in Israel since Oslo

Between the Local and the National

Mansour Nasasra

Since 1948, the Palestinian Arab minority in Israel and its political leadership has viewed itself as a distinct party to the broader Israeli-Palestinian conflict. However, Israel, the Palestine Liberation Organization (PLO) and international actors excluded them from the Oslo Accords and subsequent peace negotiations, whose focus was always on the conflict over the fate of the Palestinian territory of the West Bank and Gaza Strip occupied in 1967 (OPT). The questions of Jerusalem and the 1948 Palestinian refugees were, by contrast, recognized in the Oslo Accords as important issues to be resolved, albeit reserved until final status negotiations.

This growing minority has voiced explicit frustration regarding their exclusion from the peace process since Oslo, the signing of which sent a clear message that the fate of Palestinians in Israel was to be determined within the context of their status as Israeli citizens. Their struggle for civil rights as a national minority or otherwise was henceforth to be formally distinct from that of Palestinians in the West Bank and Gaza. This is one of the difficult truths of the framework in place since 1994 to achieve a "two-state solution," as much as this exclusion is viewed by Israel as necessary to preclude any slide toward a "one-state solution."

The Palestinian Arabs in Israel are generally viewed officially, and by most Israelis, as an ethnic or religious minority in the State of Israel, while they themselves identify simultaneously with being both an unrecognized indigenous national minority in Israel and an organic part of the Palestinian people dispersed throughout the region since 1948. Their status as Israeli citizens but a part of the Palestinian Arab people has always put them in a sensitive position, often referred to by Israeli politicians or analyzts as a potential "third column." Their national (cultural, social and political) identity as Palestinians and Arabs is something that cannot be ignored or denied. However, their exclusion from the Oslo process made it clear that they are not party to any permanent status resolution of the conflict. Despite being fragmented from other Palestinians by Oslo, as well as enduring the psychological, social and physical borders, there continues to be daily commercial, social and political interaction between Palestinians in Israel and Palestinians in the OPT, which is genuine and lively.

In analyzing political trends among Palestinian political formations in Israel, this chapter charts how the Oslo Accords promoted greater "localization" of Palestinian politics in Israel within a strictly Israeli context, and further delinkage from the broader Palestinian national movement goals and strategies. This process proceeded in parallel to the strengthening of political participation in favor of Arab parties, rather than reinforcing the position of Zionist parties dominant before Oslo. Even if not out of design, Oslo had a significant impact in terms of pushing Palestinians in Israel toward becoming more organized as a national indigenous minority at the political level. Hence, the "localization" of Palestinian politics in Israel also reinforced (paradoxically) the "national" status of their struggle and self-perception.

The politics ushered in by Oslo witnessed a significant acceleration in a process already underway among Palestinian Arabs in Israel, with increasing disassociation from Zionist parties and the emergence of a new form of grassroots indigenous politics. Oslo led to a reshuffling of the political party framework amongst the Palestinians in Israel, though along broadly the same ideological lines that had dominated preceding formations, entailing a redefinition of the goals, means and structures of the Palestinian struggle in Israel. The Arab political parties may hold differing views about the impact of Oslo on the minority, but they have shared a largely coherent and consistent position toward the PLO's political program since Oslo in terms of the two-state solution. This basic consensus, nurtured in the environment of Israeli parliamentary liberal democracy, contributed to the rise of national and civic awareness amongst the minority, and to their concern about determining their future in the Jewish State—particularly in the context of the passing of the Nation State Law in July 2018, which critics charge codifies their status as second-class citizens.

The first part of the chapter looks at the development of Palestinian Arab identity in Israel as an indigenous national minority, challenging the Zionist narrative of "Israelization." The second section highlights the historical political exclusion of the Palestinians in Israel by the state, while playing a subordinate role in PLO politics, hence setting the stage for increased reliance on "local" solutions for collective needs and political rights. Section three examines how the socioeconomic disintegration of Palestinians in Israel has perpetuated their political, cultural, geographic and social separateness from Jewish Israel, and hence a stronger shared self-consciousness. Section four assesses the Arab political parties in Israel, their core political programs, and their perspectives on the Israeli-Palestinian conflict, thus shedding further light on how the Arab party political landscape, voices and programs have shifted since Oslo. Section five highlights how the contemporary political configuration of Arab parties in Israel, the Joint List, is a mature example of a concentration of Arab political resources in order to better militate for rights in Israel

The chapter concludes by arguing that the main impact of Oslo on the Palestinian Arab citizens of Israel has been an acceleration of the localization of their struggle into one focused on rights and justice within the Jewish state—while simultaneously strengthening their Arab identity and affiliation with the parallel Palestinian struggle for national self-determination.

THE POLITICS OF IDENTITY BEFORE OSLO: PALESTINIAN ARABS, ISRAELI ARABS?

A common theme that emerges from the research for this study is that the Palestinians in Israel today must struggle for their rights as a national indigenous minority, because that is the most accurate representation of their effective status and their own perceptions of identity. While this may not be explicitly understood in so many words by the mass of Palestinians in Israel, this concept best sums up the state of the debate on the status and prospects of this population among their elites and leaders. This is not so much of a new development since Oslo, as it reflects a coalescing in recent years of well-established ideological trends within a mutually understood paradigm and unified platform for joint action at the Israeli parliamentary level in an evolving struggle for civil, political, legal, economic, social and cultural rights.

More than 20 percent of the pre-1948 Arab population of Palestine remained after the *Nakba* and the establishment of Israel, numbering around 156,000 at the time. Today, this indigenous population has grown ten-fold to 1.5 million, and it comprises 21 percent of Israel's 8.3 million population. Since 1948, different terms and definitions have been used to define them from different vantage points: Palestinian citizens of Israel; Palestinian Arabs inside Israel; Arab or Palestinian/Arab (national) minority of Israel; Palestinians of 1948.

When Israelis refer to this minority, they use a variety of terms, such as: Arab Sector; Israeli Arabs; Arab/Druze/Circassian sector; Minority Sector; Non-Jews; and, even Good Arabs.[1] When Palestinians refer to this minority, they use the terms Arabs in Israel, Palestinians from inside, Arab al-Dakhil, Arabs or Palestinians of '48 and Israel's Arabs.

In recent years, within the evolving, multi-layered dimensions of Palestinian identity in Israel, the concept has gained traction, indeed wider internal acceptance of being an "indigenous national minority"—both objectively and materially.[2]

In the first decades after 1948, the Palestinian daily struggle inside Israel was largely against exclusion and for recognition of the most basic of rights, beyond being allowed to participate in the parliamentary and local election system. At the same time as the politics of pragmatism took hold amongst most Palestinians in Israel, proud to not have fled their villages, others were simply "struggling with the very idea of a Jewish State."[3] Many were still unable to come to terms with the fall-out of the *Nakba*. The military rule that lasted until 1967 certainly intimidated Palestinians in Israel, no less than the shock of the *Nakba* itself.[4] It was also a confusing time for Palestinian identity and its Arab nationalist perspectives, amidst a matrix of complex feelings of being Arab, and yet at the same time a suspect citizen of the Jewish state—a strange and unwelcome bird in a polarized region. Indeed, during this period, the Palestinians were known in Israeli legal and official jargon as *beni miutim* (members of minorities), but were often referred to simply as *Aravim*.[5] They suffered the dual indignity of being viewed with suspicion by Arabs in the Middle East and also by their brethren in exile.

After coming under military rule, the indigenous Palestinian minority were not permitted to develop separate Arab political parties, and their elected members of the Knesset (MKs) were affiliated with Zionist parties, especially the Labor Party. As Ian Lustick has analyzed, under military rule a number of policies such as segmentation, segregation, co-optation and dependence were adopted to divide and control the Arab minority.[6] This empowered a large swathe of local leaders allied to Zionist parties through the 1970s, in a crude, paternalistic exchange of votes and communal pacification for jobs, local development funds and favors in accessing the state machinery.

The prevention of any expression of Palestinian or Arab national affinity was a key goal of Israeli policy during the early days of military rule, and indeed until Oslo. Nadera Shalhoub-Kevorkian stresses the aspects of surveillance and fear that were practiced to control the minority,[7] whilst Ahmad Sa'di highlights how state agencies adopted a strategy of banning the establishment of Arab political parties during the first two decades of the state.[8] Political exclusion and political disempowerment were thus central experiences of the Palestinian minority in Israel.[9] This political exclusion also extended to their absence from a variety of influential state bodies and key segments of the labor market.[10]

Their status as citizens who were supposed to enjoy equal legal, civil and political rights with Jewish citizens has undoubtedly improved since the first decades of the State, if not especially since Oslo.[11] Nevertheless, identification with their Palestinian and Arab brethren's origin and fate has never really dissipated.

The occupation of the West Bank and Gaza in 1967 allowed for the reunion of the Palestinian citizens of Israel with those who had lived since 1948 under Jordanian or Egyptian administration, and who were now the "population" of the "Occupied Palestinian Territory" (OPT)—in Israeli parlance referred to as the "Administered Territories" or "Judea and Samaria." As tentative reconnections ensued, it became apparent that on each side of the 1949 Armistice "Green Line," a different variant of Palestinian Arab identity had emerged. Nonetheless, both communities soon came to share similar experiences of Israeli segregation, discrimination and military rule,[12] or simply what it meant to be a Palestinian under Israeli rule. Palestinians from Israel were allowed to move with relative ease to the West Bank and Gaza (and vice versa for Palestinians from the OPT), and this led to some Israeli experts on Arab affairs at an early stage in this "reconnection" expressing concern at the "Palestinization" of Arab Israelis. Perhaps the strongest bond between Palestinians lay in their shared experience of the *Nakba*, expressed by both groups comfortable with the term "Arabs of 1948"[13] alongside those in the West Bank and Gaza who came to be known as "Arabs of 1967"[14]

Under military rule, traditional Arab politicians with family and communal power bases had constituted the municipal and parliamentary extensions of the Israeli political and security establishment within Palestinian society.[15] By the 1970s, two powerful political currents had gained footholds in the Arab political system after waging struggles mainly through the mass/popular level of support for Palestinian civil and political rights in Israel and of Arabism, especially during the heyday of Egyptian president Gamal Abdel Nasser (an icon for most Arabs in Israel, regardless of political faction).

The Communist Party of Israel was the main legally tolerated, publicly active framework for mobilizing Palestinians against Zionist parties. Prior to 1948, the Communist Party pursued a strategy of promoting joint Jewish-Arab class struggle and recognized as legitimate the claim of Jewish (Israeli) statehood. Its development and outlook was shaped both by its compromise with Zionism as well as its links to global and regional Communist and pro-Soviet tendencies and ever-changing alliances with rival Arab Nationalist (and Nasserist and Baathist) movements. It organized workers, peasants, students and women within a broad front of sympathizers and "fellow travellers," in the only legal framework for Arab, non-Zionist mobilization.

At the same time, a less centrally organized, more diffuse tendency emerged that was rooted in Arabist/nationalist ideology, a rejection of the State of Israel, and a resistance program that went beyond the "democracy and rights" championed by the Communists, and which was willing to act outside the constraints of Israeli law. This political tendency attempted to organize legally in the 1960s in different configurations under the *Al-Ard* (The Land) newspaper (and subsequently Movement, Company, Association). But their efforts to go public or broaden their popular base were banned and the leaders of the movement imprisoned, harassed, exiled or neutralized over the years. Only with the formation of *Abnaa al Balad* (Sons of the Village) at the grassroots level in the 1970s and the Progressive Movement in the 1980s at the national level did this significant political tendency find legal organizational expression for its Arab nationalist, anti-Zionist beliefs.

The events of "Land Day" in 1976 marked a turning point in the development of political awareness amongst Palestinians in Israel who, in their protest at land confiscation and Judaization of the Galilee, gained a new respect and recognition in the Arab world and among their Palestinian brethren. To counter an Israeli plan of large-scale land seizures to accommodate Jewish settlement expansion in the Galilee, in a hitherto unseen show of unity, Palestinian community leaders and factions called for a general strike, which developed into mass demonstrations around the country.[16] In the villages of Sakhnin, Arrabeh, Deir Hanna and elsewhere, the events turned violent when the Israeli military unleashed an assault that killed a number of demonstrating Palestinian citizens.

The ramifications of this confrontation were far-reaching within the community. It helped to bring to the forefront a new leadership at the local and parliamentary level, dominated by the Israeli Communist Party within a "Democratic Front" formation, alongside a reinvigorated Palestinian Arab nationalist trend which had until then been largely clandestine. The events also redefined the sense of injustice and exclusion that Palestinian Arabs in Israel continued to experience, despite official pretenses of granting equal rights.

Writing in the wake of Land Day, Mark Tessler spoke of an "identity crisis" among the Palestinian citizens of Israel.[17] Another Israeli social scientist, Sammy Smooha, similarly argued that based on his own survey research at the time, "Israelization" had been succeeding over "Palestinization."[18] Rather than cultural assimilation, this process was, for Smooha, about the intensified struggle of the Palestinians in Israel for equal rights within the Israeli framework, not outside it.

But for all the apparent localization (or domestication) of Palestinian politics in Israel through a relaunching of a Palestinian (nationalist) project inside Israel (albeit framed in terms of civil and political rights), subsequent years witnessed an accelerated "nationalization" of their struggle as they associated themselves with their Palestinian compatriots' struggle. Land Day has since been commemorated in an annual day of protest held on 30 March within

Palestinian communities inside and outside Palestine. Land Day also marked the historic moment that the different PLO factions, each from its ideological or political vantage point, began to consider the Palestinians in Israel a significant component in the Palestinian struggle.

Networking and organizational contacts between Arab political forces and parties in Israel and the different Palestinian factions expanded after the late 1970s, in a way that relinked Palestinians within a broader framework for the first time since 1948. Until Oslo at least, the dynamics of Palestinian "nationalization" of Arab political formations in Israel were very much geared to what appeared to be a joint struggle, waged simultaneously for all Palestinians everywhere by all Palestinians everywhere.

THE BITTER FRUITS OF OSLO

Despite the debates centered around the "Israelization" of the Arab minority prior to Oslo, recognition of the Palestinians in Israel as a national minority became one of the key debates that emerged amongst the Palestinians in Israel in the wake of the Accords.[19] In assessing Oslo at the time, Tamim Mansour argued that peace should start with the citizens of the Israeli state, by recognizing the Palestinians in Israel as a national minority.[20] As understood since by Hassan Jabareen, the director of Adalah, the Palestinian legal center in Israel, Oslo pushed the Palestinians in Israel toward defining themselves as a national minority for the first time, and in the direction of seeking civil liberties and group rights protection, in line with the international rise in concern with minority human rights.[21]

This view of Palestinians in Israel constituting a national minority is shared by many of the Arab MKs and activists interviewed for this study. According to *Meretz* Party MK, Issawi Freij: "Today we define ourselves as a national minority that has national rights. We also have a unified national identity and we must struggle for civil rights by using the parliamentary tools that are available for us as a minority to achieve our rights."[22] *Balad* Party MK Hanin Zoabi concurs that Palestinians defining themselves as a national minority is a result of the internal awakening of the Palestinians in Israel since Oslo.[23]

Other politicians, such as Mohamad Zidan, explicitly link the exclusion of Palestinians in Israel from the peace process to the "shift toward struggling for our equality and rights."[24] He laments the fact that although the Palestinians in Israel put a lot of effort into supporting the Palestinian cause, the PLO excluded them from the peace process and Israel continued to victimize them as a minority. Issam Makhoul, a key Communist Party leader in the 1990s and former MK, further supports the view that "as a minority we must struggle for gaining our rights as a national minority and achieving equality in the level of civil and national rights."[25] As a result, the struggle for civic rights became a more distinct, achievable goal for the Palestinian minority after Oslo, especially after hopes were dashed by the assassination of Israeli prime minister Yitzhak Rabin in 1995.[26]

Some Israeli observers and Palestinians in Israel shared a perception that the results of Oslo (i.e., peace) might imply for them greater equality and opportunity in the State of Israel. However, disillusionment with Oslo amongst Palestinians in Israel was quick to materialize. When Arab voters saw themselves again being co-opted by the Israeli left to vote for Yitzhak Rabin in 1992 and to help form what became the "Oslo two-state solution by negotiations consensus," it was clear that there would be no real change in the role and position of the Arab minority. As Sherry Lowrance highlights, marginalizing ethnic minorities only increases inter-communal tensions, so incorporating them into the body politic is important for stabilizing state-minority relations, in this case the body being that of Israel, not Palestine.[27]

The stance of the Israeli State toward the status of its Arab population in the peace equation was not at odds with the position of what the world, and now Israel, recognized as the "sole, legitimate representative of the Palestinian people." The PLO had laid aside the needs and aspirations of the Palestinian community in Israel during the negotiations, thus effectively accepting that their fate was an issue to be resolved within the framework of the sovereign State of Israel. This may have surprised some Palestinians in Israel and elsewhere, but ever since, in 1974, the PLO adopted the two-state solution focused on liberating the 1967 occupied territory, this meant effectively leaving the case of Palestinians inside Israel to some undefined future.

While strong relations developed nevertheless over the following twenty years, these were less about a shared fate than about constituting an allied struggle. The alliance entailed brave slogans that described Palestinians in Israel as "an inseparable part of the Palestinian people" and no doubt supporting Palestinian political and other activism in Israel served a useful nuisance value at least in PLO strategies. However, from the moment that both allies agreed to work toward the goal of "two states for two peoples," it was only a matter of time before the PLO-Israel track focused on the occupied territory was formally divorced from that of the Palestinian Arab struggle in Israel for equality and rights.

Certainly at Oslo the PLO maintained its representative status for Palestinians in the Diaspora through keeping the refugee return issue on the agenda (for later negotiation). However, in doing so it sacrificed any implicit claim to represent Palestinians in Israel, for recognizing Israel in 1993 meant accepting it for what it constituted then (and formally represented, including its "minority Arab" citizens). After Oslo, the PLO counselled their Palestinian "brethren" to play an active role through campaigning for peace from within Israeli politics. By leaving the Palestinians in Israel outside the framework of Oslo, the PLO and Israel pushed the minority to deal with their own politics and affairs.

Elie Rekhess notes that once the PLO started to focus on building a Palestinian state in the OPT (through the vehicle of the Palestinian Authority), "the Palestinian leadership, for its part, did not incorporate the political leadership of the Arabs in Israel as a partner in the political process."[28] However, the flipside of this is that nor were they full players in the Israeli political game. As Raja Khalidi points out, while Palestinians in Israel were "abandoned politically by the Palestinian national movement and its authority in the occupied territories, they remain on the margin of Israeli politics, society, and culture."[29] Others perceive the PLO stance regarding the Palestinians in Israel as ambiguous, despite their solidarity and support for the Palestinian cause for many years. Yezid Sayigh explained this ambiguity by arguing that, since 1993 the PLO has adopted a contradictory stance toward the Palestinians in Israel. Sometimes, the PLO encouraged the Palestinians in Israel to vote for peace through supporting the Labor Party, while also trying not to appear as if they were intervening in Israeli politics. But neither did the PLO invest its political capital in unifying the Arab parties so they could become a significant political force in Israeli politics.[30]

Some Palestinian officials, however, more candidly acknowledge that the PLO left the minority out of the framework of the peace process. A former Palestinian Authority minister and diplomat, Hind Khoury, explains: "it is true that Oslo ignored the Palestinians inside Israel, because Oslo was a compromise, because we were losing and did not think critically about our cause."[31] Indeed, as Alexander Kouttab and Mattia Toaldo point out, since Oslo, the Palestinians in Israel "no longer factor in any meaningful way in the decisions taken by the Palestinian leadership."[32]

Some Palestinian politicians in Israel during the 1990s were critical of their exclusion from Oslo, with Mohamad Zidan noting that "we struggled for many years for the Palestinian cause, and today our role in the peace process is nothing."[33] According to Salih Lutfi of the Islamic Movement in Israel, which was critical of the PLO for marginalizing the role of Palestinians in Israel within the movement, the "disaster of Oslo" was that the PLO chairman, Yasser Arafat, decided that he no longer cared about the Palestinians in Israel and instead preferred for the Palestinian minority to play a significant role in Israeli politics.[34] But there was another stream of thought, as exemplified by Sami Abu Shehada, a member of Tel Aviv Municipality and representative of Yaffa and a member of *Balad*, who argued that, "as Palestinians in Israel, we had looked at the PLO as a body that will deal with our problem once there is a possibility for resolving the conflict."[35]

As it became clear that the PLO was moving toward a peace deal with Israel, Jamal Zahalka, a *Balad* Party MK, argues that the feeling of the Palestinian Arab minority after Oslo was that "the PLO abandoned us." Zahalka notes that the immediate political shift among the Palestinians in Israel was that more joined the Labor Party and supported Rabin as a peace-maker.[36] Feelings of exclusion and being left out were more common, however, as expressed by Haneen Zoabi, a *Balad* MK, who states: "the PLO had excluded us from the struggle. You see this very clearly in the Oslo Accords. In Oslo they didn't mention us . . . the PLO treated us as an internal Israeli issue."[37]

Israel has continued since Oslo to regard the Palestinians in Israel as an internal issue and therefore they are not seen as part of the peace process. Hassan Jabareen summarizes the Israeli approach, explaining that, for Israel, "the Green Line is a matter of Israeli internal sovereignty, and thus, the status of Israel's Palestinian citizens is not part of the Oslo accords."[38] According to Israeli perceptions, Palestinian refugees, the Palestinians in the OPT and those in Israel face a different fate.[39]

After Oslo, the PLO continued to play an indirect role in the political activism of the Palestinians in Israel, encouraging them to strengthen their impact in the Israeli political system by unifying in one Arab parliamentary bloc. The PLO always sent representatives to attend Arab party conferences and mass meetings, with a message that stressed this strategy. A PLO representative to one such conference in Kafr Qara' said in 1995 that "as Palestinians we want to see more Arab MKs in the Knesset. It is important that the Arab parties get unified in one single party. Our main request is for an Arab unified party list for the next election."[40] The Palestinians in Israel were therefore invited only to celebrate Oslo, but not to be part of it. Jafar Farah, the head of Mossawa (a civil society organization promoting equal rights) confirms that after 1993 "the Palestinian leadership's language toward the Palestinian minority in Israel started to change, telling them clearly to step aside."[41]

Nevertheless, PLO representatives frequently visited Israel to share their achievement with the Palestinian minority. PLO/PA officials also attended the conferences of Arab parties as a gesture of reciprocal support and solidarity. For example, PLO officials were invited to attend the 1994 conference of the Arab Democratic Party, including the ministers of Awqaf and Justice, both of whom stressed the pre-Oslo message that all Palestinians are one community, including the Palestinians in Israel.[42] For example, in September 1994, PLO leader (now PA president) Mahmoud Abbas was hosted in Deir al-Asad, Acre and Haifa, in meetings that included leaders of the Palestinian Arabs in Israel. Abbas referred to his visit as a historic moment that symbolized the breaking of the borders between the Palestinians in the West Bank and Gaza and in Israel.[43] Arab leaders from Israel, including political figures and heads of councils and MKs, visited the OPT for the purpose of greeting Yasser Arafat upon his return to Gaza in 1994.[44] Naqabi delegations from southern Israel congratulated him for signing the peace process, while one of their leaders, Shaikh Suleiman Mustafa al-Nasasrah from the town of Rahat, delivered a speech in front of the PLO/PA leadership in Ramallah.[45]

A common program between the PLO and Palestinians in Israel may have been abandoned since Oslo, however mass protests often erupt in Arab towns in solidarity with the Palestinian cause, such as during the Intifada in October 2000 and more recently in the wake of confrontations in Gaza or Jerusalem in 2014 and 2015/2017. Most recently, in July 2017, massive demonstrations erupted in Arab towns in Israel in support of the protests at the al-Aqsa mosque in Jerusalem, provoked by the erection of metal detectors at the entrance. The act of supporting the Palestinian cause continued in December 2017, after demonstrations took place in Arab towns all over Israel against US president Donald Trump's recognition of Jerusalem as the capital city of Israel. Political statements were released by the Joint List and many other Palestinian political activists, rejecting this decision, instead insisting that East Jerusalem is the capital city of Palestine.

ECONOMIC EXCLUSION AND DISINTEGRATION

Any hopes that Oslo would lead to an improvement in the economic conditions of the Palestinian Arabs in Israel have yet to be realized. In fact, the historic economic exclusion and disintegration faced by Palestinians in Israel continues. Israeli policies regard the issue of Arab economic growth in Israel as an integrated subtheme of national development and modernization, de-linked from the issues related to the conflict since 1948 or those arising from the occupation of 1967. Despite continuing Israeli narratives of "integrating" the Arab economy, a policy stance of neglect feeds economic disintegration. Today, there is a high level of frustration amongst young Arabs in Israel, as many get training and education but find certain sectors of the job market effectively blocked. Even recent OECD reports, conducted to comply with Israel's new membership in the Organization, show that the Arabs in Israel are far from being integrated into the Israeli economy and constitute the bulk of its poorest population.[46]

The majority of the literature presents a bleak image of the state of the Arab minority's economic "integration" in Israel, characterized by poverty, discrimination and a lack of development opportunities.[47] As analyzed by

Shehadeh and Khalidi, although the participation of the Arab minority in the Israeli economy has increased since 1948 and progress has been made in absolute terms, its status does not reflect "integration, inclusion or benevolence" but rather the "segregation, marginalization and neglect" that created an economic dependency on the Jewish economy."[48]

In 2006, Arabs made up almost 20 percent of the Israeli population, but the Arab regional economy accounted for less than 8 percent of GNP,[49] and in 2015 only 3.5 percent of the industrial zone areas in Israel were in Arab communities. In 2014, the average poverty rate for Israeli families was 29 percent, but the poverty rate among Israel's Arab citizens was 57 percent.[50] While some Israeli commentators emphasize that the Netanyahu government has invested "probably more than many other governments" in the Arab minority, they are the first to acknowledge that "this has not led to a real economic integration and improvement."[51]

Economic growth in the Palestinian-Arab sector is stunted by discriminatory policies, for example the water quotas have "always been lower than those of Israeli collective farms and Kibbutzim."[52] Autonomous Arab productive capacity has been systematically limited and the State has controlled access to capital and knowledge.[53] Jewish and state interests are protected by ensuring that the building up of a Palestinian-Arab economy and market that can compete globally, regionally or even locally is "practically impossible."[54] Discriminatory economic policies have produced a de-developed Arab economy in Israel.[55] De-development, Sara Roy explains, involves a stronger dominant economy and a weaker subordinate one. The process of de-development "not only distorts the development process [of the weaker economy] but undermines it entirely."[56]

The low participation of Palestinian-Arabs in the Israeli labor force has been attributed to a low quality of education. Since 2008, government initiatives have been introduced purportedly to address this issue, and the 2016 OECD report for Israel affirms that raising the educational attainment of Arab students is essential for economic progress. While some indicators show that Palestinian-Arab students advanced faster between 2006 and 2012 than their Jewish counterparts,[57] this has yet to translate into improved economic status. The majority of Arab workers remain, as always, concentrated in the lowest-skilled occupational strata. In 2013, more than 50 percent of the employed Arab labor force were working as manual laborers, whilst only 24 percent of Jews filled such jobs.[58] The 2016 OECD report also states that since 2008 there has been increased resource allocation in housing, education and public transport,[59] but this has not improved the economic situation of the Palestinians in Israel. In December 2015, the largest ever government plan to advance the economic development of Israel's Arab population was approved by the cabinet.[60] The proposal called for $3.86 billion to be devoted to developing infrastructure, industry and health care over the following five years and to fill gaps between Israeli Jews and Arabs, including the disparity in industrial zones and public transport.

However, there is lingering scepticism as to the commitment behind these government initiatives. Many lawmakers and public figures express doubts that the latest plan would be implemented, due to rising tensions with the Palestinian-Arab minority and paralysis in the peace process, with some claiming that it was essentially motivated by a desire to increase policing in Arab communities.[61] Increased law enforcement in Arab communities is a "condition" for the funding, and addressing this, Netanyahu stated that no development projects can move forward "if we do not address the question of enforcing the laws of the State of Israel in the Arab sector."[62]

The OECD membership requirement and the pressures exerted by global economic developments are driving factors for improving and integrating the Arab economy in Israel. Another reason stated in the OECD report is that the state's two poorest demographic groups, Arabs and Haredi Jews, are "predicted to account for half the population by 2060"[63] and hence their full economic potential needs to be tapped.[64]

While acknowledging that Israel may indeed be obliged to venture where it has not dared go before (i.e., to bring the Arab economy up to OECD levels), Khalidi and Shehadeh expect that the integration of the Arab population into the Israeli economy will continue to fail.[65] A broad body of research produced within a "non-Zionist political economy" tradition shows how the state-building policy within an exclusionary and discriminatory context has created structural impediments to the political, social and economic integration of Palestinian Arabs in Israel. This means "visible ceilings" for Arab economic advancement and has led to a separate Palestinian-Arab *regional* economy that is "marginalised, impoverished and largely subservient" to the *national* Jewish/Zionist economy.[66] Shehadeh and Khalidi see two "divided and disconnected" economies: "the globalised, modern and advanced Jewish-Israeli economy and the localised and largely underdeveloped Arab economy."[67] They also highlight areas where integration is actually decreasing. For example, the increasing use of foreign labor in areas once dominated by Palestinian-Arab workers, such as construction and agriculture, is pushing them out of these economic sectors. Similarly, where Palestinian-Arab agriculture once played a role, water quotas, land confiscation and the development of highly capitalized *kibbutzim* has dwarfed Arab agriculture and prevented it from playing a part in an integrated economy.[68]

Where some Israeli commentators point to Arab human development in Israel as evidence of integration, Khalidi argues that these success stories represent an indigenous, localized economic advancement generated by "prolonged and dire hardship,"[69] whereby Israeli settlement and separation policies have resulted in fragmenting the Palestinian economy. Such economic outcomes are another unintended dimension of entrenching "indigeneity and localization" of the Arab minority in Israel. Sara Roy describes the "severing" of the Palestinian Arabs in Israel from the fate of the Palestinians in the occupied territory as a "defining economic feature of the post-Oslo period," which accelerated the process of de-development of the Arab economy in Israel by introducing "new dynamics that have further attenuated an already diminished socioeconomic base."[70]

Shalhoub-Kevorkian, Woodsum, Zu'bi and Busbridge have criticized the colonial and orientalist lens used to blame Arab and Muslim culture as being the cause and main hindrance to their full participation in the economy.[71] Regarding low economic participation and oppression as the product of religion and culture, rather than the product of historical and political forces, is a key feature of paternalistic and orientalist assumptions about how best to integrate the Arab population into the economy. In her analysis of Israeli state policies toward the Bedouin community, Shalhoub-Kerkovian argues that by focusing on cultural factors of supposed "backwardness," such assumptions serve "to centralize Jewish Israeli society as the model of modernity to which Bedouin people ought to conform,"[72] "locking them into an overall and explicit situation of de-development and slow erasure."[73]

While it is essential to document the continued economic problems of the Palestinian Arabs in Israel, Khalidi notes that Oslo also helped to create a more autonomous, indigenous and localized Arab economy, describing the Arabs in Israel in the wake of the Oslo Accords as pursuing a "self-reliant" and regional socioeconomic development strategy powered from within.[74] Moreover, economic exchanges have been "legitimized and expanded" resulting in the reconnection of fragmented Arab regional economies through a cross-border framework, highlighting a reforming Palestinian Arab shared identity.[75]

It is evident, for example, that economic and social relationships have been traditionally very intense between the Naqab and the region of Hebron. Consistently through the 1990s, Bedouin were traveling to Hebron for shopping and contributed to the development of the city's economy, but the harsh conditions in the old city of Hebron and the restrictions on movements between Israel and the West Bank have meant that business relations have recently developed differently, possibly even reversing. West Bank universities, for example Hebron, Nablus and Al Quds, also represent an important resource when it comes to higher education for Palestinians in Israel. Most Arab students in Israel study at Israeli universities and overseas, but there are also thousands who study in the West Bank; for example Hebron attracts a lot of female students from the Naqab.

ARAB POLITICAL PARTIES IN ISRAEL AND THE ROOTS OF SUPPORT FOR A TWO-STATE SOLUTION

The stance of the Palestinian Arab political parties in Israel toward the Israeli-Palestinian conflict has tracked the historical development of the main political trends in the region and the broader Palestinian national movement, while being shaped by the specific status and conditions of being Arab citizens of the Jewish State. As discussed by Sa'di and more recently by Nasasra, in the early years of the state, Palestinian national consciousness was actively suppressed, indeed outlawed, and under military rule until the mid-1960s Palestinians were not able to develop distinctly Arab institutions or political movements. Prominent Palestinian family leaders were allowed to form an "Arab List" that was part of the ruling *Mapai* party electoral slate (which later became the Labor Party) until the 1970s.[76] Until the 1970s, the majority of Arab MKs entered the Knesset affiliated with *Mapai* or other Zionist parties.[77] Although *Mapai* was keen to recruit minority votes at election time, it never accepted Palestinian Arabs as regular active members of the party.[78]

The political agendas of most Arab parties and their stance on the Israeli-Palestinian conflict have always shared a common emphasis on the historical need for justice for the Palestinians, themselves included. But positions on the desirable form of a political solution and strategies have not always been similar, indeed it is only since Oslo that Arab parties have come to endorse (almost unanimously) the two-state goal, though with different emphases and degrees of enthusiasm. Polling in 2009 indicated that 74 percent of Palestinians living in Israel supported a two-state solution,[79] while a 2017 poll showed that this had dropped to 44 percent, with the one-state alternative supported by only 26 percent of Palestinians in Israel.[80]

Regardless of the percentages, the basic premise of Arab parties' political programs today is support for a "two states for two peoples" within the context of a "just solution" of the "Question of Palestine."[81] Presenting a different view, Asad Ghanem considers that "Palestinians in Israel are the only group of Palestinians calling already for bi-nationality."[82] Support by the Palestinian Arab minority for a two-state solution has not always been unanimous, and as the polls cited above indicate, appears to be declining. Certainly, the Israeli Communist Party has been consistent in its "two-statism," indeed it could only have ever existed as a legal entity by recognition of the legitimacy of the State of Israel. This was always part of a broader program that emphasized Palestinian Arab national rights, in strict adherence to the underlying principles of the 1947 UN Partition Plan.

The only historically Jewish-Arab party, with roots going back to 1921 in Palestine, began as a pro-Soviet Jewish party that gradually attracted Arab members. Mustafa Kabha relates how, after different episodes of ideological conflict in the party, it was re-established as the Israeli Communist Party in 1949 (first called *Maki*, then *Rakah*, and today known as *Hadash*). Since its establishment, the party has been the most suitable legal vehicle for Palestinians in Israel who sought a platform for nationalist struggle albeit framed in the language and ideology of the socialist left.[83]

Hadash is today the core of the Democratic Front for Peace and Equality (DFPE), and continues, as it has since 1948, to support a two-state solution and equal rights for Palestinians in Israel.[84] Their agenda clearly states that there can be no peace without the dismantling of the Israeli settlements in the OPT, full withdrawal from the OPT, and a just solution for the Palestinian refugees in accordance with UN resolutions. They believe in the need for a united Jewish-Arab front for achieving peace, equality and democracy.[85] Since the 1980s, the party newspaper *al-Ittihad* has reported on the Party's meetings and solidarity with the PLO leadership in exile and its vigorous campaigning for a two-state solution.[86]

Meanwhile, the *Al-Ard* movement that emerged after 1960 was Palestinian-patriotic, pan-Arab nationalist and pro-Arab socialism.[87] It attracted those Palestinians who had only (grudgingly) accepted the existence of the State of Israel as a fact of life, rather than upholding the legitimacy of the Jewish State legally conceived by the UN in 1947 and accepted formally as a member in 1949. Effectively *Al-Ard* embodied the continuation of the same Arab nationalist trend that had opposed the partition of Mandate Palestine in principle and had remained unconvinced that it was a just or acceptable resolution to the situation. This was along the same lines as the PLO at the time which advocated a secular democratic unitary state (as defined by the 1964 National Charter). However, *Al-Ard*'s attempts to form legal organizations were refused and declared illegal, despite an appeal to the Supreme Court to register as a party.[88] Their attempts to field a list for the 1965 Knesset elections were blocked as well.[89] Although *Al-Ard* did not use or advocate violence against the State, it was harassed by security agencies and effectively prevented from functioning publicly.[90]

Banning *Al-Ard* in the 1960s contributed to the emergence of other manifestations of the same political trend, especially *Abnaa al-Balad* in the 1970s. As argued by one of the later leaders of the movement, *Abnaa al-Balad* was also nationalistic and had strong support amongst Arab students, rooted in the tradition of *Al-Ard*.⁹¹ As a movement amongst the Palestinians in Israel, *Abnaa al-Balad* associated itself with the PLO.⁹² *Abnaa al-Balad* supported the right of return for Palestinian refugees, and regarded the PLO to be the sole legitimate representative of the Palestinian people. It boycotted participation in the Israeli parliamentary system, focusing efforts instead at the student and local authority levels. In analyzing the ideological development from *Al-Ard* to *Abnaa al-Balad*, a current leader of the latter, Awad Abed al-Fatah, argues that while "*Al-Ard* emphasised Arab identity within Israel and pan-Arab nationalism, *Abnaa al-Balad* focused on Palestinian nationalism under the slogan 'Palestine our homeland.'"⁹³

Another joint Arab-Jewish party was spawned by the *Al-Ard* legacy in the new realities of the 1980s. Launched nationally in 1984, the Progressive Movement and its joint Arab-Jewish electoral slate, the Progressive List for Peace (PLP) was spearheaded by one of *Al-Ard*'s founders, Mohamad Mi'ari. The PLP was the first legal political party outside of the DFPE to declare full solidarity with the Palestinian cause.⁹⁴ In 1983, it secured four seats in the Nazareth elections and went on to consolidate itself as a new political force amongst Palestinians in Israel. In 1984, unifying with Jewish candidates headed by a former army general, Matti Peled,⁹⁵ the party won two seats in the 11th Knesset elections,⁹⁶ but only after it had successfully appealed to the Supreme Court to allow its participation.⁹⁷ Despite its leader being a Jewish MK, the PLP was perceived as a Palestinian nationalist movement that demanded Palestinian collective rights and autonomy within Israel and proposed a pragmatic agenda as the starting point for addressing the Palestinian Arab situation in Israel.⁹⁸ The PLP was keen to demonstrate its Palestinian nationalist credentials and connections, no less privileged than those enjoyed by the DFPE, flaunting its meetings with PLO representatives and leaders in meetings in Tunis and in Europe.

In 1988, the next Arab party established was the Arab Democratic Party, headed by Abdel Wahab Darawsha previously affiliated with *Mapai*. Darawsha refers to his decision to establish the "first recognized parliamentary Arab party in Israel" in 1988 as having been directly linked to his support for the two state solution; "after a number of years of being a member of Zionist parties, I came to a conclusion to establish an Arab party that would struggle for the civil rights of the Arab minority and put an end to the Israeli occupation that would guarantee establishing a Palestinian state in the West Bank and Gaza, including Arab Jerusalem as its capital."⁹⁹

In the wake of the 1992 elections, which brought the Labor government that signed the Oslo Accords to power, the PLP was disbanded after its voter base was fractured by the emergence of new Arab electoral lists. As Palestinians in Israel began to come to terms with their exclusion from Oslo, 1996 witnessed the emergence of new parties: the Islamic Movement (southern branch); *Balad*; and an electoral list headed by Ahmad Tibi. The new post-Oslo political climate (whereby support for the PLO was no longer illegal) marked a shift toward new forms of political expression and the consolidation of distinctly Arab political formations, as well as spurring a debate on waging elections as one unified bloc.[100]

The *Balad* list was a fusion of the wing of *Abnaa Al-Balad* that was not opposed in principle to participation in Israeli national elections and the remnants of the PLP. It chose as its leader the young, charismatic academic Azmi Bishara, who became a dominant figure in Palestinian and Arab regional politics thereafter. *Balad* contributed to creating a discourse comprised of two themes concerned with the Palestinians living as Israeli citizens: identity and citizenship, and difference and similarity. Bishara used these concepts to campaign for Palestinian cultural autonomy within Israel.[101] One of the main objectives of *Balad* was to obtain collective rights in Israel for all citizens and cultural autonomy for Arabs and Jews.[102]

Balad MK, Jamal Zahalka, confirms that "once *Balad* was established, we adopted the Palestinian national movement approach. We support a Palestinian state based on 1967 borders, dismantling the settlements and the right for Palestinian refugees to return to their homes (including inside Israel)." *Balad* also has popularized the idea of an Israeli "state for all its citizens," which became a significant rallying cry, but was regarded by the majority of Zionist parties as a challenge to the recognition of Israel as a Jewish state with certain privileges reserved purely for its Jewish citizens.[103]

A similar view of the Palestinian-Israeli conflict characterizes the political agenda of the Arab Movement for Change, headed by Ahmad Tibi, an Arab politician in Israel who worked closely for many years as an advisor on Israeli affairs to PLO chairman and first PA president, Yasser Arafat.

In 1996, the Islamic Movement (Southern Branch) established a legal political party. Though founded in the 1970s, it split into two branches in 1996 over the principle of participating in national elections, and its Northern Branch based in Umm Al Fahem continued to operate outside parliamentary politics. The Northern Branch of the movement is considered more of a civil society movement, and its leader Shaikh Raad Salah is noted as a campaigner for Islamic heritage and collective rights in Israel and Jerusalem.[104] From its inception, the Islamic Movement has focused on local municipal elections as the most effective method to improve the situation of the Arab minority.[105] The Southern Branch of the movement, headed by Shaikh Abdallah Darwish, regarded the Knesset as an avenue for improving the situation of the Arab municipalities, especially by obtaining equal budgets,[106] arguing that the interests of the Palestinian community in Israel would be best served through national representation. Shaikh Abdallah Nimer Darwish, the Movement's founder, supported Oslo, whereas the northern faction opposed the Accords, an important factor in the 1996 split.[107] According to the Northern Branch views, the disaster of Oslo was that Arafat no longer assumed the responsibility of the cause of the Palestinians in Israel and instead supported efforts by the Arab minority to participate in Israeli politics.[108]

Reviewing their political agenda, both wings of the Islamic Movement call for a just solution for the Palestinians, for East Jerusalem to be the Palestinian capital, for a two-state solution on the 1967 borders, and for the right of the Palestinian refugees to return home. While the (southern) Islamic Movement has mobilized enough votes for two Knesset seats since the late 1990s, the Northern Branch has vigorously campaigned in defense of Al-Aqsa mosque and for the right of Palestinian refugees to return to their historical villages and regain their property within the 1948 borders.[109]

After frequent Israeli attempts to restrict the Islamic Movement's activities, in November 2015 it was declared illegal, overruling the reservations of the Israeli General Security Services. This raised many questions about the vacuum left behind, mainly regarding who would run its hundreds of projects in Arab towns and villages. As reported by the Movement's media sources, on the same day the Movement was banned, the police released orders to close 23 local services institutions affiliated with the Movement., including student, welfare and humanitarian organizations, thus affecting the ability of these organizations to provide support to the 23,000 children they serve.[110] A number of the Movement's leaders were also interrogated and arrested.

In 2015, the Joint List emerged as a new political force among the Palestinians in Israel, with clear support for the two-state solution. The head of the list, MK Ayman Odeh, stated clearly that: "Between the Jordan River and the Mediterranean there is an equal number of Palestinians and Jews, and that's nothing new. That's why the crossroads where we presently find ourselves is clear: either two states based on 1967, or one state that is an apartheid state, or one democratic state in which everyone has the right to vote. There is no other option, and at least this simple truth has to be stated clearly."[111]

THE JOINT LIST OF 2015 AS A NEW POLITICAL FORCE

The transformation of the Palestinian struggle in Israel into a distinct "local" Israeli issue took a significant step forward with the successful unity pact between all Arab parties, including those with some Jewish-Israeli members such as the DFPE and *Balad*, to stand for the 2015 Knesset elections. It was established after a long process of negotiation between the different parties, sped up by the change in electoral law, whereby lists have to receive 3.25 percent of the vote in order to qualify for the Knesset, compared to 2 percent before.[112] Commenting on this change in the electoral law, which was designed to limit the representation of Arab and leftist political parties, Islamic Movement MK Talab Abu Arar believes that "one day we will come to thank Avigdor Lieberman for unifying the Arab political forces in one single party."[113] Despite the different ideologies and agendas of the Arab parties, most Arab MKs supported returning to the Knesset as members of a unified list. For example, MK Tibi said "I am in favor of going to the Knesset in a unified list, this will increase the percentage of Arabs who will come to vote. . . . Even if we sit on the opposition, we are a political and national representation of the minority and the struggle against discrimination and for equal rights."[114]

Achieving a unified parliamentary list was not an easy task. For example, resistance by the Communist Party to unite within an "Arab" identity and with Islamist allies was an important obstacle that hindered the creation of the Joint List. However, this initial reluctance was overcome, although the term "Arab" was not agreed as part of the title.

The agreement of all Arab political parties on January 22, 2015, to establish the Joint List was an unprecedented breakthrough in terms of presenting a unified position and pragmatic political manoeuvring to maintain Palestinian-Arab national political representation. MK Yousef Jabareen noted that, for the first time, the List unified the Islamic, communist, and Arab nationalist trends which dominated Arab politics in Israel.[115] This successful model, led by the once marginal Palestinians in Israel, attracted attention from the Palestinians in the OPT and worldwide.[116] As Hoffman states, while the four Arab parties comprising the list have different political agendas and programs within the Arab minority in Israel, "their joint platform calls for a just peace based on UN resolutions, ending the occupation of all land Israel captured in 1967, dismantling all settlements and the security barrier, releasing all political prisoners and forming a Palestinian state with Jerusalem as its capital." [117] A 2016 interview with MK Jabareen confirms that the Joint List also supports "a two-state solution based on 1967 borders."[118]

With 13 of the 120 seats, this third largest slate in the Knesset in 2017 is perceived as an accomplishment that will ostensibly provide Palestinian Arabs in Israel with greater legislative power and influence. As was the case with Jewish supporters of the Communist Party and the PLP, some Jewish Israelis also voted for the Joint List as the only democratic option that could strive for a state of social justice and equality, and as the only party that represents both Jews and Palestinians.[119]

An important aspect of the Joint List's achievement was the strong voter turnout amongst the Palestinian Arab community it prompted (an increase of nearly 10 percent) and the increase in votes obtained compared to those Arab votes garnered by other Israeli parties in preceding years.[120] This has helped reverse the declining turnout of Arab voters, who did not vote either because they either supported the boycott on participating in Israeli elections or because they had little faith in the political system or the Arab parties.[121] One of the lasting political impacts of Oslo was that the percentage of Arabs voting for Zionist parties dropped dramatically. For example, in 1999 the percentage had dropped to 30 percent[122] and to 28 percent by 2003.[123] This is compared with over 50 percent of the Arab vote still captured by non-Arab parties in 1992.[124]

Since its recent success, the Joint List has actively campaigned against discriminatory laws, advocated for economic improvement and appealed to the international community. This has included meetings with top EU and US officials, in order to raise awareness of the Palestinian Arab situation in Israel. After a number of Israeli legislative measures that targeted Palestinian Arab civil society activism, international fora became a key avenue for Joint List efforts to counter discriminatory policies. In 2015, for instance, MK Tibi briefed UN and US Government officials and congressmen on the status of the Palestinian minority and the discrimination faced at many levels, focusing on issues such as limited allocation of public budgets, limited job opportunities, pressures on land and housing rights and specific problems faced by the Naqab Bedouin.[125] Leader and MK, Ayman Odeh, conducted similar missions, meeting international politicians across the spectrum.[126] MK Yousef Jabareen and representatives of a number of organizations met with top EU officials, campaigning against the legislation against the Arab minority in the Knesset, such as the Nation State Law, which emphasizes Israel as a Jewish state.

Apart from the Nation State Law and its impact on the Arab citizens of Israel, the Joint List has campaigned against many other legislations and discriminatory practices experienced by Palestinian citizens of Israel. For example, it continues to campaign against the Citizenship and Entry into Israel Law (Temporary Order) 2003, which restricts marriages between Palestinians in Israel with those with West Bank and Gaza IDs, which has been criticized by the UN Human Rights Committee as being disrciminatory.[127] It has also campaigned to have 15 May designated as a national (*Nakba*) day of mourning for Palestinians living in Israel. This is a highly contentious subject, with the Israeli state in 2009 withdrawing Israeli textbooks that referred to the *Nakba*, arguing that such language promoted anti-Zionist views.[128] And it has also put serious effort into support for the recognition of Naqab Bedouin villages. The Naqab context and the struggle against the Prawer Law, which has as its goal the relocation of some 40,000 Naqab Bedouin, helped to unify the Joint List in action and lessen internal disagreements.[129] On Land Day in 2016, the majority of the MKs of the List participated in a rally held in the unrecognized Naqab village of Um al Hiran, emphasizing the common struggle for the preservation of Bedouin land, recognition of the unrecognized villages in the Naqab and opposition to the Prawer Plan.[130] MK Yousef Jabareen stated, "The Naqab context and the struggle against Prawer helps to unify us. The urgent need to deal with the situation in the Naqab is more important than our internal disagreement on various issues."[131] While efforts to relocate the Bedouin community have not ceased, the population has mobilized, and is enjoying the support of the Joint List toward this aim.

While the Joint List signals a huge achievement in partnership and collaboration between the different parties that represent the Palestinian Arab community, it has faced numerous problems. Its MKs have been subject to police investigations, harassment and criminal indictment; as well as facing constant attempts to disqualify them from participating in Israeli parliamentary elections—actions taken largely by right-wing political parties and MKs.[132] The Joint List, along with Palestinians NGOs in Israel, have led the battle and criticisms against the Nation State Law that was passed in July 2018, which codified into Israeli law that only the Jewish people had the right to exercise national self-determination, downgraded Arabic from its previous status as an "official language" to one with "special status," and established "Jewish settlement as a national value." Odeh called it "a law of Jewish supremacy" and that with its passing into Israeli law the Palestinian minority would always be regarded as "second class citizens" in Israel.[133] In a significant move, and as a joint reaction to the Israeli Nation State Law, the Palestinians in Israel across the green line declared a one day general strike in October 2018.

CONCLUSION

This chapter has argued that a consensus has coalesced since Oslo that the Palestinian minority in Israel must continue its struggle as a national minority separately from the fate of the rest of the Palestinian Arab people represented by the PLO. While Oslo did not constitute a starting point for this process, it was a milestone in a process which has been underway since the 1970s. It accelerated processes of localization and focused minds on the Palestinian Arab struggle for equality, rights and political representation as citizens of the Israeli state. However, this process of localization occurred alongside the consolidation of identification with a broader Palestinian Arab national identity.

Politically, there have been historic changes: once-rival and mutually hostile Communist, Arab nationalist and Islamist political formations have achieved a rare electoral unity at the national level, taking Arab politics in Israel into a new dimension. As exemplified by the Joint List's campaigning, the focus of the struggle of Palestinian Arabs in Israel today is on collective civil rights, whilst being less implicated in the Palestinian-Israeli peace process. Since the Oslo Accords separated the minority from the peace process, there has been an indigenization (nationalization) of voting patterns in favor of Arab parties, compared to the Zionization of their past voting behavior.

The Palestinian Arabs in Israel thus increasingly stress their collective rights within Israel, focusing on their own affairs as a national indigenous minority. Results of a poll by the Israeli National Security Center found that 69 percent of Arabs in Israel surveyed said that the struggle that mattered most to them was the struggle for equality and rights as a minority.[134] While Palestinians in Israel are less directly affected by the fate of the Palestinian national cause in the OPT as codified and represented by the PLO, a 2016 poll conducted by the Arab research center Mada al-Carmel showed that resolving the conflict remains a key matter for all Palestinian communities: Palestinians in Gaza and the West Bank, refugees, and Palestinians in Israel. According to the poll, 60 percent of Palestinians in Israeli still support a two-state solution.[135]

Whereas the specific struggle for equality and rights of the Palestinian Arab citizens of Israel is paramount to their lives and future within the Jewish state, the struggle for Palestinian rights has become more an issue of solidarity and shared cause against a common foe. Sixty years of successful Jewish state-building has rendered Palestinians in Israel as citizens without equal or full rights and Palestinians under autonomy in the OPT but subject to Israeli control. Arguably, on both sides of the Green Line Israel has succeeded in localizing Palestinian politics and daily struggles, while keeping at bay nationalistic objectives for both the minority in Israel and for Palestinians living in the area of the putative State of Palestine.

ACKNOWLEDGMENTS

The author would like to thank Raja Khalidi for incisive comments on this chapter.

NOTES

1. With reference to those Palestinians who cooperated with the state, which presumes that the rest are "bad Arabs." Hillel Cohen, *Good Arabs: The Israeli Security Agencies and the Israeli Arabs, 1948–1967* (Berkeley: University of California Press, 2010).

2. For comparison, see Amal Jamal, "Twenty Years after the Oslo Accords: A Perspective on the Need for Mutual Ethical Recognition," *Rosa Luxemburg Stiftung in Israel* 12 (September 2013).

3. Ilan Pappé, *The Forgotten Palestinians: A History of the Palestinian Minority in Israel* (New Haven: Yale University Press, 2011), 45.

4. Mansour Nasasra, *The Naqab Bedouins: A Century of Bedouin Politics and Resistance* (New York: Columbia University Press, 2017).

5. Pappé, *The Forgotten Palestinians*, 24.

6. Ian Lustick, *Arabs in the Jewish State: Israel's Control of a National Minority* (Austin: University of Texas Press, 1980).

7. Nadera Shalhoub-Koverkian, *Security Theology, Surveillance and the Politics of Fear* (Cambridge: Cambridge University Press, 2015).

8. Ahmad Sa'di, *Thorough Surveillance: The Genesis of Israeli Policies of Population Management, Surveillance and Political Control toward the Palestinian Minority* (Manchester and New York: Manchester University Press, 2014), 43.

9. Sherry Lowrance, "Being Palestinian in Israel: Identity, Protest, and Political Exclusion," 5 December, 14 Policy Analysis, el-Palestine,ges to Israel and the Palestinian leadwrship beyond the Green Line, al Quds al Ar*Comparative Studies of South Asia, Africa and the Middle East* 25, no. 2 (2005), 487–499.

10. For comparison, see Ilan Saban, "Appropriate Representation of Minorities: Canada's Two Types Structure and the Arab-Palestinian Minority in Israel," *Penn State International Law Review* 24, no. 3 (2006), 1–41.

11. For comparison, see Sammy Smooha, *Arabs and Jews in Israel: Volume 2, Change and Continuity in Mutual Intolerance* (Boulder, CO: Westview, 1992).

12. Nasasra, *The Naqab Bedouins*.

13. At once meaning Arabs in that part of Palestine "occupied in 1948" (an ideological dimension) and Arabs living within the "1948 borders" of Israel (a geographic differentiation).

14. Laurence Louër, *To Be an Arab in Israel* (Paris: Editions Balland, 2007), 9.

15. Cohen, *Good Arabs*.

16. *The Black Book: Land Day, 30 March 1976* (Nazareth: Regional Committee for the Defense of Arab Lands in Israel, 1976).

17. Mark Tessler, "Israel's Arabs and the Palestinian Problem," *Middle East Journal* 31, no. 3 (1977), 313–329.

18. Sammy Smooha, *Israel: Pluralism and Conflict* (Berkeley and Los Angeles: University of California Press, 1978), 2.

19. *al-Ittihad*, October 11, 1994.

20. *al-Ittihad*, October 11, 1994.

21. Hassan Jabareen, "20 Years of Oslo: The Green Line's Challenge to the Statehood Project," *Journal for Palestine Studies* 43, no. 1 (2013), 44.
22. Interview with Issawi Freij. Rahat, February 28, 2015.
23. Interview with MK Hanin Zoabi. Jerusalem, February 11, 2014.
24. *Davar*, August 27, 1995.
25. Interview with Issam Makhoul. Haifa, February 10, 2014.
26. Majid al-Hajj, "Education Toward Multiculturalism in Light of the Peace Process." In Menachem Mautner et al. (eds.), *Multiculturalism in a Democratic and Jewish State* (Tel Aviv: Ramot, Tel Aviv University Press, 1998).
27. Lowrance, "Being Palestinian in Israel," 487.
28. Elie Rekhees, "The Arabs of Israel after Oslo: Localization of the National Struggle," *Israel Studies* 7, no. 3 (2002), 3.
29. Raja Khalidi, "Sixty Years after the UN Partition Resolution: What Future for the Arab Economy in Israel," *Journal of Palestine Studies* 37, no. 2 (2008), 6.
30. Yezid Sayigh, *Al-Hayat*, April 2, 2015. Issue no. 18990.
31. Interview with Hind Khouri. Jerusalem, September 19, 2014.
32. Alexander Kouttab et al., "In Search of Legitimacy: The Palestinian National Movement 20 Years After Oslo: Policy Brief," *European Council on Foreign Relations* (ECFR), no. 89 (2013), 4.
33. Mohamad Zidan, *Davar*, August 27, 1995.
34. Interview with Salih Lutfi. Umm al-Fahem, May 23, 2014.
35. Interview with Sami Abu Shehada. Yafa, November 20, 2014.
36. Interview with MK Jamal Zahalka. Jerusalem, December 4, 2014.
37. Interview with Hanin Zoabi, Balad MK. Jerusalem, February 11, 2014.
38. Jabareen, "20 Years of Oslo," 48.
39. Jamal, "Twenty Years after the Oslo Accords," 4.
40. Hassan Abu Saad, "Party Meeting in Beersheba," December 7, 1995, *Al Wifaq Private Paper*.
41. Interview with Jafar Farah. Musawa, Haifa, December 9, 2013.
42. Interview with 'Abed al-Wahab Darawsha.
43. *al-Ittihad*, September 14, 1994.
44. Rekhees, "The Arabs of Israel after Oslo," 2–4.
45. Sheikh Suleiman Mustafa al-Nasasrah, Private Collection, Rahat. Accessed December 10–20, 2016.
46. "OECD Economic Surveys. ISRAEL. January 2016. Overview," *Organisation for Economic Co-operation and Development* (OECD) (2016), 30. Accessed April 5, 2016. http://www.oecd.org/israel/economic-survey-israel.htm.
47. For comparison, see Sammy Smooha, "Minority Status in an Ethnic Democracy: The Status of the Arab Minority in Israel," *Ethnic and Racial Studies* 13, no. 3 (1990), 389–413.
48. Mtanes Shehadeh et al., "Impeded Development: The Political Economy of the Palestinian Arabs inside Israel." In Mandy Turner et al. (eds.), *Decolonizing Palestinian Political Economy: De-Development and Beyond* (New York: Palgrave Macmillan, 2014), 116–119.

49. Khalidi, "Sixty Years after the UN Partition Resolution," 19.

50. Eran Yashiv, "Key Challenges Facing the Israeli Economy and their Ramifications for National Security," *Strategic Assessment* 18, no. 4 (2016), 65.

51. Interview with Don Fotterman, Head of Moriah Fund. Kfar Saba, 15 June 2015.

52. Khalidi, "Sixty Years after the UN Partition Resolution," 15.

53. Shehadeh et al., "Impeded Development," 122.

54. Shehadeh et al., "Impeded Development," 133.

55. Sara Roy, "De-development Revisited: Palestinian Economy and Society Since Oslo," *Journal of Palestine Studies* 28, no. 3 (Spring, 1999), 64–82.

56. Roy, "De-development Revisited," 65.

57. "OECD Economic Surveys," *OECD*, 30.

58. Kav LaOved, "Arab Citizens of Israel and Work: Trends of Workplace Discrimination and Violation of Labour Rights," *Worker's Hotline*, Nazareth (2013), 8.

59. "OECD Economic Surveys," *OECD*, 14.

60. Jack Khoury et al., "Israel Looks to Address Funding Gaps for Arab Community With $3.9 Billion Plan," *Haaretz*, December 28, 2015. Accessed April 3, 2016. http://www.haaretz.com/israel-news/.premium-1.694090.

61. Stuart Winer, "Israel Okays $4 billion Upgrade Plan for Arab Communities," *Times of Israel*, December 30, 2015. Accessed October 15, 2016. http://www.timesofisrael.com/government-okays-nis-15b-upgrade-plan-for-arab-communities/.

62. "Cabinet Communication," January 10, 2016. *Israel Ministry of Foreign Affairs*. Accessed April 11, 2016. http://mfa.gov.il/MFA/PressRoom/2016/Pages/Cabinet-communique-10-January-2016.aspx.

63. "OECD Economic Surveys," *OECD*, 12.

64. Raja Khalidi et al., "Israel's 'Arab Economy.'" In Nadim Rouhana (ed.), *Israel and its Palestinian Citizens: Ethnic Privileges in the Jewish State* (Cambridge: Cambridge University Press, 2017).

65. Khalidi et al., "Israel's 'Arab Economy.'"

66. Khalidi, "Sixty Years after the UN Partition Resolution," 11–19.

67. Shehadeh et al., "Impeded Development," 122.

68. Shehadeh et al., "Impeded Development," 128.

69. Khalidi, "Sixty Years after the UN Partition Resolution," 16.

70. Roy, "De-development Revisited," 64.

71. Nadera Shalhoub-Kevorkian et al., "Funding Pain: Bedouin Women and Political Economy in the Naqab/Negev," *Feminist Economics* 20, no. 4 (2014), 165.

72. Shalhoub-Kevorkian, "Funding Pain," 177–78.

73. Shalhoub-Kevorkian, "Funding Pain," 171.

74. Khalidi, "Sixty Years after the UN Partition Resolution," 13–17.

75. Raja Khalidi et al., *Strengthening Trade and Economic Interaction Between Palestinians in the West Bank and Inside Israel: An Arab "North-North" Alternative to Israelization* (Bir Zeit: Bir Zeit University Centre for Development Studies, 2014).

76. For comparison, see Sa'di, *Thorough Surveillance*; Nasasra, *The Naqab Bedouins*.

77. For comparison, see Sa'di, *Thorough Surveillance*.

78. Interview with 'Abed al-Wahab Darawsha. Iksal, October 25, 2014.

79. "New Poll Finds: Two-State Solution is the Preferred Option for Majority of Israelis and Palestinians," *Palestinian Peace Coalition, Peace Library* (2009). http://www.geneva-accord.org/mainmenu/new-poll-finds-two-state-solution-is-the-preferred-option-for-majority-of-israelis-and-palestinians.

80. Wadea Awawda, "Polling Amongst the Palestinians in Israel Highlights Two Messages to Israel and the Palestinian Leadership Beyond the Green Line," *al-Quds al-Arabi*, February 16, 2017. http://www.alquds.co.uk/?p=675353 (accessed, 20 December 2017).

81. As termed since 1949 by the United Nations.

82. As'ad Ghanem, "Israel and the 'Danger of Demography,'" In Jamil Hilal (ed.), *Where Now for Palestine? The Demise of the Two-State Solution* (London: Zed Books, 2007), 68.

83. Mustafa Kabha, "The Historical Development of the Israeli Communist Party." In Areej Sabbagh-Khoury et al. (eds.), *The Palestinians in Israel: Reading in History, Politics and Society* (Haifa, Israel: Mada al Carmel, 2015).

84. Nadeem Rouhana et al., "Settler-colonial Citizenship: Conceptualizing the Relationship between Israel and its Palestinian Citizens," *Settler Colonial Studies and Israel–Palestine* 5, no. 3 (2015), 205–225.

85. Interview with Issam Makhoul. Haifa, February 2014.

86. Interview with Issam Makhoul. Haifa, February 2014.

87. L. Dallasheh, "Political Mobilization of Palestinians in Israel: The Movement al-Ard." In Rhoda Ann Kanaaneh et al. (eds.), *Displaced at Home: Ethnicity and Gender among Palestinians in Israel* (Albany: State University of New York Press, 2010), 21–38.

88. Sabri Jiryis, *The Arabs in Israel, 1948–1966* (Beirut, Lebanon: Institute for Palestine Studies, 1969).

89. Rouhana et al., "Settler-colonial Citizenship," 7.

90. Dallasheh, "Political Mobilization."

91. Interview with 'Awad Abed al Fatah, Balad party. Nazareth, February 25, 2015.

92. Muhanad Mustafa, "Abna al Balad Movement." In Sabbagh-Khoury et al., *The Palestinians in Israel*.

93. Interview with 'Awad Abed al Fatah, the current secretary of Tajamoa party. Nazareth, February 25, 2015.

94. Rouhana et al., "Settler-colonial Citizenship," 215.

95. Aziz Haidar, "The Progressive List," In Sabbagh-Khoury et al., *The Palestinians in Israel*.

96. Amal Jamal, "The Arab Leadership in Israel: Ascendance and Fragmentation," *Journal of Palestine Studies* 35, no. 2 (2006), 6–22.

97. Rouhana et al., "Settler-colonial Citizenship," 7–8.

98. Interview with 'Awad Abed al Fatah. Nazareth, February 25, 2014.

99. Personal memories of Abed al Wahab Darawsha In The Arab Democratic Party Booklet, Third Conference of the Arab Democratic Party in Nazareth, December 15–16, 1994, 71–72 (The Challenge for Peace, 2010).

100. Kul al 'Arab, December 15, 1996.
101. Raef Zreik, "The Palestinian Question: Themes of Justice and Power. Part II: The Palestinians in Israel," *Journal of Palestine Studies* 33, no. 1 (2003), 64.
102. Zreik, "The Palestinian Question," 46.
103. Interview with MK Jamal Zahalka. Jerusalem, December 4, 2014.
104. Craig Larkin et al., "In Defense of Al-Aqsa: The Islamic Movement Inside Israel and the Battle for Jerusalem," *Middle East Quarterly* 66, no. 1 (2012), 30–51.
105. Rubin Lawrence, "Islamic Political Activism in Israel," *Centre for Middle East Policy Analysis*, no. 32 (2014).
106. Shaikh Darwish. Interviewed by Ahmad Mansour, April 28, 1999. *Al-Jazeera*. http://www.aljazeera.net/home/print/0353e88a-286d-4266-82c6-6094179ea26d/d41e56fc-8a0b-451b-a0aa-a3c9fb7bf132 (accessed April 20, 2017).
107. As'ad Ghanem et al., "Explaining Political Islam: The Transformation of Palestinian Islamic Movements," *British Journal of Middle East Studies* 41, no. 4 (2014), 335–354.
108. Interview with Salih Lutfi. Umm al-Fahem, May 23, 2014.
109. L. Barkan, "The Islamic Movement in Israel: Switching Focus from Jerusalem to the Palestinian Cause," *MEMRI Inquiry and Analysis Series Report*, no. 628 (2010).
110. "100 Days for Banning the Islamic Movement, We are Stronger than Your Banning," *Special Report by the Committee of Freedom*, Nazareth (February 2016).
111. Yotam Berger, "Figures Presented by Army Show More Arabs Than Jews Live in Israel, West Bank and Gaza," *Haaretz*, March 26, 2018. https://www.haaretz.com/israel-news/army-presents-figures-showing-arab-majority-in-israel-territories-1.5940676 (accessed March 27, 2018).
112. Jonathan Lis, "Balad Seeks to Unite Predominantly Arab Parties," *Haaretz*, September 30, 2014. http://www.haaretz.com/news/national/1.618323 (accessed April 11, 2015).
113. Lieberman had pushed the change through hoping to disqualify the Arab parties. Interview with MK Talab Abu 'Arar. Jerusalem, May 20, 2015.
114. "Interview with MK Ahmad Tibi," *Ynet*, April 9, 2014. http://www.ynet.co.il/articles/0,7340,L-4508304,00.html (accessed December 20, 2015).
115. Interview with MK Yousef Jabareen. Hura, June 25, 2015.
116. Yezid Sayigh, *Al-Hayat*, April 2, 2015. Issue no. 18990.
117. Gil Stern Hoffman, "Israel Politics: Platforms for the Politically Perplexed," *Jerusalem Post*, February 28, 2015. http://www.jpost.com/Israel-Elections/Platforms-for-the-politically-perplexed-392386 (accessed May 20, 2016).
118. Interview with MK Yousef Jabareen. Jerusalem, December 13, 2016.
119. "'Arabs Voting in Droves': Netanyahu's Fear Materializes as Joint List Wins 3rd in Israeli Election," *Democracy Now!* (YouTube), March 18, 2015. https://www.youtube.com/watch?v=tpTkGddJHEU (accessed March 12, 2016).
120. Arik Rudnitzky, "Back to the Knesset? Israeli Arab Vote in the 20th Knesset elections," *Israel Affairs* 22, no. 3–4 (September 2016), 1–14.
121. Yair Ettinger, "To Boycott or Not to Boycott," *Haaretz*, January 26, 2003. https://www.haaretz.com/1.4955472 (accessed March 14, 2014).

122. As'ad Ghanem, *The Palestinian-Arab Minority in Israel, 1948–2000: A Political Study* (Albany: State University of New York Press, 2001).

123. "Weekly Review of the Arab Press in Israel," *Arab Association for Human Rights*, Nazareth, no. 107 (2013).

124. Mtanis Shehadeh, "Reading in the Results of the 19 Knesset Elections in Israel: Elections amongst the Arab Society," *Mada Carmel* (2013).

125. *Al-Quds al-Arabi*, February 5, 2016.

126. *Al-Quds al-Arabi*, December 4, 2015.

127. "Challenging the Constitutionality of the Discriminatory Nationality and Entry into Israel Law," *Adalah Briefing Paper* (2005), 4. http://adalah.org/features/famuni/BPaper2005.pdf (accessed June 15, 2014).

128. Ian Black, "1948 No Catastrophe Says Israel, as Term Nakba Banned from Arab Children's Schoolbooks," *The Guardian*, July 22, 2009. http://www.theguardian.com/world/2009/jul/22/israel-remove-nakba-from-textbooks (accessed June 15, 2013).

129. Interview with MK Yousef Jabareen. Conference in Hura, June 25, 2015.

130. Jack Khoury, "Joint List Knows It Now Must Live Up to Voters' Expectations," *Haaretz*, March 20, 2015. https://www.haaretz.com/.premium-joint-list-leader-pledges-to-help-negev-bedouin-1.5340053 (accessed September 9, 2016).

131. Interview with MK Yousef Jabareen, Hura (March 25, 2017).

132. "Restrictions on Human Rights Organizations and the Legitimate Activities of Arab Political Leaders in Israel," *Adalah Briefing Paper* (June 23, 2010).

133. Peter Beaumont, "EU Leads Criticism after Israel Passes Jewish 'Nation State' Law." Available at: https://www.theguardian.com/world/2018/jul/19/israel-adopts-controversial-jewish-nation-state-law (accessed October 1, 2018).

134. *Al-Quds al-Arabi*, February 5, 2016.

135. Mtanis Shehadeh et al., "The Palestinians of 1948 and Their Role in the Palestinian National Project: A Reading in the Palestinian Community Positions," *Mada* (2015). http://mada-research.org/wp-content/uploads/2016/01/JDL25-8-Shehadeh-Saabneh.pdf (accessed July 20, 2016).

BIBLIOGRAPHY

al-Hajj, Majid. "Education Toward Multiculturalism in Light of the Peace Process." In Menachem Mautner, Avi Sagi and Ronen Shamir (eds.). *Multiculturalism in a Democratic and Jewish State*. Tel Aviv: Ramot, Tel Aviv University Press, 1998.

al-Nasasrah, Sheikh Suleiman Mustafa. Private Collection, Rahat. Accessed December 10–20, 2016.

Arar, Khalid and Khaled Abu-Assbah. "Not Just Location: Attitudes and Functioning of Arab Local Education Administrators in Israel." *International Journal of Educational Management* 27, no. 1 (2013), 54–73.

Arar, Khalid and Kussai Jah-Yehia. *Higher Education and the Palestinian Minority in Israel*. Basingstoke: Palgrave, 2016.

"Back to Basics: Israel's Arab Minority and the Israeli-Palestinian Conflict." *International Crisis Group*, March 14, 2012. Accessed June 14, 2014. http://www

.crisisgroup.org/en/regions/middle-east-north-africa/israel-palestine/119-back-to-basics-israels-arab-minority-and-the-israeli-palestinian-conflict.aspx.

Barkan, L. "The Islamic Movement in Israel: Switching Focus from Jerusalem to the Palestinian Cause." *MEMRI Inquiry and Analysis Series Report*, no. 628 (2010).

Berger, Yotam. "Figures Presented by Army Show More Arabs Than Jews Live in Israel, West Bank and Gaza." *Haaretz*, March 26, 2018. Accessed March 27, 2018. https://www.haaretz.com/israel-news/army-presents-figures-showing-arab-majority-in-israel-territories-1.5940676.

The Black Book: Land Day, 30 March 1976. Nazareth: Regional Committee for the Defense of Arab Lands in Israel, 1976.

"Cabinet communication," January 10, 2016. *Israel Ministry of Foreign Affairs.* Accessed April 11, 2016. http://mfa.gov.il/MFA/PressRoom/2016/Pages/Cabinet-communique-10-January-2016.aspx.

"Challenging the Constitutionality of the Discriminatory Nationality and Entry into Israel Law." *Adalah Briefing Paper* (2005), 4. Accessed June 15, 2014. http://adalah.org/features/famuni/BPaper2005.pdf.

Cohen, Hillel. *Good Arabs: The Israeli Security Agencies and the Israeli Arabs, 1948–1967.* Berkeley: University of California Press, 2010.

"Conference: The Role of Palestinians in the Palestinian National Project." *IPS and Mada al Carmel Conference*, Bir Zeit University (2015). http://mada-research.org/blog/2015/11/%D9%85%D8%A4%D8%AA%D9%85%D8%B1-%D8%AF%D9%88%D8%B1-%D9%81%D9%84%D8%B3%D8%B7%D9%8A%D9%86%D9%8A%D9%8A-48-%D9%88%D9%85%D9%83%D8%A7%D9%86%D8%AA%D9%87%D9%85-%D9%81%D9%8A-%D8%A7%D9%84%D9%85%D8%B4%D8%B1/.

Dallasheh, Leena. "Political mobilization of Palestinians in Israel: The movement al-Ard." In Rhoda Ann Kanaaneh and Isis Nusair (eds.). *Displaced at Home: Ethnicity and Gender among Palestinians in Israel.* Albany: State University of New York Press, 2010, 21–38.

Duvall, Eric. "Protestors call for Israeli investigation into Umm al-Hiran deaths." *UPI*, January 19, 2017. Accessed October 14, 2017. www.upi.com/Top_News/World-News/2017/01/19/Protesters-call-for-Israeli-investigation-into-Umm-al-Hiran-deaths/5141484847541/.

Ghanem, As'ad. "Israel and the 'danger of demography.'" In Jamil Hilal (ed.), *Where Now for Palestine? The Demise of the Two-State Solution.* London: Zed Books, 2007, 48–74.

———. *The Palestinian-Arab Minority in Israel, 1948–2000: A Political Study.* Albany: State University of New York Press, 2001.

Ghanem, As'ad and Mohanad Mustafa. "Explaining Political Islam: The Transformation of Palestinian Islamic Movements." *British Journal of Middle East Studies* 41, no. 4 (2014), 335–354.

Hussein, Cherine. *The Re-Emergence of the Single State Solution in Palestine/Israel: Countering an Illusion.* New York: Routledge, 2015.

Islamic Movement Publication. "100 days for banning the Islamic movement, we are stronger than your banning." *Special Report by the Committee of Freedom*, Nazareth (February 2016).

"Israeli Supreme Court Upholds Ban on Family Unification." *Adalah*, January 12, 2011. Accessed June 15, 2014. http://www.adalah.org/eng/Articles/1185/Israeli-Supreme-Court-Upholds-Ban-on-Family.

Jabareen, Hassan. "20 Years of Oslo: The Green Line's Challenge to the Statehood project." *Journal for Palestine Studies* 43, no. 1 (2013), 41–50.

Jamal, Amal. "The Arab Leadership in Israel: Ascendance and Fragmentation." *Journal of Palestine Studies* 35, no. 2 (2006), 6–22.

———. "Twenty Years after the Oslo Accords: A Perspective on the Need for Mutual Ethical Recognition." *Rosa Luxemburg Stiftung in Israel* 12 (September 2013).

Jiryis, Sabri. *The Arabs in Israel, 1948–1966*. Beirut, Lebanon: Institute for Palestine Studies, 1969.

Khalidi, Raja. "Sixty years after the UN Partition Resolution: What Future for the Arab Economy in Israel." *Journal of Palestine Studies* 37, no. 2 (2008), 6–22.

Khalidi, Raja and Qossay Alsattari. *Strengthening Trade and Economic Interaction Between Palestinians in the West Bank and Inside Israel: An Arab "North-North" Alternative to Israelization.* Bir Zeit: Bir Zeit University Centre for Development Studies, 2014.

Khalidi, Raja and Mtanes Shihadeh. "Israel's 'Arab Economy.'" In Nadim Rouhana (ed.), *Israel and its Palestinian Citizens: Ethnic Privileges in the Jewish State*. Cambridge: Cambridge University Press, 2017, 266–298.

Khoury, Jack. "Islamic Movement top official in Israel gets eight months in prison." *Haaretz*, March 4, 2014. Accessed June 11, 2014. http://www.haaretz.com/news/national/.premium-1.577882.

Khoury, Jack and Lee Yaron. "Israel Looks to Address Funding Gaps for Arab Community With $3.9 Billion Plan." *Haaretz*, December 28, 2015. Accessed April 3, 2016. http://www.haaretz.com/israel-news/.premium-1.694090.

Kouttab, Alexander and Mattia Toaldo. "In Search of Legitimacy: The Palestinian National Movement 20 Years After Oslo: Policy Brief." *European Council on Foreign Relations* (ECFR), no. 89 (2013).

LaOved, Kav. "Arab Citizens of Israel and Work: trends of workplace discrimination and violation of labour rights." *Worker's Hotline*, Nazareth (2013).

Larkin, Craig and Michael Dumper. "In Defense of Al-Aqsa: The Islamic Movement inside Israel and the Battle for Jerusalem." *Middle East Quarterly* 66, no. 1 (2012), 30–51.

Lawrence, Rubin. "Islamic Political Activism in Israel." *Centre for Middle East Policy Analysis*, no. 32 (2014).

Lowrance, Sherry. "Being Palestinian in Israel: Identity, Protest, and Political Exclusion." *Comparative Studies of South Asia, Africa and the Middle East* 25, no. 2 (2005), 487–499.

Lustick, Ian. *Arabs in the Jewish State: Israel's Control of a National Minority*. Austin: University of Texas Press, 1980.

Mayer, Thomas. *Hitorerut ha-muslimimb'yisrael (Islamic Awakening in Israel)*. Israel: Givat Haviva, 1988.

Nasasra, Mansour. *The Naqab Bedouins: A Century of Bedouin Politics and Resistance*. New York: Columbia University Press, 2017.

"New details emerge from Umm Al-Hiran investigation." *Israel National News*, February 22, 2017. Accessed April 14, 2017. http://www.israelnationalnews.com/News/News.aspx/225499.

"New Poll finds: Two-State Solution is the Preferred Option for Majority of Israelis and Palestinians." *Palestinian Peace Coalition, Peace Library* (2009). http://www.geneva-accord.org/mainmenu/new-poll-finds-two-state-solution-is-the-preferred-option-for-majority-of-israelis-and-palestinians.

Nikfar, Bethany M. "Families Divided: An Analysis of Israel's Citizenship and Entry into Israel Law." *Northwestern Journal of International Human Rights* 3, no. 1 (2005).

"OECD Economic Surveys. ISRAEL. January 2016. Overview." *Organisation for Economic Co-operation and Development* (OECD) (2016), 30. Accessed April 5, 2016. http://www.oecd.org/israel/economic-survey-israel.htm.

Pappé, Ilan. *The Forgotten Palestinians: A History of the Palestinian Minority in Israel*. New Haven: Yale University Press, 2011.

Pessate-Schubert, Anat. "Changing from the margins: Bedouin women and higher education in Israel." *Women's Studies International Forum* 26, no. 4 (2003), 285–298.

"Police minister maintains Bedouin car-ramming was terror attack." *Times of Israel*, January 19, 2017. Accessed September 26, 2017. https://www.timesofisrael.com/police-minister-maintains-bedouin-car-ramming-was-terror-attack/.

"Public Committee Against Torture demands Israel probe wounding of MK Odeh by police in Umm al-Hiran." *Adalah*, January 23, 2017. Accessed March 8, 2017. https://www.adalah.org/en/content/view/9010.

Rekhees, Elie. "The Arabs of Israel after Oslo: Localization of the National Struggle." *Israel Studies* 7, no. 3 (2002), 1–44.

Rouhana, Nadeem and Areej Sabbagh-Khoury. "Settler-colonial citizenship: conceptualizing the relationship between Israel and its Palestinian citizens." *Settler Colonial Studies and Israel–Palestine* 5, no. 3 (2015), 205–225.

Roy, Sara. "De-development Revisited: Palestinian Economy and Society Since Oslo." *Journal of Palestine Studies* 28, no. 3 (Spring, 1999), 64–82.

Rudnitzky, Arik. "Back to the Knesset? Israeli Arab vote in the 20th Knesset elections." *Israel Affairs* 22, no. 3–4 (September 2016), 1–14.

Saad, Hassan Abu. "Party meeting in Beersheba." December 7, 1995, *Al Wifaq Private Paper*.

Saban, Ilan. "Appropriate Representation of Minorities: Canada's Two Types Structure and the Arab-Palestinian Minority in Israel." *Penn State International Law Review* 24, no. 3 (2006), 1–41.

Sa'di, Ahmad. *Thorough Surveillance: The Genesis of Israeli Policies of Population Management, Surveillance and Political Control toward the Palestinian Minority*. Manchester and New York: Manchester University Press, 2014.

Shaalan, Hasan and Ilana Curiel. "Protests in Arab sector over Umm al-Hiran 'martyr.'" *Ynet*, January 21, 2017. Accessed September 26, 2017. http://www.ynetnews.com/articles/0,7340,L-4910556,00.html.

Shalhoub-Kevorkian, Nadera. *Security Theology, Surveillance and the Politics of Fear*. Cambridge: Cambridge University Press, 2015.

Shalhoub-Kevorkian, Nadera, Antonina GriecciWoodsum, Himmat Zu'bi and Rachel Busbridge. "Funding Pain: Bedouin Women and Political Economy in the Naqab/Negev." *Feminist Economics* 20, no. 4 (2014), 164–186.

Shehadeh, Mtanes and Raja Khalidi. "Impeded Development: The Political Economy of the Palestinian Arabs inside Israel." In Mandy Turner and Omar Shewiki (eds.). *Decolonizing Palestinian Political Economy: De-Development and Beyond.* New York: Palgrave Macmillan, 2014, 116–119.

Shehadeh, Mtanis. "Reading in the Results of the 19 Knesset Elections in Israel: Elections amongst the Arab Society." *Mada Carmel* (2013).

Smooha, Sammy. "Minority status in an ethnic democracy: The status of the Arab minority in Israel." *Ethnic and Racial Studies* 13, no. 3 (1990), 389–413.

———. *Arabs and Jews in Israel: Volume 2, Change and Continuity in Mutual Intolerance.* Boulder, CO: Westview, 1992.

———. *Israel: Pluralism and Conflict.* Berkeley and Los Angeles: University of California Press, 1978.

Speech by Abed al Wahab Darawsha, Third Conference of the Arab Democratic Party in Nazareth, December 15–16, 1994.

Staff, Toi. "Probe said to find Bedouin village incident wasn't terrorism." *Times of Israel*, February 22, 2017. Accessed September 26, 2017. https://www.timesofisrael.com/police-set-to-announce-bedouin-village-incident-wasnt-terrorism/.

Tessler, Mark. "Israel's Arabs and the Palestinian Problem." *Middle East Journal* 31, no. 3 (1977), 313–329.

"Weekly Review of the Arab Press in Israel." *Arab Association for Human Rights*, Nazareth, no. 107 (2013).

Winer, Stuart. "Israel okays $4 billion upgrade plan for Arab communities." *Times of Israel*, December 30, 2015. Accessed October 15, 2016. http://www.timesofisrael.com/government-okays-nis-15b-upgrade-plan-for-arab-communities/.

Yashiv, Eran. "Key Challenges Facing the Israeli Economy and their Ramifications for National Security." *Strategic Assessment* 18, no. 4 (2016), 59–68.

Zreik, Raef. "The Palestinian Question: Themes of Justice and Power. Part II: The Palestinians in Israel." *Journal of Palestine Studies* 33, no. 1 (2003), 42–54.

Chapter Six

A New Nationalistic Political Grammar

Jewish-Israeli Society 25 Years After Oslo

Yonatan Mendel

This chapter focuses on the dynamics of the Oslo Accords in Jewish-Israeli society, particularly focusing on the main political aspects. It starts from the premise that a paradox exists in the heart of the Israeli debate. According to the Jewish-Israeli narrative, the Oslo Accords are perceived to have been a generous and peaceful offer that was made to the other side, yet the other side did not fulfil its commitments and hence it bears responsibility for the continuation of the conflict. Simultaneously, the people most associated with the Oslo Accords and its "spirit" (in the Israeli case, especially Yitzhak Rabin, Shimon Peres, and Yossi Beilin) are regarded to be nothing but "criminals" that made an offer not for the benefit of their people but for their own personal benefits and desire for European recognition.[1] This is often expressed through the Hebrew phrase "posh'ei Oslo le-din" ("Indict the Oslo criminals"). This discourse of "crimes" and "criminals" began in 1993 and gained pace in 1994 and 1995, leading eventually to the murder of Israeli prime minister Rabin by Yigal Amir, a Jewish-Israeli national-religious person. Despite a general condemnation from Israeli politicians to the actual act of murder, the post-Oslo events have resulted in the rise of a hawkish discourse that dominates Jewish-Israeli society up until the present day; one that has made any discussion of peace with the Palestinians a particularly toxic brew in Israeli politics.

The failure of the Oslo Accords to end the conflict and lead to peaceful relations between Jewish-Israelis and Palestinians through the creation of a sovereign Palestinian state and a just and comprehensive solution to the core issues (postponed to a "later stage" that never arrived) led, in Israel, to political radicalization and an acute shift toward right-wing and extreme national-religious groups. Perhaps the starkest illustration of this is the governing coalition at the time of the Oslo Accords compared to the one in 2018.

In 1993, the Israeli parliamentarian coalition was made up of two parties only—the Labor Party (considered a center-left Zionist party) with 44 seats, and Meretz (a left-wing party, although still within the Zionist realm) with 12 seats. With the support of two Palestinian-Arab parties (the Democratic Front for Peace and Equality with three seats, and the Arab Democratic Party with two seats), which supported the government without being part of the coalition, the Rabin government enjoyed the support of 61 of the 120 members of the Knesset and was thus able to push forward the peace process. In contrast, the government in 2018 is led by Benjamin Netanyahu from the right-wing Likud Party (which has formed every coalition since 2001, with the brief exception of its offshoot Kadima in 2006–2009), and the situation is very different. The Labor Party changed its name and is now called the Zionist Camp in a deliberate bid to demonstrate its commitment to Zionism and to highlight that it is not moderate when it comes to the Palestinian issue—partly due to its association with the Oslo process.[2] But even this did not help and its support has continued to hemorrhage as indicated by the decline from 44 seats in 1993 to 24 in 2015 (even though in 2015 it united with Tzipi Livni's The Movement Party). Meretz has also lost support—down from 12 seats in 1993 to five in 2015. The shift toward the right in Israel is therefore encapsulated in the current government coalition: Likud with 30 seats, Kulanu (a centrist Zionist party whose program is dedicated mainly to the cost of living) with 10 seats, the Jewish Home (a nationalist-religious party) with eight seats, Shas (a Sephardic religious party) with seven seats, and Yahadut Ha-Torah (an Orthodox party) with six seats.

There are two other developments in Israeli politics that are crucial to the understanding of the current "post-Oslo" political situation. First, is the total delegitimization of Palestinian-Arab parties (and Palestinian-Arab citizens in Israel, in general). Second, is the paralysis that is dominating the political sphere, in which all "centrist" parties—Yesh Atid most famously, but also the Zionist Camp—do not pose a distinct opposition to the government, and instead try to gain political support by adopting similar right-wing and conservative policies. With regard to the first phenomenon, a stark example was provided by Prime Minister Netanyahu on the March 2015 election day when he called on Jewish-Israeli citizens to go out to vote because the Palestinian-Arab citizens of the state were, according to him, "heading to the polling stations in droves."[3] This message was further promoted by the popular mainstream media, which consistently portrays the Palestinian-Arab citizens of Israel as a threat.[4] Zionist opposition parties and leaders have also played a key role in this delegitimization by constantly insisting that Israel should be, first and foremost, a state for the political thought, aspirations and desires of Jewish citizens only. This, for example, can be seen in Livni's 2008 statement: "Once a Palestinian state is established, I can come to the Palestinian citizens, whom we call Israeli Arabs, and say to them 'you are citizens with equal rights, but the national solution for you is elsewhere.'"[5] This can be regarded as a clear attempt to reject the strategy of Palestinian citizens of Israel of refocusing their struggle on civil rights—and collective rights—as a response to their exclusion from the Oslo process and the PLO's national strategy (see the chapter by Mansour Nasasra in this book).[6] A similar attitude was expressed by Yair Lapid, the leader of Yesh Atid, after his success in the 2013 election. Lapid was quick to state that: "I am not going to form a coalition with the Zoabis," referring to MK Hanin Zoabi from the Arab National Democratic Party (*Balad*), thus expressing the commonly held position by Zionist parties that they are unwilling to work with Palestinian-Arab parties as a whole. It also neatly expressed the racist anti-Arab sentiment in Israel by narrowing down all Palestinian-Arabs in Israel to one name: Zoabi, who is by and large already demonized by most Israeli news channels and newspapers for her clear views against the Israeli occupation. One can only imagine the reaction in Israel if a politician in the West had said something about not forming alliances with the Cohens or the Levys.

This shift toward the right in Israel is an ongoing process. As I argued in 2015, "All Jewish parties in Israel (except Meretz, which is against the occupation and is as progressive as its Zionist boundaries allow it to be) share a desire to show that they have the guts to stand up for Israel vis-à-vis international law, and that they are anti-Arab."[7] This process has only gained strength and importance since then. Indeed, in the current Israeli political landscape there is no legitimate left-wing politics, either on the civil-society level or in public or media discourse.

This very concise summary of Israel's current political sphere does not mean that Israeli political life in the past was significantly more democratic or less anti-Arab in nature. After all, it was the Labor Party that was in office from 1948 and hence bears considerable responsibility for the ongoing Palestinian Nakba (including the rejection of the return of refugees); it led the military regime imposed on Palestinian citizens of Israel, inside Israel, from 1948–1966; furthermore, it led the government that occupied the West Bank and Gaza following the 1967 war and created the first settlements in the West Bank. Yet, having said all this, the main post-Oslo process in Israeli society is a new phase of politics—one that is right-wing and is based on a new "political grammar" to the verge of including straightforward nationalistic and fascist elements.[8] Parallel to this, the Israeli political sphere appears to be in the midst of a process of admitting (government ministers and prime minister included) that it sees no possibility for a viable peaceful and just solution to the conflict, and that it sees only a future of bloodshed and war. This situation could be regarded as one where the "masks are off," where we see increasing calls for unilateral acts, including challenging the consensus around the religious sites by permitting Jews to pray at Al-Haram Al-Sharif/Temple Mount, the annexation of Area C in the West Bank, the annexation of the whole of the West Bank including the transfer of the Palestinian population, the introduction of the death penalty to Palestinians who kill Israelis, and more.

FROM OSLO TO CAMP DAVID: READING JEWISH-ISRAELI SOCIETY

The decline of the Labor Party and the coming to dominance of the Likud (and its offshoots that appear to currently make up a considerable part of the opposition), highlights the fact that the majority of Jewish-Israelis see the Oslo Accords as a strategic error at best, or as a sham and an act of betrayal at worst.[9] This is especially the case if we look at Oslo as a process and if we include in its impacts the emerging Israeli discourse about the Palestinians, about the peace process, and about the inevitable situation of ongoing war and conflict—regarded, in Israeli eyes, as situations that have been "forced" on Israel, and never regarded as a product of Israeli actions.

In this regard, what is important for us to mention is the Israeli discourse that surrounds the Camp David 2000 summit, attended by Israeli prime minister Ehud Barak and Palestinian president Yasser Arafat, under the direction of US president Bill Clinton—a summit that must be analyzed as a continuation of Oslo, for good or bad. The summit, which eventually collapsed with both leaders blaming the other for the failed negotiations, strengthened two notions in the Israeli discourse and psyche, which are crucial to the understanding of the Oslo "legacy" in Jewish-Israeli society.

One notion was the strengthening of the "no partner" paradigm, which suggests that Israel, "as always" in Israeli minds, had its hand outstretched for peace, but it was the Palestinian side who did not want to compromise and seek peace over conflict, and hence it was the Palestinians who were responsible for the ongoing bloodshed. The conclusion that Jewish-Israelis draw from this paradigm is that Israel should therefore spend more time and effort on fighting Palestinians than on seeking neighborly relations and peace. Indeed, this is one of the insights of Avi Shlaim in *The Iron Wall*, his seminal study of Zionism and Israel's relations with its Arab neighbors.[10] According to Shlaim, the Israeli discourse of "the hand outstretched to peace" has been used to justify and legitimize the use of strong-arm military tactics and counterinsurgency violence. The second paradigm that gained pace was the "villa in the jungle" theory; again this is a perspective that is embedded in Zionist thought and which was further strengthened following the Oslo events (and peaked following the collapse of the Camp David summit in 2000). Theodor Herzl, most famously, who is considered the father of modern political Zionism, believed that a Zionist presence in Palestine would serve "as an outpost of European culture against oriental barbarism."[11] This narrative, which never really went away but which was rarely expressed publicly by the higher echelons of the Israeli government during the Oslo years, has been successfully resurrected in the twenty-first century, first by Barak, and lately by Netanyahu.[12] This metaphor vividly portrays the mainstream Jewish-Israeli attitude about itself and its neighbors, and illustrates Israel's Orientalist attitude toward the alleged impossibility of reaching peace with its Arab neighbors due to the imagined binomial oppositions and differences between the two sides. Metaphors, as Johnson and Lakoff argue, are tools that constitute meaningful political acts, and this is how they should be read here.[13]

Another important element that has had a direct influence on the image of the Oslo Accords in Israel and the rise of the right-wing, and that should not be disregarded, is the price paid by Israelis following the failures of Oslo to bring genuine peace, and the violence that spread in Israel/Palestine. Following the signing of the Oslo Accords, and due to the escalation of the security situation on the ground, which was directly related to the limitation of the agreement, many Palestinians were killed by Israeli security forces, and many Israelis were killed by Palestinians. The Oslo process deftly excluded most Palestinian factions from the negotiations and effectively offered them a stark choice between subjugation by Israel or subjugation by the Palestinian Authority. The proclamations and promises of political leaders thus began to be punctuated by dissident attacks—and the rise of suicide acts—that caused many casualties. The targets of Palestinian political violence in the 1990s and 2000s were often civilians, i.e., in streets, markets, restaurants, and buses inside Israel. These were civilians who use public transport and shop in outdoor markets; in other words, the lower middle class and the working poor—the largest and fastest growing sectors of Jewish-Israeli society due to the neoliberal economic reforms that led to greater inequality. There was also a high proportion of immigrants among these strata and among the casualties, a statistic that would reverberate forcefully in the flight of these sectors to the nationalist right. Rabin's famous promise that the Oslo Accords were "a war with no casualties, the only battle that it is a pleasure to wage, the battle for peace" quickly changed in the Jewish-Israeli experience from inspiring to grotesque.[14] Palestinian Authority president Arafat, at best on grudging probation in the Jewish-Israeli public mind, was thereafter transformed from potential peace partner to an almost treacherous "double dealer."[15] Rabin's assassination two years into the process deprived Israel of Oslo's most credible advocate, and the final collapse of the process under the leadership of Ehud Barak in 2000 underscored the point that there was no one else who could navigate the demonstrably unwieldy process to a safe conclusion.

In fact, when one analyzes the Jewish-Israeli mainstream perspective, the collapse in the credibility of the Accords was also driven by factors that were either misinterpreted or absent in the public discourse altogether. The suicide attacks were regarded as evidence of Palestinians' eternal resentment; and of Arafat's incompetence, double-dealing, or both.[16] Settlement construction—even though it grew larger not smaller after the agreement[17]—occupied less of the Israeli public attention than the violence of Palestinian individuals. Furthermore, the effects of an enhanced separation regime—and narrowing freedom of movement for Palestinians which resulted in a skyrocketing of unemployment amongst Palestinians locked out of the Israeli economy—brought an influx of guest workers from Eastern Europe and the Far East. At any rate, an often-voiced sentiment was that if Palestinians had wanted to keep working in Israel, they should not have agitated for an end to Israel's occupation and for Palestinian independence, let alone to use violence against Israelis. All this contributed to a simplistic but deeply fatalistic reading of the peace process and its discontents.

Coming back to the post-Oslo violence as experienced by the Jewish-Israeli public, the killing of Israelis had a massive influence on Israeli public opinion. See, for example, how Israeli academic, Efraim Karsh, from the Begin-Sadat Center for Strategic Studies at Bar-Ilan University, put it. According to Karsh, "[in 2006] All in all, more than 1,600 Israelis have been murdered and another 9,000 wounded since the signing of the DOP [Declaration of Principles]—nearly four times the average death toll of the preceding twenty-six years."[18] With this quote in mind, it should be highlighted that within the Israeli hegemonic discourse, Jewish-Israeli public and political perceptions tend to regard Israeli military and settler violence as always being a "response" to Palestinian violence, and they do not link the ongoing Israeli occupation to Palestinian attacks. This is encapsulated in an exchange in 2012 between Naftali Bennett, MK and leader of the Jewish Home Party, and Yossi Beilin, who is considered one of the architects behind the Oslo Accords. "The Oslo Accords resulted in 1,600 Israelis killed," said Bennett to Beilin in a live broadcast on Israel's Channel 10.[19]

What is important to highlight here is the Israeli collective memory and the automatic linkage made between the Oslo Accords, on the one hand, and the violence that erupted, on the other hand. While it is important that any analysis of the violence in Israel/Palestine should always bear in mind that there are many more Palestinians who have been killed and that Israel is the occupying power, the killing of hundreds of overwhelmingly civilian Israelis in what is regarded in Israel as the "post-Oslo context" cannot be ignored if we are to understand the social and political effects that Oslo—the actual accords or their imagined interpretations—has had on Jewish-Israeli society. It had, and still has, consequences for how Jewish-Israelis perceive the Accords, as well as on how Jewish-Israelis imagine the responsibility that Palestinians have for the ongoing violence.

The real legacy, therefore, of the Oslo Accords in Israel and within Jewish-Israeli mainstream discourse was that it reaffirmed mistrust of Palestinians and lent justification to the occupation and the lack of genuine steps by Israel toward the creation of a Palestinian state. Whether Rabin in 1993 genuinely committed Israel to supporting the creation of a sovereign Palestinian state that would emerge out of the Oslo agreements is unknown, and the Israeli hegemonic discourse that Ehud Barak offered a generous proposal at Camp David in 2000 should definitely be regarded critically. However, whether it was planned or not, the Oslo Accords and the peace negotiations that followed them, allowed Israel to accelerate rather than change its policies of building settlements in the Occupied Palestinian Territory (OPT), continuing to occupy and expropriate Palestinian land, disregard Palestinians' right and demand for self-determination, use extreme amounts of military violence, and initiate unilateral political acts.

THE OPPOSITION TO OSLO AS BEING A CONTINUATION OF THE CONFLICT BY OTHER MEANS

The prevailing Israeli opposition to Oslo, therefore, is grounded in the worst experiences of the Oslo years with a simple Jewish-Israeli reading of history and geopolitics. Palestinians, according to this line of thought, have proved they cannot be trusted because the agreement did not result in a peaceful situation, and that this would only get worse if a Palestinian state emerged because it could be used as a launching pad for more military assaults until all of historic Palestine has been recaptured—a perspective that interestingly mirrors the actual process that Israel itself followed after the 1947 UN Partition Plan. This belief feeds off of, and in turn feeds into, the existential angst that is deeply embedded within Jewish-Israeli society and politics. This existential angst, together with the belief that Israel has had a "hand outstretched to peace," as explained earlier, has allowed Israel both to ignore the Oslo Accords and to find ways to sabotage the creation of a sovereign Palestinian state.

In reality, far from facilitating Palestinian expansionism, an important result of the Oslo process was that it has permitted Israel to shrink the geographical space of any future Palestinian state. The Oslo division of the West

Bank into three different areas (Areas A, B, and C) has been used by Israel to promote the idea that some areas are "more Palestinian" and others are "more Israeli"—despite the fact that all are within the OPT. This, together with the separation between Gaza and the West Bank, has given Israel the chance to increase its grip over the land, and to push forward practically a "one state solution" in which Israel is the sole decision-maker for all the territory from the Jordan River to the Mediterranean Sea. In this context, Israel's legal procedures have followed the political aspirations of its leadership, ignoring the international community and international law.

Despite all this, the Jewish-Israeli public perceives every small compromise as a crack in the dam of hegemony that could easily spread, endangering Israeli lives in the short term, and posing a risk to Israel's very existence in the long term. Sabotaging and dismantling Oslo has therefore become a vital interest. Similarly, any attempt to reduce Israeli control has been regarded as creating the possibility of a Palestinian sovereign state—which is not the kind of "state" Israeli decision-makers mean when they say they support a "two-state solution." Instead, the hegemonic Israeli political discourse portrays that a real Palestinian sovereign state would be a threat to Israel, including a potential to act as a gateway for hostile regional forces. This dominant perception has resulted in the deep suspicion of the Jewish-Israeli public toward a peace agreement generally, and the creation of a sovereign Palestinian state more specifically.[20]

This perception has been utilized by the hegemonic political powers in Israel, particularly by the ruling Likud Party which has used it as a vehicle to preserve its dominance, as indicated by the fact that in 2018, the Likud and its political offshoots will have been in power for all of the 21st century, leading five governments in 15 years. Indeed, the 2018 government, headed by Netanyahu (who was Rabin's rival, and a virulent opponent of the Oslo "spirit") is the most staunchly nationalist one yet. This far-right bloc has solidified its grasp on power from one election to the next, wearing down the already ineffective centrist elements and achieving a robust and uniformly nationalist coalition in the 2015 elections. In the past three years, the opposition has remained bitterly divided, with its leaders, Labor chair MK Avi Gabbai and parliamentary leader MK Isaac Herzog, insisting on distancing themselves from the second largest and arguably most dynamic opposition party, the Palestinian-majority Joint List, which has been delegitimized by Likud as a matter of strategy, as mentioned earlier in this chapter, and which serves as another example of the anti-Palestinian attitude that grew in strength following the failure of the Oslo Accords.

Meanwhile, with regards to the "facts on the ground" following Oslo, the Gaza Strip has been disconnected from the West Bank, and the West

Bank is totally hollowed, to use Eyal Weizman's term.[21] Settler numbers in the West Bank have increased to just over half a million[22] meaning that not only will the settler population be difficult to displace if partition was ever to take place, but also that, statistically speaking, nearly all Jewish-Israelis now have relatives, friends, colleagues and peers from work, military service or university, who reside in settlements, a fact that has deep consequences. The proportion of Israeli settlers and their supporters in the institutions of the state has also been increasing. Indeed, the expansion and normalization of Jewish settlements in the occupied West Bank has erected a firm political and demographical barrier against Jewish-Israeli support for the creation of a Palestinian state. An analysis of this, however, is beyond the scope of this chapter.[23] In other words, the Oslo Accords and their aftermath have enabled Israel to further disconnect the areas of the OPT and Palestinian people living under occupation, and to make increasing chunks of the OPT, practically and soon also officially, part of Israel.

With the failure of the Oslo peace process to indeed bring about peace, it has therefore been extremely easy for Israeli governments after Rabin (most of which have been from the right wing) to incite against the Oslo Accords and any peace process, and at times to push the "existential threat" button, according to which there are threats and risks that Jewish-Israelis cannot accept. It is necessary to take account of the existential trauma that engulfs Jewish-Israel society as a community bruised by a genocide well within living memory. The Shoah is a trauma that has been repeatedly, habitually called on (sometimes quite callously), to explain many more recent political developments, from Israel's border wars, to Palestinian uprisings, to regional geopolitics vis-a-vis Iran. It draws on, and enhances the idea that, for Jewish-Israelis, their hegemony is inextricably conflated with survival. This perspective has been reflected with remarkable consistency in opinion polls over the past 25 years, from the Oslo Accords onward. These show that while a stable majority of people profess to support a two-state solution, a majority also opposes compromises—that according to Israelis are embedded with risks—on any of the core issues of the conflict, from the status of Jerusalem to the issue of the return of Palestinian refugees. Similarly, polls also tell us that the less chances of success a negotiating effort is perceived to have, the more support it enjoys among Israelis, and vice-versa, i.e., that the more chances there seems to be that negotiations will result in changes to the status quo, the more apprehensive Jewish-Israelis become.[24]

This cognitive dissonance also prevails in Israeli political discourse. For over two decades, the broad spectrum of Israeli politics endorsed support for the two-state solution in principle, while undermining it in practice. This was as true for Yitzhak Rabin and Shimon Peres (who built settlements even as they launched negotiations for partition), as it was for Ehud Barak, Ariel Sharon, and Ehud Olmert (who also expanded the settlements). And it is most surely doubly true for Netanyahu,[25] who voiced support for a two-state solution famously once (during a policy speech at Bar Ilan University), while in reality doing the opposite to undermine and sabotage it.[26]

Netanyahu's endorsement of the concept was lauded as the triumph of the two-state approach on both sides of the political map. Almost a decade later it seems that nothing is more powerful than an idea whose time has come—and gone. It is now perfectly safe for Netanyahu to voice support for a two-state solution, precisely because in the current post-Oslo "spirit" he has ensured he will never be required to implement it. The Israeli right openly repudiated its support for partition in the 2015 elections and in virtually every relevant policy decision it has undertaken in office.[27] Meanwhile, the parliamentary left has supported almost every use of military force, thus proving that, by and large, it offers no real alternative to current government policies as regards the OPT. And, as if it needs mentioning, this has also meant that the mainstream Israeli left has long lost any credibility it might have once had among Palestinians. For example, in the 2016 peace program presented by the Labor Party, there was a commitment to a united Jerusalem under Israeli control and a rejection of any Palestinian control (including a Palestinian capital in East Jerusalem) or shared sovereignty over parts of the city. Furthermore, in February 2016, the Labor Party conference endorsed a limited unilateral withdrawal plan, which expressly shelved a sovereignty-based two-state solution.[28] The centrist parties are obviously not much better, as indicated by the campaign of Yesh Atid which launched its campaign in Ariel, a settler city in the OPT which has become a symbol of Israeli expansionist and annexationist attitude.

Another crucial element for understanding the stagnation on the one hand, and the distancing from Palestinians (and any process with them) on the other, that exists among Jewish-Israeli society, is that within Israeli hegemonic discourse it seems there is very little incentive for Israel to change. The second decade of the twenty-first century has been a period of remarkable stability for Israel, both militarily and economically. Militarily, the conflict with Palestinians has been largely reduced to occasional flare-ups in Gaza thus serving only to entrench Jewish-Israelis in the conviction that a diplomatic track is no longer tenable.[29] Even the increase in violence since the last quarter of 2015—a largely desperate "individuals intifada" (also titled "the knives intifada")—has been surprisingly well-integrated into the surreal everyday. Netanyahu's mangling of a biblical passage to say that, yes, for the foreseeable future, Israelis would have to "live by the sword" was received with astonishing equanimity, as were the military casualties in the last war on

Gaza in 2014, during which (within six weeks) more than 2,200 Palestinians were killed, as were more than 70 Israelis, most of them soldiers.[30]

Economically, while it seems that Israel has escaped the worst of the global recession, there are a number of issues related to the neoliberal policies followed by successive governments since the early 1990s, pursued in order to open up a previously highly welfarist/Keynesian model. Israel has highly centralized retail markets that guarantee price fixing, taxation has further squeezed the secular middle class, and the lamentable state of transport infrastructure has resulted in a metropolitan housing bubble—which makes settlements a tempting fall-back plan for young Israelis struggling to get on the property ladder.

In other words, the political deadlock in the Israeli-Palestinian conflict has meant, for Jewish-Israelis, that their main concern has switched to issues such as the cost of living, the demise and hollowing out of the welfare state, and affordable housing. And while the cost of living in Israel has grown (while wages have stayed the same) the resultant backlash of popular unrest in 2011 opened up a new field of politics, i.e., a focus on the type of traditional "bread and butter" issues that have been absent from the center stage of Israeli politics at least since the First Intifada. Protests for higher wages and for efforts to solve the housing crisis revealed a much greater potential for political mobilization and room for maneuver and hope than the conflict with the Palestinians. In this process, the bits of the left that are still engaged in the struggle against the occupation have failed—or were unable and at times did not attempt—to make linkages between that and socioeconomic issues. The political revenue from the cost of living protests was picked up by centrists like Yair Lapid and by a Labor Party emphatically disinterested in the conflict. The result is that, instead of reinvigorating a broad opposition to Netanyahu's economic and military policies, the conflict is barely discussed in any substantial way, in either the day-to-day or during elections.

Furthermore, and perhaps more importantly, the stagnant stability and yet undeniable prosperity of some parts, which are steadily growing, of Jewish-Israeli society has also provided the basis by which to reject the threats and prophecies of those opposing the occupation. Israelis have been told they cannot have security and prosperity without peace, but yet they feel they do; they have been told that the world will exact a price from them for the occupation, yet the world has not; and they have been told that whatever stability they enjoy cannot last for long, but the occupation has lasted for more than half a century and is still going strong. Within this mindset, the Oslo Accords have therefore been reshaped as a naïve attempt to solve the conflict; and because it "did not work," an "Israel first" paradigm should now be followed.

THE OSLO "PEACE PROCESS" AND THE END OF PEACE

Recent polls amongst Israeli youth show that there is significant support for discriminatory practices against Palestinians, framed as a measure to safeguard Jewish-Israeli hegemony, and increasing support for state as well as grassroots violence against Palestinians.[31] Jewish-Israelis born after 1990, it is worthy of mention, are actually unlikely to have met a Palestinian living in the West Bank or the Gaza Strip—unless they are in the army as the occupying force—and that their own association with the Palestinian people is likely to have been shaped by the media, and stories of previous wars and the Second Intifada told to them by their elder siblings and parents. Indeed, one of the most worrying developments of recent years—and has to be regarded as one of the main post-Oslo failures—has been the complete disconnection between different parts of Israel/Palestine.

Despite occasional (reciprocal but by no means equal) spikes of violence, the unrelentingly increasing structural oppression of the Palestinians, and nascent signs of some international pressure on Israel, it seems unlikely that the political deadlock between Israel and the Palestinians will shift in the short term. On the Israeli side, there is neither the desire nor the vision to change direction. To borrow a phrase from Mandy Turner's chapter in this book, there is certainly no official "Plan B." The most prominently aired alternative visions from outside the Israeli government also only seek to tweak, rather than significantly challenge, the status quo. One of these visions is that of a "confederation," which suggests a more equitable and looser form of partition based on the "temporary" institutions of Oslo; however, even this model of partition-lite fails to offer Jewish-Israelis any reasons to take the risks this would entail.[32]

Other visions, provided by right-wing annexationists, offer diverse but almost always inequitable approaches to the question of Palestinian citizenship; they also do not significantly challenge the status quo. They run the gamut from offers of full citizenship, to a phased process from residency to citizenship depending on "loyalty" to the state. On the far extreme, is a plan proposed by right-wing MK Bezalel Smotrich (who also serves as the deputy speaker of the Knesset), which recommends annexation of the West Bank to Israel and either payment offered to Palestinians to emigrate or conditions imposed on them if they wish to become Israeli citizens, including being required to serve in the Israeli army before they are granted citizenship.[33]

A landmark of this annexationist drive was the passing of the "Jewish Nation-State Law" by the Knesset in July 2018. Dispensing with the traditional tension between being a Jewish state and being a democracy, this law overtly pushes the "Jewish" component of Israel over its democratic component. This was especially evident as Israeli legislators refused to include in this basic law the words "equality," "democracy," or "democratic." But the word "Jewish" is mentioned at least 15 times—for example with regard to Israel as the "homeland of the Jewish people," "the national home of the Jewish people," and "the right to exercise national self-determination in Israel is unique to the Jewish people." The law cements Jewish supremacy in all aspects of life; most notoriously, it demotes Arabic as an official language of the state (Arabic has been, until July 2018, an official language since 1948, even though Israel has never treated it as equal to Hebrew)[34] and codifies into law that while Arabic will have a "special status" only Hebrew will be the official language of Israel.

While the majority of the law can be read as focusing on Israel inside 'the Green Line,' one curious choice of language indicates a more expansionist aim. It is likely not a coincidence that the first article highlights that "the *land of Israel* is the historical homeland of the Jewish people" (emphasis mine), a clause that can be interpreted as giving Israel carte blanche to continue building Jewish settlements in the territory perceived as constituting part of the "historical homeland," but not yet annexed into the State of Israel (i.e., the majority of the Israeli settlements in the OPT). The further radicalization of Israeli politics, together with a desire to install more "facts on the ground" and not to regard Palestinians as having rights, let alone equal rights, stands at the heart of this law. This is all part and parcel of the failure of Oslo.

Nationalist, expansionist and, at times, messianic paradigms have grown louder in Israel in the last two decades, and the separatist-military discourse that drove and dominated the Oslo period has been replaced with another discourse, which is just as bad or perhaps even worse, i.e., one that does not acknowledge any limitations on the exercise of power and violence, or of the possibility of creating any Jewish-Palestinian initiatives. And it is also unapologetic in its tone. In the 2015 elections for the Knesset, for example, the Jewish Home's campaign proposed that Israel should stop apologizing—the "mafsikim le-hitnatsel" (stop apologizing) campaign was pushed forward personally by Naftali Bennett from the Jewish Home Party—for either the occupation or for Israel's use of military violence.

The likelihood of the creation of a sovereign Palestinian state is difficult to assess at the moment, to say the least. Indeed, many studies have already argued that it does not seem possible at this stage, partly due to the outcomes of Oslo and the hollowing of the OPT, but also because Israel believes, and has followed a strategy to ensure, that parts of the West Bank will become part of Israel. The Accords, in other words, intentionally or not, have helped to carve up the West Bank and make parts of it weaker thus helping to facilitate Israel's creeping annexation; and it contributed to the separation between Gaza and the West Bank as two entities which are now not even part of the same political system.

A strong sense has risen amongst Jewish-Israelis according to which the conflict is a situation that is unchangeable. Whether it was desired or planned or not, Oslo has had a negative influence on different aspects of political decision-making in Israel. It removed the idea that there was a Palestinian partner and it gave rise to a new type of thinking that is largely driven by an extreme and messianic kind of right-wing politics.

ACKNOWLEDGMENTS

I would like to thank Dimi Reider for his great help in the writing process of this article. This final version is based on previous work we have done on the subject and I would like to express my gratitude to him for his contribution, comments, and cooperation.

NOTES

1. Baruch Kimmerling, *Politicide: Ariel Sharon's War Against the Palestinians* (London: Verso, 2003), 123.
2. Meron Rapoport, "'We are not Arab Lovers': Israeli Labor's Bankrupt Efforts to Stave Off Decline," *Middle East Eye*, April 25, 2016, http://www.middleeasteye.net/columns/when-israels-main-opposition-party-has-problem-countrys-palestinian-citizens-1878921672.
3. Mairav Zonszein, "Binyamin Netanyahu: 'Arab Voters Are Heading to the Polling Stations in Droves,'" *The Guardian*, March 17, 2015, https://www.theguardian.com/world/2015/mar/17/binyamin-netanyahu-israel-arab-election.
4. Sagi Elbaz, "The Borders of National Consent: When and Why De-Legitimization of the Arab Population in Israel Began in Israel Media" [in Hebrew]. *The Seventh Eye*, November 10, 2014, https://www.the7eye.org.il/132882.
5. Tzipi Livni, "Livni: National Aspirations of Israel's Arabs can be Met by Palestinian Homeland," *Haaretz*, December 11, 2008, https://www.haaretz.com/1.5072337.
6. This was expressed even in the early years of the Oslo Accords. See Graham Usher, "Bantustanisation or Bi-nationalism? An Interview with Azmi Bishara," *Race & Class* 37, no. 2 (1995): 43–49.
7. Yonatan Mendel, "On Israeli Elections Day," *London Review of Books*, March 19, 2015, https://www.lrb.co.uk/v37/n06/yonatan-mendel/diary.
8. Zeev Sternhell, "In Israel, Growing Fascism and Racism Akin to Early Nazism," *Haaretz*, January 19, 2018, https://www.haaretz.com/opinion/.premium-in-israel-growing-fascism-and-a-racism-akin-to-early-nazism-1.5746488; Gidi Weitz, "Fascist Elements Reached a Peak in Israel War on Gaza (Protective Edge): Interview with Prof. Zeev Strenhell" [in Hebrew]. *Haaretz*, August 18, 2014, https://www.haaretz.co.il/magazine/.premium-1.2399789.

9. Avi Shlaim, "The Rise and Fall of the Oslo Peace Process," *International Relations of the Middle East*, ed. Louise Fawcett (Oxford: Oxford University Press, 2005): 241–261; Sara Roy, "Why Peace Failed: An Oslo Autopsy," *Current History* 101, no. 651 (2002): 8.

10. Avi Shlaim, *The Iron Wall: Israel and the Arab World* (New York: W.W. Norton, 2001).

11. Theodor Herzl, *The Jewish State* (London: R. Searle, 1946): 30.

12. See, for example, the following article which refers to the use of this adage by both Barak and Netanyahu as a representation of the Jewish-Israeli majority: Aluf Benn, "The Jewish Majority in Israel Still See Their Country as 'A Villa in the Jungle,'" *The Guardian*, August 20, 2013, https://www.theguardian.com/commentisfree/2013/aug/20/jewish-majority-israel-villa-in-the-jungle.

13. George Lakoff and Mark Johnson, *Metaphors We Live By* (Chicago: University of Chicago Press, 2003).

14. Rabin said this in a speech to a joint session of the US Congress on July 26, 1994, transcript at http://www.mfa.gov.il/mfa/foreignpolicy/mfadocuments/yearbook9/pages/214%20address%20by%20prime%20minister%20rabin%20to%20the%20us%20cong.aspx.

15. Especially when Israeli decision-makers referred cynically to Arafat's phrase from his 1974 speech at the UN General Assembly, as holding an olive branch in one hand and a Kalashnikov in the other. Neil MacFarquhar, "The U.N. at 50: Arafat; P.L.O. Chief, Armed With Olive Branch, Appeals for a New State," *New York Times*, October 23, 1995.

16. In one fairly representative incident, after a suicide bombing at Jerusalem's Mahane Yehuda market in 1997, Netanyahu criticized Arafat for not offering a public condemnation of the attack and for not taking "action" against terrorism. CNN, "14 Killed in Jerusalem Suicide Bombings," July 30, 1997. See also the 2002 report by Human Rights Watch, "Erased In A Moment: Suicide Bombing Attacks Against Israeli Civilians" (HRW, 2002), https://www.hrw.org/sites/default/files/reports/ISRAELPA1002.pdf.

17. Expanding settlements began then, more than before, to draw a population motivated less by politics and more by economics, against the backdrop of the rapid privatization of public housing, the booming real estate market, and the deconstruction of the welfare state within the "Green Line." According to the Israeli human rights organization B'Tselem, from 1993 to 1999, about 30 new settlements were created in the OPT "and even though they were created illegally the government did not evacuate them." B'Tselem, *Oslo: Before and After—Human Rights in the Occupied Territories* [in Hebrew] (B'Tselem, May 1999), 5.

18. Efraim Karsh, "Why the Oslo Process Doomed Peace," *Middle East Quarterly* 23, no. 4 (Fall 2016): 1–17.

19. To this accusation, Beilin responded by saying that the majority of Israelis were killed following the outbreak of the Second Intifada. Effi Avraham, "When Bennett Reminded Beilin the Israelis Murdered Following Oslo" [in Hebrew]. *Srugim website*, November 29, 2012: https://tinyurl.com/y7rugv4x.

20. Arguments about hegemony and survival have been made most cogently by Ian Lustick in *Unsettled States, Disputed Lands* (Ithaca, NY: Cornell University Press, 1993).

21. Eyal Weizman, *Hollow Land: Israel's Architecture of Occupation* (London: Verso, 2012).

22. B'Tselem estimates 547,000 Israeli settlers living beyond the Green Line at the end of 2013. B'Tselem, "Statistics on Settlements and Settler Population," May 11, 2015, http://www.btselem.org/settlements/statistics, accessed August 9, 2016.

23. For further reading, see: Dan Rabinowitz, "Postnational Palestine/Israel? Globalization, Diaspora, Transnationalism, and the Israeli-Palestinian Conflict," *Critical Inquiry* 26, no. 4 (2000): 757–772, and Adel Samara, "Globalization, the Palestinian Economy, and the 'Peace Process,'" *Social Justice* 27, no. 4 (82) (2000): 117–131.

24. Sue Surkes, "Two-state Solution Still the Most Popular Option Among Israelis and Palestinians," *Times of Israel*, February 16, 2017, https://www.timesofisrael.com/two-state-solution-still-the-most-popular-option-among-israelis-and-palestinians/.

25. Memorably described by Avi Shlaim as a man negotiating over sharing a pizza pie while eating it. Avi Shlaim, "Obama and Israel: The Pessimistic Perspective," *The Hill*, December 27, 2010, http://thehill.com/blogs/congress-blog/foreign-policy/135177-obama-and-israel-the-pessimistic-perspective.

26. Israeli Ministry of Foreign Affairs, "Address by PM Netanyahu at Bar-Ilan University," June 14, 2009, http://mfa.gov.il/MFA/PressRoom/2009/Pages/Address_PM_Netanyahu_Bar-Ilan_University_14-Jun-2009.aspx, accessed August 9, 2016.

27. Barak Ravid, "Netanyahu: Bar-Ilan 2-State Speech No Longer Relevant in Today's Reality," *Haaretz*, March 8, 2015, http://www.haaretz.com/israel-news/.premium-1.645912.

28. Jonathan Lis, "Labor Adopts Herzog's Plan for Separation From Palestinians as Party Platform," *Haaretz*, February 8, 2016, http://www.haaretz.com/israel-news/.premium-1.702002.

29. See, for instance, Anna Getmansky and Thomas Zeitzoff, "Terrorism and Voting: The Effect of Rocket Threat on Voting in Israeli Elections," *American Political Science Review* 108, no. 03 (2014): 588–604; and Claude Berrebi and Esteban F. Klor, "Are Voters Sensitive to Terrorism? Direct Evidence From the Israeli Electorate," *American Political Science Review* 102, no. 03 (2008): 279–301.

30. Barak Ravid, "Netanyahu: I Don't Want a Binational State, But We Need to Control All of the Territory for the Foreseeable Future," *Haaretz*, October 26, 2015, http://www.haaretz.com/israel-news/.premium-1.682374.

31. See the 2016 poll from the Pew Research Center, "Israel's Religiously Divided Society," March 8, 2016, http://www.pewforum.org/2016/03/08/israels-religiously-divided-society/.

32. For recent examples of these see Yuval Elyon, "An Israeli-Palestinian Confederation? Not So Fast," *+972Mag*, June 19, 2016, http://972mag.com/an-israeli-palestinian-confederation-not-so-fast/120139/; and Noam Sheizaf, "What is the Israeli Right's One-state Vision?," *+972Mag*, May 12, 2014, http://972mag.com/what-is-the-israeli-rights-one-state-vision/90755/.

33. Chaim Levinson, "Israeli Right-wing Party Wants to Pay Palestinians to Leave Israel," *Haaretz*, September 7, 2013, https://www.haaretz.com/israel-news/israeli-right-wing-party-wants-to-pay-palestinians-to-leave-israel-1.5449087.

34. For further reading, see: Yonatan Mendel, *The Creation of Israeli Arabic: Political and Security Considerations in the Making of Arabic Language Studies in Israel* (London: Palagrave Macmillan, 2014), 40–45.

BIBLIOGRAPHY

Avraham, Effi. "When Benett Reminded Beilin the Israelis Murdered Following Oslo" [in Hebrew] *Srugim website*, November 29, 2012, https://tinyurl.com/y7rugv4x.

Benn, Aluf. "The Jewish Majority in Israel Still See Their Country As 'A Villa in the Jungle,'" *The Guardian*, August 20, 2013, https://www.theguardian.com/commentisfree/2013/aug/20/jewish-majority-israel-villa-in-the-jungle.

Berrebi, Claude, and Esteban F. Klor, "Are Voters Sensitive to Terrorism? Direct Evidence From the Israeli Electorate," *American Political Science Review* 102, no. 03 (2008): 279–301.

B'Tselem, *Oslo: Before and After—Human Rights in the Occupied Territories* [in Hebrew], (B'Tselem, May 1999).

———. "Statistics on Settlements and Settler Population," May 11, 2015, http://www.btselem.org/settlements/statistics.

CNN, "14 Killed in Jerusalem Suicide Bombings," July 30, 1997.

Elbaz, Sagi. "The Borders of National Consent: When and Why De-Legitimization of the Arab Population in Israel Began in Israel Media" [in Hebrew], *Seventh Eye*, November 10, 2014, https://www.the7eye.org.il/132882.

Elyon, Yuval. "An Israeli-Palestinian Confederation? Not So Fast," *+972Mag*, June 19, 2016, http://972mag.com/an-israeli-palestinian-confederation-not-so-fast/120139/.

Getmansky, Anna, and Thomas Zeitzoff, "Terrorism and Voting: The Effect of Rocket Threat on Voting in Israeli Elections," *American Political Science Review* 108, no. 3 (2014): 588–604.

Herzl, Theodor. *The Jewish State* (London: R. Searle, 1946).

Human Rights Watch, "Erased In A Moment: Suicide Bombing Attacks Against Israeli Civilians" (HRW, 2002), https://www.hrw.org/sites/default/files/reports/ISRAELPA1002.pdf.

Israeli Ministry of Foreign Affairs, "Address by Prime Minister Rabin to the U.S. Congress, 26 July 1994," http://www.mfa.gov.il/mfa/foreignpolicy/mfadocuments/yearbook9/pages/214%20address%20by%20prime%20minister%20rabin%20to%20the%20us%20cong.aspx.

———. "Address by PM Netanyahu at Bar-Ilan University," June 14, 2009, http://mfa.gov.il/MFA/PressRoom/2009/Pages/Address_PM_Netanyahu_Bar-Ilan_University_14-Jun-2009.aspx.

Karsh, Efraim. "Why the Oslo Process Doomed Peace," *Middle East Quarterly* 23, no. 4 (Fall 2016): 1–17.

Kimmerling, Baruch. *Politicide: Ariel Sharon's War Against the Palestinians* (London: Verso, 2003), 123.

Lakoff, George, and Mark Johnson. *Metaphors We Live By* (Chicago: University of Chicago Press, 2003).

Levinson, Chaim. "Israeli Right-wing Party Wants to Pay Palestinians to Leave Israel," *Haaretz*, September 7, 2013, https://www.haaretz.com/israel-news/israeli-right-wing-party-wants-to-pay-palestinians-to-leave-israel-1.5449087.

Lis, Jonathan. "Labor Adopts Herzog's Plan for Separation From Palestinians as Party Platform," *Haaretz*, February 8, 2016, http://www.haaretz.com/israel-news/.premium-1.702002.

Livni, Tzipi. "Livni: National Aspirations of Israel's Arabs can be Met by Palestinian Homeland," *Haaretz*, December 11, 2008, https://www.haaretz.com/1.5072337.

Lustick, Ian. *Unsettled States, Disputed Lands* (Ithaca, NY: Cornell University Press, 1993).

MacFarquhar, Neil. "The U.N. at 50: Arafat, P.L.O. Chief, Armed With Olive Branch, Appeals for a New State," *New York Times*, October 23, 1995.

Mendel, Yonatan. "On Israeli Elections Day," *London Review of Books*, March 19, 2015, https://www.lrb.co.uk/v37/n06/yonatan-mendel/diary.

———. *The Creation of Israeli Arabic: Political and Security Considerations in the Making of Arabic Language Studies in Israeli* (London: Palgrave Macmillan, 2014).

Pew Research Center, "Israel's Religiously Divided Society," March 8, 2016, http://www.pewforum.org/2016/03/08/israels-religiously-divided-society/.

Rabinowitz, Dan. "Postnational Palestine/Israel? Globalization, Diaspora, Transnationalism, and the Israeli-Palestinian Conflict," *Critical Inquiry* 26, no. 4 (2000): 757–772.

Rapoport, Meron. "'We are not Arab lovers': Israeli Labor's Bankrupt Efforts to Stave Off Decline," *Middle East Eye*, April 25, 2016, http://www.middleeasteye.net/columns/when-israels-main-opposition-party-has-problem-countrys-palestinian-citizens-1878921672.

Ravid, Barak. "Netanyahu: Bar-Ilan 2-State Speech No Longer Relevant in Today's Reality," *Haaretz*, March 8, 2015, http://www.haaretz.com/israel-news/.premium-1.645912.

———. "Netanyahu: I Don't Want a Binational State, But We Need to Control All of the Territory for the Foreseeable Future," *Haaretz*, October 26, 2015, http://www.haaretz.com/israel-news/.premium-1.682374.

Roy, Sara. "Why Peace Failed: An Oslo Autopsy," *Current History* 101, no. 651 (2002).

Samara, Adel. "Globalization, the Palestinian Economy, and the 'Peace Process'" *Social Justice* 27, no. 4 (82) (2000): 117–131.

Sheizaf, Noam. "What is the Israeli Right's One-state Vision?," *+972Mag*, May 12, 2014, http://972mag.com/what-is-the-israeli-rights-one-state-vision/90755/.

Shlaim, Avi. "Obama and Israel: The Pessimistic Perspective," *Hill*, December 27, 2010, http://thehill.com/blogs/congress-blog/foreign-policy/135177-obama-and-israel-the-pessimistic-perspective.

———. "The Rise and Fall of the Oslo Peace Process," *International Relations of the Middle East*, ed. Louise Fawcett (Oxford: Oxford University Press, 2005).

———. *The Iron Wall: Israel and the Arab World* (New York: W.W. Norton, 2001).

Sternhell, Zeev. "In Israel, Growing Fascism and Racism Akin to Early Nazism," *Haaretz*, January 19, 2018, https://www.haaretz.com/opinion/.premium-in-israel-growing-fascism-and-a-racism-akin-to-early-nazism-1.5746488.

Surkes, Sue. "Two-state Solution Still the Most Popular Option Among Israelis and Palestinians," *Times of Israel*, February 16, 2017, https://www.timesofisrael.com/two-state-solution-still-the-most-popular-option-among-israelis-and-palestinians/.

Usher, Graham. "Bantustanisation or Bi-nationalism? An Interview with Azmi Bishara," *Race & Class* 37, no. 2 (1995): 43–49.

Weitz, Gidi. "Fascist Elements Reached a Peak in Israel War on Gaza (Protective Edge): Interview with Prof. Zeev Strenhell" [in Hebrew], *Haaretz*, August 18, 2014, https://www.haaretz.co.il/magazine/.premium-1.2399789.

Weizman, Eyal. *Hollow Land: Israel's Architecture of Occupation* (London: Verso, 2012).

Zonszein, Mairav. "Binyamin Netanyahu: 'Arab Voters Are Heading to the Polling Stations in Droves,'" *The Guardian*, March 17, 2015, https://www.theguardian.com/world/2015/mar/17/binyamin-netanyahu-israel-arab-election.

Chapter Seven

From Singapore to the Stone Age

The Gaza Strip and the Political Economy of Crisis

Toufic Haddad

Twenty-five years after the signing of the Oslo Accords, the Gaza Strip is trapped in an unenviable state vacillating between active military aggression on the one hand, and suffocating besiegement on the other.

A damning report published by the United Nations Country Team working across the Occupied Palestinian Territory (OPT) in July 2017 listed a shocking toll of humanitarian statistics and developmental challenges.[1]

Gaza's unemployment rate stands at 42 percent, and youth unemployment at 60 percent—among the highest in the world. Only 3.8 percent of Gaza's water is considered safe for consumption, while clean water trucked in costs 15–20 times that of water from the network. Some 80 percent of the population is food dependent, while poverty rates average around 40 percent. Gaza's population in 2020 will stand at 2.2 million persons, and 3.1 million by 2030. In the past five years alone, the population density of the Strip went up by more than one thousand persons per square kilometer—from 4383 people/km^2 to 5479 persons; 43 percent of the population is below the age of 15; unemployment rates for graduates with an Associate Diploma Certificate or above have reached 42.9 percent, while figures for women stand at 65 percent. Gaza's well-known restrictions on movement and access are not just limited to getting in and out of the Strip, but include access to 35 percent of its agricultural land and as much as 85 percent of its fishing waters. The number of Ministry of Health patient referrals for care outside of Gaza tripled in the past decade, while Israeli approval rates to exit Gaza for medical purposes dropped from 90 percent to 62 percent. Breast cancer survival rates declined from 59 percent in the 2006–2010 period, to 46 percent in 2010–2014.

While the toll of statistics illustrating Gaza's deplorable humanitarian state is well known and seemingly unending, it is made worryingly more disconcerting by the fact that there are few indications the situation will improve, and many that forebode its worsening.

Explosive conditions continue to define the Israeli-Gaza Strip bufferzone, as Palestinian protesters frequently organize demonstrations against the Israeli-imposed blockade from land, air, and sea. Military preparations continue uninterrupted on both sides, as bellicose statements by Israel and the Hamas military wing remain the norm. Outstanding issues of previous rounds of fighting remain unresolved including the issue of reconstruction, prisoners, and freedom of movement, while the main issues of contention between Israel and Palestinians as defined in the Oslo Accords—borders, settlements, refugees, water, and Jerusalem—central ones that relate to the broader question of Palestinian self-determination, have not been raised since the US-shepherded peace process effectively collapsed in 2000. Instead, Western donors maintain a "no-contact" policy with Hamas, despite having previously encouraged Palestinians to "build a functioning democracy" that resulted in the movement's rise to power. Intra-Palestinian political struggles also appear no closer to resolution, despite repeated efforts at reconciliation, as differences between Hamas and Fatah seem to have only entrenched themselves during the dozen years of their separation—discursively, financially, and institutionally.

If this were not humbling enough, the UN was forced to revise its 2012 warning that Gaza would become unlivable by 2020.[2] It now acknowledges that for most in Gaza in 2017, the territory has already crossed this dubious threshold.[3]

Things were not always this way. Ironically, the Gaza Strip was supposed to be the shining exemplar of the Israeli-Palestinian peace process. Ever since it was the first area from which Israeli troops withdrew in the summer of 1994, the territory has not escaped inflated projections that it could be transformed from a state of well-known poverty, marginalization, and violence, into a font of productivity, prosperity and peace. Singapore, Hong Kong, and a "hi-tech India on the Mediterranean" have all been invoked as possible models for Gaza by Palestinian, Israeli, and international politicians and commentators, suggesting that this possibility is both desirable, realizable, and the responsibility of Gaza's (now) Palestinian governors.

Clearly Gaza has consistently failed to meet these expectations. On the contrary, recent years have seen the abandonment of the pretense of optimism altogether as the world has increasingly witnessed the explicit and programmatic use of active and passive forms of violence against Gaza to subjugate its people, destroy its economic potential, and leverage its dependency. This is not only seen in the sensationalist rhetoric of Israeli politicians during the various military assaults launched against the territory since 2007, openly calling for Gaza to be "flattened," sent back to the "Middle Ages,"[4] and by 2014, the "stone ages."[5] It is also treated in more insidious ways as seen by the disclosures of the Israeli human rights organization Gisha, which forced Israel to reveal its military had been calculating the precise number of calories needed to ensure Gaza did not starve.[6] Gaza's misery has become a highly orchestrated and institutionalized affair, exhibiting the full attributes of rational planning.

The dramatic about-face of Gaza's fortunes raises serious questions as to the various political, economic, and historical factors that account for this reversal. How did the situation reach such proportions, and what accounts for this once-symbol of potential prosperity transmogrifying over a relatively short period of time into a situation of deliberately engineered backwardness?

HISTORICAL AND POLITICAL ECONOMIC BACKGROUND

It is important to begin by stressing that there is nothing natural about the Gaza Strip's territorial borders or the demographic composition of its population. The Gaza Strip can only be understood historically and politically as the product of the 1948 War, with about three quarters of its current population being refugees or their descendants.[7] The demographic composition of the West Bank is roughly the reverse of Gaza—with 27 percent of its total population being refugees.

The Gaza Strip's majority refugee composition has had important implications for the territory's political formation. It has meant that Gaza became the most important crucible within which the modern Palestinian national movement was formed and tested from the ruins of the Nakba. Among the factors contributing to this process were the common majority condition of exile; the defacto weak international regime established to assist refugees and protect their rights (the United Nations Relief and Works Agency for Palestinian Refugees in the Near East [UNRWA] and the defunct United Nations Conciliation Commission for Palestine [UNCCP]);[8] the dense and desperate residential conditions to emerge there as a result, with 555,000 people still living in UN-administered refugee camps (eight in total);[9] the very situatedness of Gaza within historical Palestine's borders, close to refugee homes and properties, though strictly hemmed in by Israel to the north and east, and Egypt to the south;[10] and decades of direct and indirect military occupation. Collectively these factors form the basis within which a modern and resilient national identity and movement emerged, defiantly demanding an end to occupation, the return of refugees to their homes, and the realization of these demands within a framework that asserted national self-determination.

The Gaza Strip has consistently birthed the most significant popular resistance movements against Zionist settler colonialism and occupation, and for return, given the manner in which this territory and its conditions embody the concentration of so many of the historical injustices and political contradictions of the Palestinian question today—statelessness, repeated dispossession, deplorable living conditions, and systematic oppression, combined with not insignificant amounts of shirked international responsibility and Israeli impunity.

Gaza has also consistently experienced some of the most brutal of Israel's efforts to quash Palestinian nationalism. While there is no need to go into this lengthy history, too often ignored or unrecognized in depth and character,[11] it nonetheless remains important to underscore that Palestinian national aspirations, even in their most anodyne articulation, remain antithetical to Zionist ideological and political aspirations.[12] The entire Zionist leadership in Israel has consistently and historically shared the conviction of firmly rejecting a fully sovereign Palestinian state on *any* part of the lands Israel currently controls. In turn, Israel has pursued policies that aim to weaken, control, delegitimize, or destroy Palestinian national aspirations, while equally asserting Zionist presence through the expansion of its settler colonial project across the 1967 OPT and within the remaining Palestinian-held territories inside 1948 Palestine/Israel.[13]

These factors set the Gaza Strip and Israel—as the vehicle of Zionist colonization—firmly on a collision course, and even necessitate *pro-active* Israeli approaches to the territory and its population, even in the absence of statehood or sovereignty. From an Israeli perspective, it becomes important to stem the territory's transformation into the nucleus of a national political project that could threaten Israel or spread influence beyond its current borders, especially to the West Bank where important Zionist ideological, military, religious, and geostrategic interests lie.

FROM THE ALLON PLAN TO THE OSLO ACCORDS

From these basic understandings emerge the main contours of Israel's contemporary regime of control over the OPT and Gaza in particular.

Israel's occupation of the West Bank and Gaza Strip in the 1967 War created basic demographic and political contradictions regarding Israel's self-professed "Jewish democratic" character. The existence of more than one million Palestinian Arab ("non-Jewish") residents of the OPT—represented a long-term challenge to the "Jewish majority" character necessary to maintain a "Jewish state."[14] Providing citizenship to this population would erode the "Jewish" character of the state, while denying citizenship would erode its "democratic" basis.

Faced with this predicament, Israel devised what came to be known as the 1967 Allon Plan: a strategy of indirect rule—limited autonomy without sovereignty—that allowed it to continue its settlement impetus in a long-term strategy to unite the conquests of 1948 and 1967.[15] Israel understood that it needed to create an intermediary authority between it and the local population so as to be able to statistically, institutionally, and practically remove the Palestinian population and the package of their various basic needs and rights from Israeli concern. This removal/separation however needed to take place without jeopardizing Israeli prerogatives toward the entire land between the Jordan River and the Mediterranean Sea, particularly its project to integrate the commanding heights of the West Bank topography, its water sources, and its biblically significant areas into Israel's pre-1967 "borders."[16]

Moreover, Israel needed to ensure that the West Bank and Gaza were dealt with *separately* as a means to apply leverage and division over the Palestinians. As one Israeli Labour Party Policy document from 1979 noted,

> Tying the problem of the Gaza Strip to that of the West Bank will bring about the creation of a bridge inside the state of Israel between the two concentrations of Arab population and an increase in the Palestinian population for whom a solution needs to be found. The Gaza Strip was in the past and is at present a separate unit from the West Bank—nationally, historically and politically—and there is no reason for us to be the ones to connect the two problems.[17]

Israel thus sought the geographic, institutional, and political division of the West Bank from Gaza, identifying from an early stage the importance of politically and institutionally dividing the occupied population, while allowing Israel to isolate problems, and find local solutions.

DE-DEVELOPMENT AND THE POLITICAL ECONOMY OF OCCUPATION

A natural corollary to this approach subsequently entailed the de-development of the OPT and of the Gaza Strip in particular. De-development entails "a process which undermines or weakens the ability of an economy to grow and expand by preventing it from accessing and utilizing critical inputs needed to promote internal growth beyond a specific structural level."[18] According to Roy, who coined the term, Palestinian economic relations and linkage systems in Gaza were deliberately engineered to lack "rational structural transformation, integration and synthesis" becoming and then remaining unassembled and disparate "obviating any organic congruous, and logical arrangement of the economy or of its constituent parts."[19] Gaza would increasingly become "vulnerable to and dependent upon events inside the Jewish state," with Gaza's productive sectors stultified and Gaza's labor force transformed into a cheap alternative to be employed within the Israeli economy.[20]

While these conditions would serve the interests of Israeli capital for two decades, the pre-Oslo arrangement proved increasingly untenable as the years unfolded. In particular, the high dependency of Gaza's labor force on Israeli employment would begin to raise concern within Israeli political, economic, and security circles in light of the onset of the 1987 Intifada and then the 1990–1991 Gulf War. The popular resistance witnessed in the 1987 Intifada, which began in Gaza and was fiercest and most persistent there, posed increasingly worrying moral and political questions for Israeli society and its army regarding the long-term prospects for continued direct rule over the Palestinian population. These conditions made finding or imposing a solution more pressing as the prospect of endlessly chasing Gaza's youth around labyrinthine refugee camps did not bode well for Israel's citizen army, many of whom descended from the ghettos of Europe themselves. Although Israeli defense minister, Yitzhak Rabin, had vowed to deal with the uprising with an "iron fist," the strategy was transparently futile, leading only to the budding of military groups, and the ascendancy of more radical political factions like Hamas, at the expense of Fatah, itself on the retreat after the debacle of the 1990–91 Gulf War.

The late 1980s appeal of neoliberalization to Israeli capital formations would also contribute to the impetus to restructure relations with the OPT and Gaza in particular.[21] In an era of globalizing financial capital, this neoliberalizing impetus was impeded due to the continued existence of the primary and secondary Arab boycotts. Israeli economists like Ezra Sadan began elaborating on plans to create industrial estates and free-trade zones on the "border" with the Gaza Strip, as a subcontracting solution for Israeli and international capital, that would explicitly take advantage of Gaza's deep pools of cheap refugee labor, while allowing for the circumspection of Israeli labor regulations and powerful unions.[22] Such an arrangement foresaw the need to structurally reconfigure political and economic relations between Israel and the OPT, whereby Israeli political and economic power could ally (albeit asymmetrically) with a form of Palestinian administrative power, to govern such an arrangement.

The brewing of these political, ideological, and economic contradictions would compel Israel to devise and implement its closure policy in the early 1990s, as a mechanism which enabled it to regulate and tend to these various needs.[23] Closure allowed Israel to unilaterally impose integrationist and segregationist economic, territorial, and political policies becoming "the most effective means of restricting the mobility of workers and demarcating boundaries between Palestinian and Israeli areas."[24] Gaza's labor flows to Israel would be reduced to between 45,000 and 50,000 after the start of the Intifada, and further to between 25,000 and 30,000 for the two years following the Gulf War.

FROM THE OSLO ACCORDS TO THE AL AQSA INTIFADA (1993–2000)

The percolation of these demographic, political, economic, and "security" interests, together with the externally impressed interests of Israel's most important strategic ally, the US, in the post-Gulf War era, provided the context for explaining the factors that gave birth to Israel's signing of the Declaration of Principles on Interim Self-Government Arrangements (DOP, also known as the Oslo Accords) in 1993. It was not by chance that the Gaza Strip was the first and most significant area from which the Israeli military redeployed, and in which the Palestinian Authority (PA) would be established. It was in Gaza where Israel's political, ideological, and governance contradictions were strongest. Moreover, long-term demographic and security concerns only added to the impetus for separating from Palestinians, captured in Rabin's statement of the time where he "dreamed of Gaza sinking into the sea," and that Israel needed to "get Gaza out of Tel Aviv."[25] However, even though Israel would withdraw from Gaza's most densely populated areas, it still maintained control over roughly a third of its land where 5,000 settlers resided in 21 settlements and additional military bases, together with their access routes.

Of course, packaging the political motivations and interests behind the Accords and the peace process in general took on more delicate and celebratory public forms in an attempt to win over international and domestic skeptics. The fanfare generated around the Accords by a largely uncritical international media; the issuing of the 1994 Nobel Peace Prize to Yitzhak Rabin, Shimon Peres, and Yasser Arafat; and the participation of the World Bank and IMF leading a coalition of donors to design, oversee, and finance the PA, all added to the peace process's optimism and allure. The DOP also took special care to emphasize a "liberal peacebuilding" approach, promising economic liberalization and benefits for Israelis and Palestinians, as articulated in a series of major developmental projects referred to in the Accords modeled around the US Marshall Plan.[26] The construction of the Gaza port, airport, industrial zone, and power plant were also argued to serve this end, underscoring how the peace process was intended to generate and distribute "peace dividends," whose profits would economically and socially "trickle down," consolidating a domestic constituency to support the Accords.[27]

Behind the Accord's sensationalized veneer, however, existed a series of Israeli "security" concerns that necessitated a vigilant PA policing role. In his efforts to convince the Israeli Knesset to sign on to the Oslo Accords, Rabin famously declared that "they [the Palestinians] will rule by their own methods, freeing—and this is most important—the Israeli Army soldiers from having to do what they will do."[28] No doubt Israel saw the PA as a proxy-security apparatus through which it could restructure and mediate its relations with the Palestinian people. This inherently repressive intermediary character was affirmed years later by former US Ambassador to Israel, Martin Indyk, when he noted that:

> The Israelis came to us [in 1994] and said basically, "Arafat's job is to clean up Gaza. It's going to be a difficult job. He needs walking-around money," because the assumption was he would use it to get control of all of these terrorists who'd been operating in these areas for decades.[29]

Indyk's quotation discloses that the PA's job was not only to function as a proxy security force for Israel in Gaza and across the OPT, but also that this arrangement needed to be financed through off-budget accounting. The US and Israel were consciously colluding in erecting a neopatrimonial arrangement led by PLO chairman Yasser Arafat, with this arrangement financed through less than transparent channels.[30]

By recruiting substantial sections of the grassroots Fatah movement into the PA's civil service and security apparatus across Gaza, financed through official and unofficial channels, the PA consolidated a political order that drastically differed from the existent pluralistic political arrangement that had arisen in the OPT since the early 1980s, and had crystalized during the 1987 Intifada. The latter had witnessed new political elites from all political factions emerging to challenge the quietist approach of the traditional elites who had dominated the local level since 1967, accusing them of having accommodated and even benefitted from the Israeli occupation.[31] It was these new political elites who initiated the 1987 Intifada and found ways to somewhat democratically mediate their interactions, challenging the Israeli occupation as well as the old social order.

However, the secretly negotiated Oslo Accords, and the subsequent creation of the PA, actively reversed these important sociopolitical advances. Despite the DOP being sold and driven by a "liberal peace" vision, local elections were cancelled thereby preventing the representation of this political current. Instead, elections were only held for the Legislative Council, a body whose legitimacy derived from the Oslo Accords, and which opposition factions were determined to boycott. The holding of Legislative Council elections, and the cancelling of local elections, essentially allowed Fatah to secure an overwhelming majority in the parliament, while alternatively freeing Arafat to personally appoint loyalists on the local level based on a political (Fatah) and (large) clan basis.[32] Many of these in Gaza came from the elite families that the 1987 Intifada had only recently marginalized.

Thus a hybrid social arrangement was constituted during the Oslo years (1994–2000), which saw the institutions of the PA dominated by a blend of diasporic and local Fatah leaders, together with various appointed elites, and sections of diasporic Palestinian capitalists who also largely emerged from patrician families. Arafat needed off-budget accounting to finance his patronage rule over Gaza in particular, because of the way in which Israeli troops redeployed. Unlike the West Bank, which witnessed a protracted withdrawal of Israeli troops over time that allowed for the PA to gradually centralize and consolidate its power there, in Gaza, the Israeli army redeployed rapidly from the Palestinian-populated centers to the Israeli-controlled settlements. The speed of this transition in the context of the limited nature of the autonomy enjoyed by the PA-to-be, institutionally "froze" into place the existing political and institutional forces therein. Because the autonomy extended to Palestinians across the OPT was limited in scope and nature, with Israel still controlling internal and external movement of persons and goods, the basis for the continued existence of an oppositionist political current to the Oslo process remained alive.[33]

This factor would importantly lay the basis for the gridlocked political dynamic to emerge in Gaza between Fatah and Hamas, as a consequence of the failed Oslo process. The speed of the Israeli redeployment made it difficult for the PA to centralize its rule over Gaza, and led to increasing efforts by the Authority to "buy-in" sections of Gazan society, attempting to shore up its "holding power" at the expense of the rising tides of Hamas. It also helps explain the heavier reliance upon force that the PA/Fatah exercised in Gaza (more than in the West Bank) against its opponents, resulting in unlawful arrest, torture, and even acts of shooting—notably one incident where PA policemen killed 14 Palestinians on November 18, 1994, in events which came to be known as "Black Friday."[34]

It further explains, in part, the wide varieties of persons recruited by Fatah and the PA in some capacity in Gaza, their ideological non-uniformity, and the patron-client structure of their relations to the PA/Fatah project. It may have affected the quality, capacity, and willingness of these forces to more forcefully defend the PA when clashes with Hamas eventually arose over control of the institutions of the Authority in the summer of 2007 after the

2006 election victory of Hamas, and especially the death of the Palestinian patriarch, Arafat himself.

The key political economic transition of the Oslo years is thus found in the dual maneuver of Israel restructuring its economic, political, and institutional relations with the local population (justifying this as steps toward peace and security), while simultaneously ensuring a neopatrimonial regime emerged in its place, entirely dependent upon Israel and donors for its financial and political solvency.

Closure in particular would allow for Israel to gradually incorporate its strategic interests across the OPT into pre-1967 Israel, while formalizing the fragmenting and isolating of Palestinian localities along the way. In so doing, Israel would decisively destroy the potential for the OPT, and Gaza as the center of this project, from being considered a safe investment opportunity for any economic activity that was dependent on the movement of Palestinian labor and trade flows. Closure made the OPT an unreliable destination to foreign capital investment, puncturing the Singapore mythology that had been built up to "sell" the Accords. Instead, only the most primitive investments in speculative, short return, low value-added, "lazy" investments such as real estate, telecommunications, construction of commercial and civil rental real estate, tourism, and commercial goods trade thrived. The benefits of this system also tended to flow upstream rather than down, as a small coterie of benefactors around the Authority profited.

Closure also radically transformed the structure of the Palestinian labor market. Before the 1994 Interim arrangements, 30 percent of the labor force in the West Bank and more than 40 percent in Gaza, legally worked in Israel—around 115,000 Palestinians in total.[35] But with the heavy full closures imposed in 1996–1997, these figures dropped to 18 and 6 percent respectively, spiking Palestinian unemployment to around 20 and 30 percent.[36]

The heavy Israeli closures were so economically damaging to the OPT economy that the Western donor community feared that the sudden rise in unemployment would destabilize the peace process overall. Aid interventions would suddenly shift from an initial focus on infrastructure and long-term development spending to emergency support for employment creation. Substantial numbers of Palestinians would thereafter be added to the rosters of the PA's civil and security sectors, bloating them to irrational proportions—103,000 by 2000.[37] Official statistics show that in 1995, the Gaza public sector stood at 23 percent of the workforce; by 2000 that figure jumped to 31.5 percent.[38]

Public sector employment became a means to hide Gaza's unemployment, generated by "a growing, unilaterally imposed, separation," and Israel's deliberate, broader, decades-old de-development policies.[39] The increasing isolation of Gaza would become a central part of these dynamics: unlike the West Bank, which witnessed the construction of an apartheid-like barrier only after 2001, the Gaza Strip witnessed its fencing off in 1995.[40]

This important socioeconomic and structural shift rapidly forcing Gaza's labor force away from the Israeli market and into the PA "market," paid for by international donors, is thus the most significant structural and political economic shift of the Oslo years. It represented a significant achievement for Israel to cunningly reconfigure its relations with the OPT and the rights and international obligations it was responsible for therein as an occupying power. The "security" pretext facilitated a dynamic whereby Israel oversaw the creation of an entirely dependent entity that was expected internationally to be able to manage and solve the economic and social ills of an occupied de-developed population, in an active conflict zone, without any (or almost any) of the tools that could facilitate this—beginning with sovereignty and control of borders.

THE AL AQSA INTIFADA

The Al Aqsa Intifada represented the explosion of this repressive arrangement. But it also gave Israel the opportunity and incentive to accelerate the pursuit of its pre-existing goals, in all dimensions—namely, to escalate efforts to weaken the Palestinian people, leadership, and movement while unilaterally imposing its geopolitical interests upon them.

On the political level, Arafat's rejection of the Barak-Clinton initiatives at Camp David in June 2000 and his unwillingness to crack down on the uprising once it began in September 2000, set him on a path of excommunication by Israel and the Western donor states. The Palestinian leader went from being a "partner" before Camp David, to "no longer a partner," then to being demonized, physically isolated in his compound, and then, perhaps even assassinated, as critics charge.

Israel was determined to eliminate Arafat's political power and command over the institution of the PA (both security and civil), while donors echoed this demand, doing their best to extract political and institutional "reforms" from the Palestinian leader as well.

While Israel physically attacked all PA compounds and ministries throughout its repression of the uprising, international finance institutions (IFI) began determinatively appealing to "good governance" as a means to eliminate the very sources of Arafat's financial power that these powers had provided him with when the Oslo process began. IFI reforms would centralize all revenues and investments under an IMF-audited Ministry of Finance account, create an empowered prime minister's position, and institutionally and legally restructure the PA to weaken the executive politically and financially.

Behind these maneuvers rationalized as necessary for their "anti-terror" and anti-corruption/good governance affects, lay a key strategic maneuver. The creation of the PA by the Oslo process was considered exceedingly controversial for the Palestinians, because it entailed accepting self-governance under non-sovereign conditions, while also committing the PA to Israeli security imperatives, as the weaker, occupied party. This controversial act could only have been realized thanks to the political charisma and leadership of Arafat himself, whose historical legitimacy somehow insulated and protected the decision to create the Authority under these conditions. It equally could not have come into existence were it not for the millions in Western donor aid which played a pivotal role in training, financing, and sanctioning its legitimacy internationally. This apparatus, which ultimately was seen as crucial to Israel "resolving" its Jewish democratic contradictions, was now to be extracted from the grips of its neopatron, and heavily audited and controlled by Israel and these same donors. Furthermore, the neopatrimonial manner in which the apparatus had been run under Arafat had equally exacerbated many tensions between different social, political, and economic actors, with these struggles surfacing throughout the Intifada and the years thereafter. The implications of these general trends upon the Gaza Strip were many.

Arafat's geographical isolation in his Ramallah compound during most of the Intifada, until his death, left him unable to manage the situation brewing in Gaza as a result of Israel's scorched earth policies. Casualties in Gaza were unprecedented in scope and scale, as Israel's escalating military maneuvers (particularly in house demolition, artillery shelling, and assassinations via helicopter and then drone) surpassed those in the West Bank in quantity and intensity—especially after Israel's spring 2002 offensive "Operation Defensive Shield." Some 2,998 of 4,791 Palestinians killed between September 29, 2000, and December 26, 2008 (the eve of Operation Cast Lead), were from Gaza; at least 635 of these were minors.[41]

Moreover, the failure of the Oslo process and the eruption of the Al-Aqsa Intifada vindicated Hamas and its oppositionist political stance against the Oslo process. Gaza witnessed a steady strengthening of Hamas' military strength and political popularity, but by no means was it in a position to politically eclipse Fatah while Arafat was still alive. Fatah's protean political character also allowed for elements within the movement to also claim their own anti-Oslo politics, including in the military (guerilla) arena, and substantial sections of Fatah's grassroots in Gaza joined the military activities of the Intifada. However, Fatah could never fully align its political stance with the elements of the party engaged in military activity, while Hamas of course could. Moreover, Fatah's financial dependency on Western donors also prevented this from overtly taking place, while Hamas' independent financial channels gave it a far wider margin of maneuver.

During the Oslo years, Arafat's charismatic character had been crucial to mediate and manage the often-tense relations within Fatah between competing elites, and between Fatah and Hamas, particularly during waves of PA repression against the Islamist movement. But Arafat's isolation in Ramallah weakened his ability to play this role from a distance. In his absence, and in the context of Israel's escalating military maneuvers, conditions in Gaza became increasingly unruly.

Economically and socially, things were increasingly desperate as well: 53 percent of Palestinian households in the West Bank and Gaza Strip in 2002 had to borrow money to purchase food.[42] Moreover, 22.5 percent of children below the age of five suffered from chronic (13.2 percent) and acute (9.3 percent) malnutrition. Levels were worst in Gaza where 13.3 percent of children under five suffered from acute malnutrition (a condition known as "wasting"), putting it in the company of Eritrea in 1995, and just below the Congo in 2002.[43]

By 2002, unemployment across Gaza had soared to 37.9 percent, doubling the 18.9 percent rate of 2000. Employment in the settlements had dipped to 1.8 percent of the workforce compared to 15.7 percent in 2000. GDP per capita also dropped to 959.3 in 2002 from a high of 1420 during the Oslo years (1998).[44] The Eretz industrial zone was increasingly targeted by militant activity, leading to relocation of its Israeli companies and eventual closure in 2004, losing 4,000 Palestinian jobs.[45] Israel also increasingly restricted Gaza fishermen's access to waters. Despite the Oslo Accords officially allowing Palestinians access to 20 nautical miles from the Gaza coast, this was reduced to only 12 nautical miles by 2002, and 6 nautical miles by 2006.[46] Public sector employment spiked at 41.4 percent in 2001 and remained in the high 30s until the end of 2005.

Geopolitically, while Israel accelerated its settlement expansion across the West Bank, and worked to seal it off from the 1948 areas and Jerusalem through the construction of its "separation barrier" and closure system, Gaza was shut off from all three (the West Bank, 1948 areas, and Jerusalem). Similar to the West Bank, the Israeli army also attempted to maintain control over internal movement in Gaza, cutting the Strip into four sections, utilizing its settlement infrastructure to do so.

The Israeli army made moves to geographically enforce more secure lines of movement for its army and settlers across Gaza, often doing so by bulldozing large swathes of agricultural land, homes, and farms. "Seam" zones where the Israeli army and settlers came into proximity with the Palestinian population became hyper-militarized wastelands, where untold numbers of Palestinians were killed and houses bulldozed. The Rafah border strip with Egypt (what Israel called "the Philadelphia corridor") became one of the most brutal of these frontiers, where Israeli bulldozers and tanks demolished hundreds of homes inside the UN refugee camp. For the first four years of the Al Aqsa Intifada, Israel demolished over 2,500 Palestinian houses across Gaza, nearly two thirds of these in Rafah.[47]

Aside from its expected humanitarian implications, Israel's escalating intensity of destruction began forcing new topographical realities upon the resistance formations, which emerged in Gaza during the Intifada. Pushed back from anywhere close to the settlement blocs and roads, inchoate Palestinian militant formations began to increasingly rely upon forms of attack from greater distances—namely through mortar and primitive rocket fire. These formations also began constructing underground tunnels as ways to approach and attack Israeli military installations.

This tactical shift in military strategy had important implications on Israel's holding power over its settlement project in Gaza. Settlements like Kfar Darom, Morag, Netzarim, and Gush Katif became daily targets of multiple rounds of mortar fire, with little Israel could do to prevent it. Israel was forced to restructure the nature of its hold over the territory, eventually determining that it needed to withdraw all troops and settlers from Gaza, in what became known as its "disengagement" plan. In truth, the maneuver was really a unilateral Israeli redeployment, which sealed the territory and hermetically constrained the flow of its people and goods. Israel's isolation of Gaza and its effective division of the OPT, was described by Israeli political advisor Dov Weisglas as a form of "formaldehyde" such that "there will not be a political process with the Palestinians."[48]

"Disengagement" crucially obfuscated the nature of Israel's control over Gaza, as what looked to be an act of repealed control over occupied lands, was in truth an act of strengthening its hold over these areas, by finding more efficient ways of managing them and their contradictions remotely.

THE SIEGE YEARS

The Rise of the Tunnel Economy

The 2006 Legislative Council elections held in the wake of Arafat's death, together with the unilateral Israeli redeployment from Gaza, provided the opportunity for the compounded sentiments and transformations that had taken place since Oslo to assume political expression. In truth, Hamas was the only cohesive political movement to embody an institutional capacity and political vision to pose an alternative to the status quo ante. Although it too was woefully unprepared for what would later unfold, Fatah was in even worse shape, as the movement was in the midst of weathering the political turmoil of having lost its prime regulator, while its historical, political gambit to engage in the Oslo process was in tatters. The myriad network of patrons and clients established by Arafat had unraveled after his death, with some escaping with money, others allying behind Abu Mazen, and still others jockeying for positioning against Abu Mazen and/or for other potential future Fatah leaders. Fatah's fragmentation in Gaza was so severe that it became routine before the elections for elements of the party to establish roadblocks on key routes across Gaza, as part of partisan infighting. While Hamas candidates would win the overall vote count by 44 percent to Fatah's 41 percent,[49] the actual balance of Palestinian Legislative Council seats won by each camp was more asymmetrical in Hamas's favor—74 (56 percent) to Fatah's 45 seats (34 percent). The latter (Fatah) had split its votes between different electoral slates, while Hamas's "Change and Reform" party fielded only one unified slate in each locality. Hamas's clear majority in the Legislative Council gave the movement a democratic mandate to push forward its electoral promise of instituting a series of institutional, legal, and political reforms of the Palestinian political project, including a complete deviation from the Oslo track.[50]

While Hamas's electoral victory gave expression to popular antipathy toward Oslo, the national movement's disdain of Fatah's implosion, and the rudderlessness of the post-Arafat leadership vacuum, Israel and the Western donor community saw in the victory a direct threat to their historical and political project. Their immediate response was to boycott the electoral victors, while planning for more subversive maneuvers behind the scenes. A year after Hamas and its "Executive Forces" would forcefully take over Presidential Guard and Preventative Security facilities in the summer of 2007 in a mini-civil war that saw over 200 killed, investigative journalist David Rose revealed that these elements were indeed organizing and operationalizing a coup against Hamas, led by former Gaza Preventative Security chief, Mohammed Dahlan.[51] The dramatic final escalation would unfold with Hamas personnel discovering, then stopping, a US-funded arms shipment intended for the coup-makers, instigating the latter's attack against said facilities, militarily defeating them, while Israel facilitated the coup-maker's escape to the West Bank.

Cut off from access to the world via Israeli-controlled economic channels, Gaza turned to its tunnels under the border with Egypt, transforming this once informal, survival/contraband economy into a substitute for the former "official" economy. In so doing, it inverted the previous arrangement established in the era of the Fatah-led PA, as a consequence of the 1994 Paris

Economic Protocol (see the chapter in this volume by Raja Khalidi). Hamas used its control and governance over the tunnel economy to construct its own economic arrangements, together with its various elites, working therein to construct the movement's own "political settlement."[52]

While tunnels numbered in the dozens before the siege, most of which were controlled by political factions, their numbers bloomed to more than 500 on the eve of Israel's 2008/9 military campaign, Operation Cast Lead, and to approximately 1500 by 2011.[53]

Hamas understood the strategic significance of the tunnel economy as an alternative to the previous arrangement, and made moves to formalize these routes through the establishment of a Tunnel Affairs Commission in 2009—a branch of its Ministry of Interior. This allowed it to govern the market, regulate trade, arbitrate disputes, levy customs charges, and monitor for inflation, hoarding, price-fixing, counterfeiting, and contraband. These policies lent themselves toward price stabilization, which was highly welcome in light of steep increases and volatility after the siege began. The levying of customs also enabled Hamas to secure a revenue base, which partially compensated for the loss of VAT revenues that the Fatah-led PA collected via Israeli transfers monthly (usually), but which were not sent to the Hamas government once it took power.[54] Hamas equally found a myriad of new ways to secure additional income from the tunnels, partnering with collectives of smugglers; building their own tunnels; creating import rents of their own; and facilitating the laundering of the funds generated through investments in residential and commercial real estate.

Between 1998 and 2008, the tunnel economy effectively reversed the previous economic relations that had existed between Gaza, Israel, and Egypt, substituting the latter for the former as the source of more than 95 percent of the territory's goods.[55]

The tunnel economy continued to grow, increasing ten-fold between 2008 and 2010. Tunnel quality also improved, enabling the import of livestock, cars, large quantities of raw material needed for construction, together with Egyptian government-subsidized fuel. In the case of the latter, prices undercut the previous Israeli fuel supply by as much as a quarter. Collectively these processes allowed for Gaza to reconstruct after the military assault of 2008/9, largely on its own, while spurring what the World Bank was forced to acknowledge as "exceptionally high growth"—28 percent in the first half of 2011.[56]

The tunnel economy absorbed large sections of Gaza's labor pool, employing some 5,000 tunnel owners and 25,000 workers, and supporting about 150,000 dependents, or 10 percent of Gaza's population. By subverting the political restrictions and bureaucracy created by the 1994 Paris Protocol arrangement, the tunnel economy allowed for Gaza to re-establish commercial relations with Egypt, its natural economic periphery and trading partner. It also served to sideline the elite that had hitherto dominated Gaza economically as a consequence of the previous arrangement, undercutting those who had benefitted from the politically determined capital overseen by Fatah, and indirectly by Israel and the Western donor community.

The new period was marked by the departure of Gaza's PA/Fatah-affiliated old economic and security elite after the failed 2007 coup, and the rise of a new generation of smugglers and nouveau riche benefactors to this arrangement, who derived from different social and economic backgrounds to the former elites. Tunnels became a key driver of upward mobility and social change, empowering groups "originating" from the southern Gaza strip, who had previously been marginalized at the expense of the powerful and old commercial and patrician families of Gaza City, and the elites generated by the Paris Protocol and PA economic policies.

The tunnels, and Hamas' governance over them, represented a meaningful albeit limited substitute to the ills of Gaza's economic conditions under siege, and even shed critical light on the pre-existing arrangement characterized by politically determined capital par-excellence. Moreover, Hamas showed itself capable of governing the tunnels and the rents they generated, effectively using these toward consolidating its political, economic, and social base. It nonetheless did so by utilizing a similar economic model as Fatah (control of trade rents, strategic political transfer rents, and public sector employment), albeit with its own particularities—namely, less political restrictions or oversight from its "donors': primarily the Muslim Brotherhood, Turkey, and Qatar. It also maintained an agenda to transform and incorporate its military activity into Gaza's economic activity. Public sector employment in Gaza between 2008 and 2011 was also higher than it was under Fatah rule—standing in the high 40s, thanks to the existence of parallel public sectors accountable to both Fatah and Hamas.

The Fall of the Tunnel Economy

The international pressure generated in the wake of the July 2010 killing of nine activists on the *Mavi Marmara* solidarity boat attempting to break the maritime blockade, led Israel to revise its criteria of what imports it would allow into the Strip.[57] Gazans would thereafter be allowed to import products from or via Israel, excepting a blacklist of supplies Israel claimed were directly related to military infrastructure or which could have what it regarded as a dual civilian/military use. These included basic building materials including wood, cement, and steel bars. While imports remained bureaucratic and heavily constrained by "security" procedures, this shift in the character of Israel's siege policies reopened trade channels with Israel and revived some of the commercial traders who had traditionally traded with or through it. These channels however were nonetheless still largely powerless to resist the dynamism of the tunnel trade and its cheaper supplies, leading to inevitable clashes between newly rising economic actors and more established powers within Gaza's commercial class. This clash also had inevitable reverberations upon the political and power associations of these traders, even though the class of commercial actors clearly spanned beyond those affiliated with one party or another.

Gaza's tunnels had turned the tables on the pre-existing sociopolitical arrangements established by the Paris Protocol, and overseen by Israel and donors via the PA. It created a new set of economic actors who appealed to a different legitimacy, a different set of institutions, a different set of laws, and ultimately a different monopoly on the exercise of "legitimate" violence. In this way, social and political tensions within classes between the established order and new economic actors were exacerbated, while the fault lines of political division between camps were deepening.

While these factors would lead to Hamas' effective entrenchment across the Gaza Strip, the movement was asymmetrically reliant upon the tunnel phenomenon and its revenues. Once the military junta under Abdel Fatah Al-Sisi in Egypt would rise to power in Cairo, moving against the tunnels in July 2013, dramatic economic consequences would begin to befall Gaza. Not only were 30,000 people and their dependents added (returned?) to the rosters of the unemployed, but also a cascading series of "crunches" began to take hold across Gaza's economy.

Hamas and the tunnels had facilitated a regime and economy based to significant proportions on cheap supplies of fuel, food, and construction materials obtained from Egypt. Fuel supplies had gone to meet both domestic demand for transport, cooking, and heating, while also meeting part of the fuel needs of the Gaza electricity generator—60 megawatts monthly.[58] In fact, electricity output had improved to 12–16 hr/day from 4–8 hr/day with this extra fuel supply, accumulating benefits in terms of water supply and sanitation. These gains, however, were reversed with the destruction of the tunnel economy, possibly playing a role in the rise in water-related diseases, accounting for over one fourth of illnesses and the primary cause of child mortality.[59]

The freeze on imports of Egyptian construction material combined with Israel's ban on construction imports significantly depleted supply and raised costs. This, in turn, affected construction market conditions and existing yet unrealized construction projects.[60] The crunch in building supplies was significant for the many forward and backward linkages this sector has economically and socially, especially in the context of Gaza's need for reconstruction. According to some accounts, building supplies were up to ten times their pre-siege levels.[61] Nabil Abu Mu'alaq, president of the Contractors Union, noted that the closing of the tunnel economy led to an immediate 50 percent decline in supply, forcing many projects to stop in their tracks. Only those with access to Western, Qatari, and Egyptian government supply channels remained operational. This crunch also led to conflicts between developers and builders, whereby those building their homes were forced into conflict with those they had arranged with to construct their homes (developers or contractors). The initial fixed prices settled upon by both parties, assuming market conditions of "open tunnels," were now unprofitable to pursue or continue in the context of closed tunnels. These disputes usually ended through traditional tribal mediation channels, but with both parties splitting the difference of the loss/added cost.

Operation Protective Edge

The knock-on economic and social effects of the Egyptian/Israeli siege would further be exacerbated in light of the unprecedented destruction reared as a consequence of Israel's July/August 2014 "Operation Protective Edge." These double shocks bowled over the Gaza economy and society, further deforming and stunting an already weak, de-developed, dependent economy.

"Protective Edge" was the most destructive of Israeli military assaults against Gaza since the Oslo process began, and perhaps in the history of Israeli aggression against the territory.

The Israeli army deployed 43,000 artillery shells, 39,000 tank shells, and 4.8 million bullets to the battlefield—roughly three bullets for every Gazan.[62] It flew 6,000 air attacks over the course of 51 days, utilizing an estimated 21 kilotons of high explosives.[63] By the end of the campaign, Israel was routinely using two-ton bombs on Gaza's high-rise buildings, with each one of these munitions creating 15 meter-wide craters, 11 meters deep, and spreading lethal fragments to a radius of more than a third of a kilometer.[64] On one night alone (June 19–20, 2014), the Israeli army launched a three-pronged assault against the Gaza City neighborhood of Sheja'iyya, firing over 7,000 shells, with the intensity of shelling as high as eleven shells per minute.

It is worth recounting that this unprecedented level of destruction was only made possible by previous uses of similar (albeit lesser) fire, under similarly worded "security/defensive" pretexts. This slow, accumulative permissiveness allowed for Israel to expand its margin of military maneuver against Gaza over time, truly raising the bar to seemingly genocidal proportions. The slow accumulation of permissiveness to destroy, and the justifications surrounding it, created the unique, Gaza-specific reality whereby a nuclear power could periodically pulverize a largely refugee population entitled to international protection, but denied the meaningful ability to even flee these conditions.[65]

The UN would estimate that 18,000 housing units were destroyed or rendered uninhabitable by "Protective Edge," leaving 108,000 people homeless.[66] A further 37,650 houses were damaged. Both Amnesty International and the Israeli human rights organization B'Tselem observed that the destruction of civilian property and the creation of internally displaced persons were particularly prominent features of Operation "Protective Edge," quantitatively and qualitatively distinguishing it from previous campaigns.[67] The callous indifference to human life led to the creation of the sizeable internally displaced population at the height of the war—half a million people, almost a third of Gaza's residents—and a serious housing crisis and economic burden for Gaza's Palestinian governors once the ceasefire came into effect.

Equally of note was Israel's targeting of Gaza's ability to sustain itself economically and practically, eliminating what remained of its productive sectors in particular. Gaza's fishing industry for instance had already witnessed increasing restrictions on access to the sea, as referred to earlier. But the July/August 2014 military campaign re-enforced a naval blockade *less* than 6 nautical miles from shore, while also wiping out 58 fisherman boats, and increasing the harassment of Palestinian fishermen. Indeed, one report from the Palestinian Center for Human Rights records 135 firing incidents at Palestinian fishermen between January and October 2016.[68] Other productive economic sectors were equally hit during the aggression. Ministry of Agriculture's policy and planning director, Nabil Abu Shamala, estimated losses to the agricultural sector at US$550 million, of which $350 million were in direct losses.[69] According to Abu Shamala, Israel targeted more than half of the agricultural areas in Gaza, while remaining areas were also damaged as a result of the inability of farmers to reach their crops, causing fruit and vegetables to whither on the vine. Once a formidable exporter of agricultural products like strawberries, guavas, and fresh-cut flowers to the West Bank, Israel, and beyond—9,319 truckloads worth in 2005—export traffic was reduced to a trickle, with only 136 truckloads leaving Gaza for the entirety of 2014—three quarters of which went to the West Bank.[70]

Most of Gaza's productive industries were inoperative even before the campaign. But even for those that were, the conditions of siege threatened them *in toto*. For instance, most of Gaza's 6,000 metal workshops, employing upward of 20,000 people, were threatened with closure, given the lack of electricity, metal, and welding rods, according to Mohammed Hamad, vice president of the Mineral Industry and Engineering.[71] The total number of businesses hit during the military campaign amounted to 418 establishments of which 128 were totally destroyed.[72]

While UN statistics quantify the level of destruction meted out through these campaigns, invisible to this process are the combined qualitative dimensions to them, and their implications upon Palestinian social-political life. Israel was deliberately creating a humanitarian crisis and preventing any productive capabilities in the aftermath. It also did this in a context where the international and regional conditions which frame reconstruction and its mechanisms harbored additional hidden dimensions of leverage that would have implications on the entire Palestinian national movement. That is to say, Israel knew that its besiegement of Gaza, together with Egypt, could be maintained after its decision to end the military campaign. It also knew that Western donors showed no wavering in their continued insistence on boycotting the Hamas government in Gaza, and of only working through the Fatah-led government in Ramallah. The creation of destruction on such a prolific scale, and the prevention of productive means of survival in general and thereafter, thus indicates an Israeli desire to shape the "post-war" reality of Gaza. The targets of the Israeli campaign were not to be found in the assault per se, *but in the anticipated effects of the post-conflict period* upon Gaza's society and leadership, and across the Palestinian people as a whole.

Operation "Protective Edge" created a predictable humanitarian crisis, but also an economic/fiscal one. Without international aid, there was no way Gaza could rebuild as supply routes relied upon politically conditioned arrangements established by the Western donors, with Israel and Egypt as strict on-ground enforcers. It is important to emphasize that the political conditions and timing of "Protective Edge" were qualitatively different than those of "Pillar of Defense" in 2012 and "Defensive Shield" in 2008/2009, whereby the besiegement/isolation of Gaza was close to, if not entirely, hermetic due to the political changes in Egypt. Donor insistence upon dealing with the West Bank government as the sole channel through which it would direct its aid represented a blatant attempt to undermine the delicate political reconciliation agreement forged between Fatah and Hamas on April 23, 2014, known as the Shati' Agreement, just before "Protective Edge" was waged.[73] Ever since the events of the summer of 2007, when the mini-civil war between Fatah and Hamas resulted in the institutional division of authority between the West Bank and Gaza, Palestinian grassroots and political forces had pushed the two main parties to reconcile for the greater Palestinian good. Years of costly division and bubbling popular discontent from below in both the West Bank and Gaza; shifting regional circumstances emerging in the context of the revolutionary upheavals of the Arab world post-2011, and rising financial difficulties of each party (especially Hamas, unable to meet the cost of its 40,000 public sector employees), laid the grounds for at least a tactical reconciliation between the two movements.[74] The signing of the Shati' Agreement less than three months before the military aggression began in mid-July, and based on the "Palestinian National Conciliation Accord" (itself forged from six rounds of Egyptian-sponsored dialogue in 2009), had been the painstaking result of these maturing processes, promising an end to the political and institutional division so clearly unproductive to Palestinian national ends. The agreement called for the rationalization of the split public sector payrolls, the holding of Legislative Council and presidential elections, reform of the PLO leading toward the inclusion of Hamas and Islamic Jihad, and the imposition of a new political culture across the OPT whereby both Fatah in the Gaza Strip and Hamas in the West Bank would enjoy political freedom.

Yet in the context of Israel's 2014 military assault, and the ensuing donor-imposed political conditions around reconstruction, this delicate agreement functionally imploded. The high cost of reconstruction (estimated between US$4 and 10 billion) and the immediate and predictable crisis in financial liquidity it created, especially for the Hamas government, reversed the winds of reconciliation between the two movements and set them on a course of political polarization. In the context of a delicate and unconsummated reform process, both Hamas and Fatah retreated to pre-existing narratives, tactics, strategies, institutions, and networks to try to both explain the predicament of Gaza residents, and address what they could of its needs. They equally both sought to control the conditions—and finances—of reconstruction to bolster themselves politically.

Meanwhile the international community maintains this arrangement, acquiescing to the stringent political and "security" restrictions that isolate Gaza, and forces dependency of the majority of its people on the bare minimum of humanitarian aid. Moreover, it has even acquiesced to the enforcement of Israeli security criteria in the domain of reconstruction, through the Gaza Reconstruction Mechanism established after the 2014 operation. The highly bureaucratic nature of the arrangement, its stringent checks, and the failure of donors to meet their aid commitments has led to reconstruction taking place at a snail's pace, and the creation of a black market in materials whereby it is more profitable for recipients to sell their allotment of material for much higher prices, because they are forced to feed their families.

CONCLUSION

The transformations that have taken place across the Gaza Strip since 1993 have been monumental in their scope and scale. Israel's ability to manipulate the discursive and institutional framework of the peace process has radically transformed and improved the nature and costs of its control over the OPT. Incrementally it has made strategic advances that have ultimately led to the geopolitical fragmentation of the OPT, and the isolation of Gaza as the densest concentration of Israel's very own contradictory predicament. Moreover, Israel's ability to leverage this incremental absolving of responsibility toward the occupied Palestinian people, over the PA, and ultimately upon Western taxpayers, demonstrates a remarkable sleight of hand. "Peacebuilding," "security," "development," "reform," "statebuilding," and "reconstruction" have all served as the discursive frameworks that Israel has exploited to achieve these leveraged maneuvers.

Important political, economic, and social implications for Gaza and the Palestinian movement can hence be summed up from this lengthy account of Gaza's history since the Oslo Accords were implemented.

Politically, Israel and the Western donor community have effectively overseen an arrangement that has led to the creation of parallel institutions with parallel local legitimacy, but which are equally limited in power to sovereignly govern. Instead, both sets of institutions and political powers fight each other over financial, political, tactical, and strategic questions, while attempting to manipulate their local market conditions to extract loyalty and resources for their parallel projects. This effectively means that the Palestinian political project is divided and ruled in a colonial manner by Israel (the effective sovereign) and Western donors who oversee this arrangement. Economically and socially, this has meant that Gaza has received the "stick" to the West Bank's "carrot," effectively decimating and impoverishing its people, resources, and livelihoods.

The social pressures arising from this remain explosive, and have predictably led to an explosion. On 30 March 2018, Gaza popular forces together with all political factions (including non-Abbas-linked Fatah affiliates) joined forces to launch the Great "March of Return"—a series of weekly Friday demonstrations in the buffer zone, that have led to 228 Palestinians killed, and an astonishing 5,866 injured with live ammunition as of mid-November 2018. While these demonstrations have taken on the character of a local Gaza-based Intifada, shedding light on Gaza's atrocious humanitarian situation and Israel's brutality toward Gaza, the demonstrations have yet to render changes in Israeli or the Western donor community policies vis-à-vis Gaza. Crisis and instability thus characterize the situation overall, with the situation posing the potential for yet further military escalations and challenges of different orders to the assumptions underlying the status quo—both across Gaza and the OPT overall, as well as vis-à-vis Israel and the Western donor community.

As these dynamics unfold in due course, it is fitting to end this chapter by calling upon scholars to redirect their attention from humanitarian-oriented approaches to Gaza, toward understanding and deconstructing the processes that have perpetuated the political economy of crisis—its generation, "management," and manipulation—before they do more harm. Gaza has repeatedly shown that the logics of co-optation and coercion don't work and exact an increasingly brutal toll on its people. It is in the interests of all that the political questions lying at the core of Gaza's condition be brought front and center within academic and political research and discourse. Any further denial of these questions is certain to reproduce worse variants of the status quo, which has already approached near-genocidal proportions. The implications of this are obvious not only upon Gazans themselves, but also for all those party to these crimes, and their witnessing.

NOTES

1. UN, "Gaza Ten Years Later," United Nations Country Team in the Occupied Palestinian Territory, July 2017.
2. UNRWA, "Gaza in 2020: A Livable Place? United Nations Country Team," August 2012.
3. UN, "Gaza Ten Years," 2.
4. Greg Mitchell, "Prominent Israelis: Flatten Gaza or Send It Back to the Middle Ages," *Nation*, November 19, 2012.
5. Amos Regev, "Return Gaza to the Stone Age," *Israel Hayom*, July 9, 2014.
6. GISHA, "Food Consumption in the Gaza Strip–Red Lines." Position Paper, GISHA, October 2012.
7. PCBS, "Palestinian Central Bureau of Statistics Special Statistical Bulletin On the 76th Anniversary of the Palestinian Nakba," 2015, and "About UNRWA," United Nations Relief and Works Association, Amman, 14.
8. Susan Akram, "Palestinian Refugees and Their Legal Status: Rights, Politics, and Implications for a Just Solution," *Journal of Palestine Studies* 31(3), 36–51.
9. Badil, "Survey of Palestinian Refugees and Internally Displaced Persons," Bethlehem, 2015, 34.
10. Salman Abu Sitta, *Atlas of Palestine, 1948* (London: Palestine Land Society, 2004), 121–125. Abu Sitta notes that 88 percent of all Palestinians are still in historic Palestine and in a ring of neighboring Arab countries not exceeding 150 km in width around it. He also shows their patterns of dispersion.
11. For example, until cartoonist Joe Sacco's 2009 *Footnotes in Gaza* was published, there was hardly a historical trace in English of the November 1956 Israeli massacre in Khan Younis, in which 500 Palestinians were killed in the span of a few days—this being the single deadliest massacre to take place in historical Palestine since the Nakba. Other periods in Gaza's recent history appear equally under-represented or studied. See Joe Sacco, *Footnotes in Gaza* (New York: Metropolitan Books, 2009).
12. See Moshe Machover and Emmanuel Farjoun, "The National Movement in the Arab East at the End of the Road," August 8, 1976.

13. Machover and Farjoun 1976; Gilber Achcar, "Zionism and Peace: From the Allon Plan to the Washington Accords," *New Politics* 5:3, 1995, 95–115.

14. According to Israeli statistics, Israel's population in 2015 stood at 8.34 million persons: 6.25 million Jews (74.9%) and 1.73 million Arabs (20.7%), in addition to 364,000 (4.4%) others (see http://www1.cbs.gov.il/reader/newhodaot/hodaa_template.html?hodaa=201511099). If we add the population of the West Bank and Gaza (4.55 million) to the numbers of Palestinian citizens of the state of Israel, we see that at least 6.28 million Arabs and 6.25 million Jews already live between the Mediterranean and the Jordan River.

15. Gilbert Achcar, *Eastern Cauldron: Islam, Afghanistan, Palestine and Iraq in a Marxist Mirror* (London: Pluto, 2004) 205–222.

16. Israel has not declared its official borders.

17. JPS, "A Labour Solution for Gaza," *Journal of Palestine Studies*, 9:3, 1980, 163–165. 1980 as cited in *Yediot Ahraronot*, December 12, 1979.

18. Sara Roy, "The Gaza Strip: A Case of Economic De-Development." *Journal of Palestine Studies*, 1987, 17:1, 56.

19. Sara Roy, *The Gaza Strip: The Political Economy of De-Development* (Washington, DC: Institute for Palestinian Studies, 1995), 129–130.

20. Roy, "The Gaza Strip: A Case," 57.

21. Adam Hanieh, "Global Capitalism and Israel," *Monthly Review*, 54(8) 2003a; "From State-led Growth to Globalization: The Evolution of Israeli Capitalism," *Journal of Palestine Studies*, 32(4) (2003b), 5–21.

22. Sadan would become the director general of the Israeli Ministry of Finance. Ezra Sadan, "A Policy For Immediate Economic-Industrial Development in the Gaza Strip." Ben-Ezra Consultants. August, 1991.

23. Amira Hass, "Israel's Closure Policy: An Ineffective Strategy of Containment and Repression." *Journal of Palestine Studies* (2002) 31(3): 5–20.

24. Leila Farsakh, "Palestinian Labor Flows to the Israeli Economy: A Finished Story?" *Journal of Palestine Studies*, 32:1, 2002, 13–27; *Palestinian Employment in Israel: 1967–1997. A Review*, Palestine Economic Policy Research Institute (MAS), Ramallah. 1998.

25. BBC, "Analysis: Hopeless in Gaza" *BBC News*. November 20, 2000; Aluf Benn, "Keeping the Palestinians out of Sight," *Ha'aretz*, July 20, 2007.

26. The wording "Marshall Plan" is mentioned in the DOP, Article XVI.

27. Toufic Haddad, *Palestine Ltd: Neoliberalism and Nationalism in the Occupied Territory* (London: I.B. Tauris, 2016); Adam Hanieh, "Global Capitalism and Israel," *Monthly Review* (2003a), 54(8).

28. Yediot Ahronot, September 7, 1993.

29. CBS, "Arafat's Billions," CBS News *60 Minutes*, November 9, 2003.

30. Haddad, "Palestine Ltd," 2016.

31. Glenn E. Robinson, "The Role of the Professional Middle Class in the Mobilization of Palestinian Society: The Medical and Agricultural Committees," *International Journal of Middle East Studies* (1993), 25:2, 301–326; Glenn E. Robinson, *Building A Palestinian State: The Incomplete Revolution* (Bloomington: Indiana

University Press, 1997a); Joost Hiltermann, *Behind the Intifada: Labor and Women's Movements in the Occupied Territories* (Princeton: Princeton University Press, 1991).

32. Nidal Sabri, *The Palestinian Public Sector in the Context of the Palestinian Economy* (Muwatin. Ramallah, 2003, 157–67).

33. Haddad, "Palestine Ltd," 2016, 57–80.

34. Graham Usher, "The Politics of Internal Security: The PA's New Intelligence Services," *Journal of Palestine Studies* (1996): 25(2), 21–34.

35. Joel Beinin, "Palestine and Israel: Perils of a Neoliberal, Repressive 'Pax Americana,'" *Social Justice* (1998), 4: 74, 20–39.

36. Arie Arnon, "Israeli Policy Toward the Occupied Palestinian Territories: The Economic Dimension, 1967–2007," *Middle East Journal* (2007): 61:4.

37. PCBS, 2012, 109.

38. See Palestinian Central Bureau of Statistics, "Main Statistical Indicators Gaza Strip 1993–2016": http://www.pcbs.gov.ps/Portals/_Rainbow/StatInd/gazaInd2016E.htm.

39. Arnon, "Israeli Policy," 2007.

40. See "Entry into Gaza from Israel and Jerusalem": http://www.hamoked.org/topic.aspx?tid=Topics1013.

41. See B'Tselem, "Fatalities Before Operation Cast Lead": http://www.btselem.org/statistics/fatalities/before-cast-lead/by-date-of-event.

42. CARE International, "Preliminary Findings: Humanitarian Situation in the Occupied Palestinian Territory," Johns Hopkins University/Al-Quds University CARE International, 2002a; "Health Sector Bi-Weekly Report," Johns Hopkins University/Al-Quds University CARE International, ANERA and the Maram Project (3:16), September 6, 2002b; "Nutritional Assessment of the West Bank and Gaza Strip," Johns Hopkins University/Al-Quds University, September 2002 (financed by USAID through CARE International), 2002c, 65.

43. Sara Roy, "The Palestinian-Israeli Conflict and Palestinian Socioeconomic Decline: A Place Denied." *International Journal of Politics, Culture and Society* (2004): 17, 3.

44. See Palestinian Central Bureau of Statistics, "Main Statistical Indicators Gaza Strip 1993–2016": http://www.pcbs.gov.ps/Portals/_Rainbow/StatInd/gazaInd2016E.htm.

45. "Olmert Decides to Shut Erez Industrial Zone Permanently," *Haaretz*, June 9, 2004. http://www.haaretz.com/olmert-decides-to-shut-erez-industrial-zone-permanently-1.124716.

46. OCHA, "Gaza Fishing: An Industry in Danger," Jerusalem. April 2007.

47. Human Rights Watch [HRW], "Razing Rafah: Mass Home Demolitions in the Gaza Strip," October 2004.

48. Quoted in Ari Shavit, "The Enemy Within: interview with IDF Chief of Staff Moshe Ya'alon," *Ha'aretz*, August 29, 2002.

49. NDI, *Final Report on the Palestinian Legislative Council Elections*. National Democratic Institute. January 25, 2006.

50. Khaled Hroub, "A 'New Hamas' through Its New Documents." *Journal of Palestine Studies* (2006): 35(4), 6–27.

51. David Rose, "Special Investigation: How Blair Rescued Palestine Deal Worth $200m to his £2m-a-year Paymasters." *Daily Mail*, September 12, 2010.

52. Jonathan DiJohn and James Putzel, "Political Settlements," Governance Development Resource Centre, Issues Paper, June, 2009.

53. Ensuing specific statistics on the tunnel economy derive from Nicholas Pelham's excellent 2012 study, unless otherwise noted—Nicholas Pelham, "Gaza's Tunnel Phenomenon: The Unintended Dynamics of Israel's Siege," *Journal of Palestine Studies* (2012): 41:4, 6–31.

54. MAS, *Coping Strategies Implemented by Government Employees in the West Bank in Response to Delayed Salaries*, Ramallah, 2013.

55. Nicholas Pelham, "'Gaza's Tunnel' 2012; Samir Abumdallal and Ghassan Abuhatab, "The Tunnel Economy in the Gaza Strip: A Catholic Marriage," Center for Development Studies, Birzeit University, Ramallah, 2014.

56. World Bank, "Ad Hoc Liaison Committee Report," September 14, 2011, 7.

57. COGAT [Coordinator of Government Activities in the Territories], List of Controlled Items to the Gaza Strip, *Journal of Palestine Studies* (2010): 40(1), 197–198.

58. Hassan Douhan, "Crisis of Gaza Strip Accrues After the Collapse of 'The Tunnel Economy,'" *Hayat wa Souq*, September 2013b.

59. ICG, *No Exit? Gaza & Israel Between Wars Middle East Report* 162, August 26, 2015, Geneva/Ramallah, ICG, 8.

60. Al-Qasir, Nader, "The Gaza Economy on a Hot Plate," *Hayat wa Souq*, #110, 2013, 3. http://www.alhaya.ps/sooq/HayatWaSouq110.pdf.

61. Douhan, Hassan, "Crisis of Gaza Strip Accrues After the Collapse of 'The Tunnel Economy'" *Hayat wa Souq*, September 2013. #121, 2–3. http://www.alhaya.ps/sooq/HayatWaSouq121.pdf.

62. Yoav Zitun, "Protective Edge, in Numbers," *Ynetnews*, August 14, 2014. http://www.ynetnews.com/articles/0,7340,L-4558916,00.html.

63. Rashid Khalidi, "The Dahiya Doctrine, Proportionality, and War Crimes," *Journal of Palestine Studies* (2014): 44(1). 5–13.

64. Khalidi, "The Dahiya Doctrine."

65. Prof. Richard Falk, United Nations High Commissioner for Refugees stated on 6 January 2009, that Gaza is "the only conflict in the world in which people are not even allowed to flee." See Falk, Richard. Distr. General A/HRC/12/48 Original: English Human Rights Council Twelfth Session Agenda Item 7 Human Rights in Palestine and Other Occupied Arab Territories Report of the United Nations Fact-Finding Mission on the Gaza Conflict, September 25, 2009. http://www2.ohchr.org/english/bodies/hrcouncil/docs/12session/A-HRC-12-48.pdf.

66. OCHA, "Occupied Palestinian Territory: Gaza Emergency Situation Report," September 4, 2014. www.ochaopt.org/documents/ocha_opt_sitrep_04_09_2014.pdf; OCHA, "The Gaza Strip: The Humanitarian Impact of the Blockade," July 2015(a).

67. Amnesty International, "Families under the Rubble: Israel's Attacks Against Inhabited Homes." November 5, 2014; Btselem, "Families Bombed at Home, Gaza, July–August (initial Figures)" *Btselem*, August 11, 2014; Btselem, "Black Flag: The Legal and Moral Implications of the Policy of Attacking Residential Buildings in

the Gaza Strip, Summer 2014," January (2014b); "Occupied Palestinian Territory: Gaza Emergency Situation Report," September 4, 2014, www.ochaopt.org/documents/ocha_opt_sitrep_04_09_2014.pdf; OCHA, "The Gaza Strip: The Humanitarian Impact of the Blockade," July 2015(a); OCHA, "Fragmented Lives: Humanitarian Overview 2014," March 2015(b).

68. See Palestinian Center for Human Rights, "Israeli Attacks on Palestinian Fishermen in the Gaza Strip, 01 January–31 October, 2016." http://pchrgaza.org/en/wp-content/uploads/2016/12/Report-Israeli-Attacks-against-Fishermen-2016.pdf.

69. Rasha Abou Jalal, "With $550M in Agricultural Losses, Gazans Going Hungry," *Al-Monitor*, September 17, 2014.

70. See OCHA Gaza Border Crossings Database: http://www.ochaopt.org/gazacrossing/index.aspx?id=5.

71. Badr Abdel-'Aal, "Welding Sticks Threatens 20,000 Families with Poverty." *Hayat wa Souq*, 2015. #193, 6.

72. OCHA, "Gaza Emergency," 2014.

73. See Al-Zaytouna, "Al-Shati' Agreement and Future of the Palestinian Reconciliation," Al-Zaytouna Centre for Studies and Consultations, Strategic Assessment (67), May 29, 2014.

74. See ICG, "Light at the End of their Tunnels? Hamas & the Arab Uprisings," 129, 14 August 2012. Geneva/Ramallah: ICG.

BIBLIOGRAPHY

Abdel-'Aal, Badr. "Welding sticks threatens 20,000 families with poverty." *Hayat wa Souq*, 2015. #193, 6. http://www.alhaya.ps/sooq/HayatWaSouq193.pdf.

Abou Jalal, Rasha. "With $550M in agricultural losses, Gazans going hungry," *Al-Monitor*, September 17, 2014. http://www.al-monitor.com/pulse/originals/2014/09/food-gaza-insecurity-israel-war-destruction.html#ixzz3rJZSU7rb.

Abumdallal, Samir, and Abuhatab, Ghassan. "The Tunnel Economy in the Gaza Strip: a Catholic Marriage," Center for Development Studies, Birzeit University, Ramalla, 2014.

Abu Sitta, Salman. *Atlas of Palestine, 1948* (London: Palestine Land Society, 2004).

Achcar, Gilbert. "The Washington Accords: A Retreat Under Pressure," *International Viewpoint*, 252, January 25, 1994.

———. "Zionism and Peace: From the Allon Plan to the Washington Accords," *New Politics* 5:3, Summer 1995, 95–115.

———. *Eastern cauldron: Islam, Afghanistan, Palestine and Iraq in a Marxist Mirror* (London: Pluto, 2004).

Akram, Susan. "Palestinian Refugees and Their Legal Status: Rights, Politics, and Implications for a Just Solution," *Journal of Palestine Studies* (2002): 31(3), 36–51.

Al-Mughrabi, Nidal. "A year after Gaza war, no rebuilding and an uneasy future for all," *Reuters* 8, July 8, 2015. http://www.reuters.com/article/2015/07/08/us-mideast-gaza-widerimage-idUSKCN0PI0YC20150708.

Al-Qasir, Nader. "The Gaza Economy on a Hot Plate," *Hayat wa Souq*, #110, 2013, 3. http://www.alhaya.ps/sooq/HayatWaSouq110.pdf.

al-Zaytouna. "Al-Shati' Agreement and Future of the Palestinian Reconciliation," Al-Zaytouna Centre for Studies and Consultations, Strategic Assessment (67), May 29, 2014. http://www.alzaytouna.net/en/publications/books/strategic-assessment/151706-strategicassessment-67-al-shati%E2%80%99-agreement-and-future-of-the-palestinian-reconciliation.html.

Amnesty International. "Families under the Rubble: Israel's Attacks Against Inhabited Homes." November 5, 2014. https://www.amnesty.org/en/library/asset/MDE15/032/2014/en/613926df-68c4-47bb-b587-00975f014e4b/mde150322014en.pdf/.

Antreasyan, Anaïs. "Gas Finds in the Eastern Mediterranean: Gaza, Israel and Other Conflicts," *Journal of Palestine Studies* (2012/13): 42(3).

Arnon, Arie. "Israeli Policy toward the Occupied Palestinian Territories: The Economic Dimension, 1967—2007," *Middle East Journal* (2007): 61:4.

Badil. "Survey of Palestinian Refugees and Internally Displaced Persons 2013–2015," Bethlehem, 2015.

BBC. "Analysis: Hopeless in Gaza," *BBC News*. November 20, 2000. http://news.bbc.co.uk/2/hi/middle_east/1032701.stm.

Beinin, Joel. "Palestine and Israel: Perils of a Neoliberal, Repressive 'Pax Americana,'" *Social Justice* (1998), 4: 74, 20–39.

Benn, Aluf. "Keeping the Palestinians out of Sight," *Ha'aretz*, July 20, 2007.

Btselem. "Families Bombed at Home, Gaza, July–August (initial Figures)," *Btselem*, August 11, 2014. http://www.btselem.org/gaza_strip/201407_families.

———. "Black Flag: The Legal and Moral Implications of the Policy of Attacking Residential Buildings in the Gaza Strip, Summer 2014," January. http://www.btselem.org/download/201501_black_flag_eng.pdf.

CARE International. "Preliminary Findings: Humanitarian Situation in the Occupied Palestinian Territory," Johns Hopkins University/Al-Quds University CARE International, 2002a.

———. "Health Sector Bi-Weekly Report," Johns Hopkins University/Al-Quds University CARE International, ANERA and the Maram Project (3:16), September 6, 2002b.

———. "Nutritional Assessment of the West Bank and Gaza Strip," Johns Hopkins University/Al-Quds University, September 2002 (financed by USAID through CARE International), 2002c, 65.

CBS. "Arafat's Billions," CBS News *60 Minutes*, November 9, 2003. www.cbsnews.com/stories/2003/11/07/60minutes/main582487.shtml.

COGAT [Coordinator of Government Activities in the Territories]. List of Controlled Items to the Gaza Strip, *Journal of Palestine Studies* (2010): 40(1), 197–198.

Deen, Thalif. "Cycle of Death, Destruction and Rebuilding Continues in Gaza," *Inter press Service*, October 13, 2014. http://www.ipsnews.net/2014/10/cycle-of-death-destruction-and-rebuilding-continues-in-gaza/.

DiJohn, Jonathan, and Putzel, James. "Political Settlements," Governance Development Resource Centre, Issues Paper, June 2009. http://www.gsdrc.org/docs/open/EIRS7.pdf.

Douhan, Hassan. "Collective Slaughter of Car Importers in the Gaza Strip," *Hayat wa Souq*, May (2013a), #103, 2–3. http://www.alhaya.ps/sooq/HayatWaSouq103.pdf.

———. "Crisis Of Gaza Strip Accrues After The Collapse of 'The Tunnel Economy,'" *Hayat wa Souq*, September 2013. #121, 2–3. http://www.alhaya.ps/sooq/HayatWa Souq121.pdf.

Dyke, Jon. "Donors threaten to withhold Gaza aid," *IRIN*, October 7, 2014. http://www.irinnews.org/report/100690/analysis-donors-threaten-to-withhold-gaza-aid.

Falk, Richard. Distr. General A/HRC/12/48 Original: English Human Rights Council Twelfth Session Agenda Item 7 Human Rights in Palestine and Other Occupied Arab Territories. Report of the United Nations Fact-Finding Mission on the Gaza Conflict, September 25, 2009. http://www2.ohchr.org/english/bodies/hrcouncil/docs/12session/A-HRC-12-48.pdf.

Farsakh, Leila. *Palestinian Employment in Israel: 1967–1997. A Review*, Palestine Economic Policy Research Institute (MAS), Ramallah, 1998.

———. "Palestinian Labor Flows to the Israeli Economy: A Finished Story?" *Journal of Palestine Studies* (2002) 32:1, 13–27.

Faucon, Benoit. *West Bankers* (London: Mashrek Editions, 2010).

GISHA. "Food Consumption in the Gaza Strip—Red Lines," *GISHA*, Position Paper, October 2012. http://www.gisha.org/UserFiles/File/publications/redlines/red-lines-presentation-eng.pdf.

Haaretz. "Olmert Decides to Shut Erez Industrial Zone Permanently," *Haaretz*, June 9, 2004. http://www.haaretz.com/olmert-decides-to-shut-erez-industrial-zone-permanently-1.124716.

Haddad, Toufic. *Palestine Ltd: Neoliberalism and Nationalism in the Occupied Territory*. I. B. Tauris and Center for Palestine Studies, School of Oriental and African Studies, London, 2016.

Hanieh, Adam. "Global Capitalism and Israel," *Monthly Review* (2003a), 54(8).

———. "From State-led Growth to Globalization: the Evolution of Israeli Capitalism," *Journal of Palestine Studies* (2003b): 32(4), 5–21.

Hass, Amira. "Israel's Closure Policy: an Ineffective Strategy of Containment and Repression," *Journal of Palestine Studies* (2002) 31(3): 5–20.

Hiltermann, Joost. *Behind the Intifada: Labor and Women's Movements in the Occupied Territories* (Princeton: Princeton University Press, 1991).

Honig-Parnass, Tikva, and Haddad, Toufic (eds.). *Between the Lines: Readings on Israel, the Palestinians and the US "War on Terror* (Chicago: Haymarket, 2007).

Hroub, Khaled. "A 'New Hamas' through Its New Documents." *Journal of Palestine Studies* (2006): 35(4), 6–27.

Human Rights Watch [HRW]. "Razing Rafah: Mass Home Demolitions in the Gaza Strip," October 2004. http://reliefweb.int/sites/reliefweb.int/files/resources/A6DF132792830E6385256F310072A1A9-hrw-opt-18oct.pdf.

ICG [International Crisis Group]. *No Exit? Gaza & Israel Between Wars Middle East Report* 162, August 26, 2015.

———. "Light at the End of their Tunnels? Hamas & the Arab Uprisings," 129, August 14, 2012.

JPS, "A Labour Solution for Gaza," *Journal of Palestine Studies* (1980) 9:3, 163–165.

Khalidi, Raja, and Samour, Sobhi. "Neoliberalism as Liberation: The Statehood Program and the Remaking of the Palestinian National Movement." *Journal of Palestine Studies* (2011): 40(2), 6–25.

Khalidi, Rashid. "The Dahiya Doctrine, Proportionality, and War Crimes," *Journal of Palestine Studies* (2014): 44(1), 5–13.

Khan, Mushtaq. "State Failure in Weak States: A Critique of New Institutionalist Explanations." In J. Harris, J. Hunter, and C. Lewis (eds.). *The New Institutional Economics and Third World Development* (London: Routledge, 1995), 71–86.

———. "Evaluating the Emerging Palestinian State: 'Good Governance' versus 'Transformation potential,'" in Khan, Mushtaq et al. *State Formation in Palestine: Viability and Governance During a Social Transformation* (London: Routledge-Curzon, 2004), 13–63.

Khan, Mustaq, and Hilal, Jamil. "State formation under the PNA: Potential Outcomes and their Viability." In M. Khan et al., *State Formation in Palestine: Viability and Governance During a Social Transformation* (Routledge political economy of the Middle East and North Africa series) (New York; London: RoutledgeCurzon, 2004), 64–119.

Li, Darryl. "The Gaza Strip as Laboratory: Notes in the Wake of Disengagement," *Journal of Palestine Studies* (2006) 35:2, 38–55.

Machover, Moshe, and Farjoun, Emmanuel. "The National Movement in the Arab East at the End of the Road," August 8, 1976. http://www.matzpen.org/english/1976-08-08/the-national-movement-in-the-arab-east/.

Marx, Bettina. "The back of the Gazan economy has been broken." *Deutsche Welle*. Translated from the German by John Bergeron. October 7, 2014. https://en.qantara.de/content/rebuilding-gaza-the-back-of-the-gazan-economy-has-been-broken.

MAS. "Coping Strategies Implemented by Government Employees in the West Bank in Response to Delayed Salaries Ramallah," 2013. http://www.mas.ps/files/server/20141911102840-1.pdf.

Mitchell, Greg. "Prominent Israelis: Flatten Gaza or send it back to the Middle Ages," *Nation*, November 19, 2012. http://www.thenation.com/article/prominent-israelis-flatten-gaza-or-send-it-back-middle-ages/.

NDI. *Final Report on the Palestinian Legislative Council Elections*. National Democratic Institute. January 25, 2006. Accessed at: https://www.ndi.org/files/2068_ps_elect_012506.pdf.

OCHA. "Gaza Fishing: An Industry in Danger," Jerusalem. April, 2007. http://www.ochaopt.org/documents/ocha_special_report_gaza_fisheries_april2007.pdf.

———. "Occupied Palestinian Territory: Gaza Emergency Situation Report," September 4, 2014. www.ochaopt.org/documents/ocha_opt_sitrep_04_09_2014.pdf.

———. "The Gaza Strip: The Humanitarian Impact of the Blockade," July 2015(a).

———. "Fragmented Lives: Humanitarian Overview 2014," March 2015(b).

PA and IMF. "West Bank and Gaza Economic Policy Framework Progress Report. The Secretariat of the Ad Hoc Liaison Committee, May 31, 2000." Prepared by the PA in collaboration with the staff of the International Monetary Fund, Lisbon, June 7–8, 2000.

PCBS. "National Accounts at Current and Constant Prices 1994–2000," Ramallah, Palestine, April 2003.

———. "Palestinian Central Bureau of Statistics Special Statistical Bulletin On the 76th Anniversary of the Palestinian Nakba," May 31, 2000. http://www.pcbs.gov.ps/portals/_pcbs/PressRelease/Press_En_Nakba2015E.pdf.

PECDAR. *The Palestinian Economy in the Transitional Period* (Second edition). Shtayyeh, M. (ed.). Ramallah, 2003.

Pelham, Nicholas. "Gaza's tunnels: The burrowing business," *Economist*. August 10, 2011.

———. "Gaza's Tunnel Phenomenon: The Unintended Dynamics of Israel's Siege," *Journal of Palestine Studies* (2012): 41:4, 6–31.

Razin, Assaf, and Sadka, Ephraim. *The Economy of Modern Israel: Malaise and Promise* (Chicago: University of Chicago Press, 1993).

Regev, Amos. "Return Gaza to the Stone Age," *Israel Hayom*, July 9, 2014. http://www.israelhayom.com/site/newsletter_article.php?id=18675.

Robinson, Glenn E. "The Role of the Professional Middle Class in the Mobilization of Palestinian Society: The Medical and Agricultural Committees," *International Journal of Middle East Studies* (1993): 25:2, 301–326.

———. *Building A Palestinian State: The Incomplete Revolution* (Bloomington: Indiana University Press, 1997a).

———. "The Politics of Legal Reform in Palestine," *Journal of Palestine Studies* (1997b): 27(1) 51–60.

———. "Civil Society and Local Government: An Assessment of Civil Society in Relation to Prospects for Local Government. Decentralization in the West Bank and Gaza Strip." In ARD, Inc., *Shaping Local Government Decentralization: Prospects and Issues for Local Government Decentralization in the West Bank and Gaza Strip*, Report to the US Agency for International Development, April 2000.

Rose, David. "Special investigation: How Blair rescued Palestine deal worth $200m to his £2m-a-year paymasters." *Daily Mail*, September 12, 2010.

Roy, Sara. "The Gaza Strip: A Case of Economic De-Development," *Journal of Palestine Studies* (1987) 17:1, 56–88.

———. *The Gaza Strip: The Political Economy Of De-Development* (Washington, DC: Institute for Palestinian Studies, 1995).

———. "De-development Revisited: Palestinian Economy and Society Since Oslo," *Journal of Palestine Studies* (1999): 28(3), 64–82.

———. "The Palestinian-Israeli Conflict and Palestinian Socioeconomic Decline: A Place Denied." *International Journal of Politics, Culture and Society* (2004): 17, 3.

———. *Failing Peace: Gaza and the Palestinian-Israeli Conflict* (London: Pluto, 2006).

———. *Hamas and Civil Society in Gaza: Engaging the Islamist Social Sector* (Princeton, NJ: Princeton University Press, 2011).

RT. "Bloodlust in Israel: 'Flatten Gaza, send it back to Middle Ages, they need to die!'" *Russia Today*, November 19, 2012. https://www.rt.com/news/israel-gaza-hamas-war-103/?.

Sabri, Nidal. *The Palestinian Public Sector in the Context of the Palestinian Economy*, Muwatin. Ramallah, 2003.

Sadan, Ezra. "A policy for immediate economic-industrial development in the Gaza Strip," Ben-Ezra Consultants. August, 1991.

Shavit, Ari. "The Enemy Within: interview with IDF Chief of Staff Moshe Ya'alon," *Ha'aretz*, August 29, 2002.

———. "Top PM aide: Gaza plan aims to freeze the peace process" *Ha'aretz*, October 6, 2004.

Stocker, James. "No EEZ Solution: The Politics of Oil and Gas in the Eastern Mediterranean." *Middle East Journal* (2012): 66(4), 579–597.

Strand, Trude. "Tightening the Noose," *Journal of Palestine Studies* (2014): 43(2) 6–23.

Tuma, Elias H. "The Economies of Israel and the Occupied Territories: War and Peace—A Panel Discussion." *Economic Quarterly* (1989):139, 593–606.

UN. "Gaza Ten Years Later," United Nations Country Team in the Occupied Palestinian Territory, July 2017.

UNHRC. "Human rights situation in Palestine and other occupied Arab territories: Report of the detailed findings of the independent commission of inquiry established pursuant to Human Rights Council resolution S-21/11* 2** A/HRC/29/CRP.4. Human Rights Council, Twenty-ninth session. Agenda items 7. June 24, 2015. http://gaza.ochaopt.org/2015/06/report-of-the-independent-commission-of-inquiry-on-the-2014-gaza-conflict/.

UNOG. "Gaza: Silence is not an Option, United Nations Office at Geneva," Human Rights Council—Office of the United Nations High Commissioner for Human Rights in the Occupied Palestinian Territory (OHCHR OPT), December 9, 2008.

UNRWA. "Gaza in 2020: a Livable place?" United Nations Country Team, August 2012. http://www.unrwa.org/userfiles/file/publications/gaza/Gaza%20in%202020.pdf.

———. "About UNRWA," United Nations Relief and Works Association, Amman, 2015. http://www.unrwa.org/sites/default/files/about_unrwa_2015.pdf.

UNSCO. "Gaza Reconstruction Mechanism Fact Sheet," Office of the Special Coordinator for the Middle East Peace Process, October 2014. http://www.unsco.org/Gaza%20Reconstruction%20Mechanism%20Fact%20Sheet%209%20October%202014.pdf.

Usher, Graham. "The Politics of Internal Security: The PA's New Intelligence Services," *Journal of Palestine Studies* (1996): 25(2), 21–34.

Urqhart, Conal. "Gaza on brink of implosion as aid cut-off starts to bite," *The Guardian*, April 16, 2006.

US Geological Survey. "Assessment of Undiscovered Oil and Gas Resources of the Levant Basin Province, Eastern Mediterranean," March 2010.

Wertheim, Moshe. "Can the Law Survive a Change in Political Sentiments?" *Justice*, #12, March 1997, 24–25.

World Bank. "Ad Hoc Liaison Committee Report," September 14, 2011.

Zitun, Yoav. "Protective Edge, in Numbers," *Ynetnews*, August 14, 2014. http://www.ynetnews.com/articles/0,7340,L-4558916,00.html.

Chapter Eight

Occupied East Jerusalem Since the Oslo Accords

Isolation and Evisceration

Mansour Nasasra

In the wake of the 1967 Arab-Israeli War, Israel occupied the Golan Heights, the West Bank, the Gaza Strip and the Sinai Peninsula. East Jerusalem and an additional 64 square kilometers surrounding the city—which had belonged to 28 Palestinian villages in the West Bank—were annexed by Israel on 27 June, just over two weeks after the war ended, and Israel extended its own laws to this entire area. For the price of annexing this territory, Palestinians in East Jerusalem were partially integrated into Israeli society.[1] Even though Israel has declared Jerusalem to be united and to be its capital, the UN and its member states continue to regard Jerusalem as occupied Palestinian land. Indeed, UN Security Council Resolution 478 (1980) clearly states that the annexation of East Jerusalem is a violation of international law.[2]

Since annexing East Jerusalem in 1967, Israel has expropriated 35 percent of Palestinian-owned land for settlement building and other purposes.[3] In 2015, Jabareen estimated this to constitute an area of 22,571 km^2 in East Jerusalem.[4] This facilitated the expansion of Jewish-Israeli settlements in the heart of Arab space in East Jerusalem, including occupying houses in the middle of Arab neighborhoods.[5] Israeli settlements were constructed in East Jerusalem from the very beginning of the occupation; so that by 2017 there were more than 200,000 settlers (38 percent of the total Jewish population in Jerusalem) in East Jerusalem, who reside in 15 settlements.[6] According to the UN Office for the Coordination of Humanitarian Affairs (OCHA), Israel settlers in East Jerusalem have targeted densely populated Palestinian areas such as the Muslim and Christian quarters of the Old City, Silwan, Sheikh Jarrah, Al-Tur (Mount of Olives), Wadi al-Joz, Ras al-Amud and Jabal al-Mukabbir.[7] The policy of settling Jews in Palestinian neighborhoods in East Jerusalem is supported by the Israeli State.[8]

Following a settler colonial logic, Israel has adopted a number of policies, mainly seeking to geographically divide East Jerusalem and to disintegrate Palestinian space through settlement expansions, land expropriation and territorial control. Veracini argues that "settlement, nothing else, was the absolute core of Zionist practice."[9] This is particularly true for the Jerusalem context, as settlements became one of the key mechanisms to maintain Jewish domination of the city and to expropriate more Palestinian land.[10]

Even after the occupation of 1967, East Jerusalem remained the center of Palestinian life, economy and politics: key economic, educational, civil society, Islamic courts and religious organizations were based there, and a Palestinian leadership played a significant role in the city. As Palestinian economists from the Old City recall, East Jerusalem remained the center of the Palestinian economy.[11]

During the Oslo talks, the Israeli and Palestinian negotiation teams agreed that Jerusalem would be one of the subjects to be dealt with during the permanent status talks. The Declaration of Principles on Interim Self-Government Arrangements (DOP or Oslo Accords) states that "it is understood that these negotiations shall cover remaining issues, including: Jerusalem, refugees, settlements, security agreements, border, relations and cooperation with their neighbors, and other issues of common interest."[12]

Even though Jerusalem was left out of the Oslo framework, the immediate reaction to the DOP amongst Palestinians in East Jerusalem was positive. One of the most encouraging aspects of Oslo was optimism and hope that the Palestinians who had fled from Jerusalem in 1967 would be allowed to return to the city and be reunited with their families. As 'Abdullah, a Palestinian from the Old City, remarked: "We were hoping that Oslo would reunify us with our relatives in Jordan."[13]

These hopes also encouraged some East Jerusalemites who had moved to the West Bank to return to the city. A very interesting dynamic therefore developed in Jerusalem after the Oslo agreement was signed, with an influx of Palestinians returning to East Jerusalem to buy houses and secure their positions and future in the city.[14] In practice, this created a crisis in East Jerusalem, with escalating property prices and the complications of obtaining East Jerusalem ID cards.

Running parallel to these processes, Israel has consolidated its control over East Jerusalem and has managed to create "facts on the ground" before any potential final status resolution can be reached.

According to Klein, both Palestinians and Israelis were competing in this process: "Oslo opened the competition between both sides in terms of who creates more facts on the ground to pre-empt the final status negotiations."[15] However, Palestinians were the weaker party and their position was subsequently reduced to trying simply to survive. Indeed, according to Adnan al-Hussaini, the Palestinian governor of East Jerusalem, by 2014, Palestinians in East Jerusalem resided in only 13 percent of the overall territory of Jerusalem, despite making up 40 percent of the Jerusalem population.[16] Donald Trump's statement in December 2017 that Jerusalem is the capital city of Israel enhanced the isolation of East Jerusalem from the West Bank and Gaza, leaving Palestinian Jerusalemites alone in their struggle against Israel's occupation and Judaization strategies. By declaring Jerusalem to be the capital of Israel and moving the US Embassy there from Tel Aviv, Trump made it clear that the US no longer regarded the status of the city to be part of the peace negotiations, further emphasizing the exclusion of the city from the Oslo Accords.

Since the Oslo Accords, Israel has followed a strategy that has the aim of separating East Jerusalem from the West Bank but without integration into Israel. This has led to the evisceration of the Palestinian body politic in East Jerusalem. This chapter will chart how these strategies of isolation and evisceration have been carried out through the implementation of a number of policies. The first section analyzes how Israel has employed policies of separating East Jerusalemites from the city through annexing more land and encouraging them to move to areas beyond the Separation Barrier. As part of this process of 'silent" transfer, East Jerusalemites continue to face policies of ID revocation, house demolition and difficulties over obtaining building permits. All of this has created a fragile citizenship situation for East Jerusalemite Palestinians and has increased their marginalization in terms of access and rights in the city. East Jerusalemites have no right to automatic citizenship of either Jordan, Palestine or Israel. The second section then focuses on Israel's policies of separating the East Jerusalem economy from that of the West Bank, while simultaneously keeping it isolated from the economy of West Jerusalem. Section three looks at the evisceration of the Palestinian body politic from Jerusalem, the vacuum of leadership and its impact on East Jerusalemites. Section four analyzes the struggle over the Awqaf between Jordan, Israel and the Palestine Liberation Organization (PLO)/Palestinian Authority (PA). It concludes that the struggle over control of the Awqaf has weakened Palestinian leadership in the city and limited its influence. The final section focuses on the new actors in the struggle over the Holy Basin, mainly the Palestinian-Arab members of the Knesset (MKs) and the Palestinian-Arab political parties in Israel (particularly the Islamic Movement), and argues that the emergence of these new actors is the result of the vacuum of Palestinian leadership in the city. The chapter concludes by arguing two main points: first, that the impact of the Oslo framework on East Jerusalem has been to disconnect it from the rest of the Occupied Palestinian Territory (OPT) but while not integrating it into West Jerusalem and

Israel; and second, that Israel's policies since the Oslo Accords have focused on annexing Palestinian East Jerusalem land to its sovereignty but with as few of the Palestinian population as possible. These policies of separating East Jerusalem from the rest of the OPT have led to the evisceration of the Palestinian body politic in East Jerusalem.

SEPARATION WITHOUT INTEGRATION: ISRAEL'S CONTROL OVER EAST JERUSALEMITE PALESTINIAN LIFE, LIBERTY AND PROPERTY

The process of the evisceration of East Jerusalem accelerated after the Oslo Accords through the effects of Israel's policies of "silent" transfer—i.e., revoking ID cards, preventing family reunification, house demolitions, lack of building permits, high taxes, and the continuing fragile status of residency—which has led to the 'hidden" deportation of East Jerusalemites beyond the Separation Barrier into the West Bank and further afield. Not only has the daily life of East Jerusalemite Palestinians been made fragile by these bureaucratic strategies, but continued state violence and aggression toward the population affects all levels of the community, including children and women.[17] After the Oslo Accords, Israel accelerated the process of annexing Palestinian land in East Jerusalem, with the aim of excluding its Palestinian population. East Jerusalemites today are thus separated from the rest of the OPT but are also not integrated into West Jerusalem. Yacobi and Pullan argue that the most striking and worrying Israeli policies in East Jerusalem are the restrictions on Palestinian development, its expulsion activities and house demolitions and the lack of building permits.[18] Such policies seek to maintain and expand the Jewish demographic balance and control over Jerusalem by blocking the growth of the Palestinian population through regulations and laws.

Palestinians of East Jerusalem have the status of "permanent residents" of Israel and thus have a specific East Jerusalem ID, they have neither a Jordanian passport nor a Palestinian one. But this ID is revoked by Israel if they live outside Jerusalem's boundaries (either in another country or in other parts of the OPT) for more than seven contiguous years. Therefore, to protect their residency status, East Jerusalemites need to maintain their physical presence in the city.[19] According to UNOCHA, the residency of Palestinians in East Jerusalem is conditional on them proving that Jerusalem is their "center of life." East Jerusalemites also can face their ID being revoked if they obtain residency or citizenship of another country.[20]

According to figures from the Israeli Ministry of Interior, between 1967 and 2013 the residency status of 14,200 East Jerusalemites was revoked.[21] There are also many Palestinians in East Jerusalem that have been denied East Jerusalem IDs. For instance, as a result of marriages between Palestinians from Jerusalem and Palestinians from the West Bank or Gaza, there are 10,000 unregistered children in East Jerusalem.[22] With the introduction of the Nationality and Entry into Israel Law (Temporary Order) of 2003, family reunification of East Jerusalemites with Palestinians from the West Bank and Gaza became even more restricted, and was effectively frozen in many cases, often forcing the partner without Jerusalem ID to live outside the city.[23] As a result, many families have two houses: one in Jerusalem and the other in the West Bank.[24] Revoking East Jerusalem IDs and denying family reunification is a form of forcible transfer of East Jerusalemite Palestinians.[25] Policies and actions such as these contravene international regulations that call for preventing the forcible displacement of protected persons in occupied territories.[26]

Despite the extension of the Jerusalem municipality boundaries by Israel,[27] many municipal services and resources have not reached East Jerusalem. Despite the fact that they constitute around 40 percent (more than 300,000) of the population of Jerusalem, Palestinian neighborhoods in East Jerusalem only receive 10 percent of the municipal budget.[28]

One of the most arduous and difficult processes in East Jerusalem is the obtaining of building permits. According to a 2015 report, only 7 percent of Jerusalem building permits go to Palestinian neighborhoods; in 2014, of the 3,238 building permits issued in Jerusalem, only 188 of these were for building in Palestinian neighborhoods; and from 2009–2014, 11,603 building permits were issued for the whole of Jerusalem but only 878 were for Palestinian neighborhoods.[29] Indeed, most applications from Palestinian residents for building permits in East Jerusalem are rejected. As reported by the Israeli Committee Against House Demolitions (ICAHD) in 2013, "Palestinian residents of Jerusalem cannot acquire permits to build on the 89 percent of East Jerusalem that they own."[30]

The Municipality of Jerusalem and the Israeli Ministry of Interior control all aspects of planning and building in Jerusalem.[31] East Jerusalemites are not represented in the official planning bodies, so they have no power to influence the complicated and highly centralized Israeli system of planning institutions that restricts the availability of space and takes years to navigate.[32] The total cost of a building permit can reach US$30,000, which includes applying for water, sewage services and taxes.[33] This means that the cost of building a home in East Jerusalem is extremely high, as the permit is an additional cost.

The procedural complexities of securing licenses, which are tough, expensive and protracted, have restricted East Jerusalemites from building new houses or even constructing small extensions to their existing houses.[34] The Israeli human rights organization, B'Tselem, argues that this constitutes the core reason for illegal building in Jerusalem because "Palestinians find themselves forced to build without permits because Israeli authorities, including the Jerusalem Municipality and planning bodies, practice policies that prevent them from building legally, with the stated goal of maintaining a Jewish majority in the city."[35] A further layer of obstruction also exists in that even when the municipality has been set to approve construction permits or extensions in Palestinian neighborhoods, this has often been blocked by right-wing activists and Haredi city councilors.[36] Illegal or unauthorized building in East Jerusalem is therefore directly linked to refusals to grant Palestinians building permits. As a result of this lack of permits, in 2017 it was estimated that there were around 20,000 unauthorized buildings in East Jerusalem.[37] This is the reason for the high number of house demolitions. From 2004 to August 2015, around 579 houses were demolished in East Jerusalem by the Jerusalem Municipality and the Ministry of Interior, leaving 2,133 Palestinians homeless.[38] The trauma and life instability induced by house demolitions is a reality for many Palestinians in East Jerusalem. Most of the families affected by this had nowhere else to live, and subsequently had to move outside the city borders.[39] There are thousands of demolition orders issued by the Jerusalem Municipality and the Ministry of Interior that have yet to be carried out. As evidenced by a number of interviews conducted in East Jerusalem as research for this chapter, one of the key objectives of permit obstacles, fines and house demolitions and orders, is to encourage migration outside of the city.

The Separation Barrier has also played a significant role in house demolitions and the deportation of East Jerusalemites beyond it, because it tore the eastern part of Jerusalem to shreds, and the houses of around 100 Palestinians in East Jerusalem were demolished to make way for it.[40] Another effect of the erection of the Separation Barrier has been to disconnect a number of Palestinian neighborhoods that had been part of the enlarged municipal boundaries of Jerusalem after 1967, in some cases even trapping people, despite the fact that some of their residents hold East Jerusalem ID cards. Referred to as the "seam zone," this no-man's land leaves Palestinians in a state of limbo, as confirmed by a Palestinian affected by it: "Despite that I hold Jerusalemite ID document, I found myself and my family outside Jerusalem after the Separation Wall was built. The Wall created a different form of unrecognized ID, even if we were Jerusalemite by ID."[41] Because of these types of settler colonial segregation and separation strategies, a number of Palestinian neighborhoods have not only become isolated from Jerusalem but are simultaneously neither integrated into Israel nor into the West Bank. The neighborhoods involved include: Kafr 'Aqab-Semiramis, Shuafat refugee camp, and the neighborhoods of Ras-Khamis, Ras-Shehadeh and Dahiyat al-Salaam (new Anata). According to Palestinian statistical information, as a direct result of the Separation Barrier's creation, around 130,000 Palestinians live outside the municipality's borders (i.e., on the West Bank side of the Barrier).[42] And so although some of the residents of these neighborhoods are Jerusalemites, through these processes they have been denied their rights to, and physically isolated from, the city. These policies have had a greater impact on the more vulnerable segments of Palestinian East Jerusalemites who have been unable to economically sustain living in Jerusalem, and so live in the borderlands and continue to face a fragile situation in all aspects of life. As analyzed by a number of scholars, Kafr 'Aqab is one of the most vulnerable Palestinian groups who live in such a volatile situation.[43] Interviews conducted in some of these neighborhoods show the fragility of the situation for the inhabitants, as articulated by one resident of Kafr 'Aqab: "Despite that it is cheap and easy to get housing here comparing to Jerusalem, our residency is fragile and can be revoked anytime."[44] As reported by OCHA, the municipality of Jerusalem plans to demolish more buildings in Kafr 'Aqab, further undermining the fragile situation of Palestinians in the East Jerusalem borderlands.[45] As Owais points out, disconnecting an entire section of the Palestinian population from East Jerusalem constitutes a core aspect of the fragmentation of Palestinian life.[46] Most of the neighborhoods do not receive services from the Municipality of Jerusalem, and policing and justice mechanisms for East Jerusalemites beyond the Separation Barrier is also significantly lacking, as Israel's police force has suspended all operations there.[47] There is no regular police action to maintain or enforce law and order in the area and, as a result, a criminal justice vacuum is present in these neighborhoods.[48] The vacuum extends beyond policing, i.e., there are no inspection bodies or urban planning mechanisms as a result of the lack of law enforcement.

Because of the Separation Barrier and Israel's policies of settler colonization, many young Palestinians have been encouraged to leave Jerusalem in the search for better options, e.g., living in the nearby towns of the West Bank; this thus operates as a form of (largely) invisible population transfer. But this imposes significant difficulties in getting to and from jobs as well as receiving services.[49] In a 2014 report, UNCTAD estimated that around 55,000 Palestinian Jerusalemites were directly affected by the Barrier and had to go through checkpoints, which also limits their access to health and educational facilities.[50] The physical isolation of the neighborhoods beyond the Barrier has thus left thousands of East Jerusalemites separated from Jerusalem.

ISOLATING THE ECONOMY OF EAST JERUSALEM FROM THE WEST BANK

From 1967, the Palestinian economy has experienced a number of systematic destructive policies by Israel, the occupying power, and has not been allowed to develop.[51] This is also true for East Jerusalem, although it became far worse after the Oslo Accords. East Jerusalem was part of the Palestinian economy before the Oslo Accords because Jerusalem was an open city and so Palestinian merchants and shoppers could access it easily. However, after the Oslo Accords, according to Palestinian merchants and shopkeepers in East Jerusalem, and as confirmed by available data, East Jerusalem's economy has deteriorated because of the impact of a variety of strategies used to delink and isolate it from the rest of the OPT. On the eve of the First Intifada and just before Oslo, it was estimated that the East Jerusalem economy contributed 15 percent of the GDP of the OPT, which was estimated to amount to US$250 million in 1990. By 2010, the East Jerusalem economy, compared to the rest of the OPT economy, contributed less than eight percent.[52] To support Palestinian East Jerusalem economically, international donors such as the EU contributed in 2018 alone around €14.9 million for activities in East Jerusalem.[53]

The Separation Barrier, Israeli checkpoints and the permit system have all played a significant role in separating the Palestinian economy of East Jerusalem from the rest of the OPT. This has had a significant impact on poverty rates, which in 2017 reached 79.5 percent of the Palestinian residents, including 83 percent of children.[54] The creation of the Barrier has also had a huge impact on the daily lives of Palestinians from the West Bank and Gaza in that it has restricted their access to the city, as well as reducing their economic activities and job opportunities.[55] Before the construction of the Barrier, Jerusalem functioned as the commercial, social, religious, cultural and political center of Palestinians in the West Bank and Gaza. Now access to the holy sites and the al-Aqsa mosque has been severely restricted for Palestinians from the West Bank and Gaza, who now require permits to enter Jerusalem.[56] However, this was not always the case. In interviews with East Jerusalemite Palestinian merchants and businessmen, they recall that the first few years after the Oslo Accords witnessed a growth in the Palestinian economy in East Jerusalem. The free movement of Palestinians from Gaza and the West Bank to Jerusalem was part of the mosaic of the city and this time was considered a golden era for the East Jerusalem economy.[57] But now this is no longer the case, with Israel implementing policies that have served to hinder the development of East Jerusalem's economy; and after the outbreak of the Second Intifada in September 2000 the situation worsened further.[58] In comparison with the West Bank, East Jerusalemites benefitted less economically in the era after the signing of the Accords.[59] In 2013, UNCTAD estimated that as a result of the Barrier and the various restrictive measures, economic losses to East Jerusalemites were in excess of US$1 billion, and they continue to incur losses of US$200 million per year in lost opportunities.[60] The creation of new borders, walls and checkpoints isolated East Jerusalem economically from the West Bank and Gaza.

Isolating East Jerusalem from its natural connections with the West Bank means that it is no longer connected to the Palestinian economy of the OPT. Economically, East Jerusalemite merchants struggle to keep their businesses going, and the socioeconomic level of Palestinian citizens is low.[61] The Old City, in particular, has felt the economic burden most sharply, as merchants and businessmen have experienced high levels of taxation and incur huge levels of debt. Around 40 percent of East Jerusalem's economy relies directly on tourism, while 25 percent is based on trade, 25 percent from the service sector, and less than 10 percent on handicraft and local industry. However, local Palestinian economists highlight the decline of tourism as indicated by the reduction of room reservations in small Palestinian hotels by 80 percent from 2005 to 2015. According to RaadSa'ada, in 2017, only 20 Palestinian hotels functioned in East Jerusalem.[62] It is estimated there are around 400 souvenir shops in the Old City, which constitutes 20 percent of the overall economic activities in the city, however, their economic performance is very low.[63]

In the decade after the signing of the Oslo Accords, and especially after the Second Intifada, restrictions on Palestinian access to Jerusalem were implemented, which meant that many Palestinian traders and businessmen were thereafter unable to access the city.[64] According to the NGO al-Maqdese for Society Development, between 1999 and 2015 more than 250 Palestinian businesses closed their doors because of the shrinking East Jerusalem economy.[65] As a result, many Palestinian businessmen began to invest elsewhere: in Ramallah, Bethlehem, Hebron and even outside the West Bank.[66] Furthermore, because of the high prices in Jerusalem, East Jerusalemites do more of their shopping in the West Bank, because it is cheaper, thus further impacting negatively on Palestinian businesses in Jerusalem.

According to Abu al Saud, an East Jerusalemite Palestinian economist, the economy of Jerusalem is very weak due to the lack of an Arab industrial area. Restrictions on industrial permits in East Jerusalem were a barrier to the development of industrial zones.[67] As a result, many Palestinians invest in developing their businesses in Israeli industrial areas such as Mishor Adumim and Atarot, which restricts their economic interaction with the Palestinian market.[68] Wadi al-Joz is one of the main industrial zones in Palestinian East Jerusalem, but compared to Israeli industrial zones such as Talbiyot-Talibiya, the area needs a lot of investment and development.

The East Jerusalem economy is therefore now neither integrated with the Palestinian economy in the rest of the OPT nor with the West Jerusalem (and Israeli) economy.

THE VACUUM OF LEADERSHIP: THE EVISCERATION OF THE PALESTINIAN BODY POLITIC

Israel's policies of separating East Jerusalem from the rest of the OPT have also led to the evisceration of the Palestinian body politic in East Jerusalem. Post-Oslo East Jerusalem is disconnected politically from the West Bank and Gaza. One of the direct results of the Oslo peace process was the legalization and recognition of the PLO by Israel which thus allowed it to exist in the city where previously it had been banned. However, this recognition was under attack right from the start and thus there was an ever-shrinking role permitted to the PLO in the city, and the Palestinian Authority (PA) was granted no influence at all. Israel thus managed to eventually eviscerate Palestinian political leadership from the city, including dismantling all PA/PLO institutions and closing many Palestinian civil society organizations. However, as Dumper argues, the PA has no solid and clear national strategy on how to strengthen its position in Jerusalem.[69]

Following the signing of the Oslo Accords, Palestinian political institutions were able to operate officially, but not for long. Only a few years after Oslo, the PA was forbidden from functioning in Jerusalem, leaving a leadership and power vacuum. Furthermore, the PLO's access to Jerusalem was increasingly restricted and eventually its main institutions, such as Orient House, were closed down. By weakening the PLO presence in Jerusalem and fragmenting the Palestinian body politic, Israel made it clear that the PLO would not be allowed to have a political base in the city. As reported by Madar, this also affected other Palestinian institutions, including human relief organizations, economic, media, educational and cultural organizations and services, as well as civil society organizations representing women, tourist organizations, youth and prisoners. Many Palestinian institutions were forced to move their bases to Ramallah or at least outside Jerusalem's municipal borders.[70] Palestinians were thus only allowed to develop their institutions in the OPT—and even here this was confined to Areas A and B.[71]

This political vacuum was created and unfolded almost immediately after the Oslo Accords, despite reassurances from Israel to the contrary. Writing on October 11, 1993, to Johan Jorgen Holst, the Norwegian minister of foreign affairs, Shimon Peres, Israel's foreign minister, confirmed that Palestinian institutions in East Jerusalem, including economic, cultural, social and holy places for Muslims and Christians, were important and would be protected, and further confirmed that they would continue to function as usual.[72] The clear message that should be taken from the 'Holst Letter" is that the Oslo Accords allowed for the development and preservation of Palestinian institutions in East Jerusalem.[73] Nevertheless, despite this reassurance, Israel began to close Palestinian institutions in East Jerusalem almost immediately after the peace agreement had been signed. In November 1994, the Knesset approved a law that restricted activities in Orient House,[74] and in December 1994 a further law was passed that legalized the closing of Palestinian institutions in Jerusalem. Israel's police minister, Moshe Shahal, with the support of the Israeli foreign minister and the Israeli prime minister, called for the closing of institutions affiliated to the PA.[75] In 1999, the Israeli Ministry of Interior closed three institutions based in Orient House, and in 2001 Orient House was shut down completely.[76] The ministers' aim was to restrict Palestinian efforts to establish a political presence in East Jerusalem, as part of the struggle for control.

Despite the Oslo Accords purportedly guaranteeing to protect Palestinian institutions in East Jerusalem, by 2014 Israel had closed 60 institutions (including cultural and educational organizations);[77] this included the closure of more than 22 Palestinian NGOs between 2001 to 2011.[78] This, plus the restrictions and permit obstacles put in place by the Israeli authorities, has led to a decline in the cultural life of East Jerusalem. More problematically, there is a crisis of leadership because the PLO cannot operate there. Even the role of the Palestinian governor of East Jerusalem, Adnan al-Hussaini, is restricted—he is not permitted to function in East Jerusalem and thus operates from Al-Ram (which is beyond the Separation Barrier), but without significant economic resources being made available to him by the PA. This means that Palestinians in East Jerusalem are represented by neither the Israeli political system nor by the Palestinian political system. Jerusalem residents thus perceive al-Hussaini as playing a "symbolic role" only, with one stating: "after all he has no power to help the Jerusalemites."[79]

And yet despite this official leadership gap, there are various Palestinian professional groups in Jerusalem—distributed across the economy, youth, education, civil society and tourism—that offer a significant body of grassroots leadership, although further effort is needed for them to become unified. If this leadership were to be organized under one umbrella into a new form of civil society governance, the problem of the lack of representation in East Jerusalem could be solved.[80] According to Hanadi Qwasmi, a Palestinian civil society activist from East Jerusalem, the vacuum of political leadership in East Jerusalem resulted in the emergence of youth movements that are trying to fill the leadership gap, albeit in a limited form.[81] As the gap between East Jerusalem and West Bank Palestinian communities has widened, the issue of the representation of East Jerusalem's population has become a clear concern, and was frequently mentioned during interviews with young people in East Jerusalem. One person clearly articulated the view expressed by many that: "We need a leadership that will emerge from the community rather than a non-existent leadership or a leadership that is affiliated with existing Palestinian parties."[82] This crisis of leadership is compounded by the lack of trust between the Palestinian leadership as represented by PLO/PA representatives based in Ramallah, and Palestinians in East Jerusalem. The role of the PLO and Fatah, particularly in Jerusalem, became "weak and disconnected" throughout the Oslo period, with "almost . . . no relationship and no trust with the people."[83]

While the PLO continues to encourage East Jerusalemites to boycott the Israeli political system and the municipality by not participating or voting in elections, the absence of Palestinian East Jerusalemites from political life has strengthened the control of Jewish-Israeli actors over all aspects of the city's life.[84] East Jerusalemites are permitted to vote and stand for office in Jerusalem's municipal elections, but the majority choose not to practice this right in protest against their annexation and as an act of resistance against normalization. Indeed, less than 1 percent of East Jerusalemites voted in the 2013 Municipality of Jerusalem elections.[85] This is unlikely to change in the October 2018 municipal elections, despite the fact that there are a few Palestinian candidates standing from East Jerusalem from a newly created Arab list called *Al-Quds Lilmaqdisiyeen* (Jerusalem for Jerusalemites) led by Ramadan Dabash.[86]

Through cementing its relations with Jordan and signing the 1994 Israel-Jordan Peace Treaty—also known as the Wadi 'Arab a Agreement—Israel has also tried to restrict the role of the PLO/PA in the Awqaf system. Despite that, the Awqaf in Jerusalem is the only institution that Israel cannot control, as it functions under the Jordanian Ministry of the Awqaf. The historic and important role that this institution has played, and continues to play in East Jerusalem, is the subject of the following section.

THE STRUGGLE OVER THE AWQAF: JORDAN, ISRAEL AND THE PA/PLO

One of the most contentious issues between Israel and Palestinians in East Jerusalem is over control of the Old City of Jerusalem, particularly its Muslim holy shrines, and especially the Haram ash-Sharif. This has always been a flashpoint that last escalated in the summer of 2017 as a result of the growing Israeli challenge to the status of the Haram ash-Sharif. The two weeks of peaceful Palestinian demonstrations in July 2017 against the Israeli installation of metal detectors at the gates to the al-Aqsa compound marked a new phase of conflict over the future of the waqf and the Old City. Historically, supervising the Awqaf is one of the areas of authority of the Supreme Muslim Council.[87] In East Jerusalem, the Awqaf is best known for managing and controlling the Muslim holy sites in the Old City.

The picture is complex in the Old City. Jordan has played a hugely significant role (and has done since 1924), while the PLO and the PA plays virtually none. Since the end of the British Mandate, Jordan played the most important role in maintaining and supervising the Awqaf/waqf system in Palestine. As argued by Reiter, two significant changes introduced by Jordanian rule after 1948 were that West Bank and East Jerusalem affairs were subordinated entirely to the Islamic organ in Amman; and that the Hashemite's rivals in Jerusalem, the Husaynis, were replaced with other prominent Palestinian families in the religious apparatus.[88] Since the early 1950s until the present day, therefore, the most significant role in protecting the Awqaf in Jerusalem, including the supervision and maintenance of the holy sites, has been undertaken by Jordan—despite the various political changes and developments in East Jerusalem.

During the early days of the Israeli occupation of East Jerusalem, there was no clear strategy in relation to the Awqaf.[89] After 1967, most of the religious institutions, including the Awqaf and the *shari'a* courts, remained connected to Jordanian institutions, both legally and economically. The Awqaf is the strongest and most organized local institution in East Jerusalem, and administers around 30 percent of the Islamic waqf in the Old City.[90] As well as managing the holy sites and supervising mosques, the Awqaf also runs a number of schools and *madaris shariyia*, it runs the *shari'a* courts, and colleges known as *dur al-qur'an* and *dur al-hadith*, as well as employing hundreds of people who receive their salaries from Jordan.[91] Despite Jordan's disengagement declaration from the West Bank in 1988, the *shari'a* court continued to be fully controlled by Jordan and became a branch of the Jordanian Ministry of Interior.[92] In 2015, the Awqaf employed over 420 persons in Jerusalem, who all belong to the Ministry of Awqaf in Jordan.[93] Despite being signatory to the Oslo Accords, the PLO was not granted any significant role in running the Islamic institutions in East Jerusalem. In the 1994 Wadi 'Araba Agreement, the PLO was excluded from playing any official role in dealing with the Awqaf in East Jerusalem.

Even though Israel has tried to intervene in religious matters in the Old City, the Awqaf has been able to remain independent, working directly with the

Kingdom of Jordan but not with the PA. Jordan thus plays a crucial mediating role in the event of conflict erupting between the Awqaf and the Israeli authorities.[94] The effectiveness of the Awqaf institutions is based on the fact that they report immediately to the Jordanian king and the minister of Awqaf in Jordan. As a result of this official relationship with Jordan, the Awqaf can use the diplomatic arena to deal with Israel's policies toward the al-Aqsa mosque. In a world controlled by sovereign states, the involvement of Jordan gives the Awqaf more influence. Indeed, in 2014 the Jordanian Minister of Awqaf condemned Israel for provocative actions in the Old City and around the al-Aqsa mosque, and reminded Israel to avoid any significant action that would disturb the existing order in Jerusalem.[95] Jordan's continuing power in East Jerusalem is enshrined in the 1994 Wadi 'Araba Agreement, and King Hussain's insistence on the role of Jordan taking precedence.[96]

The Wadi 'Araba Agreement between Israel and Jordan offered a "special role" for Amman to manage the Muslim Holy Shrines, but without mentioning specific details.[97] Israel's preference for granting symbolic sovereignty over the Awqaf to Jordan was linked to its wish to strengthen the Hashemite Kingdom and block the PLO having a role in East Jerusalem.[98] During discussions in the Knesset in the weeks before the 1994 peace agreement was signed with Jordan, the strategic importance of strengthening the role of the Hashemite Kingdom as a way to block the PLO's aspirations for a Palestinian state was acknowledged.[99] Israel's decision to give high priority to Jordan's historic role in protecting the holy shrines sparked tension with the PLO and also left the Islamic leadership in the Old City in a dilemma about whether to show their loyalty to the PLO or to Jordan.[100] This policy of excluding the PLO from any official role in the Awqaf has meant that Palestinians will not be granted any form of protection over the Awqaf before any final peace resolution with Israel. The Wadi 'Araba Agreement blocked any potential role for the PLO in Jerusalem and participation in the dynamics of the Holy Basin and thus initially conflict grew between the PLO/PA and Jordan over the responsibilities of the Awqaf in Jerusalem.[101] But while the Palestinian leadership sought a monopoly over the holy sites in Jerusalem, Israel would not permit the PLO to supervise the Awqaf. According to Reiter, "The agreement between Israel and Jordan included a clause that challenged the Palestinian Authority's claim to negotiate its future sovereignty over the Islamic holy places in the old city of Jerusalem."[102] Attempts by the PLO to appoint a parallel religious leadership to challenge that of Jordan led to internal divisions, and along with the apparent limited success of the Oslo Accords, it was clear that the PLO would have insufficient leverage to negotiate a strong leadership role in Jerusalem.[103] Because of the tensions, it was agreed that Jordan would continue to finance the salaries for Awqaf employees and the PA would be responsible for religious affairs in the West Bank.[104]

In 1996, Jordan promised to transfer custody of the Holy Basin to the Palestinians once they had, based on permanent status agreements, gained control over the Old City. However, given the lack of movement toward a final status agreement and growing evidence that Israel would not indeed end the occupation and annexation of East Jerusalem, in March 2013, the PLO signed a symbolic agreement supporting the right of Jordan to continue to supervise the Awqaf in Jerusalem.[105] This agreement also emphasized the principles agreed to by Jordan and Palestine to exert joint efforts to protect the Old City and its holy sites from Israel's attempts at Judaization.[106]

Jordan's commitment to the holy sites and to East Jerusalem as the capital of a future Palestinian state has been frequently expressed. In 2014, for instance, Jordanian foreign minister, Nasser Judeh, declared that for Jordan, "Jerusalem remains a red line," and that Jordan continually requests that Israel desist from any policies "that would affect Eastern Jerusalem and its holy Islamic and Christian places."[107] However, an escalation in activities by right-wing settler organizations who demand that Jews be given the right to pray in the al-Aqsa compound (which they refer to as Temple Mount), and the increasing numbers of Jewish-Israeli MKs who support this demand, has fueled fears that Israel will attempt to change the status quo in the Old City, which would endanger the Wadi 'Araba Agreement with Jordan. In response, Jordan has utilized a number of diplomatic mechanisms, including recalling its ambassador to Israel in 2014 and 2015, and appealing to the international community, particularly the UN, for action to protect the status quo.[108] Violating Jordan's status as protectors of the Awqaf in Jerusalem could risk the peace agreement with Israel. Indeed, pressure has been mounting in Jordan to cancel the peace agreement with Israel over provocations in the al-Aqsa Mosque, including in 2016 when 47 Jordanian members of parliament urged the king and his government to cancel the Wadi 'Araba Agreement.[109] However, at the time of writing the Agreement remains in place.

Rising concern at Israeli actions that challenge the status and sovereignty over the Holy Basin has even on occasion pushed US officials, including in 2014, US secretary of state, John Kerry, to intervene to try to prevent a diplomatic crisis between Israel and Jordan.[110] In all of these cases, these diplomatic efforts were conducted without official Palestinian representation—another sign of the marginal role that the PA/PLO play in East Jerusalem, and particularly the Old City, that has sparked anger and dissatisfaction.[111] Even in the current fragile situation and the ongoing debate around the future of the Awqaf and the Holy Basin, the PA/PLO has been excluded by Israel, the US and Jordan from any negotiations aimed at stabilizing the situation in East Jerusalem. As a result, on the political level, East Jerusalemites are stuck between three political entities—Israel, Jordan and the PLO/PA—without a political stake in any of these systems.

The situation as regards the status of al-Aqsa continues to be a powerful mobilizing issue for Palestinians. In July 2017, for example, after two Israeli policemen were shot dead by three young Palestinian-Arabs from the town of Umm al Fahim (in Israel), there was a major confrontation. This took the form of peaceful demonstrations, mobilized by the Waqf, in response to Israel's increased security measures around al-Aqsa, which included the installation of metal detectors and the ban on Muslim men under the age of 50 from entering. Muslims refused to enter al-Aqsa through the metal detectors, praying in the streets instead.[112] After two weeks of huge peaceful demonstrations, during which Muslim Palestinians were joined by some Palestinian Christians, Israel removed all of the new security equipment around the al-Aqsa compound, prompting a senior Waqf official to claim that Palestinian Jerusalemites were now in "a new era of victory."[113]

Over recent years, commentators have recommended that the role of the Jordanian Waqf system be "revolutionized" in order to challenge Israel effectively over the protection of the holy sites.[114] In the absence of the involvement of the PLO/PA, it is argued that Jordan should play a stronger role in East Jerusalem in order to restrict Israel's actions in the Old City. By gaining international recognition and support, Jordan could have more diplomatic power in the Old City, not only as the symbolic role of a guardianship of the Awqaf as stated in the Wadi 'Araba Agreement.

US president Donald Trump's December 2017 announcement of the US Embassy move from Tel Aviv to Jerusalem and recognition of Jerusalem as the capital city of Israel has been interpreted as the end of Oslo and the peace process. Challenging international and Muslim opinion worldwide, Trump's statement sparked anger and resistance among Palestinians in East Jerusalem and the wider OPT. The UN condemned the decision, stating clearly that the announcement undermined the peace process and damaged the position of the US as an honest broker in the conflict.[115] The EU and the pope also criticized it,[116] as did the Arab League, the Organization of Islamic Cooperation, and Turkey.[117] Jordan stated that Trump's decision contravened international law, and that it could risk the Wadi 'Araba Agreement between it and Israel.[118] However, the peaceful demonstrations in 2017 show that East Jerusalemite Palestinians will take an active role in deciding the future of their city. The status of Jerusalem therefore continues to be a powerful issue around which Palestinians and the international community are able to mobilize.

EMERGENCE OF NEW FORCES IN EAST JERUSALEM: THE PALESTINIAN ARAB PARTIES IN ISRAEL

Israel's and Jordan's policies of limiting the role of the PA/PLO in the Awqaf, and Israel's restrictions on any PLO/PA activities in East Jerusalem, has led to the emergence of new actors in the struggle over East Jerusalem, who also seek to fill the political vacuum and support East Jerusalemite Palestinians. The Palestinian citizens of Israel, including their political leaders—such as those represented by the Joint Arab List (*al Qaa'ima al Mushtaraka*) and legal organizations like Adalah—have started to play an important role in the struggle over the future of East Jerusalem. Palestinian-Arab MKs, for instance, boycotted the speech by US secretary of state, Mike Pence, in the Israeli Knesset January 2018 and strongly condemned Trump's declaration regarding the status of Jerusalem.[119]

Despite Palestinian-Arab MKs having different political agendas, they have acted as a unified body when it comes to protecting the Old City and supporting the Haram ash-Sharif.[120] According to Talab Abu 'Arar, an MK from the Joint Arab List and the Islamic Movement's southern branch, Palestinian-Arab MKs constantly stress that the al-Aqsa Mosque is a holy place for the Islamic community all over the world, and thus they present a unified stance for protecting it: "we brought the struggle over the Old City of Jerusalem to the Knesset, and made clear speeches about our rights as a Movement and as Arab MKs to protect the mosques in Jerusalem."[121] The Palestinian-Arab MKs are in direct contact with the Awqaf representatives in Jerusalem, supporting them, and have occasionally joined demonstrations in the Old City against Israel's policies of restricting Muslims from access to the mosques.

However, the MKs insist that they are not claiming political representation over Palestinian East Jerusalemites, but are simply advocating and leading a joint struggle, as Israeli citizens, using the Israeli system and political platforms. Given growing attempts to change the status of the Haram ash-Sharif compound by Jewish-Israeli parties, they are providing a frontline defense against the Israeli government officials, MKs, and Jewish religious organizations that call for full Israeli control over the Holy Basin, and wish to see a division of the al-Aqsa Mosque to open it for Jewish prayers.[122] Indeed, examining "the status of the Temple Mount" is one of the main topics constantly presented in Knesset subcommittee discussions.[123] For instance, in mid-2014, Israeli MKs such as Moshe Feiglin (at that time a Likud MK) and Hilik Bar, Labour Party, tabled proposals for imposing full Israeli sovereignty over the al-Aqsa compound by changing its current status and enhancing Jewish worship rights. Feiglin declared that: "Without the Temple Mount, we have no home."[124] Furthermore, he urged the government to strip away Jordan's role in relation to the Awqaf and impose Israeli control instead.[125] Such calls for Israeli sovereignty are considered by Palestinians and the wider Muslim and Arab world as proof of their long-standing suspicion that Israeli settlements and archaeological digs near the Holy Esplanade will eventually lead to a drastic alteration of the status quo.[126]

Feiglin's proposal sparked anger in the Arab world as well as amongst the Palestinian-Arab MKs and some Jewish MKs, one of whom, during a Knesset debate on the topic, warned of the potential risks in pursuing such a confrontational and divisive route. Meretz MK Zahava Gal-On responded to Feiglin thus: "The person who is standing at the Knesset podium is causing a provocation that has only one goal, and that is to blow up Israel's relations with the Muslim world and torpedo diplomatic negotiations." Gal-On argued that people calling for sovereignty over the Temple Mount were "throwing a match that will ignite the powder keg."[127] Supporting her position, Labour MK Nachman Shai warned that the attempt to change the situation at the al-Aqsa Mosque would "shock the entire Muslim World."[128] Feiglin's proposals, however, were blocked by the actions of the Palestinian-Arab MKs who responded by immediately withdrawing from the Knesset, thus rendering the debate irrelevant.[129] MK Ahmad Tibi has confirmed that the Arab parties would continue to campaign against such plans to gain sovereignty over the Holy Basin.[130]

In various statements that have appeared in the Arab media, MK Tibi insists on the occupied status of East Jerusalem, that settlers and right wingers are attempting to build the Temple Mount, and that the result of all these activities has been to spark hatred, racism and land confiscation.[131] The Palestinian-Arab MKs and the High Follow Up Committee for Arab Citizens of Israel (which includes local Arab leaders, mayors and Shaikhs) have also visited al-Aqsa Mosque to demonstrate a unified front from the Palestinian-Arab leadership in Israel in their rejection of any proposals for imposing Israeli sovereignty over the Holy Basin.[132]

The increase in meetings and the intensification of discussions in the Knesset concerning Israeli sovereignty over East Jerusalem and the holy sites has set the scene for an escalation in violence, including highly provocative demonstrations by right-wing groups on "Jerusalem Day," a day in which Jews celebrate what they refer to as the 'liberation of Jerusalem" in 1967, and which consistently provokes clashes with Palestinians in the Old City.[133] For example, a one-day conference in the Knesset in May 2014, again initiated by MK Feiglin, celebrating 47 years since Israel occupied East Jerusalem, proposed to debate Israeli hegemony over the mosque. Shortly after the conference, on 'Jerusalem Day," right-wing Jewish organizations called on Jews to march to al-Aqsa, which provoked clashes with Palestinians and violence in the Old City.[134] Jerusalem Day has continued to be a source of confrontation. Access to, and the status of, the Haram ash-Sharif remains a controversial issue, and is a constant flashpoint for violence.

Likewise, protecting East Jerusalem and the al-Aqsa Mosque from Judaization has been central to the Islamic Movement's activities, with leadership provided mainly by Sheikh Raed Salah, the head of the northern branch of the Islamic Movement. According to reports from the International Crisis Group, "with the PA not permitted to operate in Jerusalem per the Oslo Accords, Salah, an Israeli citizen, moved to fill the Arab leadership vacuum in the city."[135] Indeed, Dumper and Larkin argue that Jerusalem, and more specifically the al-Aqsa Mosque, have been employed by the movement as a "symbol for political empowerment."[136]

Through his role in mobilizing the Palestinian community under the political slogan "al-Aqsa in Danger,"[137] Shaikh Salah is regarded as one of the most influential characters in the struggle over the Holy Basin, despite the fact that in 2015 his movement was banned, and he was imprisoned in 2016 and again in 2017–2018 by Israel.[138] Salah managed to legitimize his role through administering a number of initiatives and projects in the Old City and al-Aqsa Mosque. Salah's speeches and articles confirm that the main focus of his activities in Jerusalem has been, and is, aimed at protecting al-Aqsa Mosque and preventing the Judaization of East Jerusalem.[139] Through the al-Aqsa Association, Salah has also managed to play a crucial role in drawing attention to Israel's plans for excavation under al-Aqsa Mosque and in the Silwan neighborhood.[140]

Before it was banned, the northern branch of the Islamic Movement coordinated and organized joint events with a number of local Palestinian institutions and the Jerusalemite leadership. For example, it liaised with Ikrima Sabri (head of the Supreme Islamic Council), Mohammed Hussein (the current mufti of Jerusalem), Adnan al-Hussaini (the PLO governor in Jerusalem), and other affiliated institutions.[141] Through its establishment of the al-Aqsa Association for Preservation of the Islamic *Waqf*, the Islamic Movement cemented its role as a key protector of the al-Aqsa. By drawing international attention to Israel's plans for dividing the mosque and opening it for Jewish prayers, the Islamic Movement has succeeded in reaching the wider Islamic and Arab world. Salah Lutfi, one of the leaders of the movement, maintains that Israel is planning to divide al-Aqsa Mosque in a similar fashion to the al-Ibrahimi Mosque in Hebron.[142] Furthermore, through the Islamic Movement's visits to Islamic and Arab countries, Salah succeeded in internationalizing the situation of Jerusalem. By using the powerful slogan "al-Aqsa is the Islamic *umma*'s main cause," or al-Aqsa is the '*umma waqf*," he has garnered international support, along with an acknowledgment of his role in Jerusalem. By hosting international and high-level diplomatic delegations from the Islamic world, as well as sending his representatives to visit Arab and Islamic countries, Salah's role was also strengthened, and the Islamic Movement was perceived internationally as the legitimate body to speak about Jerusalem.

Through its annual "al-Aqsa is in Danger" campaign, the Islamic Movement drew attention to the mosque and to its protests against the Israeli state's policies toward the Haram ash-Sharif. The campaign encouraged Muslim Palestinians in Israel to visit al-Aqsa and to attend the mosque regularly for prayers, facilitated by transport subsidized by the Islamic Movement. From 2001 to 2006, there were two million such visits to the holy sites,[143] and this increase in footfall had a positive impact on the economy of the Old City.

The Al-Aqsa Association was created with the aim of protecting Islamic sites by mapping, documenting and contesting Islamic monuments and holy places, as well as the area around the Old City. By reclaiming these places both physically and financially, Shaikh Salah, through his "re-Palestinization" of spaces in Israel, was drawing attention to Islamic and Palestinian cultural history that predated the establishment of the Israeli state.[144] While these actions ensured that the protection of the Old City and the holy sites is a central issue for the Muslim world, Salah has been criticized for using language that has alienated Israel.[145] Indeed, this is posited as one of the reasons that led to his movement being outlawed by the Israeli state in November 2015

The ongoing local and international campaigns of the Palestinian-Arab MKs in relation to the Awqaf specifically and East Jerusalem generally, has helped to strengthen the Palestinian voice in East Jerusalem. Despite the significant role they play, Jordan is not keen to recognize these actors, and appears unwilling to give any important role to Palestinian-Arab MKs that could potentially challenge its power in the Old City.[146]

CONCLUSION

After reviewing East Jerusalem from different angles, and based on extensive field research, this chapter concludes that 25 years after the signing of the Oslo Accords, East Jerusalemite Palestinians have become separated from the rest of the OPT on political, social and economic levels because Israel has pursued and accelerated policies that have separated East Jerusalem from the West Bank without integrating it into Israel. This has led to the evisceration of the Palestinian body politic in East Jerusalem. Palestinians in East Jerusalem are thus trapped between Israeli sovereignty aspirations and the lack of PLO leadership—both of which have left them weak and marginalized. As

Israel has continued its strategy of separating East Jerusalem from the West Bank, the Palestinian leadership in the West Bank has played a decreasing role in the future of the city, despite its aspirations that East Jerusalem should be the capital of a future Palestinian state. This lack of leadership has enabled a situation where the Palestinians in Israel, particularly through the Palestinian-Arab MKs and political parties, have increasingly come to play a political role, both in the Knesset and by supporting East Jerusalemites through specific projects, as well as seeking to lead campaigning activities and to fill the political vacuum in East Jerusalem.

East Jerusalemite Palestinians therefore tend to regard themselves as being stuck between two countries. Indeed, as Salah, a BeitSafafa resident, pointed out, in Jerusalem, Palestinians have no unified official ID—some have Israel citizenship, while some have East Jerusalem IDs (as well as a Jordanian passport): "It is incredible that we, as Palestinians, turned out to be holders of four or five different types of ID. We are stuck in an unimaginable situation, between Israel, Jordan and the Palestinian Authority."[147] This is all attributed to the Oslo Accords and the exclusion of Jerusalem from the peace process; Trump's 2017 assertion that Jerusalem is the capital of Israel only furthers the exclusion of Jerusalem from any future peace negotiations.

Critical Palestinian voices from East Jerusalem argue that "until today . . . we as Palestinians are still not unified, and we can continue to be disunited for the next 20 years."[148] As a result of cutting off East Jerusalem from the rest of the OPT, East Jerusalemite Palestinians "are left without the protection of an impartial arbiter and find themselves at the mercy of the occupying power."[149] However, despite all attempts to change the status and nature of the city, and separate East Jerusalem from the rest of the OPT, its inhabitants insist that they will continue resisting the occupation and the policies of isolation.

In such a precarious situation, the Palestinians of East Jerusalem continue to seek stable futures and to live better lives. But in a context where they have no influence in political institutions and where their economy is fragmenting, this will be difficult, if not impossible. Granting local leadership a greater role, and respecting Palestinian needs and demands, will be the only mechanism for stabilizing the situation in East Jerusalem.

ACKNOWLEDGMENTS

Thanks to Mandy Turner for all her support while working on this project. I would also like to thank Michael Dumper, Neve Gordon, Adnan Abed al-Razik and Qassim Harb for their great insights and support while writing this chapter.

NOTES

1. Neve Gordon, "From Colonization to Separation: Exploring the Structure of Israel's Occupation," *Third World Quarterly* 29, no. 1 (November 2008): 25–44.

2. Yosef Jabareen, "The Rights to Space Production and the Right to Necessity: Insurgent Versus Legal Rights of Palestinians in Jerusalem," *Planning Theory* 16, no. 1 (June 2015): 1–26.

3. ICAHD, "Israel's Policy of Demolishing Palestinian Homes Must End: ICAHD Submission to the UN" (The Israel Committee Against House Demolitions [ICAHD], February 2013). http://icahd.org/2013/03/03/israels-policy-of-demolishing-palestinian-homes-must-end-icahd-submission-to-the-un/ (Accessed 20 June 2017).

4. Jabareen, "The Rights to Space Production," 1–26.

5. Scott A. Bollens, "Comparative Research on Urban Political Conflict: Policy Amidst Polarization," *Open Urban Studies Journal* 2, no. 1 (2009): 1–17.

6. UNOCHA, "East Jerusalem: Key Humanitarian Concerns" (United Nations Office for the Coordination of Humanitarian Affairs [UNOCHA], August 2014). http://unispal.un.org/UNISPAL.NSF/0/D0378180CEC6DEFB85257D3800543D5A (Accessed 23 July 2017).

7. OCHA, 2017. "Significant increase in risk of displacement in East Jerusalem" (Accessed 29 March 2018). https://www.ochaopt.org/content/significant-increase-risk-displacement-east-jerusalem.

8. Nir Hasson, "The Israeli Justice Ministry's Man Who Settles Jews in Arab East Jerusalem," *Haaretz*, March 9, 2018. https://www.haaretz.com/israel-news/.premium-the-ministry-s-man-who-settles-jews-in-arab-east-j-lem-1.5888643.

9. Lorenzo Veracini, "What Can Settler Colonial Studies Offer to an Interpretation of the Conflict in Israel–Palestine?" *Settler Colonial Studies* 5, no. 3 (2015): 268–271.

10. Magali Thill, "EU Obligations and Duty to End Israeli Policies of Forced Transfer, Colonialism and Apartheid in Occupied East Jerusalem" (European Coordination of Committees and Association for Palestine [ECCP], Brussels, Belgium, September 2014).

11. Interview with Raad Sa'ada, East Jerusalemite businessman. Old City, Jerusalem, May 5, 2015.

12. Lillian Goldman Law Library, "The Declaration of Principles. Israel-Palestine Liberation Organization Agreement: 1993," Yale Law School. http://avalon.law.yale.edu/20th_century/isrplo.asp.

13. Interview in Bab al-'Amod 'Abdullah. Jerusalem, March 4, 2014.

14. Interview with Sawsan Safadi, Awqaf official. Jerusalem, February 4, 2016.

15. Interview with Menachem Klein. Jerusalem, September 19, 2014.

16. Interview with al-Ram Adnan al-Hussaini. September 11, 2014.

17. Nadera Shalhoub-Koverkian, "Children: A Universalist Perspective for How Israel is using Child Arrest and Detention to further its Colonial Settler Project," *International Journal of Applied Psychoanalytic Studies* 12, no. 3 (2015): 223–244.

18. Haim Yacobi et al., "The Geopolitics of Neighbourhood: Jerusalem's Colonial Space Revisited," *Geopolitics* 19, no. 3 (May 2014): 1–26.

19. UNCTAD, "The Palestinian Economy in East Jerusalem: Enduring Annexation, Isolation and Disintegration" (Geneva: United Nations Conference on Trade and Development, 2013). http://unctad.org/en/PublicationsLibrary/gdsapp2012d1_en.pdf.

20. UNOCHA, "East Jerusalem: Key Humanitarian Concerns" (UNOCHA, March 2011), 12–13.

21. Ehud Tagari et al., "Displaced in their Own City: The Impact of Israeli Policy in East Jerusalem on the Palestinian Neighborhoods of the City beyond the Separation Barrier" (IR Amim [City of Nations], June 2015).

22. ECCP, "EU Obligations," 13.

23. UNOCHA, "East Jerusalem," 19.

24. UNOCHA, "East Jerusalem," 12.

25. ECCP, "EU Obligations," 13.

26. ICRC, "Convention (IV) relative to the Protection of Civilian Persons in Time of War" (International Committee of the Red Cross [ICRC], August 1949). https://www.icrc.org/ihl/INTRO/380.

27. Yacobi et al., "The Geopolitics of Neighbourhood," 5.

28. Human Right Watch, "Israel: Jerusalem Palestinians Stripped of Status," August 8, 2017. https://www.hrw.org/news/2017/08/08/israel-jerusalem-palestinians-stripped-status.

29. Nir Hasson, "Only 7% of Jerusalem Building Permits Go to Palestinian Neighbourhoods," *Haaretz*, December 7, 2015. http://www.haaretz.com/israel-news/.premium-1.690403.

30. ICAHD, "Israel's Policy of Demolishing Palestinian Homes Must End: ICAHD Submission to the UN" (The Israel Committee Against House Demolitions [ICAHD], February 2013). http://icahd.org/2013/03/03/israels-policy-of-demolishing-palestinian-homes-must-end-icahd-submission-to-the-un/ (Accessed 20 July 2017).

31. Yacobi et al., "The Geopolitics of Neighbourhood," 5.

32. Jabareen, "The Rights to Space Production," 10–13.

33. Y. Odeh, *Restrictions on Palestinian Construction in Jerusalem* (Arab Studies Society [Orient House], Jerusalem, 2008).

34. B'Tselem, "Police security escort during the demolition of a home in Silwan uses violence against family members" (Jerusalem: B'Tselem, June 24, 2015). http://www.btselem.org/beating_and_abuse/20150626_police_violence_in_silwan.

35. B'Tselem, "Police security escort."

36. Nir Hasson, "Jerusalem Approves Major Housing Plan for Arab Neighbourhood," *Hareetz*, September 4, 2014. http://www.haaretz.com/news/middle-east/.premium-1.613997.

37. ACRI, "East Jerusalem: Facts and Figures 2017." May 21, 2017. https://www.acri.org.il/en/wp-content/uploads/2017/05/Facts-and-Figures-2017.pdf.

38. B'Tselem, "Statistics on Demolition of Houses Built Without Permits in East Jerusalem" (Jerusalem: B'Tselem, March 5, 2018). http://www.btselem.org/planning_and_building/east_jerusalem_statistics.

39. Meir Margalit (ed.), *Demolishing Peace: House Demolitions in East Jerusalem 2000–2010* (Jerusalem: International Peace and Cooperation Centre, 2014).

40. NRC, "The Legality of the Wall Built by Israel in the West Bank, Background Report" (Norway Refugee Council [NRC], January 2015).

41. Interview at Al Reef al Gharbi, Jerusalem, March 2015.

42. Al-'Arabi al Jadid, "Jerusalem After Oslo: Judaization, Settlement and the Absence of Palestinian Strategy," *Al-'Arabi al Jadid*, September 14, 2014. http://www.alaraby.co.uk/politics/5fd28b68-8a67-4bb5-a873-3e74ae8045a0.

43. Doaa Hammoudeh et al., "Quality of Life for Families Living in East Jerusalem's Kafr 'Aqab Urban Sprawl: A Qualitative Study," *Lancet* 390, no. 1 (August 2017): S14.

44. Interview in Kafr 'Aqab, January 5, 2016.

45. UNOCHA, "High Numbers of Demolitions: The Ongoing Threats of Demolition for Palestinian Residents of East Jerusalem" (Jerusalem: UNOCHA, January 15, 2018). https://www.ochaopt.org/content/high-numbers-demolitions-ongoing-threats-demolition-palestinian-residents-east-jerusalem.

46. Owais Abdallah, "The Wall and the Enclaves: Case Studies in Disrupted Communities," in *The Wall: Fragmenting the Palestinian Fabric in Jerusalem*, ed. Robert Brooks (Jerusalem: International Peace Cooperation Center, 2007), 98; "Shu'fat Refugee Camp Profile," United Nations Relief and Works Agency for Palestine Refugees in the Near East (UNRWA), https://www.unrwa.org/where-we-work/west-bank/shufat-camp.

47. Michael Dumper, "Policing Divided Cities: Stabilization and Law Enforcement in Palestinian East Jerusalem," *International Affairs* 89, no. 5 (2013): 1259.

48. Interview in Kafr 'Aqab with Mahmoud. March 20, 2016.

49. Israel Kimhi, "Effects of the Security Fence on Palestinian Residents, in the City and in the Jerusalem Metropolitan Area," in *The Security Fence Around Jerusalem: Implications for the City and Its Residents*, ed. Israel Kimhi (Jerusalem: Jerusalem Institute for Israel Studies, 2006), 67–118.

50. UNCTAD, "The Palestinian Economy in East Jerusalem," 11.

51. Sara Roy, *The Gaza Strip: The Political Economy of De-Development* (Washington, DC: Institute for Palestine Studies, 1995).

52. UNCTAD, "The Palestinian Economy in East Jerusalem," 11–12.

53. European Union Press Release, "New assistance package for Palestine: EU strongly committed to support socio-economic revival of East-Jerusalem," EU: Jerusalem, 01/02/2018. https://eeas.europa.eu/headquarters/headquarters-homepage/39197/new-assistance-package-palestine-eu-strongly-committed-support-socio-economic-revival-east_en.

54. Mahdi Abdul Hadi, "Reviewing the Palestinian Political Scene 2015" (Palestinian Academic Society for the Study of International Affairs [PASSIA], Jerusalem, 2015). For more figures on East Jerusalem poverty see Robert Brooks, "The Wall and the Economy of Jerusalem Governorate," in *The Wall: Fragmenting the Palestinian Fabric in Jerusalem*, ed. Robert Brooks (Jerusalem: International Peace Cooperation Center, 2007), 37–41. See also ACRI 2017, "East Jerusalem Facts and Figures." https://www.acri.org.il/en/2017/05/24/east-jerusalem-facts-and-figures-2017/.

55. ICG, "The Status of the Status Quo at Jerusalem's Holy Esplanade," International Crisis Group (ICG), *Middle East Report*, no. 159 (June 30, 2015).

56. ICG, "The Status of the Status Quo," 11.
57. Interview with Raad Sa'ada, East Jerusalemite Businessman. Old City, Jerusalem, May 5, 2015.
58. UNCTAD, "The Palestinian Economy in East Jerusalem," 11.
59. UNCTAD, "The Palestinian Economy in East Jerusalem," 12.
60. UNCTAD, "The Palestinian Economy in East Jerusalem," 13.
61. Maya Choshen et al., *Jerusalem: Facts and Trends* (Jerusalem: Jerusalem Institute for Israel Studies, 2013).
62. Assel al-Junaidi, 2017, "Tourism in East Jerusalem." *Aljazeera*, September 27, 2017. http://www.aljazeera.net/news/alquds/2017/9/27/فريسة-ةابلقدسلا-يحاة. -التحريض-الإسرائيلي.
63. Abu Halwa, "East Jerusalem Economy," *Kul al Watan*, June 1, 2015.
64. Al-Maqdese for Society Development, "Palestinian Workers Rights in the Israeli Labour Market and Settlements" (Jerusalem: Al-Maqdese for Society Development, December 2011). https://www.al-maqdese.org/AR/?page_id=924.
65. Al-Maqdese for Society Development, "Palestinian Workers Rights."
66. Al-Masri, "The Economy of East Jerusalem," *AlQuds Gateway* [in Arabic], January 2014. http://alqudsgateway.ps/wp/wp-content/uploads/2014/01/small-final-book-8.pdf (Accessed June 20, 2016).
67. UNCTAD, "The Palestinian Economy in East Jerusalem," 13–16.
68. Abu Halwa, *Kul al Watan*, June 1, 2015.
69. Michael Dumper, *Jerusalem Unbound: Geography, History, and the Future of the Holy City* (New York: Columbia University Press, 2014).
70. Buthaina Hamdan, Madar News, "Jerusalem's Institutions and the Lack of PNA support," January 12, 2017. https://madar.news/وعجز-تمويلي-حصار-القدس-مؤسسات. /و-السلطة.
71. Sami Musallam, *"The Struggle for Jerusalem: A Programme of Action for Peace"* (Jerusalem: PASSIA, 1996).
72. UNOCHA, "East Jerusalem," 8.
73. Wendy Pullan et al., *The Struggle for Jerusalem's Holy Places* (London and New York: Routledge, 2013).
74. *Al-Ittihad*, June 18, 1994.
75. Israeli Ministry of Foreign Affairs, "Police Minister Shahal Calls for Closing PA Jerusalem Institutions," *Israel Ministry of Foreign Affairs Archive*, August 14, 1995. http://mfa.gov.il/MFA/MFA-Archive/1995/Pages/Police%20Minister-%20Close%20PA%20Jerusalem%20Institutions.aspx.
76. Odeh, *Restrictions on Palestinian Construction in Jerusalem*.
77. *al-'Arabi al-Jadid*, September 14, 2014.
78. Najat Hirbawi et al., "Palestinian Institutions in East Jerusalem," *Palestine-Israel Journal* 17, no. 12 (2011).
79. Interview with Abu Ahmad and Shaikh Jarrah. May 20, 2014.
80. Interview with Raad Sa'ada. Jerusalem, May 6, 2014.
81. Hanadi Qawasmi, "Initial Review of al-Hiraq al Shababi al Falasatini in Jerusalem (in Arabic)," Masarat: The Palestinian Centre for Policy Research and Strategic Studies (2013).

82. Interview in Salah al-Din Street, January 24, 2014.
83. Interview with Menachem Klein. Jerusalem, January 20, 2014.
84. Yezid Sayigh, *Al-Hayat*, Issue no. 18990. April 2, 2015.
85. Daoud Kuttab, "Palestinians Boycott Israeli Elections in Jerusalem Again," *Huffington Post*, October 24, 2010. https://www.huffingtonpost.com/daoud-kuttab/palestinians-boycott-isra_b_4159235.html.
86. Khaled Abu Toameh, "Head of Arab List Running in Jerusalem Elections: We are not Scared,"*Jerusalem Post*, July 11, 2018. https://www.jpost.com/Arab-Israeli-Conflict/Head-of-Arab-list-contesting-Jlem-election-Were-not-scared-562244.
87. Yitzhak Reiter, *Islamic Institutions in Jerusalem: Palestinian Muslim Organizations under Jordanian and Israeli Rule* (The Hague, London and Boston: Kluwer Law International, 1999).
88. Reiter, *Islamic Institutions in Jerusalem.*
89. Michael Dumper, *Islam and Israel: Muslim Religious Endowments and the Jewish State* (Washington, DC: Institute for Palestine Studies, 1994), 107.
90. Dumper, *Jerusalem Unbound*, 119.
91. Interview with Azzam al-Khatib, Director of Awqaf. August 5, 2014.
92. Reiter, *Islamic Institutions in Jerusalem*, 21.
93. Interview with Azzam al-Khatib.
94. Nazmi Al-Jubeh, "Bab al-Magharibah: Joha's Nail in the Haram al-Sharif," *Jerusalem Quarterly*, Institute for Jerusalem Studies, 18 (June 2003): 17–24.
95. "Jordanian Minister of Awqaf: The Maximum Mosque for Muslims Only," *Ma'an*, October 13, 2014. http://www.maannews.net/arb/ViewDetails.aspx?ID=733007.
96. Yitzhak Reiter, *Sovereignty of God and Man: Sanctity and Political Centrality on the Temple Mount* (Jerusalem: Jerusalem Institute for Israeli Studies, 2001).
97. ICG, "The Status of the Status Quo," 11.
98. Menachem Klein, "The Islamic Holy Places as a Political Bargaining Card (1993–95)," *Catholic University Law Review* 45, no. 3 (Spring 1996): 747.
99. Knesset Records, July 20, 1994. http://knesset.gov.il/tql/knesset_new/knesset14/HTML_27_03_2012_06-21-01-PM/19940720@19940720030@030.html.
100. Musallam, "The Struggle for Jerusalem."
101. Musallam, "The Struggle for Jerusalem," 84–86.
102. Reiter, *Islamic Institutions in Jerusalem*, 10.
103. Michael Dumper et al., "Political Islam in Contested Jerusalem: The Emerging Role of Islamists from within Israel," *Divided Cities/Contested State Working Paper*, no. 12 (2009), 5.
104. Reiter, *Islamic Institutions in Jerusalem*, 28.
105. Associated Press, "Abbas, Abdullah Sign Pact on Protection of Jerusalem Holy Sites," *Haaretz*, March 31, 2013. http://www.haaretz.com/news/middle-east/abbas-abdullah-sign-pact-on-protection-of-jerusalem-holy-sites-1.512819; Barak Ravid et al., "Netanyahu Orders Plans Be Advanced for 1,060 New East Jerusalem Housing Units," *Haaretz*, October 27, 2014. http://www.haaretz.com/news/diplomacy-defense/.premium-1.622950.
106. Ilene Prusher, "Jordan to Safeguard Jerusalem's Islamic Holy Sites—if They're Still Standing," *Haaretz*, April 4, 2013. http://www.haaretz.com/blogs/

jerusalem-vivendi/jordan-to-safeguard-jerusalem-s-islamic-holy-sites-if-they-re-still-standing.premium-1.513531.

107. Saddam al Yahya, "The Jordanian Foreign Minister, Jerusalem is a Red Line," *al-Quds al-'Arabi*, June 16, 2014. http://www.alquds.co.uk/?p=180940.

108. ICG, "The Status of the Status Quo at Jerusalem's Holy Esplanade," International Crisis Group (ICG), *Middle East Report*, no. 159 (June 30, 2015): 2.

109. Jerusalem Post Staff, "47 Jordanian MPs Call to Cancel Israel Peace Treaty Over Knesset Temple Mount Debate," *Jerusalem Post*, February 26, 2014. https://www.jpost.com/Middle-East/47-Jordanian-MPs-call-to-cancel-Israel-peace-treaty-over-Knesset-Temple-Mount-debate-343580.

110. Al Anadol News, "John Kerry Visits Jordan for Discussing Jerusalem Crisis," *al-Quds al-'Arabi*, November 12, 2014. http://www.alquds.co.uk/?p=249207.

111. Fadi Abu Sa'ada, "Israel Removed Islamic Awqaf Camera from al Aqsa Mosque," *al-Quds al-'Arabi*, October 26, 2015. http://www.alquds.co.uk/?p=424548.

112. Independent Agency News, "Israeli Police Ban Muslim Men Aged Under 50 from Friday Prayers in Jerusalem," *Independent*, July 21, 2017. http://www.independent.co.uk/news/world/middle-east/israel-police-ban-jerusalem-friday-prayers-muslim-men-50-walled-shrine-a7852156.html.

113. Bethan McKernan, "All New Security Measures at Jerusalem Holy Site Known as Temple Mount and Haram al-Sharif Removed, Israel says," *Independent*, July 27, 2017. http://www.independent.co.uk/news/world/middle-east/israel-temple-mount-haram-al-sharif-al-aqsa-crisis-palestinian-protests-security-measures-a7862196.html.

114. Prusher, "Jordan to Safeguard Jerusalem's Islamic Holy Sites."

115. Rick Gladstone et al., "Defying Trump, UN General Assembly Condemns US Decree on Jerusalem," *New York Times*, December 22, 2017. https://www.nytimes.com/2017/12/21/world/middleeast/trump-jerusalem-united-nations.html.

116. Jason Horowitz, "U.N., European Union and Pope Criticize Trump's Jerusalem Announcement," *New York Times*, December 6, 2017. https://www.nytimes.com/2017/12/06/world/europe/trump-jerusalem-pope.html.

117. Al Jazeera, 2017. "Arab League Condemns US Jerusalem Move," *Al Jazeera*, December 10, 2017. https://www.aljazeera.com/news/2017/12/arab-league-condemns-move-dangerous-illegal-171209185754563.html.

118. Mansour Nasasra, "East Jerusalem from Oslo Until Trump's Statement," Al-Watan Newspaper, 2018. http://alwatannews.net/author/3056/1/%D8%AF.-%D9%85%D9%86%D8%B5%D9%88%D8%B1-%D8%A7%D9%84%D9%86%D8%B5%D8%A7%D8%B5%D8%B1%D8%A9.

119. Al Jazeera report, "Arab MPs Ejected after Protesting Pence Knesset Speech," *Al Jazeera*, January 22, 2018. https://www.aljazeera.com/news/2018/01/arab-mps-ejected-protesting-pence-knesset-speech-180122160854881.html.

120. Qassim Bakri, "Follow-up: We Call on the Palestinian Interior to be a "Push to the Maximum,"*Arabs48*, October 16, 2014. http://www.arabs48.com/?mod=articles&ID=1145619.

121. Interview with MK Talab Abu 'Arar. Jerusalem, February 11, 2014.

122. ICG, "The Status of the Status Quo," 10.

123. Knesset Records, October 23, 2014. http://knesset.gov.il/spokesman/eng/PR_eng.asp?PRID=11465.

124. Knesset Records, May 15, 2014. http://www.knesset.gov.il/spokesman/eng/PR_eng.asp?PRID=11172.

125. Saddam al Yahya, "The Jordanian Foreign Minister, Jerusalem is a Red Line."

126. ICG, "The Status of the Status Quo," 13.

127. Knesset Records, May 15, 2014.

128. Knesset Records, May 15, 2014.

129. Knesset Records, May 15, 2014.

130. Al Arab alaannewsa 2014, "An Arab Member of the Knesset: The proposal to impose sovereignty on the Aqsa Mosque failed and will not pass," http://www.iaanews.com/news/index?id=60209&AspxAutoDetectCookieSupport=1.

131. Moran Azolay, "MK Ahmad Tibi: 'We are not leaving the country because of Milky,'" November 3, 2014. http://www.ynet.co.il/articles/0,7340,L-4587562,00.html.

132. Ahmed Gaber, "The Delegation of the Follow-up Committee Enters the Al-Aqsa Mosque," *Panet*, October 7, 2009. http://www.panet.co.il/online/articles/1/2/S-235700,1,2.html (accessed March 20, 2017).

133. Noam (Dabul) Dvir, "Violence Mars Jerusalem Day with Temple Mount Clashes," *Ynetnews.com*, May 28, 2014. http://www.ynetnews.com/articles/0,7340,L-4524679,00.html.

134. Dvir, "Violence Mars Jerusalem Day with Temple Mount Clashes."

135. ICG, "The Status of the Status Quo," 7.

136. Dumper et al., "Political Islam in Contested Jerusalem," 1.

137. Nadev Shargai, *The 'Al-Aksa Is in Danger' Libel: The History of a Lie* (Jerusalem: Jerusalem Center for Public Affairs, 2012), 34.

138. Raef Zreik, "5 Takes on the Banning of Islamic Movement, by a Concerned Palestinian Citizen of Israel," *Haaretz*, December 22, 2015. http://www.haaretz.com/opinion/.premium-1.693102.

139. *Sawt al-Haq wa al-Huriyya*, June 6, 2014.

140. *Sawt al-Haq wa al-Huriyya*, December 18, 2009.

141. Pal48 News, "Al Aqsa Activities," June 6, 2014. http://www.pls48.net/?mod=articles&ID=1182204.

142. Interview with Salih Lutfi, Umm al-Fahem, April 21, 2014.

143. Craig Larkin et al., "In Defense of Al-Aqsa: The Islamic Movement inside Israel and the Battle for Jerusalem," *Middle East Quarterly* 66, no. 1 (2012), 40.

144. Larkin et al., "In Defense of Al-Aqsa," 39.

145. Sobhi Rayan, "Diversity" in Arab Society in Israel: The Islamic Movement as an Example," *Journal of Muslim Minority Affairs* 32, no. 1 (2012): 77.

146. ICG, "The Status of the Status Quo," 25.

147. Interview in BeitSafafa. Jerusalem, March 3, 2015.

148. Interview with Raad Sa'ada. Jerusalem, May 6, 2014.

149. Hirbawi et al., "Palestinian Institutions in East Jerusalem."

BIBLIOGRAPHY

Abdallah, Owais. "The Wall and the Enclaves: Case Studies in Disrupted Communities." In *The Wall: Fragmenting the Palestinian Fabric in Jerusalem*, edited by Robert Brooks. Jerusalem: International Peace Cooperation Center, 2007.

Abdul Hadi, Mahdi. "Reviewing the Palestinian Political Scene 2015." Palestinian Academic Society for the Study of International Affairs (PASSIA), Jerusalem, 2015.

Al-Jubeh, Nazmi. "Bab al-Magharibah: Joha's Nail in the Haram al-Sharif." *Jerusalem Quarterly*, Institute for Jerusalem Studies, 18 (June 2003): 17–24.

Al-Maqdese for Society Development. "Palestinian Workers Rights in the Israeli Labour Market and Settlements." Accessed July 1, 2014. http://www.al-maqdese.org/files/0000/0000/000000390.pdf.

al-Quds al-'Arabi, June 16, 2014. Accessed June 16, 2014. http://www.alquds.co.uk/?p=180940.

———. November 12, 2014. Accessed November 12, 2014. http://www.alquds.co.uk/?p=249207.

———. October 26, 2015. Accessed November 1, 2015. http://www.alquds.co.uk/?p=424548.

Associated Press. "Abbas, Abdullah Sign Pact on Protection of Jerusalem Holy Sites." *Haaretz*, March 31, 2013. Accessed March 31, 2013. http://www.haaretz.com/news/middle-east/abbas-abdullah-sign-pact-on-protection-of-jerusalem-holy-sites-1.512819.

Bollens, Scott A. "Comparative Research on Urban Political Conflict: Policy Amidst Polarization." *Open Urban Studies Journal* 2, no. 1 (2009): 1–17.

Brooks, Robert. "The Wall and the Economy of Jerusalem Governorate." In *The Wall: Fragmenting the Palestinian Fabric in Jerusalem*, edited by Robert Brooks, 37–41. Jerusalem: International Peace Cooperation Center, 2007.

Choshen, Maya, Michael Korach, Inbal Doron, Yael Israeli, and Yair Assaf-Shapira. *Jerusalem: Facts and Trends*. Jerusalem: Jerusalem Institute for Israel Studies, 2013.

"The Declaration of Principles. Israel-Palestine Liberation Organization Agreement: 1993." Lillian Goldman Law Library, Yale Law School. http://avalon.law.yale.edu/20th_century/isrplo.asp.

Dumper, Michael. *Islam and Israel: Muslim Religious Endowments and the Jewish State*. Washington, DC: Institute for Palestine Studies, 1994.

———. *Jerusalem Unbound: Geography, History, and the Future of the Holy City*. New York: Columbia University Press, 2014.

Dumper, Michael, and Craig Larkin, "Political Islam in Contested Jerusalem: The Emerging Role of Islamists from within Israel." *Divided Cities/Contested State Working Paper*, no. 12 (2009).

———. "Policing Divided Cities: Stabilization and Law Enforcement in Palestinian East Jerusalem." *International Affairs* 89, no. 5 (2013): 1247–1264.

Dvir, Noam (Dabul). "Violence mars Jerusalem Day with Temple Mount clashes." *Ynetnews.com*, May 28, 2014. Accessed May 28, 2014. http://www.ynetnews.com/articles/0,7340,L-4524679,00.html.

"Follow-up: We Call on the Palestinian Interior to be a 'push to the maximum.'" *Arabs48*, October 16, 2014. Accessed October 16, 2014. http://www.arabs48.com/?mod=articles&ID=1145619.

Gaber, Ahmed. "The delegation of the follow-up committee enters the Al-Aqsa Mosque." *Panet*, October 7, 2009. Accessed May 20, 2014. http://www.panet.co.il/online/articles/1/2/S-235700,1,2.html.

Gordon, Neve. "From Colonization to Separation: Exploring the Structure of Israel's Occupation." *Third World Quarterly* 29, no. 1 (November 2008): 25–44.

Hammoudeh, Doaa, Layaly Hamayel, and Rita Giacaman. "Quality of Life for Families Living in East Jerusalem's Kafr 'Aqab Urban Sprawl: A Qualitative Study." *Lancet* 390, no. 1 (August 2017).

Hasson, Nir. "Jerusalem Approves Major Housing Plan for Arab Neighborhood." *Hareetz*, September 4, 2014. Accessed December 5, 2014. http://www.haaretz.com/news/middle-east/.premium-1.613997.

———. "Only 7% of Jerusalem Building Permits Go to Palestinian Neighborhoods." *Haaretz*, December 7, 2015. Accessed February 9, 2016. http://www.haaretz.com/israel-news/.premium-1.690403.

———. "The Israeli Justice Ministry's Man Who Settles Jews in Arab East Jerusalem." *Haaretz*, March 9, 2018. Accessed March 19, 2018. https://www.haaretz.com/israel-news/.premium-the-ministry-s-man-who-settles-jews-in-arab-east-j-lem-1.5888643.

Hirbawi, Najat, and David Helfand. "Palestinian Institutions in East Jerusalem." *Palestine-Israel Journal* 17, no. 12 (2011).

International Committee of the Red Cross (ICRC). "Convention (IV) relative to the Protection of Civilian Persons in Time of War." August 1949. https://www.icrc.org/ihl/INTRO/380.

International Crisis Group (ICG). "The Status of the Status Quo at Jerusalem's Holy Esplanade." *Middle East Report*, no. 159 (June 30, 2015).

"Israeli police ban Muslim men aged under 50 from Friday prayers in Jerusalem." *Independent*, July 21, 2017. Accessed February 20, 2018. http://www.independent.co.uk/news/world/middle-east/israel-police-ban-jerusalem-friday-prayers-muslim-men-50-walled-shrine-a7852156.html.

Jabareen, Yosef. "The Rights to Space Production and the Right to Necessity: Insurgent Versus Legal Rights of Palestinians in Jerusalem." *Planning Theory* 16, no. 1 (June 2015): 1–26.

"Jerusalem After Oslo: Judaization, Settlement and the Absence of Palestinian Strategy." *Al-'Arabi al Jadid*, September 14, 2014. Accessed September 24, 2014. http://www.alaraby.co.uk/politics/5fd28b68-8a67-4bb5-a873-3e74ae8045a0.

Jerusalem Post Staff. "47 Jordanian MPs Call to Cancel Israel Peace Treaty Over Knesset Temple Mount Debate." *Jerusalem Post*, February 26, 2014. Accessed May 15, 2016. http://www.jpost.com/Middle-East/47-Jordanian-MPs-call-to-cancel-Israel-peace-treaty-over-Knesset-Temple-Mount-debate-343580.

"Jordanian Minister of Awqaf: The Maximum Mosque for Muslims Only." *Ma'an*, October 13, 2014. Accessed October 17, 2014. http://www.maannews.net/arb/ViewDetails.aspx?ID=733007.

July 20, 1994. Accessed October 28, 2014. http://knesset.gov.il/tql/knesset_new/knesset14/HTML_27_03_2012_06-21-01-PM/19940720@19940720030@030.html.

Kimhi, Israel. "Effects of the Security Fence on Palestinian Residents, in the City and in the Jerusalem Metropolitan Area." In *The Security Fence Around Jerusalem: Implications for the City and Its Residents*, edited by Israel Kimhi, 67–118. Jerusalem: Jerusalem Institute for Israel Studies, 2006.

Klein, Menachem. "The Islamic Holy Places as a Political Bargaining Card (1993–95)." *Catholic University Law Review* 45, no. 3 (Spring 1996).

Kuttab, Daoud. "Palestinians Boycott Israeli Elections in Jerusalem Again." *Huffington Post*. http://www.huffingtonpost.com/daoud-kuttab/palestinians-boycott-isra_b_4159235.html.

Larkin, Craig, and Michael Dumper. "In Defense of Al-Aqsa: The Islamic Movement Inside Israel and the Battle for Jerusalem." *Middle East Quarterly* 66, no. 1 (2012).

Margalit, Meir, ed. *Demolishing Peace: House Demolitions in East Jerusalem 2000–2010*. Jerusalem: International Peace and Cooperation Centre, 2014.

May 15, 2014. Accessed May 15, 2014. http://www.knesset.gov.il/spokesman/eng/PR_eng.asp?PRID=11172.

McKernan, Bethan. "All new security measures at Jerusalem holy site known as Temple Mount and Haram al-Sharif removed, Israel says." *Independent*, July 27, 2017. Accessed August 19, 2017. http://www.independent.co.uk/news/world/middle-east/israel-temple-mount-haram-al-sharif-al-aqsa-crisis-palestinian-protests-security-measures-a7862196.html.

Musallam, Sami. "*The Struggle for Jerusalem: A Programme of Action for Peace.*" PASSIA (Jerusalem, 1996).

Norway Refugee Council (NRC). "The Legality of the Wall Built by Israel in the West Bank, Background Report." January 2015.

October 23, 2014. Accessed October 28, 2014. http://knesset.gov.il/spokesman/eng/PR_eng.asp?PRID=11465.

"Police Minister Shahal Calls for Closing PA Jerusalem Institutions." Israel Ministry of Foreign Affairs Archive, August 14, 1995. Accessed October 20, 2014. http://mfa.gov.il/MFA/MFA-Archive/1995/Pages/Police%20Minister-%20Close%20PA%20Jerusalem%20Institutions.aspx.

Prusher, Ilene. "Jordan to Safeguard Jerusalem's Islamic Holy Sites—if They're Still Standing." *Haaretz*, April 4, 2013. Accessed October 23, 2014. http://www.haaretz.com/blogs/jerusalem-vivendi/jordan-to-safeguard-jerusalem-s-islamic-holy-sites-if-they-re-still-standing.premium-1.513531.

Pullan, Wendy, Maximilian Sternberg, Lefkos Kyriacou, Craig Larkin, and Michael Dumper. *The Struggle for Jerusalem's Holy Places*. London and New York: Routledge, 2013.

Qawasmi, Hanadi. "Initial Review of al-Hiraq al Shababi al Falasatini in Jerusalem (in Arabic)." Masarat: The Palestinian Centre for Policy Research and Strategic Studies (2013).

Ravid, Barak, and Nir Hasson. "Netanyahu Orders Plans Be Advanced for 1,060 New East Jerusalem Housing Units." *Haaretz*, October 27, 2014. Accessed October 27, 2014. http://www.haaretz.com/news/diplomacy-defense/.premium-1.622950.

Rayan, Sobhi, "'Diversity' in Arab Society in Israel: The Islamic Movement as an Example." *Journal of Muslim Minority Affairs* 32, no. 1 (2012).

Reiter, Yitzhak. *Sovereignty of God and Man: Sanctity and Political Centrality on the Temple Mount*. Jerusalem: Jerusalem Institute for Israeli Studies, 2001.

Roy, Sara. *The Gaza Strip: The Political Economy of De-Development*. Washington, DC: Institute for Palestine Studies, 1995.

Sawt al-Haq wa al-Huriyya, December 18, 2009.

———, June 6, 2014.

Shalhoub-Koverkian, Nadera. "Children: A Universalist Perspective for How Israel is using Child Arrest and Detention to further its Colonial Settler Project." *International Journal of Applied Psychoanalytic Studies* 12, no. 3 (2015): 223–244.

Shargai, Nadev. *The 'Al-Aksa Is in Danger' Libel: The History of a Lie*. Jerusalem: Jerusalem Center for Public Affairs, 2012.

Tagari, Ehud, and Yudith Oppenheimer. "Displaced in their own city: The Impact of Israeli Policy in East Jerusalem on the Palestinian Neighborhoods of the city beyond the Separation Barrier." IR Amim (City of Nations), June 2015.

Thill, Magali. "EU Obligations and Duty to End Israeli Policies of Forced Transfer, Colonialism and Apartheid in Occupied East Jerusalem." European Coordination of Committees and Association for Palestine (ECCP), Brussels, Belgium, September 2014.

United Nations Conference on Trade and Development (UNCTAD). "The Palestinian economy in East Jerusalem: Enduring annexation, isolation and disintegration." 2013. http://unctad.org/en/PublicationsLibrary/gdsapp2012d1_en.pdf.

United Nations: Office for the Coordination of Humanitarian Affairs (UNOCHA). "East Jerusalem: Key Humanitarian Concerns." March 2011.

———. "High numbers of Demolitions: the ongoing threats of demolition for Palestinian residents of East Jerusalem." January 15, 2018. https://www.ochaopt.org/content/high-numbers-demolitions-ongoing-threats-demolition-palestinian-residents-east-jerusalem.

United Nations Relief and Works Agency for Palestine Refugees in the Near East (UNRWA). "Shu'fat Refugee Camp Profile." https://www.unrwa.org/where-we-work/west-bank/shufat-camp.

Veracini, Lorenzo. "What Can Settler Colonial Studies Offer to an Interpretation of the Conflict in Israel–Palestine?" *Settler Colonial Studies* 5, no. 3 (2015): 268–271.

Yacobi, Haim and Wendy Pullan. "The Geopolitics of Neighborhood: Jerusalem's Colonial Space Revisited." *Geopolitics* 19, no. 3 (May 2014): 1–26.

Zreik, Raef. "5 Takes on the Banning of Islamic Movement, by a Concerned Palestinian Citizen of Israel." *Haaretz*, December 22, 2015. Accessed May 20, 2016. http://www.haaretz.com/opinion/.premium-1.693102.

Chapter Nine

The Politics of Being "Ordinary"

Palestinian Refugees in Jordan After the Oslo Agreement

Luigi Achilli

The signing of the Declaration of Principles on Interim Self-Government Arrangements (hereafter referred to as the Oslo Accords) in 1993 marked a radical change in the role of refugees within the Palestinian nationalist discourse and generated a profound feeling of disillusionment for politics among this scattered Palestinian community in the Arab world.[1] Relegating the status of refugees to the final stages of the negotiations, the Oslo peace agreements were, for refugees in Lebanon, Syria and Jordan, clear evidence of how the Palestine Liberation Organization (PLO) had sold off the right of return to secure the construction of a Palestinian state ostensibly on the land occupied since 1967.[2]

This feeling of disillusionment was most evident during my research in the Palestinian refugee camps of Jordan on three separate occasions spanning 2004 to 2016.[3] I was puzzled by what seemed to be an ostensible lack of interest in politics and politicking in the camp spaces, especially among young men who constituted the bulk of my informants.[4] This absence was striking. Historically, Palestinian refugee camps in the region have a reputation for being sites of political activism and nationalism.[5] Indeed, one of the most pressing debates that has occupied scholarly and public spheres (both inside and outside of Jordan) is how Palestinian refugees handle the tension between their integration and their commitment to the Palestinian national predicament and the right of return (*haqq al-'awda*).[6] Many media and academic accounts have generally tended to portray Palestinian refugees from the camps—especially young men (*shabab*)—as inherently political beings, ready to resist all attempts to annihilate their nationalist struggles.[7] In the late 1960s and early 1970s, urban camps such as al-Wihdat were even renamed "the Republic" in an overt challenge to the Jordanian monarchy.[8]

Yet, camp-dwellers appeared to reject any form of political mobilization and spoke of politics (*siyase*) as being something dirty and unprincipled; a distaste all the more striking because my fieldwork involved "young men from the camps" (*shabab min el-mukhayyamat*)—a category of people that in Jordan (as elsewhere in the Arab world) is often regarded as the embodiment of the Palestinian national predicament.[9]

Based on these observations, this chapter will offer an anthropological analysis of the consequences of Oslo on political participation among Palestinian refugees living in Jordan. It will be argued that the Accords were, for Palestinian refugees in Jordan, the culmination of a series of events that led to their disengagement from politics. A note of caution, however, is in order. The focus of this chapter is not Palestinian refugees *as a whole*, but rather those from a specific setting and a particular group: *shabab* from refugee camps in Jordan. Yet, because of their history of political mobilization, young men from the camp represent an excellent case study that ultimately allows us to infer as to the nature of Palestinian activism in Jordan and, more importantly for this book, the dramatic impact of Oslo on refugees' political participation among a category of people widely known for their political activism.

PALESTINIAN REFUGEES IN THE MIDDLE EAST

When the Jewish Agency in Tel Aviv announced the institution of the Provisional Government of Israel on 14 May 1948, the war that followed resulted in the destruction and mass evacuation of most Palestinian villages. The end of the war saw the territory of Mandatory Palestine divided between the Zionist colonies and the Arab forces that intervened on "behalf" of the Palestinian people. Whereas the former took control of the largest part of the territory, Egypt and Jordan respectively administered Gaza and annexed the West Bank. Palestinians who left their land and abandoned their houses to flee the mass persecution and atrocities perpetrated by the Haganah and other Jewish forces were prevented by the newly born state of Israel from returning to their homes and lands.[10] Palestinians from southern parts of Mandatory Palestine fled to the Gaza Strip; those from the center dispersed to the West Bank; and refugees from the north spread out into southern Lebanon and Syria.[11] Around 320,000 Palestinian refugees fled to the West Bank; 210,000 fled to the Gaza Strip, and around 280,000 to other Arab countries, including the East Bank (today's Jordan).[12]

According to the United Nations Relief and Works Agency for Palestinian refugees in the Near East (UNRWA),[13] "refugees [and the direct descendants] are people whose normal place of residence was Palestine between June 1946 and May 1948, who lost both their homes and means of livelihood as a result of the 1948 Arab-Israeli conflict."[14] Almost seven decades after the Nakba, over five million Palestinian refugees still live in exile—mostly in Jordan, Lebanon, Syria, the Gaza Strip, and the West Bank.[15] Today, in their third or even fourth generation away from their original villages, towns, and homes, refugees continue to fiercely uphold their "refugee status" as the only recognition of their rights to be repatriated or compensated.

Over the years, refugees have gained a reputation for being heralds of "Palestinianness," symbols of heroic resistance, and a source of political unrest. In a similar fashion, refugee camps have also been represented as the locus of a political agency based on the ideal of resistance.[16] This is largely explained by the importance that refugees and refugee camps have come to play in Palestinian nationalism. In the aftermath of the Nakba, the Palestinian resistance movement conceived liberation from Zionism and the right of return of the refugees to their land as the same goal. In the late 1960s, Palestinian national consciousness crystallized around the iconic figure of the refugee—especially those living in the camps (*laji'in filastinin al-mukhayyamat*). Out of the havoc and devastating defeat induced by the 1967 Arab-Israeli War,[17] in which Israel through military victory occupied the West Bank and Gaza Strip (and thus the remaining land of Mandatory Palestine), young Palestinians in exile streamed into the PLO, which had been established in 1964. During this period of mass mobilization (1969–1982), popularly known as *al-thawra* (the revolution), a triumphant narrative emerged of awakened valorized refugees as being the embodiment of Palestinian resilience and heroism.[18] This was the heyday of al-Wihdat in Jordan and Shatila in Lebanon, and other refugee camps that, like the former, became powerful symbols of Palestinian nationalism. Not anymore a miserable abode for a mass of poor displaced, they came to be known in the Palestinian nationalist discourse as "liberated zones," the furnaces of the "new men" of the revolution. The "sons of the camp," the *Fedayeen*, embodied the archetypal Palestinian. The chroniclers of the time portrayed *Fedayeen* standing firmly against the overarching forces of their prior submission, no longer brought down by the suffocating impotence and fear of the first period of exile.[19] In Jordan, the myth of the heroic guerrilla fighter from the camp resonated so powerfully in the collective imagination as to induce the late Jordanian monarch, King Hussein, to publicly declare in 1968 that "we are all Fedayeen."[20]

Camps and refugees were not simply the symbol of Palestinian resistance. When the various groups that together formed the PLO established their sanctuaries in the refugee camps, these spaces turned into operative bases for the guerrilla fighters. Camp dwellers thus became the militant and military backbone of Palestinian nationalism, and the word *"mukhayyam"* (refugee camp) stood for *"ma'askar"* (military training camp).²¹ Here, the *Fedayeen* established their headquarters and institutions: their own security apparatus (military police and a civil militia); a corollary of administrative, media, and supply centers; revolutionary courts; trade union movements; and even factories.

However, the signing of the Oslo Accords in 1993 marked a radical change in the status of Palestinian refugees within the Palestinian nationalistic predicament, discourse, and movement. The Declaration of Principles promised to initiate the gradual withdrawal of Israel from the West Bank and Gaza. Yet, it accomplished the sudden exclusion of Palestinian refugees from the national body. Postponing the discussion of the refugee issue and their right of return to a later stage in negotiations, the Palestinian leadership favored a supposedly pragmatic solution over the rights of those Palestinians evicted by Israel chiefly based on the idea of lands in exchange for peace. The right of return became, in the words of Saeb Erekat, chief Palestinian negotiator in the talks preceding the Accords, a mere "bargaining chip."²²

It is unclear why the Palestinian political leadership succumbed to such a short-sighted realpolitik that muzzled its revolutionary drive, leading up to the signing of the Oslo Accords itself, an agreement that was aptly decried by Edward Said as "the Palestinian Versailles."²³ Even more puzzling is why the PLO has been so neglectful to forget the importance of refugees and their right of return for the Palestinian national predicament. It is presumable to think that a number of concomitant and close factors caused this radical change of course.²⁴ To begin with, political events at regional and global levels profoundly weakened the PLO's relationship with, and capacity to, represent Palestinians in *al-shatat*.²⁵ Events such as the 1970–1971 Jordanian civil war (popularly known as "Black September") and the 1973 Arab-Israeli War reconfigured dramatically the political scenario in the region and prompted the PLO to reassert its role by seeking, among other things, recognition at the international level.²⁶ These events culminated in the PLO approval of the 1974 Ten Points Program—a plan that called for the establishment of a national authority "over every part of Palestinian territory that is liberated."²⁷ Accepting that the initial liberation of Palestine could be partial, the Program marked a radical shift in the center of gravity of the Palestinian national struggle from its constituencies in exile to those in the occupied territory.²⁸ The PLO exile in Tunis following Israel's three-month siege of Beirut in 1982 further contributed to this change by cutting the organization off from the Palestinian communities living in *al-shatat*. In this sense, when the Palestine National Council (PNC) in Algiers opted in favor of a two-state solution, the time was ripe for the shift from a "just solution" to an "acceptable solution."²⁹

With the Oslo agreement, the PLO abandoned refugee rights in exchange for the promise of a distinct, yet limited, territorial base to build the long sought-after Palestinian state. Sidelining refugee rights in the Oslo agreement limited the extent of the peace process, and showed its inherently flawed nature: it neither slowed down the systematic eviction of Palestinians from their lands, nor prevented the continuation of abuse and dispossession.[30] Indeed, some critics have argued that Oslo has actually undermined the creation of an independent Palestinian state—which was, ironically, its official goal and the very justification for the exclusion of refugees from its framework in the first place.[31] Put differently, engrained in the Oslo agreements and disguised under the clothes of a practical political realism were the seeds of Palestinian surrender to Israel's expansionist aims.[32] Because the creation of Israel is predicated upon the Zionist project of cleansing the land of Palestine from all its inhabitants other than Jews, getting rid of the right of return for Palestinians is an important move in the right direction, according to this logic. Saree Makdisi points out how,

> The right of return of Palestinians to their homes inside what is now Israel is anathema precisely because it would mean the end of . . . the state's claim to Jewishness. And so too, ironically, is the need to even talk about Palestinian statehood, however ephemeral or fantastical such a state may turn out to be. As it has been framed since Oslo, the point of such a state would not be to embody the rights and aspirations of the Palestinians, but rather to secure the demands and aspirations of Israelis.[33]

Unsurprisingly, the announcement of the Oslo Accords generated deep resentment and consternation among the Palestinian communities living in Syria, Lebanon, and Jordan. Refugees saw nothing for them in the agreement if not the simple fact that Arafat and his entourage had forsaken their rights and consigned them to a life in exile. Most Palestinians in Lebanon, for example, felt abandoned by the newly instituted Palestinian Authority (PA), which ultimately provoked among them the impression that they no longer belonged to the Palestinian national body.[34] In Syria, the widespread belief that the Palestinian leadership was complicit with the occupier generated a sense of profound discomfort and disillusionment among the refugee community.[35] However, while the signing of the Oslo Accords has sidelined all refugees living in exile, the response to this marginalization has been different depending on the country of displacement. As Jamil Hilal points out,

> Palestinians of the diaspora share no common social formation or common society. Leaving aside the obvious fact of dispersal among various countries with

different systems, it is only the refugee camps that have specific community features. But even there, these features vary from place to place and remain subject to the caprices of political change and upheaval.[36]

It is precisely this heterogeneity that the Trump administration wants to exploit today with the recent decision of discontinuing funding UNRWA unless the Agency would agree to downsize the number of Palestinian refugees it currently provides aid to from nearly six million to about fifty thousand.[37] This is a political move poorly disguised under economic clothes: by aiming to change the definition of a Palestinian refugee with the justification of reducing the number of UNRWA beneficiaries, the US government's ultimate goal is the dissolution of the right of return and the assimilation of the scattered Palestinian communities in their countries of exile.

Concluding this historical preamble and context, it is important to note that this chapter will not provide a comprehensive overview of forms of political participation amongst Palestinian refugees in the aftermath of the Agreements, as these were heterogeneous and multifarious. Rather, this chapter will focus on the unique experience of Palestinian refugees living in camps in Jordan, which will now be analyzed in the following section.

OSLO AND PALESTINIAN REFUGEES IN JORDAN

In 2017, there were over 2 million Palestinian registered refugees living in Jordan. Among them, nearly 370,000 registered Palestinian refugees were living in the 10 Palestinian refugee camps recognized by UNRWA in Jordan. The number of Palestinian refugees living in the Kingdom, however, is much higher if we consider that many Palestinians did not fall or did not want to fall into the category of "Palestinian refugee" set by the UN at the time of their displacement.[38]

In the aftermath of the First Arab-Israeli War, the Jordanian military annexed what remained of central Palestine. The acquisition of the West Bank required the adoption of a persuasive nationalist rhetoric to ensure the bonds of the West Bank to the East Bank. This took the form of creating a national identity that would encompass every citizen of the Kingdom. The project—pursued both by King Abdullah and, later, by his grandson, King Hussein—was based upon four fundamental premises: recognition of the Hashemite monarchy as the symbol of Jordan,[39] commitment to pan-Arab ideals, recognition of the Palestinian plight and right of return, and the unity of the two Banks.[40] The military acquisition was authorized by the signing of an addendum to the 1928 Law of Nationality, which stated that

> All those who are habitual residents, at the time of the application of this law, of Transjordan or the Western Territory administered by the Hashemite Kingdom of Jordan, and who hold Palestinian nationality, are considered as having already acquired Jordanian nationality and to enjoy all the rights and obligations that Jordanians have.[41]

The Jordanian government had a deep interest in assimilating Palestinians into Jordanian society. In order to legitimize Jordan's claim and control over the West Bank, the transformation of Palestinian refugees into disciplined subjects was paramount. With the exception of some early opposition, Palestinian refugees accepted the energetic policy of integration pursued by the government.[42]

The position of the regime toward the Palestinian population did not change in the immediate aftermath of the 1967 Arab-Israeli War, when Jordan lost control of the West Bank to Israel, a defeat that coincided with the second major Palestinian exodus commemorated as the *Naksa* (the "setback"). A new wave of refugees, approximately 388,000 people, expelled by Israel, crossed the East Bank of the Jordan River, thus raising the number of Palestinians living in Jordan to approximately 60 percent of the total population.[43]

Despite King Hussein's attempt to reaffirm sociopolitical and economic links with the West Bank, the 1967 war ushered in a new era in the development of Jordan's national identity because the monarch could not ignore Jordan's demographic and geographical contractions.[44] More importantly, the defeat of 1967 resulted in a leadership takeover and radicalization of the PLO which, in following years, led to a drastic change in the policies and attitudes of the Jordanian regime toward the Palestinian population.[45]

In the Jordanian camps, so deeply rooted and powerful was the presence of the PLO that the government found itself powerless to stop much of the militant activity carried out by the guerrilla groups in the year preceding the 1970–71 Jordanian civil war, popularly known as Black September. The spiral of tension between the Palestinian *Fedayeen* and the Jordanian army triggered a series of events that eventually culminated in a conflict that lasted until July 1971 and terminated with the eviction of the *Fedayeen* from the Kingdom.[46] It must be noted, however, that the bloody confrontation between the Palestinian guerrilla fighters and the Jordanian army did not see the juxtaposition of two distinct groups. Not only did most Palestinian-Jordanians partake in the civil strife, but a sizable minority of Transjordanians also joined the rebels in their fight against the monarchy.[47]

Nevertheless, the end of the civil war saw a radical change in Jordan's official ideological line. Under pressure from Transjordanian nationalists to distinguish Jordan from Palestine, the construction of a new national identity began to be defined almost exclusively through those attributes that celebrated a "Transjordanian nature": (East Banker) tribalism, loyalty to the Hashemites, and Islamic values as opposed to "Palestinian" urbanity, Pan-Arabism, and liberal ideologies.[48] If King Abdullah's annexation of the West Bank revolved around the creation of a collective identity encompassing Palestinian and Transjordanian elements, then Black September and the events that followed gradually precipitated a discourse of unity within the context of a guest/host relationship. In Jordan, this discourse was expressed in the terms of *muhajirin* (emigrants, i.e., the Palestinians) versus *ansar* (supporters, i.e., the Transjordanians). *Muhajirin* and *ansar* refer, respectively, to the Prophet Muhammad and his companions, who fled to Medina to escape their persecutors, and the people of Medina, who welcomed the Prophet. In the Islamic tradition, the two terms signify the establishment of the first Islamic state. The reference to these two concepts of the Islamic tradition was made for the first time by King Hussein in the wake of the civil war. While the King's intention was to invoke this distinction in order to reinforce national unity, Transjordanian nationalists reinterpreted these concepts to indicate the temporary presence of Palestinians in the Kingdom.[49]

After Black September, the government's agenda took a clear turn toward privileging non-Palestinian aspects of national identity. At the same time, further domestic and regional events fostered the weakening of the regime's inclusive policies. In October 1974, at Rabat, the Arab League recognized the PLO as the sole legitimate representative of the Palestinian people. In 1987, the outbreak of the First Intifada in the Occupied Territory struck the final blow to the Hashemites' claims over the West Bank. Not only did this Palestinian grassroots uprising question the Israeli occupation of the West Bank, but it also challenged Jordanian sovereignty over the territory. On 31 July 1988, the regime thus formally announced its disengagement from the West Bank (also known as *Qarar Fakk al-Irtibat*), and "genuinely abandon[ed] its claim to speak for Palestinians."[50] Oslo marked the end of the regime's inclusive policies. As Laurie Brand summarizes:

> [T]he signing of the Declaration of Principles (DOP) was a kind of watershed. The prospect of a Palestinian entity put the question of who would be citizens squarely on the table. In Jordan, where the Palestinians hold citizenship, the issue of Palestinian political allegiance . . . had suddenly become very real.[51]

On October 26, 1994, one year after the signing of the Oslo agreements, Jordan and Israel signed a peace treaty at Wadi Araba that laid the foundation for bilateral co-operation between the two countries and set the basis for the permanent resettlement of Palestinian refugees in Jordan. By that time, the new tendency to treat Palestinian territory and people differently than the Jordanians was firmly ingrained in the regime's agenda.[52]

Ironically, the Oslo Accords and the Treaty of Peace Between the State of Israel and the Hashemite Kingdom of Jordan (otherwise known as the Wadi Araba peace treaty) not only met the fierce criticism of the refugee community but also that of the Transjordanian nationalists who saw in the peace process the restless specter of *al-watan al-badil*: Israel's claims that Jordan is the proper homeland for Palestinians. However, Transjordanian nationalism was strengthened by Oslo. Its main concerns revolved around two intertwined issues: the Palestinian issue and the question of national identity in Jordan. Even though Transjordanian nationalists present diverse and sometimes conflicting agendas, these diverse positions all converged into one broad idea: the primacy of a national identity predicated upon the exclusion of the Palestinian "element." Such an exclusivist discourse is largely (but not exclusively) grounded on the primacy of the "tribe" (*'ashira*), where the nomadic traditions of "native" Jordanians are juxtaposed to the urban and peasant heritage of the Palestinians. As Christine Jungen points out, "the terms *'ashaari* (tribal), *watani* (patriotic) and *urduni* (Jordanian) have progressively acquired an equivalence between them."[53]

For its part, the Hashemite regime officially rejected any attempt to undermine national unity. After Oslo, King Hussein I, before, and King Abdullah II, later, promoted an inclusivist national identity that emphasized, at least rhetorically, the integration of Jordanians of Palestinian origin—provided that the latter avoided explicit invocation of a Palestinian identity and refrained from political activity against the regime.[54] After 2002, the Jordanian authorities thus sought to counter these "divisive" stances by developing a homogenizing agenda, first under the cry of "Jordan first" (*al-urdunn awalan*) and later under the slogan "We are all Jordan" (*kulluna al-urdunn*). In this context, Palestinian refugees' status as fully fledged citizens has been repeatedly confirmed through public statements such as "[Palestinian refugees are] part and parcel of the Jordanian people with the same rights and duties as any other Jordanians"; or, also, "[refugees are] a dear part of Jordan . . . that should be given the same attention and services as other parts of the country such as the countryside and the semi-desert areas."[55]

Yet, despite what the government advocated and has more or less successfully sought to accomplish, a large part of the refugee population in the country fears that the regime has ultimately surrendered to a Transjordanian exclusivist discourse. And many have been extremely sceptical of the rallying crusade of the government. In particular, the slogan "Jordan first" was interpreted in the terms of "(Trans)Jordanian first" and "Palestinian last": a clear confirmation that the government preferred "native Jordanians" before them.[56]

DEALING WITH OSLO: DODGING POLITICS

In Jordan, Oslo sanctioned dramatic transformations that were to usher in a new era in the long story of Palestinian refugees in the Kingdom. To understand its consequences on the level of refugees' political participation, we need to closely scrutinize their ambiguous status in Jordan.

It is important to remember that the situation of Palestinian refugees in Jordan differs greatly from that of Palestinian refugees living in other Arab states. In Lebanon and Syria, Palestinians have maintained a legal status as "stateless" persons. Jordan, instead, granted full citizenship to a large number of refugees. The extension of citizenship rights provided to refugees meant that they have the same rights and duties as any other Jordanian native, at least in principle. This integration policy has favored the emergence among refugees of a feeling of identification with Jordan.[57] Historically, Palestinian refugees have held important positions in the government of Jordan, e.g., as heads of the secret service, as government ministers, and even as prime ministers. Furthermore, refugee camps—often regarded as the bedrock of "Palestinianness" in exile—have become open spaces and commercial areas that more resemble a low-income residential neighborhood of Amman than a space of exception designed for control and surveillance.

On the other hand, in Jordan there is a widely held opinion that Palestinian refugees, especially camp dwellers, nurture anti-government sentiments. Loyalty to the king, the Hashemite family, and the government is, by contrast, depicted as being associated most clearly with the tribes and Bedouins, i.e., East Bank Jordanians. This claim was based on the fact that Jordanians of Palestinian origin were not sons of the tribes (*abna' al-asha'ir*) and hence not truly "Jordanians."[58] These representations are simultaneously sustained by the camps' reputation of being bastions of "Palestinianness" in exile and political unrest. This is in part true. Originally, the government sought to develop a hybrid national identity encompassing both Palestinian and Transjordanian elements. From Black September on, however, the state began to promote the creation of a national identity distinct from a Palestinian one. Oslo has sanctioned the culmination of this process: Palestinian refugees could be part of the state as long as they renounced any manifestation of "Palestinianness."

It is in the context of the refugees' desire to be both a "Palestinian refugee" and a "Jordanian citizen" that we need to situate their lack of political participation. To explain this, it is necessary to first ground ethnographically the concept of "the political." In al-Wihdat and the other refugee camps where I carried out my research, there was not a universally shared definition of what is "political": for camp-dwellers, the boundaries between what is, and what is not "political" changed over time and varied amongst people. However, my fieldwork suggests that these different interpretations all converged in the idea that "the political" to them is a thing that is liable to bring to the surface the extraordinariness of their condition: the tension between "Palestinianness" and "Jordanianness."

To understand the peculiar working of "the political" in the camps, the work of Carl Schmitt and the recent scholarship it has inspired is instructive.[59] Writing in the concluding years of the Weimar Republic, Schmitt grounded his conception of "the political" in a reworking of Hobbes' state of "Warre": "[his] critical twist was to project the state of nature depicted in Leviathan, the war of all against all in which individual agents are pitted against each other, onto the plane of modern collective conflicts: thereby transforming civil society itself into a second state of nature."[60]

For Schmitt, the condition of the political is reducible to a "friend/enemy" distinction. According to the German philosopher, such a condition "deals with the formation of a 'we' as opposed to a 'they' and is always concerned with collective forms of identification. . . . [It] can be understood only in the context of the friend/enemy grouping."[61]

Schmitt's verdict about liberal democracy and the authoritarian political conclusions he drew from this intuition are notoriously chilling, but they set an important point of departure in recent political theory. Engaging critically with the work of Schmitt, Chantal Mouffe examined the "friend versus enemy" distinction and struck a blow to deliberative theories of democracy:[62] "the we/they distinction, which is the condition of possibility of formation of political identities," she argues, "can always become the locus of an antagonism. Since all forms of political identities entail a we/they distinction, . . . antagonism is an ever-present possibility: the political belongs to our ontological condition."[63] The consequence of such an understanding is that political identities are not immanent, but that they are constituted though the work of "the political," which is inherently divisive and inescapably antagonistic. This, I will argue, helps to explain the politics of Palestinians in the refugee camps in Jordan.

As discussed at the beginning of this chapter, Palestinian camp dwellers harbor a generalized feeling of distaste for politics and politicking. This can be linked with questions of national identity and the complex politics of inclusion and exclusion that regulate the access of certain groups to political power and state resources in Jordan. Indeed, the very foundation of Hashemite governance relies on its capacity to build national constituencies by providing points of access to state resources and institutions.[64] Gaining access to state resources is not easy, especially for Palestinian refugees living in camps, where discrimination leaves them with very few opportunities to establish the right connections. This is particularly evident at the level of political participation. For example, although in recent years the government has promoted the creation of political parties and the development of parliamentary institutions, these are widely regarded by camp dwellers as ineffective. In fact, the exclusivist attitude as promoted by the regime since Oslo and discussed in the previous section, has resulted in a massive purge of Jordanian-Palestinians from the state apparatus, which has meant that "citizens of Trans-Jordanian origin . . . are almost twice as likely to vote as Jordanians of Palestinian origin, who generally have less influence in the government."[65]

This experience of exclusion helps to explain refugees' lack of political involvement in Jordanian politics. If you do not have access to patron-client relationships, avenues to political participation remain limited, if not absent. However, the eagerness of many in the camp to distance themselves from what they see as the unsavory and dangerous world of politics can also be explained by the specific understanding of "the political" as being fundamentally based on the dichotomy of "friend/enemy." The difference between "enemy" and "friend" should be thought of as being intrinsic to Palestinian refugees' status. This distinction is played out in the tension between "refugee-ness" and "citizenship"; between "Palestinianness" and "Jordanianness"; between the effort of living a life in the context of integration in Jordan and the nationalistic struggles of an exiled and marginalized community. An obvious demonstration of what this means lies in the fact that in Jordan there is a popular conflation between "being Palestinian" and "being disloyal"—i.e., any assertion of "Palestinianness" is perceived by the authorities as a manifestation of disloyalty; and any manifestation of political dissent is often seen as an expression of "Palestinianness." A case in point was the sit-in held on March 24, 2011.

In the wake of the Arab revolutions that were sweeping across the region, anti-government demonstrations were held every Friday in Wasat al-Balad (downtown) of Amman, with unexpected regularity. Although generally quite small in numbers of participants, a sit-in held on March 24, 2011, at the Dakhilliyye Circle led to a tent encampment named "Tahrir Square" after the Cairo square that hosted the revolt against Egyptian president Hosni Mubarak's regime and the political demonstration that followed his deposition. Like the demonstrations and protests in other Arab countries, the sit-in was initially organized by various social networks and blogs, and comprised a disparate coalition of people named "The March 24 Youth Movement." Originally planned as ongoing until their demands were met, it lasted for only a couple of days. On March 25, the participants were attacked by a group of counter-demonstrators (the "Loyalty March"), allegedly loyal to King Abdullah II. Eventually both groups were dispersed by the police in the ensuing chaos. Despite being comprised of different groups with diverse ethnic and political backgrounds, the participants of the sit-in were rapidly identified by the counter-demonstrators as Palestinians aiming to overthrow the monarchy and establish an alternative homeland.[66]

What this episode tells us is that the working of "the political" produces adversarial positions, and these—especially after Oslo—are frequently translated in the dichotomy "Palestinian" versus "Jordanian." Because of its agonistic nature, the political cankers that set off tensions leave little space for Palestinian refugees to establish the kind of flexibility they need to live harmoniously as both Palestinian refugees and Jordanian citizens. In this context, politics—understood as formal political action—is simply the arena in which the political tension between competing acts of loyalty is most forcefully re-enacted. Engaging in "politics" therefore manifests itself as camp dwellers being constantly asked to whom they pledge allegiance— the Jordanian state or Palestinian nationalism? In a country dominated by the logics of patrimonialism, such a question is not reduced to a merely procedural issue about defining "who is who." It is, as we have seen above, a distinction that determines forms of discrimination and that can also regulate access to state resources.

It comes as no surprise, therefore, that many in the camps expressed only a mild interest in the kind of protests witnessed across the region. Echoing the thoughts of many, a respondent in al-Wihdat refugee camp expressed the popular sentiment by confirming the point: "This is not like Egypt and Tunisia: we don't want the revolution here!"[67] Even more surprising was a comment made by another, more radical respondent who, when referring to the "March 24" sit-in, commented: "Don't worry about it . . . it's only a group of *dawawin* [troublemakers] clashing with other *dawawin* [referring to the counter-demonstrators and police officers]."[68]

Politics requires taking a firm stand either as a Palestinian refugee or a Jordanian citizen that camp dwellers are unwilling to take. However, I argue that a descent into the mundane and apparently trivial gives them hopes of transcending the incommensurability of the rhetoric of "Palestinians" versus "Jordanians." There is good reason for this—the accomplishment of a hyphened national identity (Jordanian-Palestinian) bears with it both the promise of socioeconomic integration in Jordan and cultural authenticity as a Palestinian refugee. I will show what I mean with this in the following section.

A NON-POLITICAL ORDINARINESS

One of the most considerable achievements of poststructuralist political anthropology is the recognition of the artificiality of the "non-political." In this context, rather than being perceived as something natural, the non-political is an inherently political act of depoliticization of a given political reality.[69] However, as Matei Candea puts it, "the pitfall in this denaturalization of the nonpolitical, however, lies in a concomitant naturalization of the political."[70] To readdress this "shortcoming," I intend to draw an analogy between the "ordinary," as it is perceived in al-Wihdat, and Jameson's "suspension of the political" as the refusal to play the game of politics.[71] The "suspension of the political" has been a useful analytical tool employed by recent anthropological literature to understand change in regimes that are experienced as totalitarian and immutable. Alexei Yurchak, for example, shows how the members of an artistic movement during late Soviet socialism in Russia undermined the power of a seemingly totalitarian state, constituting a new space of subjectivity and agency, by refusing to engage anything they regarded as political.[72] My case diverges from his insofar as the suspension of the political was not a form of resistance vis-à-vis the assimilationist practices of the state or against the normative pressures of Palestinian nationalism. It was, instead, an opportunity to enact these simultaneously constitutive but apparently contradictory forces rather than acting against them. However, it dovetails his argument, as the refugees' descent into what they perceived to be a nonpolitical ordinariness is deeply transformative, for it creates the possibility for new forms of political subjectivity. But what exactly does "being ordinary" entail for camp dwellers?

Many people in al-Wihdat perceive the "ordinary" (*'adı*) as substantially non-political and largely encompassed within the prospect of full socioeconomic integration in Jordan, with all this might entail—owning a flat, getting married, gaining a decent professional status, but also being able to fulfil other desires, such as having fun or being free to choose a specific dress code. Against the backdrop of declining economic standards in Jordan, active militancy and overt forms of resistance are no longer discussed strategies for pursuing nationalist goals and socioeconomic integration; in fact, they generate suspicion, and often disapproval. According to respondents in the camp, people do not have time to waste on politics, as they have to cope with other more urgent matters, such as working to maintain their families. As one respondent put it, "now there are no more Fedayeen in al-Wihdat because they need to find a job to live . . . now, life is more expensive, we don't have time to waste on politics!"[73]

Deprived of guidance and ideals, young men in the camp gradually sink into despair and apathy generated by a lack of economic means. The results of the overt independence and hostility of those labelled as "troublemakers" (*dawawin*) are clear and plain for all to see: entire families lacking a fatherly example and stable financial support; children and adolescents devoid of proper guidance, who fill their time running across the streets of the camp; male youth lying on the sofas of barber's shops or idling on footpaths.

A true Palestinian and a "proper" man is, instead, perceived as he who provides for his family rather than searching for political legitimacy in the marginality of his condition. For this "ordinariness" to be assured in a context marked by declining economic standards, however, people in the camp need to work hard. By pursuing renovations within the camp and its integration into the surrounding urban neighborhoods, camp dwellers seek to challenge the socioeconomic marginality of al-Wihdat and, ultimately, further their integration in Jordan. But in this process refugees have also found the energy to uphold their nationalist predicament. Far from interpreting the physical precariousness of al-Wihdat as a token of their temporary stay in Jordan, many of the people I spoke with in al-Wihdat perceived the camp's deteriorating infrastructure and its low standards of environmental health as an attempt to liquidate the Palestinian issue and sink refugees into despair and oblivion. Poverty and the lack of decent infrastructure were often held by camp dwellers as the main sources of social problems and immorality among the youth and the ultimate threat to the Palestinian nationalist struggle. As an old man in his seventies said to me while sitting, lethargically, on a curb and staring at a bunch of children who were playing amidst a pile of garbage and debris tossed in the middle of a narrow alley in al-Wihdat:

> I am afraid for the future. If you live in a bad environment, you grow wild; and if you are poor, you don't eat; and if you don't eat, you cannot sleep. So what do you do? You think, and you get angry, more and more, until . . . until something bad will happen. It's not still the worse, but we are close to it. Once people will get [to] the bottom, they will start making trouble, maybe kill each other. . . . This is what they [Israel and the USA] want. They want us to kill each other![74]

Marginalized by the Oslo agreements and faced with the gradual decay of their living conditions, camp dwellers have regarded the socioeconomic rehabilitation and physical upgrading of al-Wihdat—a symbol of Palestinian nationalism—as a way forward to preserve their nationalist ideals in the context of assimilation.

Perhaps nothing expresses with greater clarity the attempt to ground "Palestinianness" into urban integration than al-Wihdat market (*suq al-wihdat*). Cross-cut by al-Nadi Street, the souk is split into two main sections: the northern part with the food and kitchen articles (*suq al-khudra*, i.e., vegetable market), and the southern part with the clothing and other items (*suq al-malabes*, i.e., cloth market). Anybody who steps into the market for the first time would be bewildered by the number of things and people in the street. The intense sociality of the souk is striking. Shops, fast foods, stalls, and street sellers are distributed across the market, selling virtually everything, from potato peelers to bright velvet corduroy pants, from sexy lingerie to little pictures that frame the most common hadiths of the Prophet or the word "Allah." Men selling various objects compete to shout the loudest about the price of their merchandise, while others sit and gaze passively. An important area of the food market is covered. Here, among stands, hawkers, and small shops there is also a modern supermarket. In *suq al-malabes*, amidst miserable shops and wrecked stands, there are fancy boutiques that recall high street shops like H&M or Zara. In this noisy and teeming labyrinth, animals such as rabbits, chickens, and even lambs and sheep are exhibited for sale.

At the time of my research, refugees took evident pride in claiming how the products sold in the market not only competed with but actually outmatched those in the fanciest and richest zones of Amman. The souk was the ultimate token of their hyphened national identity as Jordanian-Palestinians: a symbol of their integration into Jordan and the capacity of Palestinians to struggle against the adversities of a life in exile. This mixture of resilience and integration is what—according to the words of a fifty-year-old Palestinian refugee previously employed in the UN compound in the camp—endows Al-Wihdat with its characteristic family likeness:

> For those who have never stepped a foot into it, it is difficult to distinguish the camp from any other poor neighborhood. But for us who have lived and worked in the camp, al-Wihdat is home. You can distinguish the camp for its vegetable market, for the women who dress with Palestinian traditional dresses, for the [Palestinian] way of speaking of the people and the way they shout when they sell their products.[75]

Remarkably, when I then asked if there were differences between refugee camps and the rest of the city, the man added: "No, there is no difference, the camp is like the *balad*."[76] By saying so, he was drawing a link between the commercial zone of the camp and the old city of Amman, which is commonly known as *balad* and where an important open market of the capital city is located, a place of business and trade. But in Arabic, the term *balad* connotes also "village," "homeland," and "place of origin." By stating that al-Wihdat was only another *balad*, he was also indirectly referring to the fact that the camp had become an alternative city center in Amman: the center of a Palestinian space and a symbol of Palestine itself. The association of al-Wihdat with the *balad* of Amman is an expression of the twofold nature of the camp: a space of "Jordanianness" and "Palestinianness." "Jordanian" and "Palestinian" as opposed collectivities do not represent self-contained groups whose divisions can somehow be healed by political processes. Quite the contrary, they are often a consequence of the working of the political. Living an "ordinary life" (*haya 'adiye*) represents precisely an attempt to limit, control, and hold back the upsetting dynamics of the we/they distinction.

Of course, an objection may be raised regarding my proposal that we think of the "ordinary" in terms of a suspension of the political. We may be hence tempted to step back from this and redescribe what I define as "the pursuit of the ordinary" as "political" because of the political implications that such an endeavor has for camp dwellers. However, I think that we should resist this temptation for a number of reasons. First, the risk would be to misunderstand or even ignore local categories of the political that do not neatly conform to the categories of a Western ethnographer, for most of the people in al-Wihdat would not normally consider an ordinary activity such as owning a vegetable stand as a political activity. If we disregarded the refugees' attempt to limit the disturbing workings of the political, we would also make their willingness to live as Jordanian citizens unintelligible. Another problematic weakness of such an analytical approach is to represent people's lives as being excessively austere. Politics certainly shapes many aspects of the Palestinian refugees' everyday lives, but to reduce most of their existence to the political would contribute to reproducing one-sided depictions of their lives—popularly conveyed, for example, in the stereotype of refugees as irreducible dissidents.[77] Finally, such a reading would prevent us from understanding a crucial dimension of my analysis: the role of the non-political in fashioning a hyphenated identity as Palestinian-Jordanians—what many in the camp aimed to do especially after the Oslo Accords when even the already tenuous prospects of repatriation succumbed to the PLO's short-sighted realpolitik.

CONCLUSION

When the winds of the Arab revolts hit the Middle East in 2011, the storm left Jordan apparently unharmed. Despite the escalation of protests that led many demonstrators to demand the abdication of King Abdullah II and the end of Hashemite rule in the winters of 2012 and 2013, the protests in Jordan have failed to produce the massive political upheaval seen elsewhere in the region. Along with Jordan's fragmented political field and the security forces' deftness, commentators and scholars hold the political disengagement of the largely Palestinian population of East Amman and central Irbid mostly accountable for the split of the protest into a number of isolated demonstrations. This is arguably true, and it certainly accounts for a great deal of the outcome. Oslo has cankered the tension intrinsic to the status of Palestinian refugees in Jordan, and substantially contributed to curbing political activism among Palestinian refugees. The last episodes of "uprising" that most of my informants in the camp recollect dated back to 2004 when Jordanian flags were burned in al-Wihdat following the assassination of the historical leader of Hamas, Shaykh Yassin. The issue was eventually solved at an official level by camp leaders (*makhatir*) who put the blame on alleged agitators coming from outside the camp.[78]

However, the lack of sustained protest does not mean that nothing happened. Lured by the spectacular clarity of political demonstrations and acts of violence that have dramatically upset Tunisia, Egypt, and Syria, many Middle East scholars and political analysts have, with few exemptions, missed the reverberation of the Arab Spring in Jordan. Inspired by the Arab revolts in the region, a number of Palestinian youth decided to renegotiate their inclusion in the national polity and the revitalization of Palestinian struggles for liberation. Toward this end, groups of demonstrators from the camps took to the streets in November 2012 together with groups of Transjordanians and demanded the end of Hashemite rule. This participation could be the foundation stone for the development of cross-cutting socio-ethnic alliances, the same alliances that have toppled regimes and overthrown presidents in other Arab countries, and could have dramatic transformative capacities in the revitalization of the Palestinian liberation project and political participation of Palestinian refugees in Jordan. However, it is hard to foresee whether these short-lived protests will trigger a more active political participation of Palestinian refugees from camps. An analysis of this kind goes beyond the scope of this chapter.

The present analysis has instead sought to address how camp dwellers have dealt with the complexities associated with their ambiguous status in Jordan in the aftermath of the Oslo Accords. While the *Nakba* evicted Palestinians from their lands, Oslo doomed them to a life in exile. By undermining the basis upon which their hope for return lay, it triggered among refugees a profound rethinking of their status in Jordan. In this context, the whole nationalist project became difficult to imagine, and their heroic heydays painful to remember. Oslo and the spectre of *al-watan al-badil* led to a substantial disengagement of refugees from politics. This disengagement, I argued, was largely explained by the attempt of Palestinian refugees to limit, control, and hold back the unsettling dynamics of the "friend/enemy" distinction. If "the political" requires a positioning either as a Palestinian refugee or as a Jordanian citizen that camp dwellers are unwilling to take, a descent into "the ordinary" gives them hopes of transcending the absolute political incommensurability of "us" versus "them." In this sense, Palestinian refugees have never ceased to demonstrate their allegiance to Palestinian nationalism, which remains a central constitutive element of their political subjectivity. However, the momentary suspension of "the political" creates new spaces of agency that allow refugees to accommodate their need to live an ordinary life as Jordanian citizens with their "extraordinary" existence as living symbols of Palestinian nationalism.

NOTES

1. See, for example, Randa Farah, "Palestinian Refugees: Dethroning the Nation at the Crowning of the 'Statelet'?" *Interventions* 8, no. 2 (2006): 228–252; Laleh Khalili, *Heroes and Martyrs of Palestine: The Politics of National Commemoration*, vol. 27 (Cambridge: Cambridge University Press, 2007); Ghada Hashem Talhami, *Syria and the Palestinians: The Clash of Nationalisms* (Gainesville: University Press of Florida, 2001).

2. Salim Tamari, *Palestinian Refugee Negotiations: From Madrid to Oslo II* (Washington, DC: Institute for Palestine Studies, 1996).

3. After conducting preliminary research in the Palestinian refugee camps of Jordan from May to December 2004, field research referred to in this chapter was carried out in the al-Wihdat refugee camp from July 2009 to September 2010—a camp set up in 1955 on the outskirts of Amman, the capital of Jordan, which gradually became an integral part of the city. During these periods, I lived mostly in al-Wihdat. My research was complemented by several visits throughout 2011–2016 to other refugee camps in the Kingdom—most notably, Baq'a, Suf, and Hussein camps.

4. My field trajectory led me to adopt a privileged focus on young men and adolescents of the camp to the detriment of other categories, most notably that of women. When the occasion arose, I spoke with women in the camps too. However, due to the patterns of gender segregation and standards of modesty, as a male researcher I experienced difficulty in carrying out an investigation of this kind. As such, I want to emphasize that this study tackles the issue of political participation among young men from the camp, which—albeit exemplificative—is not representative of Palestinian politics at large.

5. See, among others, Julie Marie Peteet, *Landscape of Hope and Despair: Palestinian Refugee Camps* (Philadelphia and Bristol: University of Pennsylvania Press, 2005).

6. Kamal Salibi, *A Modern History of Jordan* (London: I. B. Tauris, 1993).

7. Over the past years, a large range of studies have focused on camps and refugees as crucial sites of Palestinian political mobilization and empowerment. See, among others, George E. Bisharat, "Displacement and Social Identity: Palestinian Refugees in the West Bank," *Center for Migration Studies Special Issues* 11, no. 4 (1994): 163–188; Randa Rafiq Farah, "Popular Memory and Reconstructions of Palestinian Identity, Al-Baq'a Refugee Camp, Jordan" (University of Toronto, 2000); Peteet, *Landscape of Hope and Despair: Palestinian Refugee Camps*; Maya Rosenfeld, "Power Structure, Agency, and Family in a Palestinian Refugee Camp," *International Journal of Middle East Studies* 34, no. 3 (2002): 519–551; Rosemary Sayigh,

Palestinians: Prom Peasants to Revolutionaries: A People's History (London: Zed Press, 1979).

8. Luigi Achilli, *Palestinian Refugees and Identity: Nationalism, Politics and the Everyday* (I. B. Tauris, 2015).

9. Iris Jean-Klein, "Mothercraft, Statecraft, and Subjectivity in the Palestinian Intifada," *American Ethnologist* 27, no. 1 (2000): 100–127; Joseph Massad, "Conceiving the Masculine: Gender and Palestinian Nationalism," *Middle East Journal*, 1995, 467–483; Julie Peteet, "Male Gender and Rituals of Resistance in the Palestinian Intifada: A Cultural Politics of Violence," *American Ethnologist* 21, no. 1 (1994): 31–49.

10. Both Israeli and Palestinian historians have criticized official Israeli claims that Palestinians left their houses and land following their own decision or on the order of Arab leaders. In contrast, these authors have pointed out how the attacks and raids perpetrated by Zionist forces were at the origin of this exodus. Farah, "Palestinian Refugees: Dethroning the Nation at the Crowning of the 'Statelet'?"; Rashid Khalidi, *Palestinian Identity: The Construction of Modern National Consciousness* (New York: Columbia University Press, 2010); Baruch Kimmerling and Joel S. Migdal, *Palestinians: The Making of a People* (Cambridge, MA: Harvard University Press, 1993); Benny Morris, *The Birth of the Palestinian Refugee Problem, 1947–1949*, vol. 15 (Cambridge: Cambridge University Press, 1987); Ilan Pappe, *The Making of the Arab-Israeli Conflict, 1947–1951* (London: I. B. Tauris, 1992).

11. Kimmerling and Migdal, *Palestinians: The Making of a People*.

12. Elia Zureik, *Palestinian Refugees and the Peace Process* (Washington, DC: Institute for Palestine Studies, 1996).

13. UNRWA is a relief and human development agency established in December 1949. The agency today provides education, health care, social services, and emergency aid to Palestinian refugees in its five fields of operation—namely Jordan, Lebanon, Syria, the Gaza Strip, and the West Bank.

14. It must be noted that this was simply an operational definition employed by UNRWA to establish the parameters for determining who was entitled to receive its services. As Palestinian refugees fell under the general assistance mandate of UNRWA when the United Nations High Commissioner for Refugees (UNHCR) was established, they were not included in the official definition of refugee. This has had important consequences. First, Palestinian refugees are not entitled to those fundamental rights enjoyed by those who meet the criteria set by the 1951 Convention relating to the Status of Refugees—i.e., repatriation, permanent resettlement in country of residence, or resettlement in a third country. Second, unlike the UNHCR, UNRWA does not provide protection of refugees, and its mandate is limited only to basic services.

15. UNRWA, "Jordan," 2017, https://www.unrwa.org/where-we-work/jordan.

16. Nearly one-third of registered Palestine refugees, around 1.5 million individuals, live in 58 recognized Palestine refugee camps in Jordan, Lebanon, the Syrian Arab Republic, the Gaza Strip, and the West Bank, including East Jerusalem. Designed as transit centers to host and prepare Palestinian refugees for local integration, refugee camps in the Middle East have become what Julie Peteet has recently described as "oppositional spaces appropriated and endowed with alternative meanings." Peteet, *Landscape of Hope and Despair: Palestinian Refugee Camps*, 3.

17. Also known as the 1967 Arab-Israeli War, the "Six-Day War" was fought in June 1967 between Israel and the neighboring states of Egypt, Jordan, and Syria.

18. Khalili, *Heroes and Martyrs of Palestine: The Politics of National Commemoration*; Sayigh, *Palestinians: From Peasants to Revolutionaries: A People's History*.

19. Muhammad Siddiq, *Man Is a Cause: Political Consciousness and the Fiction of Ghassān Kanafānī* (Seattle: University of Washington Press, 1984).

20. Yezid Sayigh, *Armed Struggle and the Search for State: The Palestinian National Movement, 1949–1993* (Oxford: Clarendon Press, 1997), 179.

21. Khalili, *Heroes and Martyrs of Palestine: The Politics of National Commemoration*.

22. In Saree Makdisi, "Oslo and the Systematic Exclusion of Refugee Rights," *Special Issue "20 Years Since Oslo: Palestinian Perspectives,"* 2013, 94.

23. Edward Said, "The Morning After," *Special Issue "20 Years Since Oslo: Palestinian Perspectives,"* 2013, 16.

24. Mjriam Abu Samra, "The Road to Oslo and Its Reverse," *Allegra Lab* (blog), October 29, 2015, http://allegralaboratory.net/the-road-to-oslo-and-its-reverse-palestine/.

25. *Al-shatat* can loosely be translated as "diaspora." However, I will not refer to Palestinians as a diasporic group, though their exodus presents many characteristics typical of such groups; see Clifford (1994). For geographic, temporal, semantic, and political reasons specific to the Palestinian case, the employment of the concept of diaspora would mask more than unveil the political issues behind their flight; see Julie Peteet, "Problematizing a Palestinian Diaspora," *International Journal of Middle East Studies* 39, no. 4 (2007): 627–646; see also Sari Hanafi, "The Palestinians in Syria and the Peace Process," in *Homelands and Diasporas: Holy Lands and Other Places*, by Andre Levy and Alex Weingrod (Stanford: Stanford University Press, 2003), 97–122; Tareq Arrar, "Palestinians Exiled in Europe," *Al Majdal* 29 (2006): 41–45.

26. Ronald R Macintyre, "The Palestine Liberation Organization: Tactics, Strategies and Options toward the Geneva Peace Conference," *Journal of Palestine Studies* 4, no. 4 (1975): 65–89.

27. Text of the Ten Point Program, June 8, 1974.

28. Jamil Hilal, "PLO Institutions: The Challenge Ahead," *Journal of Palestine Studies* 23, no. 1 (1993): 46–60.

29. Al Hout, in Abu Samra, "The Road to Oslo and Its Reverse."

30. In this sense, far from being a failure, the process of peacebuilding in Palestine has been a success—from the Israeli point of view. Indeed, as Mandy Turner points out, there is a "deep structural symbiosis in the philosophy and methods of counterinsurgency and peacebuilding that lie in securing the population against unrest through the implementation of governance, development and security strategies that instill acquiescence and ensure control." Mandy Turner, "Peacebuilding as Counterinsurgency in the Occupied Palestinian Territory," *Review of International Studies* 41, no. 1 (2015): 97.

31. See, among others, Makdisi, "Oslo and the Systematic Exclusion of Refugee Rights."

32. Joseph Massad, "Oslo and the End of Palestinian Independence," *Al Ahram Weekly Online* 982, no. 21 (2010): 10.

33. Makdisi, "Oslo and the Systematic Exclusion of Refugee Rights," 94.

34. Khalili, *Heroes and Martyrs of Palestine: The Politics of National Commemoration*, 27:58.

35. Talhami, *Syria and the Palestinians: The Clash of Nationalisms*.

36. Hilal, "PLO Institutions: The Challenge Ahead," 50.

37. Al Jazeera News, "Wishing away Palestinian refugees: End of US' UNRWA aid explained," *Al Jazeera*, 26 September 2018, https://www.aljazeera.com/news/2018/09/unrwa-funding-cut-deeply-regrettable-shocking-180901071620633.html.

38. For this reason, with the term "Palestinian refugees," I am here referring to all those people that have been evicted from their lands by Israel in the context of its occupation and colonial practices.

39. The Hashemites are the Jordanian royal family, originally coming from the Hejaz region of Saudi Arabia.

40. Laurie A. Brand, "Palestinians and Jordanians: A Crisis of Identity," *Journal of Palestine Studies* 24, no. 4 (1995): 50–52.

41. Article 2, in Joseph Massad, *Colonial Effects: The Making of National Identity in Jordan* (New York: Columbia University Press, 2001), 39.

42. Adnan Abu-Odeh, *Jordanians, Palestinians & the Hashemite Kingdom in the Middle East Peace Process* (Washington, DC: United States Institute of Peace, 1999); Avi Plascov, *The Palestinian Refugees in Jordan 1948–1957* (London: F. Cass, 1981).

43. Massad, *Colonial Effects: The Making of National Identity in Jordan*, 233.

44. Abu-Odeh, *Jordanians, Palestinians & the Hashemite Kingdom in the Middle East Peace Process*.

45. Iris Fruchter-Ronen, "Black September: The 1970–71 Events and Their Impact on the Formation of Jordanian National Identity," *Civil Wars* 10, no. 3 (2008): 244–260.

46. Sayigh, *Armed Struggle and the Search for State: The Palestinian National Movement, 1949–1993*.

47. The term "Transjordanian" has been used to indicate the population that became citizens of the State of Transjordan, and later citizens of the Hashemite Kingdom of Jordan, by virtue of the nationality laws of 1928 of the Emirate of Jordan. There is not an exact equivalent Arabic term for "Transjordanians" used in Jordan. In daily usage, Palestinian refugees who want to set themselves apart from "local" Jordanians use the general term of *urduniyyın* (which literally means "Jordanians") or *badawi* (Bedouins).

48. See, for example, Abu-Odeh, *Jordanians, Palestinians & the Hashemite Kingdom in the Middle East Peace Process*.

49. Abu-Odeh, 211–212.

50. Stefanie Nanes, "Choice, Loyalty, and the Melting Pot: Citizenship and National Identity in Jordan," *Nationalism and Ethnic Politics* 14, no. 1 (2008): 91.

51. Brand, "Palestinians and Jordanians: A Crisis of Identity," 57.

52. While the Hashemites never really ceased to rhetorically uphold the discourse of unity between Transjordanians and Jordanians of Palestinian origin (i.e., refugees and displaced people from the 1948 and 1967 wars), the regime showed a clear indul-

gence toward the manifestation of Transjordanian chauvinism. Brand, "Palestinians and Jordanians: A Crisis of Identity."

53. Christine Jungen, "Tribalism in Kerak: Past Memories, Present Realities," in *Jordan in Transition*, by George Joffe (London: Hurst and Company, 2002), 201.

54. It should be noted also that by generally supporting the manifestation of Transjordanian nationalism, the Hashemites—who do not come from Jordan but from the Hijaz in Saudi Arabia—also exploited intercommunal tension in order to achieve specific goals, such as the prevention of alliances between Palestinians and Transjordanians or the strengthening of the PLO's authority over the territory. Brand, "Palestinians and Jordanians: A Crisis of Identity."

55. Respectively, Abdel-Karim Abul Heija (director of the Jordanian Department of Palestinian Affairs in Arab al-Yawm) and Ma'rouf Bakhit (ex-prime minister). In Jalal Al-Husseini, "The Evolution of the Palestinian Refugee Camps in Jordan. Between Logics of Exclusion and Integration," *Collections Électroniques de l'Ifpo. Livres En Ligne Des Presses de l'Institut Français Du Proche-Orient*, no. 6 (2011): 181–204.

56. Achilli, *Palestinian Refugees and Identity: Nationalism, Politics and the Everyday*.

57. Abu-Odeh, *Jordanians, Palestinians & the Hashemite Kingdom in the Middle East Peace Process*; Achilli, *Palestinian Refugees and Identity: Nationalism, Politics and the Everyday*; Massad, *Colonial Effects: The Making of National Identity in Jordan*.

58. Jungen, "Tribalism in Kerak: Past Memories, Present Realities," 201.

59. E.g., Giorgio Agamben, *Homo Sacer: Sovereign Power and Bare Life* (Stanford: Stanford University Press, 1998); Chantal Mouffe, *The Democratic Paradox* (London: Verso, 2000).

60. Perry Anderson, *Spectrum* (New York: Verso, 2005), 5.

61. Carl Schmitt, *The Concept of the Political* (New Brunswick, NJ: Rutgers University Press), 35.

62. Mouffe, *The Democratic Paradox*; Chantal Mouffe, *On the Political* (London: Routledge, 2005).

63. Mouffe, *On the Political*, 16.

64. Andrew Shryock, *Nationalism and the Genealogical Imagination: Oral History and Textual Authority in Tribal Jordan* (Berkeley: University of California Press, 1997).

65. Ellen Lust-Okar, "Reinforcing Informal Institutions through Authoritarian Elections: Insights from Jordan," *Middle East Law and Governance* 1, no. 1 (2009): 13.

66. Jadaliyya Reports, "Jordan's March 24 Youth Sit-in Violently Dispersed," *Jadaliyya*, 26 March 2011, http://www.jadaliyya.com/pages/index/1012/jordans-march-24-youth-sit-in-violently-dispersed-.

67. Interview with young man, anonymous, Amman, September 20, 2011.

68. Interview with young man, anonymous, Amman, June 20, 2011.

69. James Ferguson, *The Anti-Politics Machine: Development, Depoliticization, and Bureaucratic Power in Lesotho* (Minneapolis: University of Minnesota Press, 1994).

70. Matei Candea, "'Our Division of the Universe' Making a Space for the Non-Political in the Anthropology of Politics," *Current Anthropology* 52, no. 3 (2011): 320.
71. Alexei Yurchak, *Everything Was Forever, until It Was No More: The Last Soviet Generation* (Princeton: Princeton University Press, 2013).
72. Yurchak, *Everything Was Forever*.
73. Interview with young man, anonymous, Amman, April 2, 2014.
74. Interview with old man, anonymous, Amman, December 19, 2010.
75. Interview with former UNRWA field officer, Amman, September 18, 2010.
76. Interview with former UNRWA field officer.
77. See, for example, Sami Al-Khazendar, *Jordan and the Palestine Question*, 1997.
78. Al-Dustour, "Al-Dustour's Opinion: Investigating the Al-Wihdat Events," *Al-Dustour*, March 30, 2004.

BIBLIOGRAPHY

Abu-Odeh, Adnan. *Jordanians, Palestinians & the Hashemite Kingdom in the Middle East Peace Process*. Washington, DC: United States Institute of Peace, 1999.

Abu Samra, Mjriam. "The Road to Oslo and Its Reverse." *Allegra Lab* (blog), October 29, 2015. http://allegralaboratory.net/the-road-to-oslo-and-its-reverse-palestine/.

Achilli, Luigi. *Palestinian Refugees and Identity: Nationalism, Politics and the Everyday*. I. B. Tauris, 2015.

Agamben, Giorgio. *Homo Sacer: Sovereign Power and Bare Life*. Stanford: Stanford University Press, 1998.

Al-Dustour. "Al-Dustour's Opinion: Investigating the Al-Wihdat Events." *Al-Dustour*, March 30, 2004.

Al-Husseini, Jalal. "The Evolution of the Palestinian Refugee Camps in Jordan. Between Logics of Exclusion and Integration." *Collections Électroniques de l'Ifpo. Livres En Ligne Des Presses de l'Institut Français Du Proche-Orient*, no. 6 (2011): 181–204.

Al Jazeera News, "Wishing away Palestinian refugees: End of US' UNRWA aid explained," *Al Jazeera*, 26 September 2018, https://www.aljazeera.com/news/2018/09/unrwa-funding-cut-deeply-regrettable-shocking-180901071620633.html.

Al-Khazendar, Sami. *Jordan and the Palestine Question*, 1997.

Anderson, Perry. *Spectrum*. New York: Verso, 2005.

Arrar, Tareq. "Palestinians Exiled in Europe." *Al Majdal* 29 (2006): 41–45.

Bisharat, George E. "Displacement and Social Identity: Palestinian Refugees in the West Bank." *Center for Migration Studies Special Issues* 11, no. 4 (1994): 163–188.

Brand, Laurie A. "Palestinians and Jordanians: A Crisis of Identity." *Journal of Palestine Studies* 24, no. 4 (1995): 46–61.

Candea, Matei. "'Our Division of the Universe' Making a Space for the Non-Political in the Anthropology of Politics." *Current Anthropology* 52, no. 3 (2011): 309–334.

Farah, Randa. "Palestinian Refugees: Dethroning the Nation at the Crowning of the 'Statelet'?" *Interventions* 8, no. 2 (2006): 228–252.

Farah, Randa Rafiq. "Popular Memory and Reconstructions of Palestinian Identity, Al-Baq'a Refugee Camp, Jordan." University of Toronto, 2000.
Ferguson, James. *The Anti-Politics Machine: Development, Depoliticization, and Bureaucratic Power in Lesotho*. Minneapolis: University of Minnesota Press, 1994.
Fruchter-Ronen, Iris. "Black September: The 1970–71 Events and Their Impact on the Formation of Jordanian National Identity." *Civil Wars* 10, no. 3 (2008): 244–260.
Hanafi, Sari. "The Palestinians in Syria and the Peace Process." In *Homelands and Diasporas: Holy Lands and Other Places*, by Andre Levy and Alex Weingrod, 97–122. Stanford: Stanford University Press, 2003.
Hilal, Jamil. "PLO Institutions: The Challenge Ahead." *Journal of Palestine Studies* 23, no. 1 (1993): 46–60.
Jadaliyya Reports. "Jordan's March 24 Youth Sit-in Violently Dispersed." *Jadaliyya*, March 26, 2011. http://www.jadaliyya.com/pages/index/1012/jordans-march-24-youth-sit-in-violently-dispersed-.
Jean-Klein, Iris. "Mothercraft, Statecraft, and Subjectivity in the Palestinian Intifada." *American Ethnologist* 27, no. 1 (2000): 100–127.
Jungen, Christine. "Tribalism in Kerak: Past Memories, Present Realities." In *Jordan in Transition*, by George Joffe, 191–207. London: Hurst and Company, 2002.
Khalidi, Rashid. *Palestinian Identity: The Construction of Modern National Consciousness*. New York: Columbia University Press, 2010.
Khalili, Laleh. *Heroes and Martyrs of Palestine: The Politics of National Commemoration*. Vol. 27. Cambridge: Cambridge University Press, 2007.
Kimmerling, Baruch, and Joel S. Migdal. *Palestinians: The Making of a People*. Cambridge, MA: Harvard University Press, 1993.
Lust-Okar, Ellen. "Reinforcing Informal Institutions through Authoritarian Elections: Insights from Jordan." *Middle East Law and Governance* 1, no. 1 (2009): 3–37.
Macintyre, Ronald R. "The Palestine Liberation Organization: Tactics, Strategies and Options toward the Geneva Peace Conference." *Journal of Palestine Studies* 4, no. 4 (1975): 65–89.
Makdisi, Saree. "Oslo and the Systematic Exclusion of Refugee Rights." *Special Issue "20 Years Since Oslo: Palestinian Perspectives*," 2013.
Massad, Joseph. *Colonial Effects: The Making of National Identity in Jordan*. New York: Columbia University Press, 2001.
———. "Conceiving the Masculine: Gender and Palestinian Nationalism." *Middle East Journal*, 1995, 467–483.
———. "Oslo and the End of Palestinian Independence." *Al Ahram Weekly Online* 982, no. 21 (2010): 10.
Morris, Benny. *The Birth of the Palestinian Refugee Problem, 1947–1949*. Vol. 15. Cambridge: Cambridge University Press, 1987.
Mouffe, Chantal. *On the Political*. London: Routledge, 2005.
———. *The Democratic Paradox*. London: Verso, 2000.
Nanes, Stefanie. "Choice, Loyalty, and the Melting Pot: Citizenship and National Identity in Jordan." *Nationalism and Ethnic Politics* 14, no. 1 (2008): 85–116.

Pappe, Ilan. *The Making of the Arab-Israeli Conflict, 1947–1951*. London: I. B. Tauris, 1992.
Peteet, Julie. "Male Gender and Rituals of Resistance in the Palestinian Intifada: A Cultural Politics of Violence." *American Ethnologist* 21, no. 1 (1994): 31–49.
———. "Problematizing a Palestinian Diaspora." *International Journal of Middle East Studies* 39, no. 4 (2007): 627–646.
Peteet, Julie Marie. *Landscape of Hope and Despair: Palestinian Refugee Camps*. Philadelphia and Bristol: University of Pennsylvania Press, 2005.
Plascov, Avi. *The Palestinian Refugees in Jordan 1948–1957*. London: F. Cass, 1981.
Rosenfeld, Maya. "Power Structure, Agency, and Family in a Palestinian Refugee Camp." *International Journal of Middle East Studies* 34, no. 3 (2002): 519–551.
Said, Edward. "The Morning After." *Special Issue "20 Years Since Oslo: Palestinian Perspectives*," 2013.
Salibi, Kamal. *A Modern History of Jordan*. London: I. B. Tauris, 1993.
Sayigh, Rosemary. *Palestinians: From Peasants to Revolutionaries: A People's History*. London: Zed Press, 1979.
Sayigh, Yezid. *Armed Struggle and the Search for State: The Palestinian National Movement, 1949–1993*. Oxford: Clarendon Press, 1997.
Schmitt, Carl. *The Concept of the Political*. New Brunswick, NJ: Rutgers University Press, 1976.
Shryock, Andrew. *Nationalism and the Genealogical Imagination: Oral History and Textual Authority in Tribal Jordan*. Berkeley: University of California Press, 1997.
Siddiq, Muhammad. *Man Is a Cause: Political Consciousness and the Fiction of Ghassān Kanafānī*. Seattle: University of Washington Press, 1984.
Talhami, Ghada Hashem. *Syria and the Palestinians: The Clash of Nationalisms*. Gainesville: University Press of Florida, 2001.
Tamari, Salim. *Palestinian Refugee Negotiations: From Madrid to Oslo II*. Washington, DC: Institute for Palestine Studies, 1996.
Turner, Mandy. "Peacebuilding as Counterinsurgency in the Occupied Palestinian Territory." *Review of International Studies* 41, no. 1 (2015): 73–98.
UNRWA. "Jordan," 2017. https://www.unrwa.org/where-we-work/jordan.
Yurchak, Alexei. *Everything Was Forever, until It Was No More: The Last Soviet Generation*. Princeton: Princeton University Press, 2013.
Zureik, Elia. *Palestinian Refugees and the Peace Process*. Washington, DC: Institute for Palestine Studies, 1996.

Chapter Ten

No "Plan B" Because "Plan A" Cannot Fail

The Oslo Framework and Western Donors in the OPT, 1993–2017

Mandy Turner

> *Mehdi Hassan:* "I always hear US officials saying this: the window is closing, the time's running out, the point of no return is being reached. At what stage does it become too late, in your view?
>
> *Martin Indyk:* "I honestly don't know. What I know is, when we get to that point, the two-state solution will be resurrected. It's like the kings and queens of England, you know. The peace process is dead, long live the peace process. It keeps on coming back. Amazing thing, Mehdi, amazing thing."
>
> —Mehdi Hassan interviews Martin Indyk, "Should the US be neutral on Israel-Palestine?" *Head to Head, Al-Jazeera,* May 13, 2016.[1]

The Oslo peace paradigm—which includes the structures created by the various agreements signed between the Palestine Liberation Organization (PLO) and Israel from 1993, as well as its ideological underpinnings and assumptions—has been remarkably resilient. As clearly articulated in the epigraph to this chapter by Martin Indyk (US special envoy for Israeli–Palestinian Negotiations 2013–2014, and US ambassador to Israel 1995–1997, 2000–2001), despite regular epitaphs being written on the death of the two-state solution (and thus the peace process and the Oslo framework), it will be continually resurrected as the "Plan A" par excellence, because it serves three important political purposes. First, it allows the continuation of Western foreign policy prerogatives of supporting the state of Israel while simultaneously recognizing that there needs to be a solution to the "Palestine Question." Second, it provides the justification for the extensive involvement of Western donors and multilateral agencies in the Occupied Palestinian Territory (OPT) because the expansion of services for Palestinians under the guise of "peacebuilding" and "self-governance" through the Palestinian Authority (purportedly in anticipation of full sovereign statehood) has provided the foundation for stability. Third, despite constant violations of the principles of the Oslo framework by Israel, as well as statements by government ministers (including Prime Minister Benjamin Netanyahu) that there will be no Palestinian state, a negotiated two-state solution remains Israel's official position—although by May 2018 more practices and policies were pointing to it being completely abandoned, particularly given the US administration's position under the presidency of Donald Trump. And while the PLO/Palestinian Authority leadership has turned toward international agencies such as the UN Security Council, and International Criminal Court, and has, on occasion, threatened to disband the Palestinian Authority and turn the struggle for Palestinian national rights into a struggle for Palestinian civil rights—the two-state solution also remains its official policy.[2] Indeed, two states—Israel and Palestine, living side by side in peace ("Plan A")—is the stated preferred option of the two leaderships and the main third party actors. However, the reason for its lack of implementation is beyond the scope of this chapter (please see the chapter by Diana Buttu in this book).

Other chapters in this book explore the experiences and responses of Israeli and Palestinian communities to the hugely significant geographic, economic, and political changes that came in the aftermath of the signing of the Declaration of Principles on Interim Self-government Arrangements (hereafter the DOP, otherwise known as the Oslo Accords) in 1993. This chapter has a different focus—it analyzes Western donor and multilateral involvement based on the observation that these actors have played a crucial role in creating and sustaining the particular type of colonial "peace" that exists in 2018. Western donor and multilateral agencies have underwritten the creation and maintenance of the Palestinian Authority, the building of infrastructure and economic development, support for civil society organizations, and security sector reform—activities normally included in the Western donor peacebuilding matrix. While the majority of research and writing on aid to the OPT has focused on its lack of "effectiveness" to bring about peace or development, this chapter takes a different approach.[3] It takes as its starting point that the evaluation of "effectiveness" is problematic—"effective" in what way and for whom? The chapter instead focuses on understanding the political motivations (declared or undeclared) behind aid and how they have played out in the OPT. And so the analysis provided is not technical or policy-orientated; its overt focus is not on the amount, channels, or sectoral distribution of international assistance, nor of the performance (positive or negative) of economic and social indicators—unless they tell us something interesting about donor priorities.

Graphs of donor aid from 1993 to 2017 are provided in this chapter, however it is important to remember that aid data is notoriously incomplete and inaccurate. This applies even more so in the OPT, where the large number of aid actors, the amount of aid (per capita), and its politicized nature (even more so than with other aid contexts) has made it difficult to track. A more extensive tracking system was put in place in the late-2000s, but still no one really knows how much aid is coming into the OPT.[4] This chapter focuses specifically on Western donors and multilateral agencies because they have largely set the agenda for aid that has sustained the Oslo framework, and so while other donors have certainly played an important role (particularly from the Arab world) these will not be analyzed here. While aid has declined in the past few years (see graphs 2 to 4), the involvement and commitment of donors continues. Indeed, it is important to acknowledge that without donor assistance neither the Oslo framework nor the Palestinian Authority would have survived this long. The donors are thus central to the longevity and sustainability of the Oslo peace paradigm.

The main focus of this chapter is thus two-fold. First, it will provide an analysis of why, how, and with what impacts Western donors have sought to put in place the foundations for the successful implementation of "Plan A." Second, at a time when the possibility of a two-state solution is being increasingly questioned, it will assess whether and in what forms alternative strategies are being developed. The argument developed in this chapter is the product of a structural analysis based on 12 years of research on Western donor interventions in the OPT plus semi-focused interviews conducted with senior aid coordination officials from the main multilateral and Western donor agencies operating in the OPT. All interviews were conducted "Chatham House Rules" with reference made to those interviewed as being "senior Western aid officials" in order to protect anonymity. This is because of the nature of the topic and the desire to receive an honest opinion from the respondents. Indeed, nearly all respondents admitted they would not have agreed to be interviewed otherwise, or could only have parroted the official line of their governments. The interviews probed the policies that Western and multilateral aid agencies have followed since the DOP, the guiding rationale for them, and their attitude toward the Oslo peace paradigm and the two-state solution particularly as it pertains to the continuation of their involvement through aid support. The interviews neatly intersect with the structural analysis in that they confirm Western donor focus on stabilization, that their involvement and mandate is tied to the implementation of "Plan A," and that there are huge obstacles to them talking about (let alone developing) an official alternative plan due to the politics tied up with the DOP and the two-state solution.

In order to develop these arguments, the chapter is split into three sections. The first section focuses on how to understand the key Western aid actors and their strategies, including their stated policy aims and objectives. The second section analyzes what I consider to be the most important impacts of 25 years of Western donor activities in the OPT. Section three then looks at what donors think of the Oslo peace paradigm and the two-state solution nearly 20 years after the interim period was supposed to end (in 1999). The chapter concludes that, despite senior Western aid officials being acutely aware of the problems with the Oslo peace paradigm and the potential for a Palestinian state, their governments and agencies remain committed to it; that any policy changes implemented have been in an attempt to save this framework; and that even when the peace process appears to be dead, it is necessary to continue with "Plan A" and the façade that it is leading somewhere because it cannot be acknowledged to have failed. However, in the absence of final status negotiations and Palestinian sovereign statehood, donor support for the two-state solution in practical terms has morphed into support for the DOP and the Oslo framework. Western donors and multilaterals have therefore assisted in creating a colonial peace by supporting the persistence of a peace accord and framework that has allowed Israel to control Palestinians while continuing to grab land and expand settlements.

FUNDING THE OSLO FRAMEWORK: WESTERN PEACEBUILDING STRATEGIES AND ACTORS

While there are, of course, differences between the various actors, the long-term stated objective of Western aid interventions in the OPT has been to support and underpin the Oslo peace paradigm and framework, which was the practical outcome of the peace agreements signed between Israel and the PLO beginning with the DOP in 1993. This framework, which was supposed to last only until 1999, was based on resolving the issue of the status of the territories occupied after 1967. These agreements committed Israel and the PLO to track-one bilateral negotiations toward a resolution of the conflict (overseen by the US), the creation of a form of partial self-government for the Palestinian people (the Palestinian Authority), an economic customs union (through the Paris Protocol), and a phased withdrawal of Israel's occupation forces that justified a "zoning" of the OPT into Areas A, B, and C (each with different modalities of governance). Israel retained control over 70 percent of the West Bank as well as over all the borders including entry and exit points, and control over land and other natural resources. The Palestinian Authority was established as an interim administration, with tight restrictions on its powers, but with governance functions over small pockets of territory that were not contiguous. Access to and from these Palestinian high-density population areas in the West Bank remain under Israeli military control through the use of internal "borders" created and policed by checkpoints and roadblocks.[5]

The 1994 Paris Protocol on Economic Relations is the framework that governs economic relations between the Palestinian Authority and Israel through a joint customs union and a tax transfer scheme where Israel collects and passes to the Palestinian Authority the taxes and custom duties on Palestinian imports from or via Israel, and income tax from Palestinian workers in Israel (see the chapter by Raja Khalidi in this book).[6] Despite it being almost 20 years since the original cut-off interim date of 1999, this framework remains in place.

But Israel and the PLO/Palestinian Authority are not the only actors in this process. Into the context and framework provided by the DOP, around 40 donor countries and dozens of UN and other multilateral agencies have provided aid and "experts" to the OPT.[7] This has taken the form of two kinds of aid: the first is for humanitarian activities (which includes emergency response, reconstruction, relief and rehabilitation, and disaster prevention and preparedness), the second is for peacebuilding (which includes the wider governance and development aspects that are supposed to follow directly on from reconstruction in the relief to development continuum, i.e., building infrastructure and services, government and civil society assistance, as well as private sector development). This chapter focuses on peacebuilding aid and activities as it is these that have attempted to mold circumstances rather than merely respond to them.

Some activities that have been undertaken under the peacebuilding rubric have a long pedigree—particularly propping up preferred elites, using aid to promote a particular type of development trajectory, and training militaries. But in the post-Cold War period, peacebuilding became a distinct policy field that adopted and adapted many conceptual assumptions and questionable theories from development studies, but with the addition of unique ingredients based on largely liberal understandings of what causes conflict and peace to make a particularly toxic recipe.[8] Indeed, as with other disciplines, academic studies in this area have been used *selectively* to underpin and justify decisions related to foreign assistance and peacebuilding that have less to do with the requirements of the aid-receivers and more to do with the objectives of the aid-givers.[9] From the late 1990s, "matrixes" and "toolkits" of the different tasks and their desired outcomes were created, with each multilateral agency, donor, and INGO promoting their own particular version. These "toolkits" promote a particular model of neoliberal capitalism and governance. Western peacebuilding is therefore not neutral nor as benign as it presents itself. As Woodward points out, it is a transformation agenda that builds "market economies and market-friendly states through domestic laws and procedural rules, technical assistance, and identification and support for 'reform leaders.'"[10] However, in addition, its purpose is also stabilization hence the large amount of aid assistance and donor focus on statebuilding and the security sector.[11] So while there is a lot of rhetoric and policy documents that state the importance of promoting democracy, human rights, and economic development, the most resilient parts of the peacebuilding matrix are those related to the pursuit of an aggressive economic liberalization agenda and governance strategies focused on enhancing instruments of state coercion.[12] This has become more pronounced in the post-9/11 world.

Donor policies and strategies in the OPT have been no different in this regard in that they have followed general peacebuilding principles as applied in other war-torn societies. However, they have developed in certain ways and with certain impacts—particularly because, as confirmed by a senior aid official, "it has always been a highly politicized development project."[13] Indeed, many involved in Western donor agencies in the OPT acknowledge that they are not "operating or implementing a development mandate."[14] This has led to some interesting twists and turns in donor policies and practices (unpacked in the following section), which would appear to be contradictory, but are not when viewed through a structural lens that regards them as the product of the underlying goal of stabilization. Many Western donors regard the OPT as a foreign policy priority—and this has underpinned their extensive involvement and large financial commitment since 1993.

Organizationally, Western donors and multilateral agencies created aid coordination structures to manage their involvement and interaction (see figure 10.1). This is standard practice in a situation with so many actors. One small glance at the aid governance graph shows the plethora of organizations involved and their slightly different priorities and foci; however, the main actors that have set the agenda and guided peacebuilding activities in the OPT are the UN, the World Bank, the EU, and the US—thus reflecting global structures of power as they manifest themselves in the region. One senior aid official thus summed it up: "Here we have big power politics at play. So we can't be surprised that politics plays a huge influence."[15] The US and the EU are the two biggest Western donors; and the UN and the World Bank are the two most important multilateral implementing agencies—a brief analysis of these actors is thus illustrative.

The UN has had the longest standing involvement, and has continually proposed and supported a two-state solution as codified in its 1947 Partition Plan for Palestine adopted through UN Resolution 181, and endorsed in sub-

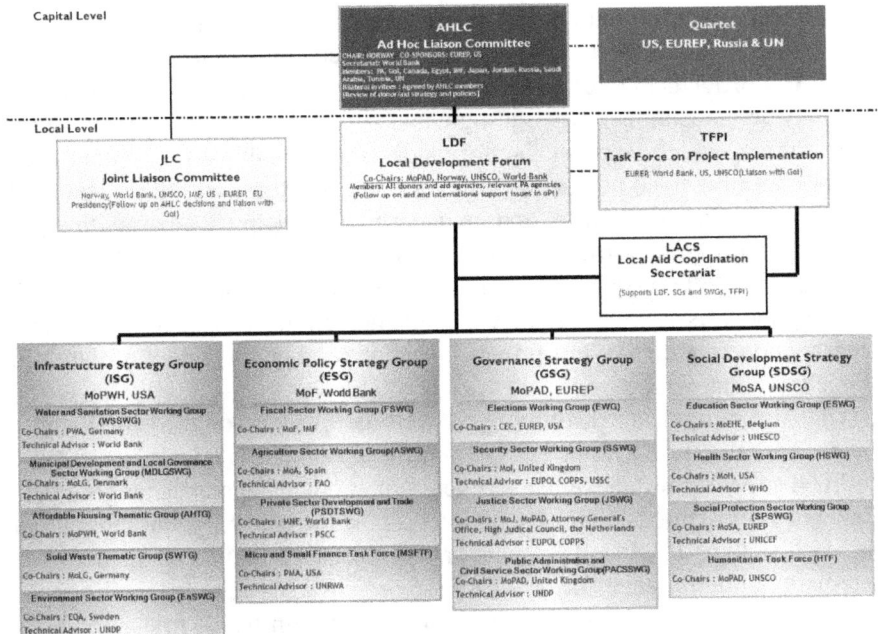

Figure 10.1. Aid Management Structure in State of Palestine
Source: Local Aid Coordination Secretariat (LACS) in Ramallah, Palestine

sequent resolutions, particularly UN Resolution 242. The UN was also one of the first actors involved in providing humanitarian and development support, initially and continually through the United Nations Relief and Works Agency for Palestinian Refugees in the Near East (UNRWA), which was created in 1949 to provide assistance to the refugees created by the Nakba and the establishment of the State of Israel. Then in 1978, the United Nations Development Programme–Programme of Assistance to the Palestinian People (UNDP-PAPP) was established to improve the economic and social conditions of Palestinians resident in the OPT.[16] After 1993, there was a huge expansion of UN agencies—to over 20—operating in the OPT; these are overseen by the UN Special Coordinator Office for the Middle East Peace Process (UNSCO), which was established in the aftermath of the DOP to enhance the involvement of the UN during the interim period.[17] And yet despite its leading role as an aid provider and coordinator of extensive peacebuilding and humanitarian activities in the OPT, as well as its leading role in brokering peace deals worldwide, the UN does not have a diplomatic role. Israel has continually resisted a greater role for the UN in the peace negotiations, as it regards the UN to be biased against it. Indeed, Israel's fraught relations with the UN but its close relations with the US have created a difficult operating environment for UN agencies—and this has been continually highlighted by senior UN officials in interviews I have conducted over a 12-year period, i.e., that they are constantly in the spotlight and subjected to microscopic enquiry and critique, which imposes caution and self-censorship to an extent seen in very few other contexts. Nevertheless, despite these problems, the UN endorses the Oslo framework and its underlying principles, albeit with some of its agencies being critical of its restrictions; this gives "Plan A" credence and legitimacy. The creation of the Quartet (which includes the UN, the EU, the US, and Russia), to oversee the implementation of the 2003 Roadmap, merely added another layer of donor oversight and endorsement of the Oslo framework and assumptions.

The EU, through its institutions as well as through some of its member states, has also had a long engagement. The Venice Declaration of 1980 codified support for Palestinian self-determination and against changes in the status of Jerusalem, as well as signaled support for the PLO; and throughout the 1980s, the EU (and its precursor, the EEC) continually called for an international conference for Middle East peace.[18] But neither Israel nor the US wanted the European community to play a significant role during the 1991 Madrid Conference or subsequently.[19] The EU has therefore largely been sidelined in the diplomatic arena. However, its mission to the OPT has grown exponentially due to the huge volume of aid disbursed and number of technical experts dispatched since 1993. The European Commission has consistently been the largest donor to the OPT; total EC commitments from 1994 until the end of 2017 exceeded 7.1 billion Euros (US$8.12 billion), and continued at a rate of around 300 million Euros per year from 2014 to 2017 (see figure 10.2). A significant number of European governments also have a substantial bilateral commitment. There are, of course, differences between the European donors. The UK and Germany, for instance, are regarded as "pro-Israel," while others are regarded as being more critical of Israel. These distinctions are rooted in divergent opinions and interests, as well as historical connections. Initially, the majority of EU aid was channeled into construction, infrastructure, and natural resource management. But in the post-Second Intifada period, this shifted toward high levels of budget support to the Palestinian Authority.[20] The EU has continually supported the Palestinian Authority, particularly in times of crisis, or more accurately a Palestinian Authority that supports the Oslo process and parameters. In 2006, for instance, the EU diverted aid via a "Temporary International Mechanism" (TIM) that was created to bypass the Hamas government that had been elected on an anti-DOP platform, and give support directly to the office of the president under the control of Mahmoud Abbas. While this was touted as a "humanitarian"

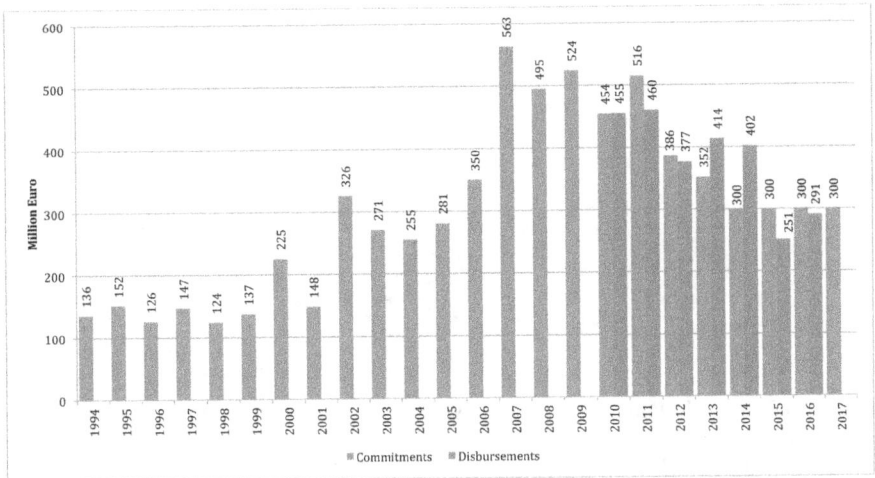

Figure 10.2. Financial Commmitments of EC to Palestine, 1994–2017
Total Commitments: 7.168 Billion Euro
*Disbursements only available from 2010–2017: 2.65 Billion Euro
Source: https://ec.europa.eu/neighbourhood-enlargement/neighbourhood/countries/palestine_en; constructed by Dana Erekat

measure at the time, it was clearly a deeply political act designed to support Palestinian political elites preferred by the Western donors and Israel, and it contravened the "good governance" measures the EU had promoted only a few years before. The TIM changed its name to PEGASE in 2008 and, as with many so-called "temporary measures" introduced to the OPT, it became the EU's permanent system of direct financial assistance to the Palestinian Authority.[21] For both the EU and for many EU member states, a resolution to the conflict is a foreign policy priority and so financial and technical assistance has been extensive and continuous.

Another key actor is the World Bank. Its 1993 study *Developing the Occupied Territories: An Investment in Peace* formed the basis for the first donor pledging conference and the initial aid framework for the OPT; it administers multi-donor trust funds; it is the leading multilateral actor in donor coordination; and its reports and policy recommendations shape the aid agenda.[22] It is estimated that between 1993 and 2018 the World Bank disbursed nearly US$3.8 billion (see figure 10.3).[23] The World Bank also plays an influential role in the development of the Palestinian Authority's economic and policy strategies.[24] Indeed, the Palestinian Authority's first minister of planning, Nabil Sha'ath, stated: "Palestine, in the peace process, was economically somehow given to the World Bank."[25] This relationship helped institute a two-way process of the World Bank coaxing the Palestinian Authority

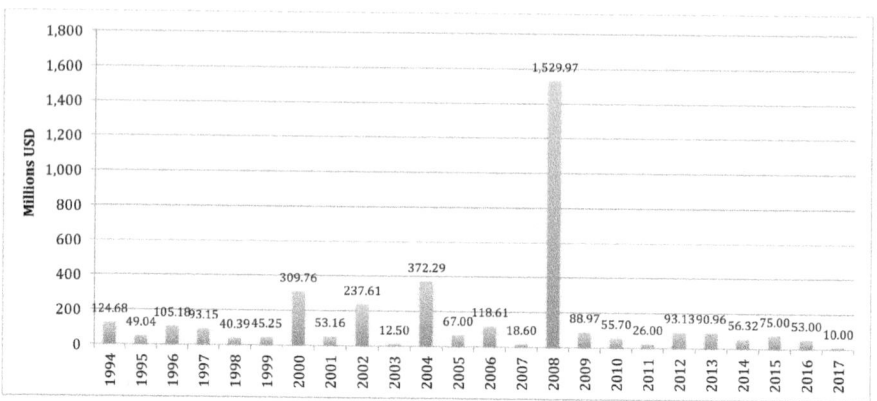

Figure 10.3. World Bank Funding to West Bank and Gaza, 1994–2017 (includes other donors support)
Total: 3.726 Billion USD
Source: The World Bank; constructed by Dana Erekat

to accept certain policies, and Palestinian political elites internalizing and promoting the dominant development fashions.[26] But while the World Bank normally promotes policies for private-sector-led growth, it acknowledged that in the case of the OPT the public sector had to take a leading role: first, due to the dire state of the economy and infrastructure after 26 years of occupation; second, because of the problem of encouraging private investment in such a situation; and third, because of the lack of an "enabling environment" or policy framework.[27] This meant that budget support to the Palestinian Authority and the building up of its institutions was of immense importance. And so the stringent types of aid conditionalities imposed in other developing or conflict contexts (as well as measures of "aid effectiveness") were not applied to the OPT because the main goal of aid was to underpin the DOP and the Oslo framework and so the strategy that was developed focused on promoting political and economic stability in the OPT.[28] The World Bank has played a key role in the OPT that has exceeded its involvement in other war-torn contexts; indeed, many innovations were made to allow its involvement in the OPT that were thereafter introduced elsewhere, such as the creation of multi-donor trust funds.

The most important third party actor is obviously the US. It plays a dominant role as the overseer of the bilateral negotiations, and as the supervisor and guarantor of security coordination between Israel and the Palestinian Authority. It regards Israel to be a very close ally, and thus bestows seemingly unconditional support on it, i.e., close military relations (which includes billions of dollars per year in military aid with special spending arrangements, joint military exercises and training, and cooperation on military technology), as well as diplomatic and political support.[29] Because of this, the role of the US as an "honest broker" has been questioned.[30] However, it also gives significant amounts of aid to the OPT, particularly after the beginning of the Second Intifada, and which reached new heights after the administrative split between the West Bank and Gaza in 2007. The total aid committed from 1993 to 2018 by the US government is approximately $7.75 billion, making it the largest bilateral donor to the Palestinian people (see figure 10.4); it has also been the largest donor to UNRWA, contributing over $364 million in 2017 alone, although this was cut in 2018.[31] In all US congressional reports on US aid to the OPT, it is stated that aid is intended to promote three US priorities: the first is to prevent attacks on Israel, the second is to foster "stability, prosperity, and self-governance that may incline Palestinians toward peaceful coexistence with Israel and a 'two-state solution'" (although support for a two-state solution only became official US policy in 2002); and the third is to "maintain humanitarian needs."[32] Toward this end, aid is channelled through three funding routes—through the Economic Support Fund (for development, governance, and civil society), through the International Narcotics Control and Law Enforcement Fund (for the training and advising of the Palestinian

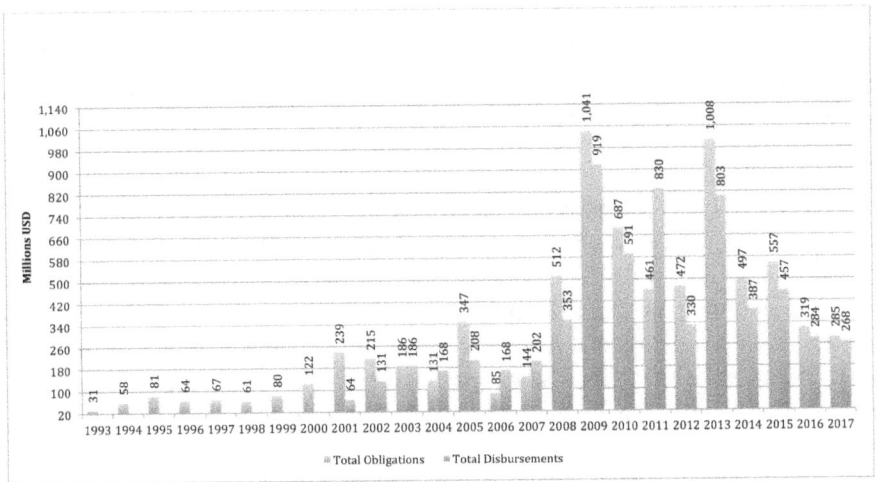

Figure 10.4. US Support to Palestine, 1993–2017
Total Obligations: 7.75 Billion USD

*Disbursements only available from 2001–2017. Total: 6.349 Billion USD
Source: https://explorer.usaid.gov/cd/PSE?fiscal_year=2017&implementing_agency_id=1&measure= Disbursements; constructed by Dana Erekat

security forces through the United States Security Coordinator program), and through the Migration and Refugee Funds (for UNRWA).[33] There is a continual vetting and freezing out of Palestinians that do not agree with the DOP and the Roadmap, which was enhanced by the "Anti-Terrorism Certificate" introduced in 2002 that requires all USAID implementing partners to sign. Critics argue that this has turned implementing partners (including international and Palestinian NGOs) into surveillance agencies as they are required to gather information for USAID in order to ensure compliance, which then shares this information with the Israeli military authorities, i.e., the Coordinator of Government Activities in the Territories (COGAT).[34] Aid to the OPT is *the* most rigorously vetted USAID program worldwide,[35] and funds have been occasionally withheld as part of the US's "carrot and stick" approach to the Palestinian Authority.[36] The US also has laws to restrict funding to any UN agency that allows Palestine to become a member; indeed in 2017 the US withdrew its membership and funding from UNESCO for this reason. However, despite the US's partisan practices, it is unlikely that a settlement will be reached without its involvement.[37]

The heterogeneity of donor agendas and priorities (with some focusing on governance and security, others focusing on civil society and municipalities, and others on health and social services), plus the amount of money pouring in, fuels competition. As one senior Western aid official stated: "There is an oversupply of donors which makes it a 'beauty contest' where there is too much aid offered."[38] While it is important to remember the fact that donors compete and have different agendas, the following section highlights the general goals and impacts of Western aid in the OPT.

SECURING AND STABILIZING: THE POLITICAL ECONOMY OF WESTERN DONOR AID IN THE OPT

The peacebuilding and statebuilding activities funded and implemented by the donors are heavily circumscribed and structured by the geographic, economic, and governance limitations imposed by the Oslo framework. The lack of control that Palestinians have over their resources (both natural and human), creates the necessity for large and continuing amounts of aid. In the context of the Oslo framework and restrictions, and the overarching focus on security and stabilization, Western donor policies have manifested themselves in particular ways and with certain impacts. There have been some changes in focus in the past 25 years—with the Interim period (1994–1999) emphasizing infrastructure building; the Roadmap period (2003–2006) focusing on governance reforms; and the West Bank First period (2007–present day) underpinning statebuilding. Nevertheless, the underlying strategies have remained the same: supporting "partners for peace," infrastructure and private sector development, and security sector enhancement and coordination. This section will briefly outline the rationale and impacts of each of these strategies.

International donors have a huge influence on Palestinian politics in the OPT through what I have labelled the "partners for peace" discursive framework (because of the constant use of this phrase).[39] While it is common practice in peace processes to use aid to prop up "preferred partners," the preferred Palestinian "partners for peace" are those with which Israel will negotiate and who are acceptable to important donors. The "partners for peace" discursive framework has provided the ideological rationale and basis for the convergence of strategies between Israel and the donors, and is used to control and manipulate Palestinian political elites. At its most extreme, it has been used to justify the removal (or downgrading) of particular political leaders and parties in a more subtle (and less visible) form of intervention than a coup or a military operation. A less extreme, but more frequently used (and effective) mechanism is when Israel uses the phrase to refuse to cooperate with the Palestinian Authority or certain Palestinian political elites, and to justify blocking/stalling/delaying the transfer of revenue it collects on behalf of the Palestinian Authority and codified through the Paris Protocol. The most obvious example of how this discursive framework has been used to promote regime change is after the election of Hamas in 2006 on an anti-DOP platform.[40] Arguing that it had a popular mandate from the Palestinian people, Hamas refused to adhere to the "Quartet Principles" (that a Palestinian state must: (1) recognize the state of Israel, (2) abide by previous diplomatic agreements, and (3) renounce violence as a means of achieving goals); it was thereafter boycotted by the main Western donors and Israel. This created the conditions for Hamas to be forced out of office and eventually restricted to the Gaza Strip. Western donor aid restrictions on Hamas continue to apply thereby ensuring that political reconciliation between Fatah and Hamas and thus the administrative reconciliation of the West Bank and Gaza Strip is extremely difficult if not impossible, as a unity government that includes any Hamas members or results from an agreement with Hamas would again trigger sanctions.[41] This means that Western donors have endorsed the lack of elections, or at least remained silent, due to the fear of another Hamas electoral victory. While many senior aid officials acknowledge the problems with this strategy, it is, according to them, Hamas's opposition to the Oslo framework that drives their policy of exclusion.

There are numerous other less malignant but nevertheless still significant examples where the "partners for peace" discursive framework has been used to control and cajole Palestinian political elites to take certain decisions and act in particular ways that are not always the best ones for their local legitimacy or indeed their struggle for statehood. For instance, in October 2009, UN secretary-general Ban Ki-moon called Palestinian Authority president Mahmoud Abbas a "credible partner for peace."[42] This praise came after Abbas, under heavy US pressure, had withdrawn Palestinian Authority support for a resolution that called on the UN Human Rights Council to adopt the Goldstone Report into war crimes committed by Israel and Hamas in the 2008–2009 Israeli war on Gaza. But while Abbas enjoyed praise abroad from the US and UN, at home the response was different: there were demonstrations against the decision, posters of Abbas's face with the word "traitor" emblazoned across it appeared on walls across the OPT, Palestinian NGOs were vocal in their criticisms, and Palestinian Authority ministers and ambassadors resigned in protest.[43] Thus a phrase that appears incredibly benign can, in its operation, be disturbingly malignant in its impact—at least for Palestinians. While Palestinian political elites have also attempted to use the "partners for peace" discursive framework to criticize the Israeli leadership, they are unable to impose any political consequences as they lack the power to do so.

In terms of economic development, in the initial period after the DOP, resources focused on building infrastructure, because after 26 years of military occupation the OPT had a de-developed economic infrastructure and industrial base due to low levels of investment, as well as decades of Israeli policies designed to ensure a captive market in the OPT for Israeli goods and deny any economic basis for Palestinian self-determination. Until relatively recently, most Western donor aid and activities were largely focused on Areas A and B, where the PA is allowed to provide services (although not security in Area B), and not in Area C. This created pockets of prosperity that some writers have referred to as "bubbles."[44] In the areas excluded from the Oslo aid framework, i.e., Area C, Palestinians struggle to make a living and remain there. It was only after 2012 that the donors recognized this as constituting a problem for the two-state solution because of the centrality of Area C to Palestinian statehood; attempts were made thereafter to help Palestinian communities in Area C (but with only small-scale projects). This strategy comes with substantial risks: permits for any buildings or construction must be applied for from the Coordinator of Government Activities in the Territories (COGAT), and these are virtually impossible to obtain for Palestinian communities.[45] While some donors only fund projects with COGAT permits, some support small-scale projects without permits.[46] However, many of these projects, usually buildings, have been demolished by Israel, as recorded by the UN Office for the Coordination of Humanitarian Affairs in the OPT (UNOCHA OPT).[47]

The possibility of building productive capacity in the OPT is circumscribed, because it is restricted by the Oslo framework. As expressed by one senior Western aid official: "Perhaps we have reached the limits with what we can do with the development framework."[48] Indeed, one donor project to build an agro-industrial park in Jericho took more than 10 years to gain permission from the Israeli authorities to build an access road that crosses Area C from the park to the King Hussein/Allenby Bridge to allow the export of goods to Jordan and beyond.[49] Lack of control over borders, and the internal checkpoints that were the product of the division of the OPT into Areas A, B, and C, increases the price of transport exponentially thereby adding costs that make Palestinian products uncompetitive. The service sector is one of the few areas of the OPT economy where you can see the most significant rates of growth (particularly telecommunications, IT, retail, real estate, and financial services). While the expansion of the service sector is a generic global development trend promoted by neoliberal economic models, it is particularly pronounced in the OPT. While the vast majority of the OPT economy is made up of small businesses (mostly family-run), there are other highly profitable sectors dominated by business groups and business elites are intricately intertwined with the political elite who are rewarded through privileged access and monopolies. This particular form of "crony capitalism" was consciously developed as part and parcel of the political allegiances and economic alliances that underpin the structures created by the Oslo process.[50] Public criticism from Western donors over corruption, monopolies, and cronyism, which dominated the Roadmap period, have almost disappeared, although all of these relationships and practices remain albeit in a different format, and concerns are still expressed in private. This is because, in the post-Fayyad era, Western donors are more concerned about the viability of the Oslo framework and the two-state solution—and thus propping up the Palestinian Authority and ensuing stability is the primary focus. As explained by one senior Western aid official: "People are focused on the political. They are more interested in how this affects the peace process. It has not been balanced out with a focus on the nuts and bolts of development questions of accountability and transparency."[51]

The third pillar of Western peacebuilding strategies—particularly supported by the US and the EU—has been to create a Palestinian security force and so the Palestinian security sector has continually annually received around US$1bn of the Palestinian Authority's budget (around 30 percent of all international aid).[52] While reform or construction of the security sector is central to most donor peacebuilding and statebuilding programs, the specific environment of dependency, occupation, and colonization that exists in the OPT has meant that the role of the Palestinian security forces has been to protect the Palestinian Authority and its elites, and to prevent unrest against the Israeli army and Israeli settlers—the latter of whom has more than doubled in numbers in the past 25 years to nearly 600,000 in the OPT.[53] The main function of the Palestinian Authority security forces is not to protect the

Palestinian population against external threats (which come from the Israeli military and settlers) but to ensure stability and repress dissent.[54] This was written into the peace agreements; for instance, the 1998 Wye River Memorandum equated all forms of resistance with terrorism.[55] Arafat was initially given a free rein to create his own security forces, the numbers and units of which proliferated vastly.[56] While the CIA was heavily involved in this initial period, the US in general played a much bigger role in the supervision of the Palestinian Authority security forces after the Second Intifada was crushed. Indeed, EU and US funding and involvement was essential to rebuild the security forces after Israel's 2002 military campaign "Operation Defensive Shield" during which the Israeli army destroyed most of the Palestinian Authority's security infrastructure. After 2005, a US team (the Office of the US Security Coordinator, or USSC) led the rebuilding and restructuring of the Palestinian security forces, while the EU led on the reform of the civil police (through the EU Coordinating Office for Palestinian Police Support, known by its acronym EUPOL COPPS). Both of these missions are conducted within strict limits set by Israel.

The EU-funded and staffed EUPOL COPPS mission has provided assistance for building a security infrastructure of prisons, police stations, and training colleges, as well as justice reform including the drafting of criminal justice legislation.[57] Its budget doubled from 6.1 million Euros in 2007 to 12.372 million in the period July 2016 to June 2018; and since 2012 it has employed around 70 international staff and around 45 national staff, most of whom are based at its HQ in Ramallah.[58] Simultaneously, the USSC has focused on rebuilding a Palestinian security force loyal to President Mahmoud Abbas (including training, equipping, and advising nine special battalions and two presidential guard battalions), and coordinating and overseeing security arrangements between Israel and the Palestinian Authority.[59] Initially referred to as "the Dayton Mission" (after the first USSC chief, Lt. General Keith Dayton), its HQ is in the US Consulate in West Jerusalem and its staff are mostly American and Canadian (but with some British and Turkish) military officers.[60] Both Israel and the US have stated frequently that the security coordination that has developed since 2005 with the Palestinian security forces has been, for them, the most important component of the current framework.[61] As revealed by "The Palestine Papers," published by the news agency *Al-Jazeera*,[62] Palestinian security forces are primarily targeting opponents of the DOP and Oslo framework, particularly Hamas (but also other groups such as the Popular Front for the Liberation of Palestine and Islamic Jihad), which has had thousands of its members arrested and many jailed or killed.[63] Under conditions of Israel's occupation and colonization practices, and in a context where the Palestinians lack democratic governance and thus no civilian oversight of the security sector, some critics charge that the conditions have been created for authoritarianism and a police state.[64] It is difficult to avoid this conclusion given that by 2016, it was estimated that there were 83,276 Palestinian security sector personnel, of which 65,463 receive a salary from the Palestinian Authority (the rest, based in Gaza, receive their salary from Hamas).[65] This is a huge number given that there is an estimated Palestinian population in the OPT of only 4.45 million.[66]

In this context, the political economy that has emerged in the West Bank is that of a neopatrimonial governance structure (a non-sovereign "quasi-state") that uses violence and nepotism to suppress or buy-off opposition, a business class that is in a co-dependent relation with the Palestinian Authority in order to access resources and markets (through trading monopolies, aid, and export permits), a civil environment that has been depoliticized through aid dependency, and a highly policed society where dissent is not tolerated. Some senior aid officials interviewed for this chapter were fully aware that their policies and strategies are supporting one party (Fatah) to dominate the Palestinian political arena unchecked and unchallenged. Indeed, one stated, "If you ask: what are we building here? A dictatorial system."[67] Mostly all senior aid officials interviewed were remarkably candid in their acknowledgment that the main reason for them being in the OPT and the underlying rationale for their programming was stabilization. "Our strategy is to keep on supporting the Palestinian Authority and stabilizing and maintaining the situation," confirmed one senior aid official.[68] This is in a context where leading aid officials also acknowledge that the two-state solution could be beyond repair or achievement. "We are aware and fighting the fact that things are eroding and getting worse. But we do not want to reach the conclusion that a Palestinian state is not possible anymore," admitted another official.[69] Normal donor practice in other situations would necessitate the creation of a "Plan B" or at least discussion of an alternative plan for future strategies; the following final section thus explores this issue.

SHORING UP "PLAN A"

The absence of a peace process, constant epitaphs being written on the death of the two-state solution, and statements from Israeli politicians (including one in February 2017 from Israeli prime minister Benjamin Netanyahu) that Israel will only grant Palestinians a limited form of sovereignty (a "state minus")[70] all indicate the failure (or at the very least a stasis) of "Plan A." So where and what is "Plan B'; where are the alternative strategies and plans that are made in all other aid contexts? Responses to this question from senior western aid officials fell into three categories. The first group argued that there was little point in broaching the subject of an alternative "Plan B" due to the foreign policies of their countries. The second group revealed they had tried to discuss a "Plan B" but there was opposition from their foreign ministries back home. As one senior aid official confirmed: "I ask the minister about Plan B; he says there is no Plan B. But it does exist, it comes from us here."[71] This sentiment also crosses the third set of responses, i.e., that a potential "Plan B" had been discussed at the local (Ramallah/East Jerusalem) level but not further. As disclosed by one senior Western aid official: "The Consulate ensured that we were given a mandate that was sufficiently open and flexible to design a Plan B if it is needed."[72] In a typical example of fudging the issue, many senior Western aid officials revealed that while their HQs would not consider a "Plan B," they had been given permission to be "inventive," i.e., to introduce policies that would shore up "Plan A" and prevent the situation from deteriorating further. "Here, me and my project leader discuss and reflect on how we work in this reality, but this is not in the capital," said one senior official.[73] These responses reveal a disjuncture between those working on in-country missions and their HQs/governments. Although, of course, this is the case in most aid contexts, this is extremely pronounced in the situation of the OPT. One senior aid official summed this up: "Donors are questioning why they are here. They are talking to their HQs and asking to change the mandate and allow them to do development."[74] What was clear from all the interviews was that all Western donors remain fully committed to "Plan A," i.e., the two-state solution and the DOP. Any discussions that have taken place about potentially developing a "Plan B" have been about defending "Plan A" and shoring it up. As confirmed by one senior Western aid official: "The international community has invested billions in developing a Palestinian state, so they wouldn't allow it to collapse."[75] Thus, in pursuit of saving "Plan A," incremental changes in aid practices have taken place since 2015. Three main ones will be briefly explored here: working in Area C, expanding work in East Jerusalem, and supporting local municipalities.

By 2017, most donors reported doing aid work in Area C. This is a big change from recent years, despite there being no alterations in Area C's status or indeed in the abilities to undertake development work there unhindered. Before 2010, almost no Western donors were working in Area C.[76] The problems in Area C and the threat to the two-state solution if nothing is done have been continually identified in reports by the EU heads of mission since 2011.[77] Doing development work in Area C is regarded by many as a test of Western donor commitment because of the problems provoked by this strategy, including Israeli obstructions and the lack of building permits. Some donors have subsequently engaged in aid work in Area C without permits, arguing that international humanitarian law is guiding their activities not Israeli military law. For example, structures funded by Western donors and built for Bedouin communities near Ma'ale Adumim and E1 have been criticized by Israel and its supporters including accusations that they are illegal and should be demolished.[78] This has led to further confrontations between Israel and the EU, which has been the most active and has put its logos on some of the structures in the (largely mistaken) belief that this might protect them from demolition. The threat (and reality) of the destruction of donor-funded infrastructure means that aid here falls outside of the rubric of normal development work. As confirmed by one senior Western aid official, "It is not how we understand conventional development work. But it is important that we are involved in these areas even if what we do is destroyed."[79] Donors recognise that without Area C, particularly agriculturally rich areas in the Jordan Valley, the potential for a sustainable Palestinian state is limited and so most emphasized that "working in Area C is a strategic decision."[80] This change in donor strategy is driven by political calculations on what is required to shore up the two-state solution.

While Western donor activities in Area C are fairly recent, they have been present in East Jerusalem for longer through their support for Palestinian hospitals, schools, and civil society organizations. This aid has helped to shore up the Palestinian presence in East Jerusalem which would clearly have been in a much worse situation without their involvement.[81] Regular EU Heads of Mission reports on East Jerusalem, which have been produced since 2005, outline their main concerns regarding the negative trends taking place, particularly the economic, social, and political exclusion of Palestinians from the political economy of the city as a whole and the deterioration in the economy of East Jerusalem specifically. The 2012 EU Heads of Mission report thus recommended a "more active and visible implementation of EU policy on East Jerusalem" as pertains to ensuring that East Jerusalem remains "the future Palestinian capital."[82] One senior Western aid official insisted that they had been forced into this stance because: "East Jerusalem is declining rapidly and there is no coordinated action."[83] Western donor programs will therefore continue and probably even expand because the future status of East Jerusalem is clearly a crucial one. Israel insists that Jerusalem is its "undivided capital," and that it will never agree on its (re)division. The Palestinian leadership insists that East Jerusalem must be the capital of a Palestinian state. The international consensus is that the status of Jerusalem can only be decided by Israel and Palestine based on international law and appropriate UN resolutions. By implementing the US Embassy Act that recognized Jerusalem as the capital of Israel and facilitated the moving of the US Embassy from Tel Aviv to Jerusalem in May 2018, the US seriously challenged the status quo regarding the future of Jerusalem and violated international law. In response to this, the EU and the UN have intimated that they intend to continue to follow international law and the international consensus as relates to the status of Jerusalem, and thus will help shore up the Palestinian presence based on the belief that no Palestinian leadership will sign a peace deal that leaves out East Jerusalem as the capital of a Palestinian state.

Commitment to the Palestinian Authority remains resolute amongst Western donors (even amongst those that do not supply direct budget support). Nevertheless, there is acute awareness of the debates regarding the potential collapse or deliberate dissolution of the Palestinian Authority, and problems that would arise from this, as initially explored in the 2014 report "The Day After" published by the Palestine Center for Policy and Survey Research (which interviewed many donors and multilateral agencies).[84] This report identified the key challenges faced if the Palestinian Authority ceased to exist, and what donors would be required to do to ensure that social services continued to reach Palestinians in the OPT thereafter. However, as confirmed by one senior aid official: "If the Palestinian Authority collapsed I can't see the international community taking over the functions, and Israel neither."[85] This realization has fueled a shift, by some, toward supporting municipalities as well as expanding social work through civil society and NGOs. "We won't scale down, but it might be that we entirely shift our focus away from certain PA institutions toward more civil society institutions," confided one senior aid official.[86] Donor funding has thus nearly doubled to local municipalities from 51,457 Euros disbursed in 2008 (97,069 Euros pledged) to 93,148 Euros disbursed (145,847 Euros pledged) in 2016.[87] The Municipal Development and Lending Fund was established in 2005 to coordinate and channel funds between the donors, the Palestinian Authority, and local municipalities; there is no data prior to this. The setting up of this Fund was in itself a shift toward decentralization.

These new aid trends indicate that Western donors are focused on shoring up the DOP and the two-state solution by developing Area C and East Jerusalem, as well as supporting the Palestinian Authority and local municipalities.

All senior aid officials interviewed expressed the opinion that there were two main things blocking discussions of a "Plan B" (never mind the development of one): the most important one was the foreign policy of their countries (i.e., committed to "Plan A"—the two-state solution); but the other one was the fact that the Palestinian Authority leadership also had no "Plan B." Most were skeptical of the Palestinian Authority disbanding, as summarized by one senior aid official: "I see it as an empty threat, because there would be major economic consequences which will also affect people within the Palestinian Authority, including Abbas and his sons."[88] Many stated that they could not move beyond what was proposed by the Palestinian Authority leadership, despite any prognosis or change in policy they might propose to their capitals back home. Some pointed to the huge amount of pressure on the Palestinian leadership not to abandon the DOP, and not to embrace an approach based on civil rights or the principles of the Boycott, Divestment and Sanctions Movement (BDS), which is a global grassroots movement initiated by Palestinian civil society in 2005 campaigning for sanctions, divestment, and boycott of Israeli institutions based on the South African anti-apartheid campaign model. Many of the aid coordination officials interviewed for this chapter revealed that the Israeli-led campaign against the BDS Movement was creating pressures on their governments to impose a "no-BDS clause" on their aid funding and programs.[89] In late 2017, for instance, Denmark announced that it was introducing more oversight for its funding for Palestinian civil society groups because of this.[90] Given that Palestinian NGOs are highly dependent on Western aid, more and more will be forced to accept this clause or lose funding. This may well be one of the main reasons that the Palestinian Authority itself does not express support for BDS although it does support a boycott of Israeli settlement produce.[91] And it is this precarious balancing act that the Palestinian Authority is continually being forced to practice.[92] Quite aside from the fact that the current political elite might not agree with BDS, the Palestinian Authority is trapped in a corner: if it gives support to BDS it risks losing Western donor aid funding and support; and without donor funding and support, there is no more Palestinian Authority.

Aid has therefore deliberately been used to direct and control Palestinian politics, i.e., to bolster Palestinian political elites who support the DOP and the two-state solution, while isolating/removing those that do not. Donors have a lot of power to set the political agenda to which those across the political spectrum (from elites in the PA to civil society organizations) must adhere in order to continue to receive funding; those who do not are simply excluded.

Many senior Western aid officials interviewed for this chapter expressed the opinion that what their programs were doing is neither "traditional" development, nor is it sustainable, but that it was politically necessary for stabilization waiting on a political solution. As vocalized by one senior aid official: "People are fatigued and there is a sense of despair. This is just to keep the peace and to keep the status quo."[93] Most senior aid officials stated that their governments were committed to staying, and did not envisage a time when they might pull out, although a couple of those interviewed referred to the abandonment of the Quartet Principles or the end of security coordination by the Palestinian Authority as being potential triggers for their departure. While the Palestinian Authority/PLO has made some announcements regarding rescinding these measures, particularly in response to US president Trump's

Jerusalem announcement, they have yet to be taken. In this context, therefore, senior aid officials conclude that what is likely in the current circumstances is an eroding status quo (in development terms) and that aid had to be used to delay this. And yet the desire to stop the eroding developmental context does not extend beyond the incremental measures reviewed in this section, and certainly do not overshoot the framework and limitations set by the DOP. As revealed by one senior aid official: "We did a peace and conflict assessment. The advisers tried to talk about a Plan B, but the only consensus we could find was an eroding status quo. We are already starting to focus on social work and humanitarian work. This is not a Plan B but just what we do with the money."[94] Indeed, to have or admit to having a "Plan B" would be highly symbolic in that it would signal the abject failure to achieve the two-state solution.[95] And thus it is, at present, unlikely. UN secretary-general Antonio Guterres reconfirmed the dominant Western perspective in February 2018 by stating, "There is no Plan B. . . . A two-state solution is the only way to achieve the inalienable rights of the Palestinian people and secure a sustainable solution to the conflict."[96]

CONCLUSION: "THE PEACE PROCESS IS DEAD, LONG LIVE THE PEACE PROCESS"

Western donor and multilateral aid agencies have clearly played an important role in the political economy of the OPT in the past 25 years, and thus have also been an important part of the story from the Jordan River to the Mediterranean Sea. In recognition of this influence, this chapter set out to do three things. First, to chart the official rationale for the huge amounts of involvement and assistance of Western donors and multilateral agencies in the OPT. This was framed in terms of their commitment to "Plan A," i.e., the DOP and the two-state solution. Second, to draw out the main structural impacts of Western donor strategies in the governance, economy, and security realms. And third, to probe the future of Western donor and multilateral strategies in the OPT in the light of the increasing amounts of epitaphs on the death of the two-state solution, and particularly whether any were developing a "Plan B." It was concluded that they were not, and that "Plan A" was continually being adapted in order to shore it up under conditions that were ultimately destroying it. A clear message from the interviews conducted was that, despite glossy donor reports, all these senior Western aid officials recognized the stasis of the current situation and were cynical about the potential for "Plan A" to be implemented and achieved. And yet despite this recognition, or perhaps *because* of it, "Plan A" staggers on like a zombie that refuses to die while also ensuring that all alternatives are destroyed or neutralized, particularly those that are opposed by the US and Israel. Meanwhile, Israel has continued to expand its state and secure dominance over the land and resources of the OPT through colonization and counterinsurgency strategies, and blockading and regularly bombarding the Gaza Strip after its military disengagement and withdrawal of settlers in 2005.

Western donor aid priorities in the OPT in the past 25 years have not changed: the underlying rationale remains focused on supporting the DOP, stabilization, and underpinning the two-state solution. Because of this, it is difficult not to conclude, as Martin Indyk does in his cynical, yet revealing, reply to Mehdi Hassan which served as an epigraph to this chapter: "The peace process is dead; long live the peace process." In the absence of an alternative plan for how to reach the two-state solution, it only remains for the donors to continue to support the DOP and its framework. There is little to suggest that this will alter in the near future unless there is a drastic change in the political landscape.

ACKNOWLEDGMENTS

I would like to thank Dana Erekat for constructing the donor aid graphs for this chapter, and the Local Aid Coordination Secretariat in Ramallah for kindly allowing me to reproduce their aid coordination diagram. I would also like to thank Michael Pugh for comments made on an earlier version of this chapter. However, all opinions and mistakes are my responsibility.

NOTES

1. Al-Jazeera, "Should the US be Neutral on Israel-Palestine?," Mehdi Hassan interviews Martin Indyk, Head to Head, *al-Jazeera*, May 13, 2016.

2. It is hard to discern where the PLO ends and the PA begins in terms of international strategy and negotiations. The PLO remains the official negotiating partner as defined by the DOP, but there is so much overlap in terms of personnel and mandates that this chapter uses the PA/PLO in order to avoid confusion, but when it is one particular aspect of this combination this will be emphasized.

3. Anne Le More, *International Assistance to the Palestinians After Oslo: Political Guilt, Wasted Money* (Oxon: Routledge, 2008); Mushtaq H. Khan, George Giacaman and Inge Amundsen (eds.), *State Formation in Palestine: Viability and Governance During a Social Transformation* (Abingdon: Routledge Curzon, 2004); Sara Roy, *Failing Peace: Gaza and the Palestinian-Israeli Conflict* (London: Pluto Press, 2007); Sahar Taghdisi-Rad, *The Political Economy of Aid in Palestine: Relief from Development or Development Delayed?* (London: Routledge, 2011).

4. Interview with Dana Erekat, Head of Aid Management and Coordination Directorate and Special Adviser to the Minister, Ministry of Planning and Finance, Palestinian Authority, June 3, 2016, Ramallah, Palestine.

5. Neve Gordon, *Israel's Occupation* (Berkeley: University of California Press, 2007).

6. Hiba Husseini and Raja Khalidi, "Fixing the *Paris Protocol* Twenty Years Later: Frequently Asked Questions for Diehard Reformers," *Jadaliyya*, February 6, 2013.

7. Le More, *International Assistance*.

8. For an example of this, see the work of Paul Collier. For a critique of his work, see Astri Suhrke, Espen Villanger and Susan L. Woodward, "Economic Aid to Post-conflict Countries: A Methodological Critique of Collier and Hoeffler," *Conflict Security and Development* 5, no. 3 (2006): 329–361.

9. William Easterly, *The White Man's Burden: Why the West's Efforts to Aid the Rest Have Done So Much Ill and So Little Good* (New York: Penguin, 2006), 39–43.

10. Susan L. Woodward, "The Political Economy of Peacebuilding and International Aid," in *Routledge Handbook of Peacebuilding*, Roger Mac Ginty (ed.) (Abingdon: Routledge, 2013): 325–335, 332.

11. Woodward, "The Political Economy of Peacebuilding and International Aid," 325.

12. Michael Pugh, Neil Cooper and Mandy Turner (eds.), *Whose Peace: Critical Perspectives on the Political Economy of Peacebuilding* (Hampshire: Palgrave Macmillan, 2008).

13. Senior Western aid official, Interview C, December 15, 2014.

14. Senior Western aid official, Interview B, January 20, 2015.

15. Senior Western aid official, Interview G, December 3, 2014.

16. Raja Khalidi, "The United Nations, Palestine, Liberation, and Development," in *Land of Blue Helmets: The United Nations and the Arab World*, Karim Makdisi and Vijay Prashad (eds.) (Berkeley: University of California Press, 2017): 409–429.

17. Until 1999, it was called the Office of the Special Coordinator in the Occupied Territories.

18. Dimitris Bouris, *The European Union and the Occupied Palestinian Territories: Statebuilding Without a State* (New York: Routledge, 2013): 49–51.

19. Costanza Musu, *European Union Policy Toward the Arab-Israeli Peace Process: The Quicksands of Politics* (Hampshire: Palgrave Macmillan, 2010): 49–50.

20. Le More, *International Assistance*, 88–89.

21. European Court of Auditors, "European Union Direct Financial Support to the Palestinian Authority," Special Report No.14 (2013), Luxembourg.

22. Rex Brynen, "International Aid to the West Bank and Gaza: A Primer," *Journal of Palestine Studies* 25, no. 2 (1996): 46–53.

23. Dana Erekat, "Interview."

24. Mandy Turner, "Creating 'Partners for Peace': The Palestinian Authority and the International Statebuilding Agenda," *Journal of Intervention and Statebuilding* 4, no.1 (2011): 1–21.

25. Quote in Toufic Haddad, *Palestine Ltd: Neoliberalism and Nationalism in the Occupied Territory* (London: I. B. Tauris, 2016): 84.

26. Raja Khalidi and Sobhi Samour, "Neoliberalism and the Contradictions of the Palestinian Authority's Statebuilding Programme," in *Decolonizing Palestinian Political Economy: De-development and Beyond*, Mandy Turner and Omar Shweiki (eds.) (Hampshire: Palgrave Macmillan, 2014).

27. Haddad, *Palestine Ltd*, 65.

28. After the outbreak of the Second Intifada, donors started to attach conditionalities to their aid, leading the World Bank to establish a multi-donor trust fund with conditionalities in 2004. Le More, *International Assistance*, 147–148.

29. J.M. Sharp, "US Foreign Aid to Israel," CRS Report RL33222 (Washington, DC: Congressional Research Service, February 26, 2018). See also, John Mearscheimer and Stephen Walt, "The Israel Lobby," *London Review of Books* 28, no. 6 (2006); Ilan Pappe, "Clusters of History: US Involvement in the Palestine Question," *Race and Class* 48, no. 3 (2007): 1–28.

30. Rashid Khalidi, *Brokers of Deceit: How the US Has Undermined Peace in the Middle East* (Boston: Beacon Press, 2013); Mandy Turner and Mahmoud Muna, "The United States Recognition of Jerusalem as the Capital of Israel, and the Challenge to the International Consensus" (Middle East Research and Information Project, Washington, DC, May 16, 2018).

31. UNRWA, "Top 20 Donors 2017 Pledges to UNRWA, December 31, 2017," UNRWA.

32. Jim Zanotti, "US Foreign Aid to the Palestinians" (US Congressional Research Service, Washington, DC, December 16, 2016): 1. Although support for a "two-state solution" only became official US policy in 2002.

33. Zanotti, "US Foreign Aid to the Palestinians," 2016.

34. Lisa Bhungalia, "Managing Violence: Aid, Counterinsurgency, and the Humanitarian Present in Palestine," *Environment and Planning A* 47 (2015): 2308–2323, 2316.

35. Jim Zanotti, "US Foreign Aid to the Palestinians" (US Congressional Research Service, Washington, DC, August 12, 2010): 5.

36. Ha'aretz, "Report: US Blocks $200 Million in Aid to Palestinian Authority," *Haaretz*, October 1, 2011.

37. Eric Cortellessa, "Rebuffing Abbas Gambit, US Says Europe Knows It Can't Be Lead Peace Broker," *Times of Israel*, January 23, 2018; AFP and TOI Staff, "Jordan King Says No Israel-Palestinian Peace Without US Role," *Times of Israel*, February 4, 2018; David Rosenberg, "Netanyahu to Abbas: No Peace Talks Without the US," *Arutz Sheva: Israel National News*, January 21, 2018.

38. Senior Western aid official, Interview C, December 15, 2014.

39. Turner, "Creating 'Partners for Peace.'"

40. After the election, acting Israeli prime minister, Ehud Olmert, said: "A Hamas-led Palestinian Authority is not a partner," quoted in Aaron Pina, "Palestinian Elections" (US Congressional Research Service, Washington, DC, February 9, 2006): 11.

41. Zanotti, "US Foreign Aid to the Palestinians 2016," 7.

42. Tovah Lazaroff, "Ban Supports Abbas on Goldstone Report," *Jerusalem Post*, October 13, 2009, https://www.jpost.com/International/Ban-supports-Abbas-on-Goldstone-report.
43. Jack Khoury and Ari Issacharoff, "Abbas aide: Deferring Action On Goldstone Report Was a Mistake," *Ha'aretz*, October 7, 2010.
44. Kareem Rabie, "Ramallah's Bubbles," *Jadaliyya*, January 18, 2013.
45. UNOCHA, "Under Threat: Demolition Orders in Area C of the West Bank," *In the Spotlight* (East Jerusalem: UNOCHA OPT, September 2015).
46. Senior Western aid official, Interview B, January 20, 2015.
47. UNOCHA, "Record number of demolitions and displacements in the West Bank during 2016" (UNOCHA OPT, East Jerusalem, January 2017).
48. Senior Western aid official, Interview F, January 20, 2015.
49. Interviews with Mitsui San, director of JICA, October 19, 2016; and Ali Shaath, director of PIEFZA, October 25, 2016.
50. Tariq Dana, "The Palestinian Capitalists That Have Gone Too Far," *Alshabaka*, January 14, 2014.
51. Senior Western aid official, Interview G, December 3, 2014.
52. Alaa Tartir, "Criminalizing Resistance: The Cases of Balata and Jenin Refugee Camps," *Journal of Palestine Studies*, 46, no. 182 (2017).
53. Peter Beaumont, "Israel Announces 2,500 More West Bank Settlement Homes," *The Guardian*, January 24, 2017.
54. Yezid Sayigh, "'Fixing Broken Windows': Security Sector Reform in Palestine, Lebanon and Yemen" (Washington, DC: Carnegie Endowment for International Peace, October 2009).
55. Naseer Aruri, "The Wye Memorandum: Netanyahu's Oslo and Unreciprocal Reciprocity," *Journal of Palestine Studies* 28, no.2 (1999): 136.
56. Sayigh, "Fixing Broken Windows."
57. Dimitris Bouris, *The European Union*, 108–114.
58. Bouris, *The European Union*, 110; EUPOLCOPPS, "Mission Facts and Figures," http://eupolcopps.eu/en/content/what-eupol-copps. Accessed 19 February 2017.
59. Melissa Boyle Mahle, "A Political-Security Analysis of the Failed Oslo Process," *Middle East Policy* 12, no.1 (2005): 79–96, 81.
60. Nathan Thrall. "Our Man in Palestine," *New York Review of Books*, October 14, 2010.
61. Zanotti, "US Foreign Aid to the Palestinians 2016," 16; Thrall, "Our Man in Palestine."
62. The "Palestine Papers" were the leak of 1,600 internal confidential documents from the Israel-Palestine negotiations from 1999–2010; they were published by *al-Jazeera*.
63. Mark Perry, "Dayon's Mission: A Reader's Guide," *The Palestine Papers*, January 25, 2011, *al-Jazeera*.
64. Sayigh, "Fixing Broken Windows"; Tzvi Ben Gedalyahu, "US Trained Armed Forces Turning PA into Police State," *Arutz Sheva* (Israel National News), November 23, 2011.

65. Tartir, "Criminalizing Resistance."
66. CIA Factbook, 2016.
67. Senior Western aid official, Interview C, December 15, 2014.
68. Senior Western aid official, Interview F, January 20, 2015.
69. Senior Western aid official, Interview J, December 4, 2014.
70. Reuters, "Netanyahu Opposes Palestinian State, Israeli Cabinet Minister Says," *Jerusalem Post*, February 13, 2017.
71. Senior Western aid official, Interview A, December 2, 2014.
72. Senior Western aid official, Interview A, December 2, 2014.
73. Senior Western aid official, Interview J, December 4, 2014.
74. Senior Western aid official, Interview B, January 20, 2015.
75. Senior Western aid official, Interview F, January 20, 2015.
76. Mandy Turner, "Challenges of Implementing the Statebuilding Programme," Presentation to the UN Seminar on Assistance to the Palestinian People, Helsinki, April 28–29, 2011; Senior Western aid official, Interview B, January 20, 2015.
77. EU Heads of Mission, "Report on East Jerusalem," 2011.
78. Herb Keinon, Tovah Lazaroff, "EU Building Hundreds of Illegal Structures for Palestinians in Area C of the West Bank," *Jerusalem Post*, May 2, 2015.
79. Senior Western aid official, Interview G, December 3, 2014.
80. Senior Western aid official, Interview E, November 28, 2014.
81. Michael Dumper, "Jerusalem Unbound: Geography, History and the Future of the Holy City," book launch and lecture, September 10, 2014, Kenyon Institute, East Jerusalem.
82. EU Heads of Mission, "Area C and Palestinian Statebuilding" (July 2012).
83. Senior Western aid official, Interview A, December 2, 2014.
84. Palestine Center for Policy and Survey Research, "The Likelihood, Consequences, and Policy Implications of PA Collapse or Dissolution" (Ramallah, February 4, 2014).
85. Senior Western aid official, Interview F, January 20, 2015.
86. Senior Western aid official, Interview F, January 20, 2015.
87. Municipal Development and Lending Fund Annual Reports, Compilation of figures from 2008 and 2016 reports (the first and last reports available at time of writing) (MDLF, Al-Bireh, Palestine).
88. Senior Western aid official, Interview F, January 20, 2015.
89. Senior Western aid official, Interview F, January 20, 2015.
90. Noa Landau, "Denmark Says It Will Tighten Conditions for Financial Aid to Palestinian NGOs," December 23, 2017, *Haaretz*.
91. Yoel Goldman, "Abbas: Don't boycott Israel," December 13, 2016, *Times of Israel*.
92. Interviews with senior Western aid officials, December 2014 to January 2015.
93. Senior Western aid official, Interview G, December 3, 2014.
94. Senior Western aid official, Interview J, December 4, 2014.
95. Thanks to Michael Pugh for this point.
96. AFP, "UN Chief Warns Consensus on Two-State Solution May Be Eroding," *Times of Israel*, February 6, 2018.

BIBLIOGRAPHY

AFP, "UN Chief Warns Consensus on Two-State Solution May Be Eroding," *Times of Israel*, February 6, 2018, https://www.timesofisrael.com/un-chief-warns-consensus-on-two-state-solution-may-be-eroding/.

AFP and TOI Staff, "Jordan King Says No Israel-Palestinian Peace without US Role," *Times of Israel*, February 4, 2018, https://www.timesofisrael.com/jordan-king-says-no-israeli-palestinian-peace-without-us-role/.

Aruri, Naseer. "The Wye Memorandum: Netanyahu's Oslo and Unreciprocal Reciprocity," *Journal of Palestine Studies* 28, no. 2 (1999).

Beaumont, Peter, "Israel Announces 2,500 More West Bank Settlement Homes," *The Guardian*, January 24, 2017, https://www.theguardian.com/world/2017/jan/24/israel-announces-2500-more-west-bank-settlement-homes.

Ben Gedalyahu, Tzvi. "US Trained Armed Forces Turning PA into Police State," *Arutz Sheva* (Israel National News), November 23, 2011, www.israelnationalnews.com/News/News.aspx/140787#.U6wqtbHvKSo).

Bhungalia, Lisa. "Managing Violence: Aid, Counterinsurgency, and the Humanitarian Present in Palestine," *Environment and Planning A* 47 (2005): 2308–2323, 2316.

Bouris, Dimitris. *The European Union and the Occupied Palestinian Territories: Statebuilding without a State* (Abingdon: Routledge, 2013).

Brynen, Rex. "International Aid to the West Bank and Gaza: A Primer," *Journal of Palestine Studies* 25, no. 2 (Winter, 1996): 46–53.

CIA Factbook, 2016, https://www.cia.gov/library/publications/the-world-factbook/geos/we.html.

Cortellessa, Eric. "Rebuffing Abbas Gambit, US Says Europe Knows it Can't Be Lead Peace Broker," *Times of Israel*, January 23, 2018, https://www.timesofisrael.com/rebuffing-abbas-us-says-europe-knows-it-cant-lead-peace-broker-role/.

Dana, Tariq. "The Palestinian Capitalists That Have Gone Too Far," *Alshabaka*, January 14, 2014, https://al-shabaka.org/briefs/palestinian-capitalists-have-gone-too-far/.

Dumper, Michael. "Jerusalem Unbound: Geography, History and the Future of the Holy City," book launch and lecture, September 10, 2014; Kenyon Institute, East Jerusalem.

Easterly, William, *The White Man's Burden: Why The West's Efforts to Aid the Rest Have Done So Much Ill and So Little Good* (New York: Penguin, 2006).

EUPOLCOPPS. "Mission Facts and Figures," http://eupolcopps.eu/en/content/what-eupol-copps. Accessed February 19, 2017.

European Court of Auditors, "European Union Direct Financial Support to the Palestinian Authority," Special Report No.14 (Luxembourg, 2013).

EU Heads of Mission, "Report on East Jerusalem 2011," http://www.thecepr.org/images/stories/pdf/eu%20homs%20jerusalem%202011.pdf.

———. "Area C and Palestinian Statebuilding," July 2012, http://www.thecepr.org/images/stories/pdf/area%20c%20%20final%20report%20july%202011.pdf.

Goldman, Yoel. "Abbas: Don't Boycott Israel," *Times of Israel*, December 13, 2016, http://www.timesofisrael.com/abbas-we-do-not-support-the-boycott-of-israel/.

Gordon, Neve. *Israel's Occupation* (Berkeley: University of California Press, 2007).

Ha'aretz, "Report: US Blocks $200 Million in Aid to Palestinian Authority," October 1, 2011, http://www.haaretz.com/israel-news/report-u-s-blocks-200-million-in-aid-to-palestinian-authority-1.387480.

Haddad, Toufic. *Palestine Ltd: Neoliberalism and Nationalism in the Occupied Territory* (London: I.B. Tauris, 2016).

Hassan, Mehdi, "Interviews Martin Indyk: Should the US Be Neutral on Israel-Palestine?," Head to Head, *al-Jazeera*, May 13, 2016, http://www.aljazeera.com/programmes/headtohead/2016/06/transcript-martin-indyk-israel-1606130824 08332.html.

Husseini, Hiba, and Raja Khalidi, "Fixing the *Paris Protocol* Twenty Years Later: Frequently Asked Questions for Diehard Reformers," *Jadaliyya*, February 6, 2013.

Keinon, Herb, and Tovah Lazaroff, "EU Building Hundreds of Illegal Structures for Palestinians in Area C of the West Bank," *Jerusalem Post*, May 2, 2015, http://www.jpost.com/Arab-Israeli-Conflict/Report-EU-building-hundreds-of-illegal-structures-for-Palestinians-in-Area-C-of-West-Bank-390184.

Khalidi, Raja. "The United Nations, Palestine, Liberation, and Development," in *Land of Blue Helmets: The United Nations and the Arab World*, Karim Makdisi and Vijay Prashad (eds.) (Berkeley: University of California Press, 2017): 409–429.

Khalidi, Raja, and Sobhi Samour, "Neoliberalism and the Contradictions of the Palestinian Authority's Statebuilding Programme," in *Decolonizing Palestinian Political Economy: De-development and Beyond*, Mandy Turner and Omar Shweiki (eds.) (Hampshire: Palgrave Macmillan, 2014).

Khalidi, Rashid. *Brokers of Deceit: How the US has Undermined Peace in the Middle East* (Boston: Beacon Press, 2013).

Khan, Mushtaq H., George Giacaman and Inge Amundsen (eds.). *State Formation in Palestine: Viability and Governance During a Social Transformation* (Abingdon: Routledge Curzon, 2004).

Khoury, Jack, and Ari Issacharoff, "Abbas Aide: Deferring Action on Goldstone Report Was a Mistake," *Ha'aretz*, October 7, 2010, http://www.haaretz.com/news/abbas-aide-deferring-action-on-goldstone-report-was-a-mistake-1.6532.

Landau, Noa. "Denmark Says It Will Tighten Conditions for Financial Aid to Palestinian NGOs," December 23, 2017, *Haaretz*, https://www.haaretz.com/middle-east-news/palestinians/.premium-denmark-says-will-tighten-conditions-for-finan cial-aid-to-palestinian-ngos-1.5629446.

Lazaroff, Tovah. "Ban Supports Abbas on Goldstone Report," *Jerusalem Post*, October 13, 2009, http://www.jpost.com/International/Ban-supports-Abbas-on-Goldstone-report.

Le More, Anne, *International Assistance to the Palestinians After Oslo: Political Guilt, Wasted Money* (Oxon: Routledge, 2008).

Mahle, Melissa Boyle. "A Political-Security Analysis of the Failed Oslo Process," *Middle East Policy* 12, no.1 (2005): 79–96.

Mearsheimer, John, and S. Walt, "The Israel Lobby," *London Review of Books* 28, no. 6, March 23, 2006.

Municipal Development and Lending Fund Annual Reports, Compilation of figures from 2008 and 2016 reports, MDLF, Al-Bireh, Palestine. http://www.mdlf.org.ps/Details.aspx?LangID=en&PageID=121.

Musu, Costanza. *European Union Policy Toward the Arab-Israeli Peace Process: The Quicksands of Politics* (Hampshire: Palgrave Macmillan, 2010).

Palestine Center for Policy and Survey Research, "The Likelihood, Consequences, and Policy Implications of PA Collapse or Dissolution," February 4, 2014, Ramallah, http://www.pcpsr.org/sites/default/files/finalreport.pdf.

Pappe, Ilan, "Clusters of History: US Involvement in the Palestine Question," *Race and Class* 48, no. 3 (2007): 1–28.

Perry, Mark. "Dayon's Mission: A Reader's Guide," *The Palestine Papers*, January 25, 2011, AlJazeera, http://www.aljazeera.com/palestinepapers/2011/01/2011125145732219555.html.

Pina, Aaron. "Palestinian Elections" (Washington, DC: US Congressional Research Service, February 9, 2006).

Pugh, Michael, Neil Cooper and Mandy Turner (eds.). *Whose Peace: Critical Perspectives on the Political Economy of Peacebuilding* (Hampshire: Palgrave Macmillan, 2008).

Rabie, Kareem. "Ramallah's Bubbles," *Jadaliyya*, January 18, 2013, http://www.jadaliyya.com/pages/index/9617/ramallah%E2%80%99s-bubbles.

Reuters, "Netanyahu Opposes Palestinian State, Israeli Cabinet Minister Says," *Jerusalem Post*, February 13, 2017, http://www.jpost.com/Israel-News/Netanyahu-opposes-Palestinian-state-Israeli-cabinet-member-says-481400.

Rosenberg, David. "Netanyahu to Abbas: No Peace Talks Without the US," *Arutz Sheva: Israel National News*, January 21, 2018, https://www.israelnationalnews.com/News/News.aspx/240980.

Roy, Sara. *Failing Peace: Gaza and the Palestinian-Israeli Conflict* (London: Pluto Press, 2007).

Sayigh, Yezid, "'Fixing Broken Windows': Security Sector Reform in Palestine, Lebanon and Yemen" (Washington, DC: Carnegie Endowment for International Peace, October 2009).

Sharp, J. M. "US Foreign Aid to Israel," Congressional Research Services Report RL33222 (Washington, DC: Congressional Research Service, 26 February 2018).

Suhrke, Astri, Espen Villanger and Susan L. Woodward, "Economic Aid to Post-conflict Countries: A Methodological Critique of Collier and Hoeffler," *Conflict Security and Development* 5, no. 3 (2006): 329–361.

Taghdisi-Rad, Sahar, *The Political Economy of Aid in Palestine: Relief from Development or Development Delayed?* (London: Routledge, 2011).

Tartir, Alaa. "Criminalizing Resistance: The Cases of Balata and Jenin Refugee Camps," *Journal of Palestine Studies* 46, no. 182 (2017).

Thrall, Nathan. "Our Man in Palestine," *New York Review of Books*, October 14, 2010, http://www.nybooks.com/articles/2010/10/14/our-man-palestine/.

Turner, Mandy. "Creating 'Partners for Peace': The Palestinian Authority and the International Statebuilding Agenda," *Journal of Intervention and Statebuilding* 4, no. 1 (2011): 1–21.

———. "Challenges of Implementing the Statebuilding Programme," Presentation to the UN Seminar on Assistance to the Palestinian People, Helsinki, April 28–29, 2011.

Turner, Mandy, and Mahmoud Muna, "The United States Recognition of Jerusalem as the Capital of Israel, and the Challenge to the International Consensus," May 16, 2018, *Middle East Research and Information Project*, https://www.merip.org/mero/mero051618.

UNOCHA, "Under Threat: Demolition Orders in Area C of the West Bank," *In the Spotlight* (East Jerusalem: UNOCHA OPT, September, 2015), https://docs.google.com/viewerng/viewer?url=https://www.ochaopt.org/sites/default/files/demolition_orders_in_area_c_of_the_west_bank_en.pdf&chrome=true.

———. "Record Number of Demolitions and Displacements in the West Bank During 2016" (East Jerusalem: UNOCHA OPT, January 2017), https://www.ochaopt.org/content/record-number-demolitions-and-displacements-west-bank-during-2016.

UNRWA, "Top 20 Donors 2017 Pledges to UNRWA, 31 December 2017," https://www.unrwa.org/sites/default/files/top_20_donors_overall_2017.pdf.

Woodward, Susan L, "The Political Economy of Peacebuilding and International Aid," *Routledge Handbook of Peacebuilding*, Roger Mac Ginty (ed.) (Abingdon: Routledge, 2013): 325–335.

Zanotti, Jim. "US Foreign Aid to the Palestinians" (Washington, DC: US Congressional Research Service, December 16, 2016).

———. "US Foreign Aid to the Palestinians" (Washington, DC: US Congressional Research Service, August 12, 2010).

INTERVIEWS (MOST ANONYMIZED)

Erekat, Dana. Head of Aid Management and Coordination Directorate and Special Adviser to the Minister, Ministry of Planning and Finance, Palestinian Authority, Interview, Ramallah, June 4, 2016.

Hulileh, Samir. Director of PADICO, Interview, Ramallah, November 5, 2016.

San, Mitsui, Director of Japan International Cooperation Agency (JICA), Interview, Ramallah, October 19, 2016.

Senior European diplomat, Interview H, Ramallah, January 21, 2015.
Senior Western aid official, Interview A, East Jerusalem, December 2, 2014.
Senior Western aid official, Interview B, East Jerusalem, January 20, 2015.
Senior Western aid official, Interview C, East Jerusalem, December 15, 2014.
Senior Western aid official, Interview D, East Jerusalem, December 3 2014.
Senior Western aid official, Interview E, East Jerusalem, November 28, 2014.
Senior Western aid official, Interview F, East Jerusalem, January 20, 2015.
Senior Western aid official, Interview G, Ramallah, December 3, 2014.
Senior Western aid official, Interview I, East Jerusalem, December 1, 2014.
Senior Western aid official, Interview J, East Jerusalem, December 4, 2014.
Senior Western aid official, Interview K, East Jerusalem, December 11, 2015.

Shaath, Ali. Director of Palestinian Industrial Estates and Free Trade Zones Authority (PIEFZA), Interview, Ramallah, October 25, 2016.

Chapter Eleven

The Single-State Solution

Vision, Obstacles, and Dilemmas of a Re-Emergent Alternative in Flux

Cherine Hussein

The single-state movement re-emerged in the aftermath of the Oslo Accords largely as an academic debate, based upon a critique of Zionism and the principle of separation upon which the paradigm of the accords themselves were based.[1] As such, it is a movement defined by the intellectuals powering it forward as a decolonizing, counterhegemonic struggle of resistance based upon the political desire to de-Zionize Palestine/Israel. This is rooted in the belief held by single state intellectuals that it is political Zionism that stands in the way of justice, equal citizenship, and the liberation of both peoples' common humanity from oppression. As such, the struggle for a single-state solution in Palestine/Israel represents not only a struggle of Palestinian resistance and liberation—which, of course, it primarily is—but one of Jewish-Israeli-liberation as well. For as Edward Said highlighted in 1999, if this more inclusive worldview is to emerge as an effective force, it is imperative that injustice is jointly countered by both Israelis and Palestinians who seek an alternative pathway to real self-determination for all.[2] Ilan Pappe stated some years later, "the very composition of this movement must be a model for the future."[3] In 2009, Omar Barghouti also argued that this movement would only be able to translate itself into a political force if it succeeded in fusing a unified vision with organized, grassroots action:

> Ethical decolonization, anchored in international law and universal human rights, is a profound transformation that requires above everything else a principled and popular Palestinian resistance movement with a clear vision for justice and a shared society, and an international movement supporting Palestinian rights and struggling to end all forms of Zionist apartheid and colonial rule.[4]

Indeed, Barghouti renamed the two-state solution (as it was conceived of in the Oslo Accords) as "the apartheid solution," and detailed Israel's as a "three-tiered" form of apartheid, consisting of:

> The occupation and colonization of the 1967 territory; the system of racial discrimination against Palestinian citizens of Israel, which is the Zionist form of apartheid; and the total denial of refugee rights, particularly the right to return home and to reparations.[5]

It follows from the above, then, that the reunification of the fragmented Palestinian national collective is a central driving force in the single-state movement's struggle against Oslo. For by centering the struggle against Zionism and its multiple forms of apartheid, the rights and aspirations of all three segments of the Palestinian people are taken into account, and the struggle for Palestinian liberation is realigned into one that is mutually inclusive, and more powerful. Moreover, the movement for a single democratic state in all of historic Palestine begins from the premise that the reality in which Palestinians and Jewish-Israelis live today is one of a de facto single apartheid state. Hence, both its vision and activism aim to erase the "green line," and to wage a struggle for equal citizenship for all of the inhabitants of historic Palestine that is relocated within the framework of international law in an effort to dismantle the Israeli state's form of Zionist apartheid in the name of a unitary democratic state for all.

In this chapter I begin by giving a brief snapshot of the recent re-emergence of the single-state solution as a potential political force, and of its alternative intellectual worldview against the Oslo Accords. Predominantly powered forward by the Palestinian Diaspora within the international arena today, it is this unified vision that holds the whole of the alternative together as a movement of resistance. Centering political Zionism and its processes of separation as the central obstacles to justice and equality in Palestine/Israel, in the second section I proceed to highlight the core elements of this worldview, and the strategies of resistance that emerged as channels through which to begin to transcend Zionism. In the final section of this chapter, I argue that in the single-state alternative's struggle to erase the "green line," and to wage a struggle for equal citizenship for all of the inhabitants of historic Palestine, the role of Palestinian-Israelis is central.[6] However, it is also within the dilemmas and divisions of this role that many of the obstacles facing the single-state alternative within the geography of Palestine/Israel itself can be seen. As such, in juxtaposing the voices of a selection of prominent Palestinian-Israeli intellectuals presently involved in the creation of a grassroots national movement for equal citizenship with those of others within the land of Palestine/Israel itself, I seek to underline the main obstacles and divisions the movement is currently facing across the fragmented geographies of the land. In doing so, I hope to be able to create space for strategies forward from within the terrains of the single-state alternative's present failure to transform its original potential into a coherent movement for social change within the geography of the contested land itself.

THE SINGLE-STATE SOLUTION: A SNAPSHOT OF A RE-EMERGENCE POWERED BY THE DIASPORA

In November 2007, the Annapolis Conference was applauded for creating history by being the first conference between Israel and the Palestinians (within the framework of the US-sponsored peace process) to directly endorse a two-state solution to the Israeli-Palestinian conflict. Aimed at demonstrating international support for the two-state solution at a time when US secretary of state Condolezza Rice warned that the window for the creation of a viable solution was closing,[7] the conference's joint declaration was strongly supported by the Middle East Quartet. Made up of the United States, the European Union, the Russian Federation, and the UN, the Quartet also "took note of the broad international support for the Annapolis Conference" and "affirmed its commitment to seize this opportunity to mobilize international support to achieve meaningful progress toward a just and lasting negotiated settlement to this conflict."[8]

In parallel to Annapolis though, a different group of Israelis and Palestinians came together in a self-financed conference hosted by the School of African and Oriental Studies (SOAS) in London. Entitled, "Challenging the Boundaries: A Single State in Palestine/Israel," this conference was put together by students of the newly created London One State Group and the SOAS Palestine Society. Organized as a follow-up to the Madrid Conference in July of that same year, it aimed at creating "a platform for a broad debate on democratic alternatives to the two state paradigm, and mak(ing) those ideas more accessible to the general public."[9] Bringing together many of the prominent Israeli and Palestinian academics and activists who have spoken out and written against the peace process since Oslo, the conference aimed at highlighting the fact that the two-state solution had failed to bring about peace and justice for Palestinians and Jewish-Israelis.

The main arguments underlying the single-state critique of the international hegemonic consensus surrounding the Oslo Accords can be summarized into three main points of contention. The first of these revolves around the generally accepted idea that Oslo represents the launching of a process of peace. Thus, it is important to underline that for single-state intellectuals, the peace process since Oslo does not reflect the launching of a comprehensive process for peace based upon the desire for justice and reconciliation, but a process of separation and fragmentation. The reason for this is rooted in the Accords' choice of historical point of beginning. Hence, single-state intellectuals argue that beginning the peace process in 1967 (as opposed to 1948) results in the erasure of the Palestinian Nakba, by absolving Israel of any responsibility for the ethnic cleansing of 1948, and as such closes a significant door for justice and reconciliation between the two people. Moreover, beginning the peace process in 1967 also denies Palestinian history and rights to self-determination by setting the Occupied Palestinian Territory (OPT) as the only territorial part of historic Palestine over which negotiations can be held.

Thus, the peace process involved negotiations that would lead to further territorial concessions and fragmentation within the West Bank and Gaza Strip (WBGS) from its start. Furthermore, by erasing the realities of 1948, it was also based on the fragmentation of the Palestinian collective from the beginning—excluding both the Palestinians inside Israel, and the Palestinian refugees from the negotiating table. As such, the single-state movement is an effort to relocate the search for peace and justice between Israelis and Palestinians in 1948, and opposes the principle of geographically partitioning the land into two states for two peoples upon which the Oslo Accords were based.[10] Hence, it mirrors Edward Said's assertion that by embracing the principle of separation, the peace process since Oslo has in fact delayed the "real reconciliation that must occur if the 100 year war between Zionism and the Palestinian people is to end."[11] Said writes,

> Palestinian self-determination in a separate state is unworkable, just as unworkable as the principle of separation between a demographically mixed, irreversibly connected Arab population without sovereignty and a Jewish population with it. The question is not how to devise means for persisting in trying to separate them but to see whether it is possible for them to live together.[12]

As such, for single-state intellectuals, the question revolves around how to begin again to talk about sharing the land "in a truly democratic way, with equal rights for each citizen."[13] Thus they assert, "the beginning is to develop something entirely missing from both Israeli and Palestinian realities today: the idea and practice of citizenship, not of ethnic or racial community, as the main vehicle of coexistence."[14] In this vein, and perhaps most crucially, the single-state movement also represents a force that seeks to reunify the Palestinian collective around an idea that serves the rights, agenda, and aspirations of all Palestinians.

In parallel to this, single-state intellectuals argue that it is only by beginning in 1948 that true processes of justice and reconciliation can be launched between the two peoples. Thus, Israeli activist and founder of Zochrot,[15] Eitan Bronstein, argues:

> One state is the only arrangement that will permit Palestinian refugees to realise their right to return. The implementation of this right is both moral and a necessary step toward ending the conflict and reconciliation between Israelis and Palestinians. It also gives the Israelis the opportunity to be true inhabitants of this land rather than settlers or colonisers.[16]

As such, the One State Declaration[17] stipulates that any process of peace must begin in 1948, and involve all of the inhabitants of what was Mandate Palestine, regardless of ethnicity, religion, and current citizenship status.

The second point of contention revolves around the fact that while Oslo was applauded by the international community as the beginning of a two-state solution to the Israeli-Palestinian conflict, single-state intellectuals argue that it represented the exacerbation of Zionist processes of separation and colonization. While a detailed exposition of these processes themselves is beyond the scope of this chapter[18] (see Diana Buttu's chapter in this book), they have famously been argued to represent a modified Allon Plan by Edward Said,[19] and can be summarized in the words of Amnon Raz-Krakotzin on the motivation behind Yitzhak Rabin's recognition of the Palestine Liberation Organization (PLO) at the time:

> Rabin was a follower of Yigal Allon, who after the 1967 war outlined a plan according to which the district of Jerusalem, as well as parts of the Hebron district and the Jordan Valley, would be kept under Israeli sovereignty. The remaining territory . . . would become an autonomous Palestinian area, with a link to Jordan. Rabin considered the Oslo framework to be one which would enable him to achieve, via different tactics, the policy he had always favored.[20]

It is important to note that single-state intellectuals view the fact that the peace process is officially accepted as one that will lead to a two-state solution as both a "misnaming" of the two-state solution itself, and as a deflection from the realities within Palestine/Israel that have made a two-state solution territorially and economically unviable. In parallel to this, single-state intellectuals regard the concessions made by PLO chairman Yasser Arafat—in order to be able to return to the OPT and wage a war of position from within—as the beginning of the emergence of a Palestinian Authority (PA) that was placed in an inevitable position of collaboration with Israeli occupation and colonization, while simultaneously sidelining Palestinian popular resistance. To this effect, Said famously wrote,

> The sudden transformation of Arafat from freedom-fighter and "terrorist" into an Israeli enforcer and a guest at the White House has been difficult for Palestinians to absorb . . . most Palestinians saw the new Arafat as the symbol of defeat.[21]

Hence, the single-state movement is also an attempt to reignite nonviolent Palestinian mass resistance to the continuing processes of separation and colonization. Intertwined with this is a call for both abolishing the PA and creating a debate around who represents the Palestinian people today,[22] as well as interrogating the possibility of redemocratizing the PLO into an organization that represents, empowers, and reunifies the whole Palestinian collective.[23]

Thirdly, single-state intellectuals highlight that it was only Yasser Arafat and his small entourage in Tunis who were involved in the acceptance of the terms of the Oslo Accords on behalf of the PLO—which resulted in a crisis of representation within the Palestinian national collective, as well as a questioning of the legitimacy of a leadership that viewed the internationally recognized rights of its collective as bargaining chips that could be compromised. Thus, at the SOAS One State conference, Joseph Massad stated,

> To date, no Diaspora Palestinian has proposed to Israel that if Israel grant the Diaspora a right of return, in exchange, it could deny West Bank and Gaza Palestinians their right to self-determination, and continue to colonize their land. Why then does the leadership of the West Bank believe that it can compromise the rights of Palestinians it does not even represent?[24]

In accepting the terms of Oslo and after, the PLO officially accepted the fragmentation of the Palestinian collective and the erasure of the rights of the Palestinian Diaspora, Palestinian refugees, and Palestinian-Israelis. Therefore, single-state intellectuals argue that the view that the PA represents the Palestinian people today is one that only holds if the only people recognized as Palestinians are Palestinians in the West Bank and Gaza Strip. In this vein then, only WBGS Palestinians would be set to benefit from the peace process. However, single-state intellectuals point out that even these Palestinians' lives have been made significantly worse by the processes of Oslo, with the "only hope awaiting them being an apartheid Bantustan solution."[25] It is from within this context that single-state intellectuals seek to throw the PA into the "dustbin of history,"[26] and to ignite a debate surrounding leadership, collective representation, and the possibility of redemocratizing the PLO. More significantly, it is also from within this context that the single-state movement can be seen as one initially launched as a war of position of the Palestinian Diaspora, Palestinian refugees, and Palestinian-Israelis.

Hence, to return to the SOAS single-state conference, these intellectuals fleshed out and debated the points of contention expressed above—while stressing that it is those Palestinians who have been historically silenced by Oslo who must now become central agents in the articulation, mobilization, and creation of a more just alternative to the status quo. Thus, they argued that the two-state solution served to distract from the territorial and political realities on the ground; to distract from the fact that the processes unleashed by Oslo "entrenche[d] and formalize[d] a policy of unequal separation on a land that has become ever more integrated territorially and economically";[27] and to distract from the fact that an independent Palestinian state appeared no longer viable. Moreover, they argued that the process of the solution is based upon a false premise of equality in terms of both power and morality between "a colonized and occupied people on the one hand and a colonizing state and military occupier on the other."[28] Indeed, according to their critique, the Oslo process's historical point of beginning and terms of reference are set within "the unjust premise that peace can be achieved by granting limited national rights to Palestinians living in the areas occupied in 1967, while denying the rights of Palestinians inside the 1948 borders and in the Diaspora."[29] In view of this, these intellectuals argue that a just and liberating alternative must be found to counter this paradigm of peacemaking and its deflection from the continuing processes of separation and colonization.

To this end—after two days of debate—the conference culminated in the drafting of "The One State Declaration."[30] This declaration set out the principles upon which all of the participants of both conferences in Madrid and London agreed that an alternative democratic single-state solution should be mobilized for, and created. These principles included the fact that any process of justice had to historically begin in 1948, and affirm the fact that the land of Palestine historically belongs "to all who live in it and to those who were expelled or exiled from it since 1948, regardless of religion, ethnicity, national origin or current citizenship status";[31] that any system of government must be based upon the principle of equality in all of its diverse arenas; that the Palestinian right of return must be implemented; that any form of state must be nonsectarian; that a process of justice and reconciliation must be launched; and, significantly, that the segments of the Palestinian collective that have been historically silenced by Oslo—the Palestinian Diaspora, the Palestinian refugees, and the Palestinians inside Israel—must be centrally involved in the articulation of the outlines and contents of such a solution. It is these principles that remain the basis of unity within the vision, strategies, and initiatives of this group of intellectuals and activists—despite their divisions, lack of centralized coordination and, at times, shifts in emphasis or direction. In the conference's closing session, the London One State Group stated:

The two days of discussions in London proved that there's a growing movement among Palestinians and Israelis that calls for thinking about their common future in terms of equality and integration, rather than separation and exclusion.[32]

While Palestinian-Israelis were originally acknowledged to be the central force behind the re-emergence of the single-state idea, it is Diaspora Palestinians who are its fastest growing proponents. Thus, at a single-state conference in Boston, Ghada Karmi states, the "constituency where the one state has got the most currency . . . is the Palestinian Diaspora."[33] This is illustrated in the fact that they visibly reflect the largest constituency of single-state intellectuals present at publicly organized single state events—such as the fast-growing network of conferences aimed at expanding the single-state movement.[34] While this visibility could be linked to their geographical locations and mobility—this rapid expansion is also reflected in the growing number of single-state initiatives and networks within which the Diaspora are involved.[35]

A CRITIQUE OF ZIONISM AND SEPARATION

As highlighted above, one of the central unifying themes of the single-state movement is that it is a struggle of resistance aimed at dismantling Zionism's hegemony and interlinked processes of separation upon the land and its inhabitants. Following the *Encyclopedia Hebraica*, Uri Davis defines Zionism as "a Jewish national movement emerging at the end of the nineteenth century" that had as its objective "returning the people of Israel to their historical homeland in the land of Israel."[36] This return was inspired by "a vision of return to Zion (a synonym for Jerusalem)."[37] Of the various schools of thought that this definition encompasses, it was "political Zionism, founded by Theodor Herzl, [which] became the hegemonic and dominant mainstream."[38] Political Zionism itself represents a school of thought and interlinked practice that,

> Is committed to the normative statement that it is a good idea to establish and consolidate in the country of Palestine a sovereign state, a Jewish state, that attempts to guarantee in law and in practice a demographic majority of the Jewish tribes in the territories under its control.[39]

As Ilan Pappe argues, this form of Zionism is a "secularized and nationalized Judaism."[40] According to Judaism itself, "Palestine had been revered throughout the centuries by generations of Jews as a place for holy pilgrimage, never as a future secular state."[41] Furthermore, "Jewish tradition and religion clearly instructs Jews to await the coming of the promised Messiah . . . before they can return to Eretz Israel as a sovereign people . . . [which]

is why today several streams of Ultra-Orthodox Jews are either non or anti-Zionist."[42] As such, the single-state alternative seeks to highlight the important distinction between Zionism and Judaism, as well as the fact that Zionism goes against the central tenets of Judaism and, as such, should not be allowed to speak for—or act in the name of—those who belong to the Jewish faith. In this vein, at the single-state Madrid Conference in 2007, Steven Freedman argued that Zionism represented a revolt against the mainstream and widely held beliefs of Judaism. Thus,

> It is very important that Zionism, as the leading force of the essentialization process that has taken place within Jewish identity, be undone and deconstructed, in order to erase its structural and fundamental characteristics (colonialist, separatist, racist), which are indeed the main obstacles to a just and long-term solution in the region.[43]

Similarly, while Zionism emerged due to the growing persecution of Jewish people in Europe in the late 1880s,[44] many single-state Jewish-Israeli intellectuals argue that it simultaneously has a complex inter-relationship with anti-Jewish racism itself.[45] Thus, Davis highlights that though political Zionism is based upon the premise that it can offer a solution to anti-Jewish racism, it is in fact interlinked to this racism—since they both "share a common worldview on the existential status of Jewish minority communities in non-Jewish societies."[46] He elaborates,

> Both the political Zionist and the anti-Jewish racist believe that, given the fundamental racial incompatibility of Jews and non-Jews, Jews . . . cannot . . . be equal citizens and free minority communities within a non-Jewish society and polity. . . . For the political Zionist, Jewish society must also be segregated outside the body of "Gentile" society, in this case in Palestine.[47]

Haim Bresheeth echoed this analysis at the single-state Madrid Conference, arguing that Zionism and anti-Semitism have in common that they both agree upon the distressing notion that Jewish people must, and want to, separate themselves from the rest of humanity.[48]

In a different vein, Pappe underlines that while the impulses from within which Zionism emerged as a movement can be argued to have been both fair and humanistic, the moment it decided that its aims would be implemented on the land of Palestine, Zionism was transformed into a settler-colonial movement.[49] Elaborating upon this point, Davis writes that Political Zionism's solution to anti-Jewish racism involved:

> The transformation of the Arab country of Palestine . . . into the Jewish land of Israel, through the dispossession and mass transfer of the native indigenous Pal-

estinian Arab population out of Palestine, the mass migration of Jews the world over into Palestine, and the establishment, through the Jewish colonization of Palestine of a sovereign Jewish state.[50]

While the Zionist colonization of Palestine reflected European practices of colonization, single-state intellectuals emphasize that there was one crucial difference—namely that Zionism did not colonize the land in order to dispossess and exploit the indigenous population, but to dispossess and replace, or exclude them. It is from within this context that Jamil Hilal argues that Zionism is a special branch of European settler colonialism—one that is an exclusivist ethno-religious state building project.[51]

Similarly, it is from within this context that Pappe contends that the real source of the Palestinian tragedy is rooted within the fact that the Jewish population of Mandatory Palestine was so small—coupled with the Zionist movement's insistence upon creating both an exclusively ethnic Jewish state, as well as a democratic state. It is this irreconcilable logic that led to the ethnic cleansing of the Palestinians in the past—and that lies at the core of the continued Israeli policies of ethnic cleansing against the Palestinians, due to the above mentioned paradox of a continued desire for more land, yet less Palestinians. Moreover, on this obsession with a "demographic danger" within Israel, As'ad Ghanem writes,

> The discourse on the future of Israel is based, according to most of Israel's leaders, elite, and average public, on what is known as the "demographic danger." Related to the "demographic danger" is the fear that Israel, within its extended borders, including the West Bank and Gaza, or within the limits of the borders before the June 1967 war, would sooner or later turn into a "bi-national" state.[52]

As Ghanem argues, the ideas and actions of Ariel Sharon himself were a reflection of Israel's irreconcilable dilemma since its 1967 occupation of the WBGS—namely a belief in the "Greater Land of Israel," coupled with a fear of a bi-national reality and a desire to maintain both the Jewish and democratic character of the Israeli state.[53] Disengagement represented the answer to these irreconcilabilities, based upon a vision, "to withdraw from the Gaza Strip and 42 percent of the . . . West Bank in return for annexing those Palestinian areas where Jewish settlements are established and other West Bank areas with coveted resources."[54] As Jewish-American Tony Judt wrote, in an article that triggered the ire of many within the US and sparked an urgently overdue debate about the nature of the Israeli regime,

> The very idea of a "Jewish state"—a state in which Jews and the Jewish religion have exclusive privileges from which non-Jewish citizens are forever excluded—is rooted in another time and place. Israel, in short, is an anachronism.[55]

It is precisely this anachronism that single-state intellectuals attempt to unveil, and struggle against, with their alternative anti-Zionist worldview.

As highlighted above, the core elements of this worldview include: emphasizing the distinction between Zionism and Judaism; highlighting both the settler-colonial and ethnically exclusionary nature of political Zionism; and underlining the dangers linked to ethnic cleansing and population transfer that this form of exclusionary settler-colonialism represents when it is coupled with the equally entrenched Jewish-Israeli desire to create a Jewish democracy upon as much of the land of "Greater Israel" as possible. From within this critique—much of which was aimed at dealing a blow to the consensus surrounding both Zionism's worldview and the idea of separation as the only viable solution to the conflict within the civil societies and publics of the West—single-state intellectuals agreed upon several strategies of resistance aimed at transcending Zionism. These strategies primarily centered upon breaking the taboo of critically and publicly engaging with the nature of Zionism and the Israeli state in Europe and North America, and its links to settler-colonialism and separation. Paralleling this was an effort to "South Africanize" the Israeli-Palestinian conflict in order to unveil the specific nature of Zionist apartheid and Palestinian fragmentation and dispossession—and make a case for the launching of a boycott, sanctions and divestment (BDS) strategy of resistance to it. The move to the apartheid paradigm gained much traction in the post-Oslo period—and is especially advocated by scholars who believed that this paradigm shift was the only avenue left from within which Palestinians could hope to break through the intransigent wall of US elite support for Israel and their inaccurate reflection, and hence popular understanding, of the occupation-liberation paradigm within this specific conflict. Moreover, as single-state intellectuals underline, it is also the most accurate reflection of the obscured reality on the ground in Israel/Palestine. On this paradigm shift, George Bisharat states,

> One of the reasons that the anti-apartheid movement in the US reached such heights was because it resonated with the American civil rights movement. . . . Unfortunately, that's not the way Israel/Palestine reads to Americans . . . if you talk to Americans about settlers or settlements some of them actually have a positive connotation of that, because it reminds them of the American west and pioneering settlers—it's not a bad term. Apartheid however, they all know that apartheid is bad. They all respond to it. So, yes, I think that analogy . . . is a valuable tool. And it's not just a valuable tool, it's accurate.[56]

Similarly, Barghouti underlines the importance this paradigm shift represents in terms of the moral and legal power it contains for Palestinians within the realm of the established legal conventions of the "international community":

The significance to the Palestinian struggle for self-determination of the fact that international law considers apartheid a crime against humanity that therefore invites sanctions . . . cannot be overemphasized. The UN and the international community know full well . . . how to deal with apartheid; all Palestinians and defenders of justice have to do is prove . . . how Israel's own . . . [regime] constitute[s] apartheid.[57]

Intertwined with this push to "South Africanize" the conflict was the unanimous agreement of single-state intellectuals upon the centrality of launching a BDS campaign against the state of Israel as one of the collective's central weapons of nonviolent resistance. While the surprising subsequent take-off of the BDS campaign, and its transformation into a powerful, expanding global movement is beyond the scope of this chapter, it should be highlighted that the BDS strategy was originally developed as a central component of the single-state movement. Thus, as Haim Bresheeth succinctly put it, "Boycott is a tactic, and the strategy is one state."[58] Elaborating upon this point further, Bresheeth states,

There are many diverse groups within Israel that are against the occupation—soldiers, women, doctors, architects, lawyers, Peace Now, etc.—but there are no linkages among the separate groups, and they don't gain any support in Israel because most Israelis financially depend on the occupation. This is why there must be structural change in Israeli lives, and why this is a South African moment in which the BDS movement is so crucial.[59]

Thus, single-state intellectuals seek to aid any dissent that exists within Israel by launching a tactic for external pressure against Zionism and its practices. Perhaps most crucially of all though is Palestinian civil society's BDS call in 2005—which represented the first unified Palestinian national call to unite all segments of the Palestinian people within it, and calls for the achievement of the rights of all three segments of the Palestinian collective.[60]

These goals (which significantly mirror those of the single-state alternative) are: the inalienable right to Palestinian self-determination; ending the Israeli occupation and colonization of all Arab lands, and dismantling the Wall; the recognition of the fundamental rights of the Palestinian citizens of Israel to full equality; and the implementation of the Palestinian right of return as stipulated in UN General Assembly Resolution 194.[61] Speaking on the significance of this call, Nadia Hijab states, "This is perhaps the most significant national document since the national movement was founded. It establishes a clear set of goals for the entire Palestinian people. This clear set of goals is the first most crucial source of power of the Palestinian people."[62] Moreover, single-state intellectuals developed the tactic of BDS as a central weapon of resistance as a result of their disillusionment with the PA and the international community's complicity with Israeli policies, as well as their interlinked failure to hold Israel accountable for its actions under international law. Thus, this campaign primarily targets civil societies in Europe and North America in an effort to transcend the dominant view of the conflict among their citizens, and transform them into social forces of change against their governments' complicity with Israeli policies. It also seeks to create this change in tactic within all of the organizations, institutions, associations, and groups that support Palestinian rights, and are involved in Palestinian solidarity campaigns.[63]

In parallel with these shifts, this tactic seeks to shame the PA as a collaborator leadership—and to present an alternative for those within the PA who realize that the peace process is dead; feel the need to reformulate their positions; and can be influenced to actively join the recentering of the Palestinian struggle for self-determination around a unified, grassroots Palestinian (and anti-Zionist Israeli) collective, waging a nonviolent struggle for a decolonized liberation.

Moreover, while single-state intellectuals stand against partition on the grounds that it is interlinked with practices of population transfer and ethnic cleansing, they also stress the fact that the people of Mandate Palestine have always been too intertwined for such a solution to succeed. Fused with this worldview is an argument that seeks to stress that identities themselves are fluid, intertwined, and complex, and that the binary opposition between "Arabs" and "Jews" that underpins much of the commonly understood notions of the Israeli-Palestinian conflict does not reflect the reality on the ground.[64] For single-state intellectuals, nothing epitomizes the erasure of this complexity more than the negating of the identity and history of the Arab-Jewish people (i.e., Jews that came from the Arab world).[65] Thus, one of the most interesting threads within the anti-Zionism of single-state supporters revolves around the countering of the hegemonic European Ashkenazi depiction of Jewish-Israeli history and identity,[66] the rearticulation of the identities and voices of Arab-Jews, as well as the reinsertion of the history of coexistence between Arabs and Jews in the Arab world within public arenas, public consciousness, and written interventions.[67]

Hence, describing what he argues is a state-sponsored project to de-Arabize Mizrahim Jewish communities in Israel more concretely, Jewish-Israeli filmmaker and academic Eyal Sivan states,

> The idea of a Jewish state today is that of a non-Arab state. It's not a Jewish state in any religious definition. The history of the people, the history of the country, is the history of the European in the land, and before they came to the land ... this is [reflected in the] system of education, a system that is built on the fact that "we," this common we, have one history which is a European history. This

brought us to the situation that today, every descendant of an Iraqi-Jewish family in my class would say, "but when we were in Poland we were persecuted." This means that the personal "we" transforms every Israeli into a European with a European heritage.[68]

In 2010, Azmi Bishara elaborated upon how this state-sponsored project of de-Arabization affected the dynamics between Palestinian-Israelis and Arab-Jewish communities in Israel,

> The Palestinian has learned to recognize the Mizrahi as the extremist Israeli. And the Palestinian understands that the Mizrahi is in a predicament, since he constantly tries to distinguish himself from the Arab in his Arab-ness. The Ashkenazi does not have to emphasize his Jewishness, for it is obvious to him that he is not Arab. . . . Yet, the Mizrahi resembles the Arab in looks, customs, dialects and other aspects that force him to differentiate himself from the Arab in order to win equality on the basis of national identity. If the criterion for equality is nationalism, then they must prove their nationalism.[69]

It is in this context that, in 2007, Joseph Massad argued for a single-state Jewish-Israeli strategy that would counter this de-Arabization of Arab-Jewish communities,

> There's been much ambivalence within the Mizrahi population toward Ashkenazi hegemony and more generally with regards to their Arab culture. I think this is a population that is mobilizable despite the racist Ashkenazi depiction of the Mizrahim as something of a right-wing Zionist racist . . . and I think that's the work of our Israeli colleagues and friends.[70]

For single-state intellectuals, the revival of the Arab-Jewish identity is interlinked with the broader discussion of equal citizenship and the fluid, intermingled identities of much of the population of Palestine/Israel. Underlining the complexity of identities (especially those of Palestinian-Israelis and Arab-Jews) also helps attack the argument of many single-state opponents that a homogenous block of "Israelis" would never accept a single-state solution, remaining forever united in a static (Orientalist and racist) political Zionism.

THE ROLE OF PALESTINIAN-ISRAELIS: DILEMMAS AND OBSTACLES FROM WITHIN

As highlighted above, one of the premises of the One State Declaration revolves around the fact that "those who have been historically excluded from decision-making [by the Oslo Accords]—especially the Palestinian Diaspora and its refugees, and Palestinians inside Israel—must play a central role"[71] in its rearticulation and mobilization as a unifying democratic solution for the whole Palestinian national collective. In its struggle to de-Zionize Israel/Palestine, the single-state alternative also places one of its central points of beginning in the necessity to develop the notion and practice of equal citizenship as the main channel forward toward sharing the land in a truly democratic way among all of its inhabitants.[72] Thus, while currently it is the Palestinian Diaspora who have become the single-state alternative's most potent driving force forward—it is in this context that Palestinian-Israelis were originally acknowledged to be the catalysts behind the re-emergence of the single-state idea. For, as Asa'ad Ghanem underlines, "Palestinians in Israel are the only group of Palestinians calling clearly for bi-nationality."[73] This can be argued to stem from their own peculiar fate as Palestinians confined within the Israeli state, and frequently perceived as an enemy threat within it.[74] Having been rendered invisible by the PLO after Oslo, they were separated from their own Palestinian people, while being subjected to Zionist processes of de-Arabization.[75] In being Israeli second-class citizens and subjects under what Oren Yiftachel termed an Israeli system of creeping apartheid[76]—they also, though, have at their disposal certain points of access into the political process. This led to their development of "a collective political agenda based on grounding their status as a national homeland minority . . . determined to achieve equality and recognition."[77]

The fact that Palestinian-Israeli citizenship is structurally limited by the inherent contradiction within Israel's simultaneous self-definition as an exclusionary Jewish and a democratic state [78] also provided much of the groundwork for single-state efforts to highlight what Barghouti has described as Zionism's form of apartheid, and the fact that it is Jewish structural privileges that stand in the way of justice and equality for all. Within this context then—in the single-state struggle to create alliances and solidarity between themselves and marginalized Jewish groups within Israel against state-sponsored racism—the role of Palestinian-Israeli single-state supporters against apartheid is central both historically and in the present. Their potential political role—and geographic location as an indigenous community that has managed to remain upon its land despite the Israeli ethnic cleansing of 1948—also reflects both the political defeats of the Arab world and of the Palestinian national movement in liberating Palestine, as well as the biggest contradictions and divides that the single-state movement faces in its efforts to erase the "green line."

As Awad Abdel-Fattah, secretary-general of the Palestinian-Israeli political party, Tajamuu' (also known by its Hebrew name *Balad*), recounts, the idea of the single democratic state was first taken up by Abnaa El-Balad when the movement was established in 1969. It adopted the idea from Fatah, which had itself rearticulated the vision in that same year. Fatah's vision became the PLO's official position in 1971 "under the slogan of a democratic state in Palestine inclusive of Jews, Muslims, and Christians."[79] As Leila Farsakh writes, this rearticulation constituted a shift from the PLO's position to liberate all of historic Palestine, to one that acknowledged the Jewish presence within the land. Thus "the democratic state represented the first Palestinian attempt to come to terms with the reality of Jewish presence on the land rather than negate it, albeit from within a nationalist Palestinian paradigm."[80] As such, the Jewish community within this paradigm of a secular democratic state was considered Palestinian.

Mirroring this shift in the Palestinian national movement's position, Abnaa El-Balad was established as a grassroots movement in the village of Umm el-Fahm in 1969, made up of both Palestinian-Israelis and Jews who identify themselves as Jewish-Palestinians. It views itself as an integral part of the Palestinian national movement,[81] and grew out of the Palestinian student movements in the 1960s and 1970s, with the aim of preserving the collective identity of the Palestinians inside Israel, linking their struggle with that of their Palestinian brothers and sisters in the West Bank and Gaza Strip, and with that of the Palestinian refugees.[82] It supports the Palestinian right of return, recognizes the PLO as the legitimate representative of the Palestinian people, and advocates for the principle of equality within the Israeli state—which it argues was forcibly imposed upon Palestinians in 1948, and which it does not recognize as legitimate. The signing of the Oslo Accords constituted a blow to the growing strength of Abnaa El-Balad and the movements affiliated with it inside the "green line," as Abdel-Fattah states,

> The demise of the Palestinian national movement with the signing of the Oslo Accords had a deep effect upon us. Oslo suddenly painted us, Abnaa el-Balad, as traitors—both to the Palestinian cause and to our own rights here. It was a big blow to a comprehensive one-state solution, and we were unable to continue with the same power and momentum, as Palestinians inside of Israel. In the '50s and '60s it was different, because people here did not take the idea of Israeli citizenship seriously.[83]

He continues,

> In the new reality that emerged after Oslo, we were placed in a very weak position, and we realized that we could no longer call for big visions like the one-state solution. So we shifted our tactics and strategies, and began to accept the fact that Israel is here to stay. We brought together a large coalition of forces that had been with us in Abnaa el-Balad, and part of the Azmi Bishara group that had left the Communist Party, and others—and we decided

to create a Palestinian democratic party that underlined our national identity, but also took our Israeli citizenship seriously. . . . So the language of struggle shifted into one that spoke of citizenship and equality, but was also a much more intricate conversation about what this citizenship and equality actually means. So we stopped talking about the liberation of all of Palestine, and began to say that we call for the establishment of a Palestinian state in the West Bank and Gaza Strip, and demand equal citizenship in Israel and oppose the idea of an ethnically exclusive Jewish state.[84]

However, even then, the newly created democratic alliance failed to build any momentum, or to move any closer toward becoming a grassroots movement within Palestinian-Israeli communities,

Originally, we planned our party as a grassroots form of political activism and had no intention of joining the Knesset. Five or six years later, after we failed to create any kind of momentum from the outside, we decided to join the Knesset and to take our nationalist-democratic project of equality to the government. The intent behind this move was to turn the space of the Knesset into an arena of ideological confrontation, and to defy Israel from inside. And that's what happened. Azmi Bishara was our first candidate in the Knesset, and due to his academic background, and his intimate knowledge of both Zionism and the state of Israel as a colonial-settler state, his success was incredible, and it shamed liberal Zionists even more than it shamed the right. Because, of course, liberal Zionists used to say, OK we are a Jewish state—but we are a democratic and Jewish state, and a democracy just like the democracies of the West. His being there though made it very obvious that Israeli democracy was a sham, that Israeli citizenship was defined through ethnicity, that Arabs were second class citizens, and that the time had come to erase these Jewish privileges because they are the root cause of injustice and inequality. And so this confrontation, with this novel articulation, was suddenly ignited in the public for the first time ever.[85]

Today, this confrontation with Jewish privileges continues inside the "green line," and these divisions within the Palestinian-Israeli community on the most realistic way forward continue to structure the differences among single-state intellectuals of this community in terms of strategy and tactics. This particular history of struggle also forms the basis of divisions between Palestinian-Israelis and other Palestinian single-state intellectuals—most notably on the topic of bi-nationalism itself. Thus, while many of their counterparts within the OPT view bi-nationalism as a "Zionist solution,"[86] many Palestinian-Israeli activists and intellectuals continue to be wary of advocating for a single democratic state, and prefer to support bi-nationalism as a necessary "transitional phase" toward the establishment of a single democratic solution. As Nidal Othman from Mossawa states, for example,

> The one state solution for me is the solution we are striving toward as a long-term goal for the whole of the land of mandatory Palestine, because our sense of belonging as Palestinians and to the land of Palestine is much larger than anything that can be fragmented. . . . In my opinion though, talking about a shared future in the context of a two-state solution—which for me is just a transitional phase—creates the foundational groundwork for struggling for a one-state solution. . . . If even amongst ourselves within Israel we can't create this shared future, how can we create it among all of the inhabitants of historic Palestine? It's impossible. So this is our terrain of struggle, and the hope is to be able to go from here to the larger terrain in the future.[87]

Elaborating further on the strategy behind Mossawa's struggle for creating a shared future within Israel, Othman elaborates,

> We've succeeded today in creating alliances with groups of Jewish-Arabs, with Ethiopians, and with Russians too. Jewish-Arabs are 35–40 percent of the Israeli-Jewish population. Russian speaking Jews are around 20 percent of the population. And Ethiopians are around 1.5 percent. Put together, all of us make up around 70 percent of the population. So, we target these groups and try to build common ground with them in terms of solidarity against racism, and by highlighting the fact that we are all victims. And we do find people who join us, but it's not widespread, and we have failed to transition into a more widespread grassroots movement. But we try to build alliances around specific rights. So in 2011, during the wave of social protests against housing prices here, we brought in a lot of Palestinians, and Palestinians from the Naqab, from Arakib, to jointly protest with Arab-Jewish groups in public spaces and in front of the house of the housing minister, and its our belief that these kinds of initiatives are a way of contributing to a way forward, and for especially Jewish-Arabs to stop perceiving Palestinians and Arabs as their enemy. But the problem is that this is a very long process. We know that we need to create a grassroots movement and that real transformation must come from the bottom up. If we fail to create this movement, even a one-state solution will be an apartheid solution.[88]

This strategy is of course paralleled by Jewish-Israeli single-state intellectuals, who argue that they must also work within their communities in order to create a grassroots movement against apartheid and for democracy within Israel. As such, in 2007, Eyal Sivan stated,

> In this transformation of the one (apartheid) state into a democratic state, we have to sell to the privileged ones (we, the Israelis) the benefits of transformation into a one democratic state. We have to know who can benefit from this transformation. I would think of populations like the non-Jewish Zionists for example—the new immigrants from Russia, who are having a lot of problems in terms of identity, marriage, work, language, cultural autonomy. The huge population of

Arab-Jews that continue to be discriminated against inside Israel culturally and economically. Israel's population is still ruled by us—the Ashkenazi Jews.[89]

However, in practice, many Palestinian single-state activists today argue that Jewish-Israeli single staters have not done enough work on transforming the worldview of their own communities, and have chosen instead to coresist with Palestinians in places like East Jerusalem for example. This perceived failure on the part of Jewish-Israelis to activate this aspect of the single-state movement's strategy of building a movement has created much frustration toward the idea of joint struggle among new generations of Palestinian activists—especially in Jerusalem. As an activist in East Jerusalem elaborates,

> I agree that it's hard to change public opinion on the Israeli side, and to convince them of supporting a one-state solution. This is a great challenge [for Jewish-Israeli single-state supporters]. But this doesn't mean that they should work on transformation with Palestinian communities instead. It's great that they work with international civil society too, but that doesn't replace the need for them to work with their own people. I know they find it easier to work with Palestinians, which is how this whole era of activism and discourse around "co-resistance" began. They started coming to Sheikh Jarrah, or to the protests in Bil'in, and Nabi Saleh and Nil'in. . . . But who is going to convince the Israeli side of the one state solution then? If it's not their responsibility, then whose is it?[90]

While cognizant of the fact that coresistance has become a trend in the world of activism right now, young Palestinian activists in both Jerusalem and the OPT are concerned that this form of resistance structurally results in disempowering Palestinian popular resistance. Hence,

> There are people today who believe that it's time for us to co-resist. From experience though, even when it comes to co-resistance [as opposed to co-existence] any group between Palestinians and Israelis inevitably reflects the power relations on the ground. No matter how hard Israelis try to make our relations artificially equal, the outside world always has an effect. For example, the latest pictures of co-resistance today from Bil'in and Nil'in and Nabi Saleh have been black balloons being released in the sky, and tear gas canisters being turned into flower pots. Gas canisters as flower pots is a great idea. But is it Palestinian popular resistance? Of course not. . . . What happens on the ground is that internationals and Israelis are the ones who are shaping the identity of popular resistance in Palestine today. As a result popular resistance is becoming less popular, and less Palestinians are joining it. So how are these Jewish-Israelis working with me on transformation? They're harming me and my struggle just to be able to clear their conscience and feel like they deserve the place that they occupy here in Palestine. And they're mostly unwelcome.[91]

For their part, younger Jewish-Israeli anti-Zionists criticize Palestinians for not engaging in joint struggle with them more often, arguing that the lack of actual alliances with Palestinians makes them look less credible within their own communities. However, as has been highlighted above, while this may be the case for Palestinians in Jerusalem and the OPT, Palestinian-Israelis have been both attempting to educate Jewish publics on the inherent racism within Zionism and to create alliances with anti-Zionist and marginalized Jewish communities since the signing of the Oslo Accords, with very little success. While to a large extent this failure can be attributed to a lack of resources and to state-sponsored repression, it is also a reflection of a lack of consensus on the way forward even among different groups of Palestinian-Israelis. For example, Othman argues,

> Many [Palestinian groups and institutions inside Israel] can't believe that we would even compare the racism we face as Palestinians with that faced by the diverse marginalized Jewish communities. When you compare them, and engage in joint struggle with them, you're effectively giving up on your Palestinian identity. So we don't have the same approach to the problem, and they refuse the premise of solidarity with these diverse groups as a strategy for transformation. This is the case for lots of Palestinian civil society groups in '48.[92]

In many ways, this impasse among Palestinian-Israeli intellectuals and civil society institutions can be paralleled with the weariness of Palestinian single staters in the OPT of speaking in terms of bi-nationalism as a way forward (as opposed to a "one-person-one-vote" democracy). Hence, as Barghouti argues,

> I'll be very honest, the divide is between Zionists versus anti-Zionists, and I'm sorry to say that some Palestinians have been Zionized. Some Palestinians are using terms such as self-determination to describe the rights of Jewish colonizers in Palestine, which is incredible to me. How can the indigenous accept the colonizers as having equal national rights? Equal rights, yes. But national rights is not acceptable.[93]

Similarly, on whether or not prominent anti-Zionist Jewish-Israelis are part of their movement, Radi Jarai, a single-state intellectual in the OPT, stresses that while they are all technically involved in the same struggle, they do not agree on bi-nationalism,

> The problem with bi-nationalism is that it takes us back to two-states, and the principle of self-determination. If we support bi-nationalism, we are effectively saying that each nation has the right to have an independent state (and giving our colonizers national rights which they are not entitled to). So the democratic solution is more ideal, and it doesn't negate anyone's identity.[94]

These obstacles and divisions magnify the argument of most older generation Jewish-Israeli single staters (the majority of whom can be described as Marxist or anti-imperialist in political orientation) that a global BDS movement is the most potent tactic within the strategy toward a one-state solution—precisely due to the fact that they are pessimistic about the possibility of change from within Israeli society itself.[95]

It should perhaps also be noted here that all single-state intellectuals support BDS[96] as a central tool of nonviolent resistance, as well as the Palestinian right of return. They also all agree that one major obstacle to moving forward is represented by the existence of the PA and its strategy to create a security apparatus that involves coordination with Israel and under the supervision of the USA, which is designed to police Palestinian resistance. According to Jarai, this is a strategy aimed at enabling the oppression of Palestinian society, and any revolutionary potential within it, as efficiently and effectively as possible.[97] And while most Palestinian activists have no illusions that the PA would ever walk away from the peace process that enables its existence, most Jewish-Israeli activists have little hope that change will come from within Israeli society. Hence, Bresheeth's argument that the impulse for social transformation must come from the Palestinians themselves,

> The key for transformation now is the Palestinians, not the Israelis. They must support the one state idea, they must refuse to be partners in the "two-state" peace process, and they must refuse to play by Israel's rules and create a new framework for peace.... Change will not come from within Israel. For Israelis, changing their position as a public has to come from intense pressure—inside and outside.[98]

As previously emphasized, this has led Palestinian single staters in the OPT to call for the abolishment and dismantling of the PA, and has ignited an internal debate surrounding the possibility of the redemocratization of the PLO.[99]

However, while some elements of Fatah have become open to the idea of a single-state solution,[100] the real dilemma remains that the idea has failed to galvanize any real grassroots momentum within the OPT due to the fact that no political parties or politicians have embraced it as a solution to the conflict. On this obstacle of a vacuum of political leadership, Barghouti makes the point,

> There is no political party, no politicians for one state. We got close. Before he passed away, Haidar Abdel-Shafi, one of the most influential Palestinian civic leaders ... spoke to me and said there's nothing in the one state declaration that he disagrees with. I'm an old communist, he said, and this is what we dreamed of, a democratic society for all, with the refugees' right of return.

... I'm glad you're doing this work, and I hope to support it publically. Then he passed away. He would have been the only mainstream voice who would have helped in supporting one state. We don't have anyone now. I mean Palestinian intellectuals, academics on the outside, are not very influential inside. They unfortunately do not carry much weight here.[101]

Within the context of the geographic theatre of Palestinian-Israelis, Awad Abdel-Fattah[102] also argues,

There is no one right now in terms of political parties that can take the leadership role in a one-state movement. In terms of academics, there are many who speak about this topic, but they have been unable to have an effect beyond these elite circles. So who can take leadership of this kind of movement? I don't know. On my side, we are trying to push our party in this direction now, but we also feel like we are on the cusp of an explosion, and a new reality that none of us will be able to control and so we are partly waiting to see where the chips fall. Ultimately, I think that the leadership of this movement will have to be found in the new generation of Palestinians. Our role as politicians and intellectuals is to push toward unification under the umbrella of a struggle for equal rights. If we fail to ignite a grassroots movement right now, the next generation will not. In my opinion, the coming reality will force this upon them—it will unite the whole Palestinian national collective in one project of liberation: the single democratic state.[103]

Thus, the question of the lack of a political leadership for the single-state solution remains an open one as of this writing—one whose lack of resolution is argued by all single staters to be a crucial factor in the failure of any real grassroots movement for unity, democracy, and equal rights for all to emerge on either side of the "green line," and activate any real potential for transforming the increasingly untenable status quo.

CONCLUSION

While the re-emergent single democratic state idea has been largely successful in creating an alternative vision capable of unifying its supporters both within Palestine/Israel and among the Diaspora, it has yet to find any success in translating this vision into a grassroots popular resistance movement capable of reunifying the fragmented Palestinian national collective, and galvanizing either political leadership or momentum aimed at walking away from the (currently nonexistent) peace process. This conundrum is perhaps best voiced in single-state intellectual Radi Jarai's statement, "Where we propose the idea, we find supporters—from university campuses to the refugee camps.

The challenge we face though is one of organization—how do we organize our supporters effectively when there is no political leadership or party supporting one state?"[104]

And while this question of why they have been unable to create a grassroots movement on either side of the "green line" in Palestine/Israel consumes all Palestinian single-state intellectuals, the simple answer seems to be that they remain unsure as to why they have not been able to galvanize more success as a political force.[105] This is especially so in the context of a time in which youth movements, especially those linked to the struggle against the Prawer Plan in the Naqab, have largely succeeded in engaging in resistance that has erased the "green line," and of the (arguably) low-intensity Palestinian Intifada that has been unleashed in the wake of the Israeli state's latest escalation of violence and Palestinian dispossession. The demise of both the peace process and of any Israeli pretense of a willingness to negotiate a two-state solution, or of its need for the PA to camouflage the fact that it currently rules over a de facto single apartheid state in Palestine, should have also opened up spaces for more mobilization. And while in this chapter I have endeavored to highlight both the coherence of the single state vision itself as a potent alternative, and the main dilemmas it faces in its strategies within the land—perhaps it is the words of the secretary-general of Tajamuu' which ring the most true. While it has been the role of this generation of activists and intellectuals to push toward Palestinian reunification in the framework of a struggle for equal rights, it will be the new generation's role to mobilize from the bottom up and take the struggle forward for a single democratic state.

NOTES

1. As argued by Amnon Raz-Krakotzin, a prominent Jewish-Israeli single-state intellectual himself, "the principle of separation was the essence of the logic of the Oslo Agreement from the Israeli point of view. . . . Both "right" and "left" accept the desire for separation as a starting point. [Thus] the reality of separation which was formed after the Oslo Accord actually diminished the differences between the main political powers in Israel concerning the future of the Occupied Territories." Raz-Krakotzin argues that the motivating factor which brought both Labor and Likud around to accepting the solution offered by Oslo was "a rejection of a bi-national state . . . they all agreed that Jerusalem and most of the settlements should remain in Israeli hands." Amnon Raz-Krakotzkin, "A Peace without Arabs: The Discourse of Peace and the Limits of Israeli Consciousness," in *After Oslo: New Realities, Old Problems*, ed. George Giacaman and Dag Jrund Lonning (London: Pluto Press, 1998), 65.

2. Edward Said, "Truth and Reconciliation," *Al-Ahram Weekly*, January 14–20, 1999, http://weekly.ahram.org.eg/1999/412/op2.htm.

3. Ilan Pappe, "Proposal For A New Israeli Political Organization: Building A Movement For The One State Solution," paper presented at *One State for Palestine/Israel: A Country for all its Citizens?* (Boston, MIT, 2009).

4. Omar Barghouti, "Organizing for Self Determination, ethical De-Zionization & Resisting Apartheid," paper presented at *One State for Palestine/Israel: A Country for all its Citizens?* (Boston, MIT, 2009).

5. Barghouti, "Organizing for Self Determination."

6. This chapter was written before the passing of the new Jewish Nation-state Law by the Israeli Knesset in July 2018, which may serve to add further momentum to the centrality of the role of Palestinian-Israelis within this particular struggle.

7. Scott Macleod, "Rice's Fear of the One-State Solution—The Middle East Blog," *Time*, 2007, http://mideast.blogs.time.com/2007/10/25/rices_fear_of_the_one state_sol/.

8. The Quartet, "Middle East Quartet Expresses Support for Annapolis Conference," News and Media Division, New York: UN Secretary-General: Department of Public Information, 2007, http://www.un.org/News/Press/docs/2007/sg2133.doc.htm.

9. The London One State Group, "Challenging the Boundaries: A Single State in Israel/Palestine," 2007, http://www.onestate.net/.

10. For a more in-depth interrogation of what she argues are the "two conjoined premises" underlying the acceptance of geographic partition as the only way forward for peace since the Oslo Accords—namely Israeli sovereignty in parts of Mandate Palestine since 1967, and the acceptance of the principle of national self-determination by the international community for the essentialist identity of a binary opposed Jewish people and Palestinian people—see Virginia Tilley, "After Oslo, a paradigm shift? Redefining "peoples," sovereignty and justice in Israel-Palestine," in "Palestine/Israel after Oslo: Mapping transformations and alternatives in a time of deepening crisis," eds. Mandy Turner and Cherine Hussein, *Conflict, Security and Development* 15, no. 5 (December 2015): 425–453.

11. Said, "Truth and Reconciliation."

12. Said, "Truth and Reconciliation."

13. Said, "Truth and Reconciliation."

14. The London One State Group, 2007.

15. Zochrot, or "Remembering," was founded by Eitan Bronstein in Tel Aviv in 2002, and is made up of a group of Israeli citizens dedicated to raising the awareness of the Jewish-Israeli public about the Palestinian Nakba of 1948 as a fundamental first step toward peace and reconciliation. Zochrot does this through hosting conferences, panels and research initiatives—as well as through direct action initiatives that involve using Jewish-Israeli public spaces in order to showcase that the land upon which every Israeli lives, simultaneously tells the story of Palestinian ethnic cleansing and dispossession. Zochrot supports the Palestinian right of return. To read more about them, go to, http://zochrot.org.

16. Eitan Bronstein, "One State from Within: Civil Society Social Movements, and Grassroots Activism," paper presented at *Challenging the Boundaries: A Single State in Palestine/Israel* (London, SOAS, 2007).

17. To read the One State Declaration, go to, http://electronicintifada.net/content/one-state-declaration/793.

18. For detailed expositions of these processes, see for example, Jamil Hilal, *Where Now for Palestine? The Demise of the Two-State Solution* (London: Zed Books, 2007).

19. Edward Said, "The Morning After," *London Review of Books* 15, no. 20 (October 1993): 3.

20. Raz-Krakotzkin, "A Peace without Arabs," 61.

21. Edward Said, "On Lost Causes," in *Reflections on Exile and Other Literary and Cultural Essays* (London: Granta Books, 2001), 551.

22. Osama Khalil, "Who are you, The PLO and the Limits of Representation," *Al Shabaka*, March 18, 2013, https://al-shabaka.org/briefs/who-are-you-plo-and-limits-representation/.

23. For an account of these debates, see for example, Rana Barakat et al., "An Open Debate on Palestinian representation," *Al Shabaka*, May 1, 2013, https://al-shabaka.org/roundtables/open-debate-palestinian-representation/.

24. Joseph Massad, "A Matter of Immediate Urgency, not a Distant Utopia," paper presented in *Challenging the Boundaries: A Single State in Israel/Palestine* (London, SOAS, 2007).

25. Massad, "A Matter of Immediate Urgency."

26. Massad, "A Matter of Immediate Urgency."

27. Ali Abunimah et al., "The One State Declaration," *Tadamon!*, 2007, http://www.tadamon.ca/post/1047.

28. Abunimah et al., "The One State Declaration."

29. Abunimah et al., "The One State Declaration."

30. To read the One State Declaration, go to, http://electronicintifada.net/content/one-state-declaration/793.

31. Abunimah et al., "The One State Declaration."

32. The London One State Group, 2007.

33. Ghada Karmi, "Building an International Movement To Promote the One State Solution," paper presented in *One State for Palestine/Israel: A Country for all its Citizens?* (Boston, MIT, 2009).

34. It is important to note that besides being instrumental in drafting the One State Declaration itself, this network of conferences was instrumental in revealing a platform from within which anti-Zionist activists, academics, organizations, students and individuals involved in Palestine/Israel could locate each other, share stories, find common ground, and create what some have referred to as an almost cathartic single state "grassroots network." They also triggered a flurry of debates that broke through the taboo on critically discussing the nature of Zionism in the West, and are a central arena within which both academics and activists meet to fuse theory and practice in the elaboration of their strategies and political programs.

35. For more on the role of the Diaspora in taking the single state alternative forward, see Cherine Hussein, "The Single State Alternative in Palestine/Israel," in "Palestine/Israel after Oslo: Mapping transformations and alternatives in a time of deepening crisis," eds. Mandy Turner and Cherine Hussein, *Conflict, Security and Development* 15, no. 5 (December 2015): 521–547.

36. Uri Davis, *Apartheid Israel: Possibilities for the Struggle Within* (London: Zed Books, 2003), 7.
37. Davis, *Apartheid Israel*, 7.
38. Davis, *Apartheid Israel*.
39. Davis, *Apartheid Israel*.
40. Ilan Pappe, "Zionism and the Two-State Solution," in *Where Now for Palestine? The Demise of the Two-State Solution*, ed. Jamil Hilal (London: Zed Books, 2007), 11.
41. Pappe, "Zionism and the Two-State Solution," 10.
42. Pappe, "Zionism and the Two-State Solution."
43. Omar Salamanca, "The Madrid Conference: Translating the One-State Slogan into Research and Political Agendas," *Arab World Geographer* 10, no. 1 (January 2007): 57–80.
44. Pappe, "Zionism and the Two-State Solution," 10.
45. The term "anti-Jewish racism" is used here rather than the more widely used "anti-Semitism" as it was the term the Jewish-Israeli anti-Zionists quoted and interviewed for this chapter used. This may be because it is more specific/correct than the category of "Semites" which would technically also include Arabs, and so is possibly more clear/useful in the context of discussions on Zionism and different forms of racism.
46. Davis, *Apartheid Israel*, 11.
47. Davis, *Apartheid Israel*.
48. Salamanca, "The Madrid Conference."
49. Ilan Pappe and Uri Avnery, "Two States Or One State: A Gush Shalom Debate," *Countercurrents*, June 2007, http://www.countercurrents.org/pappe110607.htm.
50. Davis, *Apartheid Israel*, 19.
51. Jamil Hilal, ed., *Where Now for Palestine? The Demise of the Two-State Solution* (London: Zed Books, 2007).
52. Asaad Ghanem, "Israel and the 'danger of demography,'" in *Where Now for Palestine? The Demise of the Two-State Solution*, ed. Jamil Hilal (London: Zed Books, 2007), 48.
53. Ghanem, "Israel and the 'danger of demography,'" 52.
54. Ghanem, "Israel and the 'danger of demography.'"
55. Tony Judt, "Israel: The Alternative," *New York Review of Books* 50, no. 16 (October 2003), http://www.nybooks.com/articles/2003/10/23/israel-the-alternative/.
56. George Bisharat, interview with author, Toronto, June 2009.
57. Omar Barghouti, *Boycott, Divestment, Sanctions: the Global Struggle for Palestinian Rights* (Chicago: Haymarket Books, 2011), 63–64.
58. Haim Bresheeth, interview with author, London, April 2008.
59. Bresheeth, interview with author, London, April 2008.
60. Nadia Hijab, "Modes of Non Violent Activism to Achieve Palestinian Human Rights," paper presented in *One State for Palestine/Israel: A Country for all its Citizens?* (Boston, MIT, 2009).
61. To read the BDS Call go to, http://www.bdsmovement.net/call.
62. Hijab, "Modes of Non Violent Activism."
63. Ilan Pappe, interview with author, Brighton, September, 2009.

64. Said, "Truth and Reconciliation."
65. For more detailed expositions of this topic see, for example, the work of Smadar Lavie and of Sami Shalom Chetrit.
66. Eyal Sivan, "One State from Within: Civil Society Social Movements, and Grassroots Activism," paper presented at *Challenging the Boundaries: A Single State in Palestine/Israel* (London, SOAS, 2007).
67. Sivan, "One State from Within."
68. Sivan, "One State from Within."
69. Sami Shalom Chetrit, "Intra-Jewish Conflict in Israel: White Jews, Black Jews," Filmed in 2010, at Arabic Hour. Video, http://www.arabichour.org/Video/2011/AH_01_22_2011/AH_01_22_2011.wmv.
70. Massad, "A Matter of Immediate Urgency."
71. One State Declaration, http://electronicintifada.net/content/one-state-declaration/793.
72. The London One State Group, 2007.
73. Ghanem, "Israel and the 'danger of demography,'" 68.
74. Nadim Rouhana and Nimer Sultany, "Redrawing the Boundaries of Citizenship: Israel's New Hegemony," *Journal of Palestine Studies* 33, no. 1 (Autumn 2003): 6–10.
75. Oren Yiftachel, "Voting for Apartheid: The 2009 Israeli Elections," *Journal of Palestine Studies* 38, no. 3 (Spring 2009): 72–85.
76. Oren Yiftachel, "'Ethnocracy' and Its Discontents: Minorities, Protests, and the Israeli Polity," *Critical Inquiry* 26, no. 4 (Summer 2000): 725–756.
77. Yiftachel, "Voting for Apartheid," 72–85.
78. Yiftachel, "Voting for Apartheid."
79. Laila Farsakh, "The One-State Solution and the Israeli-Palestinian Conflict: Palestinian Challenges and Prospects," *Middle East Journal* 65, no. 1 (Winter 2011): 65.
80. Farsakh, "The One-State Solution," 65.
81. Abnaa El-Balad, "Abnaa El-Balad Movement," http://www.abnaa-elbalad.org/harakeh.htm.
82. Abnaa El-Balad, "Movement."
83. Awad Abdel-Fattah, interview with author, Nazareth, December 2014.
84. Abdel-Fattah, interview with author, Nazareth, December 2014.
85. Abdel-Fattah, interview with author.
86. Omar Barghouti, interview with author, Ramallah, November 2014.
87. Nidal Othman, interview with author, Haifa, March 2015.
88. Othman, interview with author, Haifa, March 2015.
89. Sivan, "One State from Within: Civil Society, Social Movements, and Grassroots Activism," paper presented at *Challenging the Boundaries: A Single State in Palestine/Israel* (London, SOAS, 2007).
90. Anonymized activist, interview with author, East Jerusalem, June 2015.
91. Anonymized activist, interview with author, East Jerusalem, June 2015.
92. Othman, interview with author, Haifa, March 2015.
93. Barghouti, interview with author, Ramallah, November 2014.
94. Radi Jarai, interview with author, Al-Bireh, March 2015.
95. Bresheeth, interview with author, London, June 2007.

96. To read more about the link between the global BDS movement and the single state solution, see chapter 5 in Cherine Hussein, *The Re-Emergence of the Single State Solution in Palestine/Israel: Countering an Illusion* (London: Routledge, 2015).

97. Jarai, interview with author, Al-Bireh, March 2015.

98. Bresheeth, interview with author, London, June 2007.

99. Barghouti, interview with author, Ramallah, November 2014.

100. As of this writing, both Hamas and the Islamic Movement in Israel remain excluded from within the single state idea due to the fact that most single state intellectuals argue that while they both oppose partition and appear to be open to democratic models of statehood, their preference remains for a single Islamic state. The exclusion of Hamas from within this alternative by Palestinians in Palestine/Israel also specifically hardened after the rise and fall of the Muslim Brotherhood in Egypt.

101. Barghouti, interview with author, Ramallah, November 2014.

102. Since the writing of this chapter, Awad Abdel-Fattah has been instrumental in the founding of a new One Democratic State Initiative (within the "green line") along with Ilan Pappe and Jeff Halper (among others). For more information on this initiative go to: https://mondoweiss.net/2018/08/democratic-organizational-perspectives/.

103. Abdel-Fattah, interview with author, Nazareth, December 2014.

104. Jarai, interview with author, Al-Bireh, March 2015.

105. It should be noted here that the intensification of Israeli repression, especially with regards to Palestinian-Israelis and Palestinians of East Jerusalem, also played a significant role in making it much more dangerous and difficult for single staters, and was a significant obstacle to their mobilizing at the grassroots. The appeal of the single state vision was also significantly dimmed in the context of populations of Palestinians who are simply struggling to survive on either side of the "green line," and uninterested in discussing political visions. Hence, this question did not seek to take away from these facts—but probes the strategy and tactics of the intellectuals involved in creating the movement themselves, and building (or hoping to build) collective Palestinian political agency today.

BIBLIOGRAPHY

Abnaa El-Balad. "Abnaa El-Balad Movement." http://www.abnaa-elbalad.org/harakeh.htm.

Abunimah, Ali, et al. "The One State Declaration." *Tadamon!*, December 8, 2007. http://www.tadamon.ca/post/1047.

Barghouti, Omar. *Boycott, Divestment, Sanctions: the Global Struggle for Palestinian Rights*. Chicago: Haymarket Books, 2011.

———. "Organizing for Self Determination, ethical De-Zionization & Resisting Apartheid" (Paper presented at *One State for Palestine/Israel: A Country for all its Citizens?*, Boston, MIT, 2009).

Bronstein, Eitan. "One State from Within: Civil Society, Social Movements, and Grassroots Activism" (Paper presented at *Challenging the Boundaries: A Single State in Palestine/Israel*, London, SOAS, 2007).

Chetrit, Sami-Shalom. "Intra-Jewish Conflict in Israel: White Jews, Black Jews," Filmed in 2010, at Arabic Hour. Video, http://www.arabichour.org/Video/2011/AH_01_22_2011/AH_01_22_2011.wmv.

Davis, Uri. *Apartheid Israel: Possibilities for the Struggle Within*. London: Zed Books, 2003.

Farsakh, Laila. "The One-State Solution and the Israeli-Palestinian Conflict: Palestinian Challenges and Prospects," *The Middle East Journal* 65, no. 1 (Winter 2011): 55–71.

Ghanem, Asaad. "Israel and the 'danger of demography.'" In, *Where Now for Palestine? The Demise of the Two-State Solution*, edited by Jamil Hilal, 48–74. London: Zed Books, 2007.

Giacaman, George and Jrund Lonning, Dag, eds. *After Oslo: New Realities, Old Problems*. London: Pluto Press, 1998.

Hijab, Nadia. "Modes of Non Violent Activism to Achieve Palestinian Human Rights" (Paper presented at *One State for Palestine/Israel: A Country for all its Citizens?*, Boston, MIT, 2009).

Hilal, Jamil, ed. *Where Now for Palestine? The Demise of the Two-State Solution*. London: Zed Books, 2007.

Hussein, Cherine. *The Re-Emergence of the Single State Solution in Palestine/Israel: Countering an Illusion*. London: Routledge, 2015.

———. "The Single State Alternative in Palestine/Israel." In, "Palestine/Israel after Oslo: Mapping transformations and alternatives in a time of deepening crisis," edited by Mandy Turner and Cherine Hussein, *Conflict, Security and Development* 15, no. 5 (December 2015): 521–547.

Judt, Tony. "Israel: The Alternative," *New York Review of Books* 50, no. 16 (October 2003), http://www.nybooks.com/articles/2003/10/23/israel-the-alternative/.

Karmi, Ghada. "Building an International Movement To Promote the One State Solution" (Paper presented in *One State for Palestine/Israel: A Country for all its Citizens?*, Boston, MIT, 2009).

Khalil, Osama. "Who are you, The PLO and the Limits of Representation," *Al Shabaka*, March 18, 2013, https://al-shabaka.org/briefs/who-are-you-plo-and-limits-representation/.

The London One State Group. "Challenging the Boundaries: A Single State in Israel/Palestine," 2007, http://www.onestate.net/.

Macleod, Scott. "Rice's Fear of the One-State Solution—The Middle East Blog," *Time*, 2007, http://mideast.blogs.time.com/2007/10/25/rices_fear_of_the_one state_sol/.

Massad, Joseph. "A Matter of Immediate Urgency, not a Distant Utopia" (Paper presented in *Challenging the Boundaries: A Single State in Israel/Palestine*, London, SOAS, 2007).

Pappe, Ilan. "Zionism and the Two-State Solution." In, *Where Now for Palestine? The Demise of the Two-State Solution*, edited by Jamil Hilal, 30–47. London: Zed Books, 2007.

———. "Proposal for a New Israeli Political Organization: Building a Movement for the One State Solution" (Paper presented at *One State for Palestine/Israel: A Country for all its Citizens?*, Boston, MIT, 2009).

Pappe, Ilan and Avnery, Uri. "Two States Or One State: A Gush Shalom Debate," *Countercurrents*, June 11, 2007, http://www.countercurrents.org/pappe110607.htm.

The Quartet. "Middle East Quartet Expresses Support for Annapolis Conference," News and Media Division, UN Secretary-General: Department of Public Information, November 27, 2007, http://www.un.org/News/Press/docs/2007/sg2133.doc.htm.

Raz-Krakotzkin, Amnon. "A Peace without Arabs: The Discourse of Peace and the Limits of Israeli Consciousness." In, *After Oslo: New Realities, Old Problems*, edited by George Giacaman and Dag Jrund Lonning, 59–76. London: Pluto Press, 1998.

Rouhana, Nadim and Nimer Sultany. "Redrawing the Boundaries of Citizenship: Israel's New Hegemony," *Journal of Palestine Studies* 33, no. 1 (Autumn 2003): 6–10.

Said, Edward. "Truth and Reconciliation," *Al-Ahram Weekly*, January 14–20, 1999, http://weekly.ahram.org.eg/1999/412/op2.htm.

———. "On Lost Causes." In, *Reflections on Exile and Other Literary and Cultural Essays*, edited by Edward Said, 527/553. London: Granta Books, 2001.

———. "The Morning After," *London Review of Books* 15, no. 20 (October 1993): 3.

Salamanca, Omar. "The Madrid Conference: Translating the One-State Slogan into Research and Political Agendas," *Arab World Geographer* 10, no. 1 (January 2007): 57–80.

Sivan, Eyal. "One State from Within: Civil Society, Social Movements, and Grassroots Activism" (Paper presented at *Challenging the Boundaries: A Single State in Palestine/Israel*, London, SOAS, 2007).

Tilley, Virginia. "After Oslo, a paradigm shift? Redefining "peoples," sovereignty and justice in Israel-Palestine." In, "Palestine/Israel after Oslo: Mapping transformations and alternatives in a time of deepening crisis," edited by Mandy Turner and Cherine Hussein, *Conflict, Security a nd Development* 15, no. 5 (December 2015): 425–453.

Yiftachel, Oren. "Voting for Apartheid: The 2009 Israeli Elections," *Journal of Palestine Studies* 38, no. 3 (Spring 2009): 72–85.

———. "Ethnocracy" and Its Discontents: Minorities, Protests, and the Israeli Polity," *Critical Inquiry* 26, no. 4 (Summer 2000): 725–756.

INTERVIEWS

Abdel-Fattah, Awad. Interview with author, Nazareth, December 2014.
Anonymous activist. Interview with author, East Jerusalem, June 2015.
Barghouti, Omar. Interview with author, Ramallah, November 2014.
Bisharat, George. Interview with author, Toronto, June 2009.
Bresheeth, Haim. Interview with author, London, April 2008.
Jarai, Radi. Interview with author, Al-Bireh, March 2015.
Othman, Nidal. Interview with author, Haifa, March 2015.
Pappe, Ilan. Interview with author, Brighton, September 2009.

Index

Abbas, Mahmoud, 11, 26, 31, 53, 71–73, 75, 77, 78, 81, 85, 86, 119, 134, 278, 284, 286, 290, 300
Abdel-Fattah, Awad, 317, 318, 330
Abdulhadi, Rabab, viii
Abnaa al Balad, 130, 131, 133, 134, 140–43, 161, 256, 260, 317
Abu Arar, Talab, 144
Abu Ali Mustafa Brigades, 84
Abu Mazen. *See Mahmoud Abbas*
Abu Shehada, Sami 133
Adalah, 131, 156
agriculture, 111–13, 117, 137
aid: conditionalities 280; coordination 273, 276, 277, 291, 293; dependency 106, 287
Aker, Mamdouh, 26
Al Aqsa Intifada. *See* Second Intifada
Al-Aqsa mosque, 86, 135, 143, 220, 226, 227, 229–31
Al-Aqsa demonstrations (2017), 228
Al-Ard, 130, 140, 141
al-Hussaini, Adnan, 215, 223, 231
al-Shatat. *See* diaspora
Al-Sisi, Abdel Fatah, 196
Allon Plan, 1, 182, 183, 307
Annapolis Conference (2007), 305

Annexation, 162, 170, 171, 213, 224, 227, 252
anti-Semitism, viii, ix, 311
Anti-Terrorism Certificate, 282
anti-Zionism, 59, 130, 145, 311, 313, 315, 322, 328
apartheid, 12, 23, 32, 51, 143, 303, 304, 308, 313, 314, 317, 320, 325
Arab Democratic Party, 134, 141, 160
Arab Higher Follow Up Committeee, 54, 230
Arab League, 20, 46, 228, 252
Arab Liberation Front (ALF), 46, 53
Arab Peace Initiative, 31
Arafat, Yasser, 1, 17, 25, 49, 52, 59, 72, 73, 75–78, 102, 119, 133, 135, 142, 143, 162–64, 185–93, 249, 286, 307, 308
Arar, Talab Abu, 144, 229
Ashkenazi, 4, 315, 316, 321
autonomy, 46, 118, 141, 142, 147, 183, 187, 320
Awqaf, 215, 224–30, 232

Backwardness, 138, 181
banking, 72, 100, 102, 106
bantustan, 308

bantustanisation, 51
Barak, Ehud, 162–65, 168
Barghouti, Mustafa, 85
Barghouti, Omar, 303, 304, 313, 317, 322, 323
bedouin community, 4, 138, 146, 254, 289
Beilin, Yossi, 159, 164, 173
Bennett, Naftali, 164, 171
Bethlehem, 78, 221
bi-nationalism, 319, 322
Bishara, Azmi, 142, 316, 318, 319
Bisharat, George, 263, 313
Black September, 248, 251, 252, 254
Bourdieu, Pierre, 41
Boycott, Divestment, and Sanctions (BDS), 31, 32, 291, 313, 314, 323, 330
boycott of Hamas, 81, 199
Bresheeth, Haim, 311, 314, 323
Bronstein, Eitan, 307
building permits in East Jerusalem, 217, 218
Bush, George W., 21
B'Tselem, 173, 198, 218

Camp David summit (2000), 30, 31, 48, 58, 69, 162, 163, 165, 189
Canary Mission, viii
Central Intelligence Agency (CIA), 286
checkpoints, 21–23, 34, 51, 53, 117, 119, 219–21, 275, 285
citizenship, 12, 97, 142, 145, 170, 182, 183, 215, 216, 233, 252, 254, 256, 303, 304, 306, 307, 309, 316–319
civil rights, 54, 125, 131, 141, 147, 161, 291, 313
civil society, 7, 26, 41, 66, 84, 86, 134, 145, 161, 222, 223, 255, 272, 275, 281, 282, 287, 289–91, 314, 321, 322
class formation, 6, 120
class struggle, 129
Clinton Parameters. *See* Camp David summit (2000)

colonial peace, 274
colonization, 1, 3, 6, 7, 29, 43, 53, 63–65, 86, 98, 102, 117, 119, 182, 219, 285, 286, 293, 304, 307–309, 312, 314
contraband economy, 193, 194
Coordinator of Government Activities in the Territories (COGAT), 282, 284
corruption, 65, 68, 73, 74, 285
counterinsurgency, 4, 12, 64, 162, 293, 298

Darawsha, Abdel Wahab, 141, 149, 151, 157
Darwish, Mahmoud, 1, 142, 143
Darwish, Shaikh Abdallah, 142, 143
Davis, Uri, 310, 311
de-arabization, 316, 317
Declaration of Principles on Interim Self-Government Arrangements (DOP), 1, 18, 19, 22, 27, 28, 32, 41, 49, 74, 103, 164, 185, 214, 225, 229, 245, 248, 252, 272, 278
de-development, 8, 97, 109, 138, 183, 188
de-development in Gaza, 183–88
de-industrialization, 105
Democratic Front for Peace and Equality (DFPE), 140, 141, 143
Democratic Front for the Liberation of Palestine (DFLP), 46, 49, 52, 53, 59
demographic threat, 20, 24, 34, 185, 310, 312
diaspora, 2, 10, 56, 67, 68, 70, 80, 132, 249, 304, 305, 308–310, 316, 317, 324, 327
displacement, 55, 217, 249, 250
dispossession, 11, 43, 56, 182, 249, 311, 313, 325
donors, 5, 10, 11, 65, 66, 70, 71, 73, 75, 81, 84, 180, 185, 188–91, 195, 196, 199–201, 220, 273–93
Druze, 4, 127

East Jerusalem, 2, 3, 9, 22, 27, 50, 86, 117, 135, 143, 168, 214–18, 220–25, 227, 229, 233, 289, 290, 321, 330
East Jerusalem economy, 220–22
economic dependency, 54, 71, 74, 85, 96, 98, 99, 102, 104, 106, 114, 136, 287
economic growth, 3, 96–98, 102, 104–6, 109–11, 113, 114, 117–19, 135, 136, 183, 216, 220, 280, 285
economic peace, 7, 72, 96, 106, 119
education, 26, 44, 105, 112, 113, 135, 136, 138, 223, 315
Egypt, 44, 45, 48, 57, 58, 82, 181, 192–96, 199, 246, 257, 262, 330
Erekat, Saeb, 31, 248, 301
ethical decolonization, 303
ethnic cleansing, 34, 42, 43, 51, 55, 56, 306, 312, 313, 315, 317, 326
European Commission, 278
European Union (EU), 52, 75, 82, 145, 220, 228, 276–79, 285, 286, 288–90, 305
EU Coordinating Office for Palestinian Police Support (EUPOL COPPS), 286
EU Heads of Mission, 288, 289
Exports, 109–10, 115–16, 120

facts on the ground, 23, 28, 59, 63, 95, 166, 171, 214
Falk, Richard, 205
family reunification, 3, 216, 217
Farsakh, Leila, 318
Fatah, 2, 25, 46, 49, 52–55, 57, 65, 66, 73, 76–83, 85, 180, 184–87, 191, 193, 195, 199–201, 224, 283, 287, 318, 323
Fayyad, Salam, 71, 72
Fedayeen, 247, 248, 251, 258
Feiglin, Moshe, 229, 230
Finkelstein, Norman, viii
First Intifada, 49, 54, 76, 79, 111–13, 169, 184, 186, 187, 252
foreign investment, 71, 72

fragmentation, 9, 11, 41, 43, 45, 50, 53, 55, 65, 81, 86, 193, 308, 313
free market, 71, 96, 97, 99, 104, 114, 277
Friedman, David, 11

Gal-On, Zahava, 230
Galilee, 7, 120, 130
Gaza blockade, 3, 82, 86, 180, 195, 198
Gaza tunnel economy, 192–97
Gaza unemployment figures, 179
Gaza-Jericho agreement, 18, 36
gender, 56, 263, 270
Germany, 278
Ghanem, Asad, 139, 312, 317
globalization, 6, 97, 99, 101, 105, 111, 112, 114
Goldstone, Report, 284
Governance, 66, 71–73, 79, 81, 82, 97, 102, 189, 190, 194, 195, 223, 255, 265, 274–77, 279, 281, 282, 286, 287, 292
green line, 4, 7, 29, 129, 134, 146, 147, 171, 304, 317–319, 324, 325, 330
Gulf War (1991), 22, 99, 111, 184, 185
Guterres, Antonio, 292

Hadash, 140
Haifa, 118, 134, 332
Hamas, 25, 49, 52–55, 57, 60, 65, 66, 68, 73, 77, 79–83, 85, 180, 184, 187, 188, 190–96, 199, 200, 262, 278, 283, 284, 286, 330
Haram ash-Sharif, 162, 224, 227–32
Haredi, 3, 4, 137, 218
Hashemite Kingdom of Jordan. *See* Jordan
Hawking, Stephen, viii
health care, 26, 105, 113, 137, 219, 259, 264, 282
Hebron, 18, 138, 139, 221, 231, 307
Herzl, Theodor, 163, 310
Hijab, Nadia, 314
house demolitions, 12, 23, 51, 190, 215–18, 289

human rights, 25, 26, 131, 181, 198, 218, 276, 277, 335
Human Sciences Research Council of South Africa, 12
Hussein, Mohammed, 231
al-Hussaini, Adnan, 215, 223, 231

Imports, 101, 105, 108, 110, 112, 113, 115, 116, 120, 195, 196, 275
indigeneity, 7, 125–28, 138, 147, 311, 312, 317, 322
industry, 113, 117, 137, 198, 221
Indyk, Martin, 25, 186, 271, 293
injustice, 130, 303, 319
institution-building, 67, 71, 74, 76
intellectuals, 10, 303–316, 319, 320, 322–325, 330, 336
Interim Agreement on the West Bank and the Gaza Strip (1995), 18, 19, 21, 23, 27, 28, 36, 70
International Criminal Court, 272
International Holocaust Remembrance Alliance, ix
international law, 23, 28, 119, 161, 166, 213, 228, 289, 290, 303, 304, 314, 315
International Monetary Fund (IMF), 108, 121, 185, 189
Iraq, 2, 44, 46, 54, 57, 58
Islamic Jihad, 52, 53, 68, 77, 80, 81, 200, 286
Islamic Movement (Israel), 133, 142–44, 215, 229, 231, 232, 330
Israel-PLO Letters of Mutual Recognition (1993), 18, 19
Israeli Communist Party, 59, 130, 139, 140
Israeli disengagement from Gaza (2005), 21, 192, 293
Israeli military campaigns: Operation 'Cast Lead' (2008–2009), 190, 194 Operation 'Defensive Shield' (2002), 190, 199, 286 Operation 'Pillar of Defense' (2012), 75, 79, 199, 285

Operation 'Protective Edge' (2014), 197–99
Israeli redeployment, 18, 19, 27, 28, 187, 192
Israelization, 126, 130, 131
Izz ad-Din al-Qassam Brigades, 80

Jabareen, Hassan, 134, 213
Jabareen, Yousef, 144–46
Jericho, 18, 22, 33, 36, 85, 285
Jerusalem Day, 230–31
Jewish Agency, 246
Jewish Home Party, 160, 164, 171
Joint List, 7, 54, 127, 135, 143–47, 166
Jordan, 9, 20, 42–45, 48, 54, 56, 58, 224–28, 232, 233, 245–63
Jordan first policy, 253
Jordanianness, 255, 256, 260
Jordan River, 4, 143, 166, 183, 251, 292
Jordan Valley, 2, 29, 30, 51, 289, 307
judaization, 9, 86, 130, 215, 227, 231

Kadima, 160
Karmi, Ghada, 310
Khoury, Hind, 133
kibbutzim, 136, 137
King Hussain of Jordan, 226, 247, 250–53
Knesset, 4, 9, 23, 29, 54, 55, 128, 134, 139–45, 160, 171, 186, 215, 223, 226, 229, 230, 233
Kulanu, 160
Kuwait, 2, 50, 54

labor market, 102, 117, 128; 188
Labor Party (Israel), 7, 128, 133, 134, 139, 160, 161, 162, 168, 169
Lamont Hill, Marc, viii
land confiscation, 34, 103, 117, 130, 137, 230
Land Day (1976), 130, 131, 146
Lapid, Yair, 161, 169
Lebanon, 44, 47–49, 54, 55, 57, 58, 99, 245–47, 249, 254

legitimacy, 67–69, 78, 140, 187, 190, 196, 201, 259, 278, 284, 308
liberalization, 96, 101, 105, 111, 113, 185, 276, 277
Libya, 54, 57
Likud, 8, 160, 162, 166, 229, 325
Livni, Tzipi, 160
localization, 6, 7, 41, 126, 127, 130, 138, 146, 147
London One State Group, 305, 309, 332
Lustick, Ian, 128

macro-economy, 104–7, 110, 117, 118
Mada al-Carmel 147,
Madrid Peace Conference (1991), 45, 99, 100, 278, 305, 309
Makhoul, Issam, 131
malnutrition, 191
manufacturing, 105, 112, 113
March 24 Youth Movement, 256
Massad, Joseph, 264–66, 308, 316
Mavi Marmara, 195
McGreal, Chris, viii
Mediterranean Sea, 4, 8, 143, 166, 180, 183, 292
merchandise, 115, 116, 120, 260
Meretz Party, 131, 160, 161
Mizrahim, 3, 4, 315, 316
monopolies, 65, 285, 287
Morrison, Toni, viii
Mossawa, 134, 319, 320
Mouffe, Chantal, 255
Muslim Brotherhood, 42, 79, 82, 195
Mustafa, Abu Ali, 84

Nakba, 6, 42, 43, 57, 58, 127–29, 145, 161, 181, 247, 277, 306
Nation-State Law (2018 Israel), 4, 7, 8, 42, 126, 145, 146
Naqab, 118, 138, 139, 145, 146, 320, 325, 337
nationalization, 7, 130, 131, 147
neoliberal capitalism, 3, 57, 187, 275, 285

neoliberalism, 3, 6, 7, 55, 66, 71–73, 105, 106, 112, 163, 169, 184, 275, 285
neopatrimonial, 77, 186, 188, 190, 287
nepotism, 73, 287
Netanyahu, Benjamin, 25, 72, 136, 137, 160, 163, 166, 168, 169, 272, 287
NGOs, 65, 66, 84, 146, 221, 223, 282, 284, 290, 291
normalization, 167, 224

Odeh, Ayman, 143, 145, 146
occupation, 3, 6, 11, 24, 27, 29, 44, 50, 51, 56, 57, 65, 76, 79, 96– 98, 102–6, 111–19, 129, 135, 141, 144, 161, 164–71, 181–83, 186, 213–15, 225, 227, 233, 274, 280, 284–86, 304, 307, 312, 314
Olmert, Ehud, 168
one state, 10, 115, 125, 139, 316, 318, 320, 321, 324
Orient House 222, 223
Oslo Accords. *See* Declaration of Principles on Interim Self-Government Arrangements (1993)
Othman, Nidal, 319, 320, 322

Palestinian-Arabs in the Israeli labor force, 136–37
Palestinian Authority, 2, 5, 6, 11, 18, 21, 23–27, 29, 31, 32, 42, 65, 95, 133, 163, 185, 187, 188, 190, 215, 222, 226, 233, 249, 272–75, 278–80, 282–87, 290, 291, 307, 335
PA authoritarianism, 72, 73, 75, 77
Palestinian Basic Law, 52, 68, 82, 97
Palestinian exports, 110, 115, 116, 120
Palestinian Gross Domestic Product (GDP), 106–15, 191, 220
Palestinian Gross National Disposable Income (GNDI), 106, 109
Palestinian Gross National Income (GNI), 106–10, 117
Palestinian Liberation Front (PLF), 53, 59, 304

Palestinian Legislative Council (PLC), 52, 53, 73
Palestine Liberation Army, 41
Palestinian Monetary Authority, 102
Palestinian Municipal Development and Lending Fund, 290
Palestinian national consciousness, 139, 247, 332
Palestinian National Charter, 41, 43, 44, 140
Palestinian National Council (PNC), 41, 45, 46, 49, 50, 58, 68, 85, 248
Palestinian national identity, 42, 43, 55, 57, 58, 69, 80, 125–29, 131, 138, 141, 144, 147, 181, 250, 252–55, 257, 260, 315, 316, 318, 319, 321, 322
Palestinianness, 247, 254, 259
Palestinian People's Party (formerly the Communist Party), 45, 46, 49, 53, 129, 131
Palestinian security sector, 19, 25, 27, 72, 75, 76, 282, 285–87
Palestinian security forces. *See* Palestinian security sector
Palestinian trade deficit, 110, 115
pan-arabism, 44, 47, 140, 141, 250, 252
Pappe, Ilan, 57, 310, 311, 312, 336
Paris Protocol, 6, 8, 18, 95, 97–99, 101–5, 114, 116, 193–96, 274, 275, 283
patrimonialism, 257
peacebuilding, 65, 66, 71, 185, 271, 272, 274–77, 282, 285, 301
Peres, Shimon, 159, 167, 185, 222
PLO bureaucratization, 47
PLO Charter, 19
pluralism, 47, 64, 65, 67, 72, 82
polarization, 200
Popular Front of the Liberation of Palestine (PFLP), 45, 46, 49, 52, 53, 58, 59, 66, 83–86
PFLP-General Command, 53
Popular Struggle Front (PSF), 53
Prawer Plan, 146, 325

prisoners, 25, 36, 85, 144, 180, 222
private sector, 71, 72, 113, 275, 283;
public sector, 74, 76, 96, 98, 107, 111, 114, 188, 191, 195, 200
Progressive List for Peace (PLP), 141, 151
Proportionality, 205, 209
Protocol Concerning the Redeployment in Hebron (1995), 18
Protocol on Economic Relations. *See* Paris Protocol

Quartet on the Middle East, 278, 305
Quartet Principles, 278, 283, 291, 305, 326
quasi-state, 31, 76, 287
Qurei, Ahmed, 30, 31, 99

Rabin, Yitzhak, 1, 2, 17, 23, 24, 27, 29, 76, 102, 132, 134, 159, 160, 163, 165–67, 184–86, 307
racism, 230, 311, 317, 320, 322, 328
Raz-Krakotzin, Amnon, 307, 325
real estate, 112, 113, 173, 188, 194, 285
reconciliation (Hamas-Fatah), 7, 180, 199, 200, 283
reconstruction, 101, 102, 180, 197, 199–201, 275
refugees, 245–70
right of return, 20, 30, 31, 51, 58, 69, 141, 245, 247–50, 308, 309, 314, 318, 323, 326
remittances, 47
resistance, 10, 24, 26, 32, 43, 44, 79–81, 84, 99, 144, 182, 184, 247, 258, 303, 304, 307, 308, 310, 313, 314, 323–325
restructuring, 4, 68, 75, 188, 286
roadblocks, 22, 193, 275
Roy, Sara, 8, 136, 138, 236, 244, 293, 300
Russia, 258, 278, 320

Sa'adat, Ahmad, 84, 85
Sa'di, Ahmad, 128, 139

Said, Edward, 1, 18, 27, 32, 64, 104, 248, 303, 306, 307, 336
single-state solution. *See* one-state
Salah, Shaikh Raad, 142, 231–33
Salaita, Steven, viii
Sarsour, Linda, viii
Sayigh, Yusef, 75, 99, 133
Schmitt, Carl, 255
Second Intifada, 8, 30, 52, 69, 75, 77, 78, 80, 81, 84, 85, 103, 109, 135, 173, 185, 189, 190, 192, 221, 225, 281, 286, 325
security coordination, 11, 26, 74, 78, 86, 280, 286, 291
segregation, 128, 129, 136, 218, 263
separation barrier, 51, 53, 103, 117, 144, 189, 191, 215, 216, 218–21, 223
separation wall. *See* separation barrier
services economy, 105, 108, 110–13, 115
settlements, 3, 4, 17, 18–23, 27–30, 50, 63, 69, 70, 81, 102, 117, 130, 138, 140, 142, 144, 146, 161, 164–71, 180, 183, 185, 187, 191–94, 213, 214, 230, 274, 282, 291, 298, 305, 312, 313, 325
settler colonialism, 12, 43, 44, 47, 50, 51, 56, 65, 97, 114, 118, 119, 182, 311–313
Shalhoub-Kevorkian, Nadera, 128, 138
Sharm el-Sheikh Memorandum (1999), 19, 27, 28
Sharon, Ariel, 168, 172, 176, 312
Shas, 160
Shlaim, Avi, 162
Shoah, 167
Shuafat refugee camp, 219
Sivan, Eyal, 315, 320
solidarity, 49, 133–35, 140, 141, 147, 195, 315, 317, 320, 322
Soviet Union, 3, 49, 50, 55, 58, 83, 100, 258
statebuilding, 1, 45, 50, 52, 65–67, 71, 73, 76, 84, 97, 118, 137, 147, 201, 276, 277, 282, 283, 285
subjectivity, 258, 262

support for a two-state solution, 139–44, 168, 281
surveillance, 128, 254, 282
Syria, 4, 46, 54, 55, 57, 58, 245, 246, 247, 249, 254, 262, 263

Taba negotiations (2001), 30
taxation, 72, 82, 101, 116, 169, 216, 217, 221, 275
telecommunications, 116, 188, 285
Temple Mount. *See* Haram ash-Sharif
Temporary International Mechanism (then PEGASE), 278; 279
Ten Point Political Programme, PLO (1974), 248
Terrorism, 18, 22, 25, 51, 81, 186, 286, 308
'The Day After' Report (2015), 290
Tibi, Ahmad, 142, 144, 145
tourism, 113, 188, 221, 223
trade deficit, 110, 115
trade unions. *See* unions
tribalism, 74, 252
Trump, Donald, 11, 17, 26, 52, 135, 215, 228, 272
Tunisia, 20, 44, 58, 76, 257, 262
tunnels, 82, 192–97

unemployment, 104–8, 119, 164, 179, 188, 191
United Arab List. *See* Joint List
United Nations Conciliation Commission for Palestine, 181
United Nations Development Programme—Programme of Assistance to the Palestinian People (UNDP-PAPP), 277
United Nations Economic and Political Commission for Western Asia, 14, 16, 35
United Nations General Assembly, 31, 46, 52, 314
United Nations High Commissioner for Refugees (UNHCR), 264
unions, 41, 42, 47, 184

United Nations Office for the Coordination of Humanitarian Affairs (UNOCHA), 216, 284
UN Partition Plan (1947), 11, 140, 165, 276, 277
United Nations Relief and Works Agency for Palestinian Refugees in the Near East (UNRWA), 44, 181, 246, 250, 277, 281, 282
UN General Assembly Resolution 194 (1948), 31
United Nations Security Council, 7, 18, 20, 28–32, 36, 77, 121, 213, 272
UN Security Council Resolutions 242 (1967), 18, 28, 29, 31, 33, 36, 277
UN Security Council Resolutions 338 (1973), 17, 18, 33, 36
UN Security Council Resolution 478 (1980), 213;
US Jerusalem Embassy Act (1995), 1, 52, 215, 228, 289
US, 9, 11, 12, 17, 20, 21, 25, 26, 27, 28, 30, 32, 45, 48, 50, 52, 53, 64, 73, 75, 76, 83, 85, 100, 135, 145, 162, 180, 185, 186, 193, 215, 218, 227, 228, 229, 250, 259, 271, 272, 274, 276, 278, 280, 281, 282, 284, 285, 286, 289, 291, 293, 305, 312, 313, 323
USAID, 282
United States Security Coordinator (USSC), 286

Venice Declaration (1980), 278
violence, 12, 44, 72, 102, 140, 162–65, 168, 170, 171, 180, 196, 216, 230, 231, 262, 283, 287, 325
voting, 7, 145, 147, 224

Wadi 'Araba Agreement (1994), 224–28, 252, 253
Waqf, Jerusalem Islamic, 225, 228, 231
Waters, Roger, viii
Welfare, 96, 98, 118, 143, 169, 173
White, Ben, viii
Al-Wihdat Camp, 45, 247, 254, 257–62
women, 41, 43, 46, 57, 129, 179, 216, 222, 260, 314
World Bank, 71, 100, 116, 185, 194, 276–80
World Trade Organization (WTO), 101
Wye River Memorandum (1998), 19, 20, 27, 74, 286

Yahadut Ha-Torah, 160
Yarmouk refugee camp, 55
Yesh Atid, 60, 161, 168
Yemen, 57
youth, 46, 60, 170, 179, 184, 222, 223, 256, 259, 262, 325

Zahalka, Jamal, 134, 142
Ze'evi, Rehbavam, 84
Zidan, Mohamad, 131, 133
zionism, 10, 19, 129, 160, 162, 163, 247, 303, 304, 306, 310–314, 316, 319, 322
The Zionist Camp, 160
zionization, 7, 147
Zoabi, Hanin, 131, 134; 161
Zochrot, 307
Zoning (Areas A, B and C), 21, 22, 24, 27, 69, 70, 118, 162, 166, 274, 284, 285, 288, 289, 290

About the Contributors

Luigi Achilli is a Marie Curie Fellow at the European University Institute in Italy and San Diego State University in California. He holds a PhD in political anthropology from the School of Oriental and African Studies (SOAS), University of London. He has taught at Cambridge, SOAS, and various universities in the Middle East. His research and writing focus on the Palestinian issue, irregular migration and smuggling networks, refugee studies, political engagement, and nationalism in the Middle East.

Diana Buttu is a Canadian-Palestinian attorney specializing in human rights and negotiations. In 2000, she moved to the occupied West Bank where she served as a legal advisor to the Palestinian negotiating team and later to the Palestinian Authority president. She resigned from her post in 2005 and remains a frequent commentator on Middle East politics and human rights. Her op-eds have been published in the *New York Times*, *The Washington Post*, *The Guardian*, BBC, CNN, and Aljazeera, among others.

Tariq Dana is a faculty member in the MA program in Conflict and Humanitarian Studies, Doha Institute for Graduate Studies, Qatar. Previously, he was director of the Center for Development Studies and a senior research fellow at the Ibrahim Abu-Loughod Institute of International Affairs, Birzeit University, Palestine. He is also a policy adviser for the Palestinian Policy Network (Al-Shabaka), and has published extensively on Palestine and Arab affairs.

Toufic Haddad is deputy director of the Kenyon Institute (Council for British Research in the Levant) in East Jerusalem. He is the author of *Palestine Ltd: Neoliberalism and Nationalism in the Occupied Territory* (2016) and co-editor of *Between the Lines: Israel, the Palestinians and the US War on*

Terror (2007). He holds a PhD in development studies from the School for Oriental and African Studies (SOAS), University of London, and formerly worked as a journalist, editor, and researcher in the Occupied Palestinian Territory, since 1997.

Jamil Hilal is a Palestinian sociologist who has published a number of books and numerous articles (in Arabic and English) on Palestine, Israel, and the Arab world. His publications include: *The Formation of the Palestinian Elite: from the Palestinian National Movement to the Rise of the Palestinian Authority* (2002) and *Across the Wall: In Search of a Shared View of Palestinian-Israeli History* (2010), co-edited with Ilan Pappe. Hilal has lectured in British and African universities, and is a senior associate research fellow at a number of Palestinian research institutions.

Cherine Hussein is associate postdoctoral fellow in the Swedish Institute of International Affairs' program on Middle East politics. She holds a PhD in international relations from the University of Sussex. Her research focuses on the politics of social transformation in the Middle East, with a particular interest in the writings of Antonio Gramsci and Edward Said, as well as the role of organic intellectuals in instigating social change. She is the author of *The Re-Emergence of the Single State Solution in Palestine/Israel: Countering an Illusion* (2015).

Raja Khalidi was trained as a development economist at Oxford University and the School of Oriental and African Studies (SOAS), University of London. He has conducted research and published and lectured widely on Palestinian economic conditions. He worked with the United Nations Conference on Trade and Development (UNCTAD) from 1985 to 2013 as coordinator of its Programme of Assistance to the Palestinian People and as a senior economist. He is currently research coordinator at the Palestine Economic Policy Research Institute (MAS) in Ramallah, Palestine.

Yonatan Mendel is a senior lecturer in the Department of Middle East Studies at Ben-Gurion University of the Negev, Israel, and the director of the Arabic-Hebrew Translators' Forum at the Van Leer Jerusalem Institute. His research interests include the sociology of language, focusing on the status and history of the Arabic language in Palestine/Israel. Mendel is author of *The Creation of Israeli Arabic* (2014), co-author (with Ronald Ranta) of *From the Arab Other to the Israeli Self* (2016), and co-editor (with Abeer AlNajjar) of *Language, Politics and Society in the Middle East* (2018).

Mansour Nasasra is a lecturer in Middle East politics and international relations in the Department of Politics and Government, Ben Gurion University of the Negev, Israel. Before that, he taught at the University of Exeter and Plymouth University (both in the UK), and was a research fellow at the Council for British Research in the Levant in East Jerusalem. He is author of *The Naqab Bedouins: A Century of Politics and Resistance* (2017), co-editor of *The Naqab Bedouin and Colonialism: New Perspectives* (2015), and co-editor of *The Routledge Handbook on Middle East Cities* (2019).

Mandy Turner is director of the Kenyon Institute (Council for British Research in the Levant) in East Jerusalem. Her research and publications focus on the politics of international intervention and the political economy of development in war-torn societies with a country focus on the occupied Palestinian territory, but also comparatively. She is the co-editor of *The Politics of International Intervention: The Tyranny of Peace* (with Florian P. Kuehn, 2016); *Decolonizing Palestinian Political Economy: De-development and Beyond* (with Omar Shweiki, 2014); and *Whose Peace? Critical Perspectives on the Political Economy of Peacebuilding* (with Michael Pugh and Neil Cooper, 2008). She lives and works in East Jerusalem.

www.ingramcontent.com/pod-product-compliance
Lightning Source LLC
Chambersburg PA
CBHW052056300426
44117CB00013B/2155